AF411960

# Personality Coherence
# and Incoherence
## A Perspective on Anxiety and Depression

# Personality Coherence and Incoherence
## A Perspective on Anxiety and Depression

Małgorzata Fajkowska
*Institute of Psychology*
*Polish Academy of Sciences*
*Warsaw, Poland*

Foreword by Philip J. Corr

ELIOT WERNER PUBLICATIONS, INC.
CLINTON CORNERS, NEW YORK

Library of Congress Cataloging-in-Publication Data

Fajkowska, Malgorzata.
Personality coherence and incoherence : a perspective on anxiety and depression /
Malgorzata Fajkowska, Institute of Psychology, Polish Academy of Sciences,
Warsaw, Poland.
pages cm
Includes bibliographical references and index.
ISBN 978-0-9797731-4-3
1. Personality.   2. Anxiety.   3. Depression, Mental.   I. Title.
BF698.F255 2013
152.4'6 – dc23                                                                        2012027529

ISBN-10: 0-9797731-4-8
ISBN-13: 978-0-9797731-4-3

Copyright © 2013 Eliot Werner Publications, Inc.
PO Box 268, Clinton Corners, New York 12514
http://www.eliotwerner.com



Printed in the United States of America

# Foreword

Personality psychology is the science of describing and explaining individual differences in affect, cognition, and behavior, and specifically with the *patterning* of these differences across situations and over time. This science deals with complex phenomena, entailing person and environmental factors and their interactions. Any theory that attempts to account for these factors must be conceptually sophisticated yet empirically testable, especially in relation to how interacting components make up the higher-level integrated organization that is manifest in personality and associated phenotypes (e.g., anxiety and depression). However, the development of any such a theory is a daunting undertaking and certainly not one for the dispositionally faint hearted. Małgorzata Fajkowska has risen to this challenge with aplomb.

The theory detailed in this book sets out to address four major problems in personality psychology: (a) personality as a complex system; (b) the multiple levels of structure and causal processes (i.e., biological, psychological, and situational mechanisms); (c) stability and change over time; and (d) coherence and incoherence in structures and processes. A central theme running through the theory is the necessity of viewing personality as an organized system with interrelating variables that interact with the external world. Fajkowska adumbrates a System of Regulation and Integration Stimulation as a fundamental personality architecture. Its major function is to attain and maintain (a) the optimal level of activation and arousal to achieve the optimal level of functioning of the whole system and (b) intraindividual coherence and behavioral integrity. These functions are achieved by two sets of processes: an attentional system and temperament traits.

Of special note, the theory attempts to account for these complex, higher-level phenomena through the lens of Systems Theory, which emphasizes the coordinated action of interconnected subsystems. This perspective has been applied—with some success—to many diverse areas, including robotics, biological systems, and even economic systems. Fajkowska provides a novel application of this perspective to one of the major problems in personality psychology: coherence and incoherence. A fresh perspective on this long-standing problem is indicated by the fact that psychologists still struggle with it—and not only with its solution, but also with its definition. Any theory that can throw new light on this problem would be a major contribution. For sure, we shall have to wait for future research to announce the final verdict on the scientific power of the theory outlined in this book, but no waiting time is needed to recognize the fact that Fajkowska has provided a new way to look at an old problem.

The emphasis of the theory on highly interdependent subsystems, all working together to produce the final psychological output, makes good scientific sense because it is necessary in personality psychology—as in other areas of psychology—to consider the system as whole rather than as merely a collection of isolated subsystems. This emphasis sidesteps the pitfalls of the strictly analytical approach, preferring instead a synthetic approach that views parts of the system as meaningful only in terms of the workings of the whole system. Too often lip service is paid to this dictum, but frequently it is forgotten in the everyday business of research. But systems thinking should be paid more attention, and for several reasons: it forces us to focus on the related superordinate functions of the parts and whole of the system, and it encourages us to consider the longer-term outcomes of the operation of the whole system. This perspective is especially vital since personality is concerned with longer-term stabilities and not just with immediate, short-term outcomes. The fact that personality scores are able to predict outcomes many years ahead underscores the value of any theory that can provide a viable account of these longer-term stabilities and outcomes. Yet at the same time, personality is not "set in stone"; it does change and in meaningful ways. Explaining immediate (state) processes, and how they lead to both stability and instability in longer-term (trait) outcomes, is one of the major strengths of this book.

To illustrate the above points, consider defensive behaviors. Although there are many different kinds of these behaviors, their coherence can only be meaningfully seen in terms of their related superordinate functions. For example, in the case of freezing and flight that are seen in the face of intense and immediate threat, although they are apparently quite different, they serve the same function of avoiding/escaping danger—albeit by different behavioral strategies demanded by immediate environmental demands (freezing when flight is not a viable option, flight when escape is possible). Looking at each of these specific processes outside a systems framework is bound only to lead to confusion—and this is exactly what is seen with the continued confusion in psychology and psychiatry between fear and anxiety: although superficially very similar, they have different superordinate goals (avoidance/escape in the case of fear, cautious approach in the case of anxiety). Thus behaviors can appear different but serve the same functional goal, or they can appear highly similar but serve different functional goals.

There is another reason why a theory that explains coherence in personality structure and processes is so important; this relates to differences between the patterns of within-person and between-persons covariation. Although we might assume that the covariance structures within the person should be reflected in population-level trait structures, this is not the case. Partly, this might be a result of the fact that within-person covariation reflects dynamics in the time domain of repeated measures of a single person, whereas between-person differences relate to the study of a large group of people who have been measured (usually only once). It is also possible that there are heterogenous subsamples in the population that have different covariance structures, and this confuses the picture at the population (trait) level. But these explanations are unlikely to be the whole story. Although it must logically be the case that the source of personality traits measured at the population level must come from within-person dynamics, we lack a theoretical model of how to relate these two levels. It will be important to see if the theory proposed in this book is able to shed new light upon this important problem.

Fajkowska expands the basic concepts of her model to account for the clinical conditions of anxiety and depression that, even to this day, resist adequate explanation and treatment. Of particular interest here, the author uses the theory to propose different forms of these clinical disorders: the Arousal Type of anxiety, Apprehension Type of anxiety, Anhedonic Type of depression, and Valence Type of depression. She shows that these types are related to specific attentional patterns of stimulation processing. These novel postulates clearly need empirical scrutiny, but their theoretical novelty should orient the attention of investigators to new research questions.

In this detailed and thought-provoking book, Małgorzata Fajkowska provides a unique perspective on personality and its expressions in anxiety and depression. Her theory is well founded, resplendent in factual description and theoretical nuance, and bound to stimulate new thinking and research.

PHILIP J. CORR
*City University London*
*London, United Kingdom*

# Preface

Writing this book I was guided by the belief that the field of personality and individual differences should be formed in the manner of an integrative discipline. Thus when I began working on this volume some years ago, I made an assumption that it is valuable to adapt systems thinking to understanding personality and individual differences—more specifically, that a systems approach potentially might advance the core concerns of this branch of psychology, with a priority on personality coherence and incoherence.

This book is about personality coherence and incoherence and their role in explaining anxiety and depression. The operative words in the previous sentence are "personality coherence and incoherence." There are only a few works designed to introduce readers to the topic of personality coherence; these books are organized according to the integrative theories that have been of great importance in shaping and defining this field. However, any theoretical discussion of personality coherence in these books includes temperament and the attentional system—within the same framework—as the basic elements of personality coherence. Furthermore, none of these publications explain personality incoherence.

I have tried to propose an alternative. Obviously, the question of what personality coherence and incoherence are was the major motivating factor to write this book. Also, I was puzzled by the question about the functional role of personality coherence and incoherence and how it relates to the quality and dynamics of performance. Thus my primary goal in this volume is to establish the theory of personality coherence/incoherence. In addition, I introduce the affective traits (anxiety and depression) to this theory as elements of intraindividual coherence/incoherence, with the intention of offering a more complete explanation for the functional links between negative affectivity and attentional processing. Thus my secondary goal in this book is to integrate anxiety and depression into a more comprehensive scheme—a personality system—that better captures their complex nature and their relation with cognitive performance.

To some extent this book builds on the foundation provided by my earlier studies, papers, and monograph. However, it represents a more ambitious undertaking. I am uncomfortably aware that my proposition is only a modest attempt to illuminate some phenomena connected with personality and individual differences and mood traits. I would like to leave a critical evaluation of this volume in the hands of readers.

With reference to prospective readers, the book is intended for a range of audiences—including researchers and advanced students in personality and individual differences psychology, colleagues in other areas of psychology, and professionals in related disciplines.

The preparation of this work benefited enormously from the knowledge of various people who are experts in personality, individual differences, cognition, mood disorders, and statistics. They very kindly lent their assistance by commenting on some of the draft chapters of the book. Among those to whom I am truly grateful for such assistance are Philip Corr, Ewa Domaradzka, Andrzej Eliasz, Michael Eysenck, Piotr Jaśkowski, Joanna Kantor-Martynuska, Shulamith Kreitler, Jan Strelau, Agata Wytykowska, Anna Zagórska, and Marzenna Zakrzewska. I also thank publisher Eliot Werner for his tremendous devotion to the editorial work on this volume, and the late Gloria Brownstein for her editorial assistance.

I also wish to thank the Polish Ministry of Science and Higher Education (grant #N–N106432633) and the Institute of Psychology, Polish Academy of Sciences, for their financial support of this publication.

Writing such a complex book has influenced my personal life. On one hand it was a great intellectual adventure, but on the other it robbed me of time that I could spend with my family and friends. Thus I wish to thank my husband Marek and my daughter Weronika for sharing the enthusiasm and confusion of months of writing. I am also very grateful to Reverend Witold Świąder and Helena Krysiak for their prayers and encouragement. But above all I thank God and my late father for giving me the strength to finish the project.

I dedicate this book to my daughter Weronika, who has the most beautiful personality I have ever seen.

# Contents

## Part II. Anxiety and Depression in the Complex-System Approach to Personality

### Introduction.
### Introducing anxiety and depression: The complex phenomena



### Chapter 3.
### Anxiety and depression within the System of Regulation and Integration Stimulation



### Chapter 4.
### Anxiety and depression within the structure of coherent and incoherent types of personalities

## *Part III. Epilogue*

**Chapter 6.**
**Looking to the future: A need for integrative**
**models of personality** . . . . . . . . . . . . . . . . . . . . . . . . . . . . . . . . . . .  233

# PERSONALITY COHERENCE AND INCOHERENCE

## A Perspective on Anxiety and Depression

# Personality coherence and incoherence: An overview of the book

In this book personality coherence and incoherence are viewed through a systems framework. What are the unique aspects of systems thinking? Why is systems thinking valuable? Can the systems approach offer a better understanding of personality coherence and incoherence?

Let us deal with the first question. Generally, systems thinking is a way of understanding reality. Reality as a whole is composed of highly interdependent subsystems. Systems thinking is an approach to problem solving, based on the belief that the components of a system can be better understood in the context of relationships with each other and with other systems, rather than in isolation. In other words, in contrast to René Descartes's scientific analysis, to fully understand why a problem occurs and persists is to understand the parts in relation to the whole, and to examine the linkages and interactions between the elements that compose the entirety of the system. Potentially, systems thinking offers a new perspective, a specialized language, and tools that one can use to address specific everyday or scientific problems.

This brings us to the second question: the value of systems thinking. From the perspective of many scientists, including me, systems thinking is extremely valuable. It gives a more accurate picture of reality and encourages us to think about problems and solutions with an eye toward the long view. But far more important is the fact that systems thinking is founded on some basic, universal principles that one can detect in all areas of life. It appears that systems thinking "procedures" may be used to study any kind of system. Historically, the elements of systems thinking might be identified in the works of—for example—Isaac Newton (physicist), Karl Ludwig von Bertalanffy (biologist), William Ross Ashby (psychiatrist), Gregory Bateson (anthropologist and social scientist), Edward Norton Lorenz (mathematician and meteorologist), and Stanisław Lem (writer).

Thus here is the third question: why not apply this approach to personality psychology and to one of its cardinal concerns, personality coherence and incoherence? I think that the utility of systems thinking in personality psychology seems to be quite clear. In essence, if this branch of psychology is truly concerned with personality stability versus variability, personality coherence versus incoherence, and individuality, the principles that one discovers within a systems approach should at some point shed light on these issues. The accuracy of this statement is underscored by the content of the present book.

The book is organized into three parts. In Part I, I outline my own approach, which I refer to as the Complex–System Approach to Personality (C-SAP). In general, the C-SAP is a psychological paradigm that is designed to reconcile the stability and coherence of personality or behavior with their concomitant variability and incoherence. I believe that this theoretical framework can stand as a shared paradigm for personality psychology and the fields of psychology that explore the cognitive, affective, and social mechanisms of behaviors. Thus individual differences, as well as patterns of intraindividual variability/stability and coherence/incoherence, can be understood by fitting them into specific individual differences dimensions and biological and psychological mechanisms and processes. The study of complexity in nonlinear, dynamic systems (e.g., Bak & Chen, 1991; Bateson, 1972, 1979; Carver & Scheier, 1998, 2002; Cervone, 1997, 2005; Nowak & Vallacher, 1998; Skyttner, 2006; von Bertalanffy, 1950, 1955; Weinberg, 2001), with special reference to the social cognitive theories of personality (e.g., Bandura, 1986, 2006; Cervone, 2004, 2008; Shoda, 1999) and the Transactional Model of Temperament (Eliasz, 1981, 1985, 1992, 1995, 2004), provided a major impulse to the formulation of the C-SAP. I believe that the C-SAP advances other system approaches to personality (e.g., Mayer, 2006; McAdams, 2006) and represents one of many possible strategies for building an explanation of the functional meaning of personality coherence versus incoherence.

In Chapter 1, I consider personality organization and development from a meta-theoretical perspective. I articulate and extend four propositions: (a) personality is a complex system; (b) personality has a three-level organization; (c) personality develops and changes over time; and (d) personality reflects either coherent or incoherent structure. In short, personality as a system is a high-level organization of a set of variables standing in interrelation among them and with the environment. I claim that personality is organized into three levels: Level L-1 denotes biological, psychological, and situational mechanisms and processes; Level L represents structures; and Level L+1 indicates behaviors and actions. The relative stability of personality is explained by employing the compositional (scalar) hierarchy of system, while personality changes over time and across situations are explained by recruiting the subsumptive (specification) hierarchy of system. From a meta-theroretical perspective, three defining features of personality coherence are proposed.

- Personality coherence/incoherence emerges as a high-ordered property (Level L); is relatively stable, with an organized structure formed by a specific set of internal mechanisms (Level L-1); and expresses itself in overt responses and behaviors (Level L+1).

- Personality represents functional coherent or incoherent integration between different personality qualities.
- Highly integrated personality coherence or incoherence reflects functional correspondence or conflict (respectively) between composing complex personality qualities.

Chapter 2 focuses on the System of Regulation and Integration Stimulation (SRIS) as a fundamental structure of personality architecture. I advocate that the SRIS's major function is an effort allocation to attain and maintain (a) the optimal level of activation and arousal to achieve the optimal level of functioning of the whole system and (b) intraindividual coherence and behavioral integrity. It may be reached by its two basic elements: attentional system and temperament traits located on the processes (L-1) and structures (traits; L1) levels, respectively. These elements of the SRIS, based on the arousal and activation processes, are suggested to have a substantially important role in forming personality coherence/incoherence. However, I consider personality coherence as the consistency of traits in their controlling functions over stimulation (functional simplicity) and personality incoherence as the inconsistency of traits in their controlling functions over stimulation (functional complexity). On a more elaborated level, I claim that intraindividual personality coherence/incoherence is built upon functional consistency/inconsistency over stimulation processing between temperament and other, stimulation processing-related personality traits. And this functional consistency is analyzed in light of the complexity of traits (how many functional components might be distinguished in them) and the dominant function (reactive, regulative, or self-regulative) that they play in controlling stimulation.

Thus the dominant controlling function over stimulation in temperament type is a foundation for assessing personality coherence and incoherence. Different structures of temperament represent different controlling functions over stimulation. Based on the arousal related theories of temperament—Pavlovian, Eysenckian, and Strelauvian—I assume that the harmonious melancholic and disharmonious choleric types are more reactive (avoiding stimulation) than regulative (seeking stimulation) types of temperament, while the harmonious sanguine and disharmonious phlegmatic types seem to be more regulative (seeking stimulation) than reactive (avoiding stimulation) types of temperament.

I also suggest criteria for how to theoretically analyze the functional significance of personality coherence/incoherence. First, I postulate an exploration of correlational relations among controlling functions in focal traits, informing us about functional simplicity (coherence) or complexity (incoherence) of the personality system and their influence on quality of stimulation processing. Second, I propose the analysis of interactive (additive, synergistic, or antagonistic) relations among dominant controlling functions of temperament and other personality traits in coherent/incoherent types of personality. The latter provides an indicator of the dynamics of processes engaged in processing stimulation.

Part II of the book illustrates selected theoretical assumptions presented in Part I. Chapter 3 explores the modulatory role of anxiety and depression[1] as elements of the SRIS. It documents that these mood traits contribute to stimulation processing via the fact that as dimensional emotional phenomena they relate to arousal and activation and to activity in different neurobiological and physiological systems. I assume that if the biological mechanisms of arousal and activation bind temperament traits, moods traits, and attentional processes, a strong interrelation would be expected between them in response to (emotional) stimulation. Both mood traits are recognized as complex heterogeneous phenomena and their subtypes are proposed. Four of them—Arousal Type of anxiety and Apprehension Type of anxiety, and Anhedonic Type of depression and Valence Type of depression—are included in the theoretical analysis. It is shown that anxiety and depression subtypes produce specific attentional patterns of stimulation processing. The identification of these patterns allowed establishing the dominant controlling functions of each subtype: reactive rather than regulative in arousal anxiety and valence depression, and regulative rather than reactive in apprehension anxiety and anhedonic depression.

Chapter 4 is focused on constructing theoretical relations among four temperament types and anxiety and depression subtypes, which allows for building the specific structures of coherent/incoherent personalities. To be more precise, it looks for functional correspondence—or lack of it—among four temperament types (regulative sanguine and phlegmatic, and reactive melancholic and choleric) and mood subtypes (regulative apprehension anxiety and anhedonic depression and reactive arousal anxiety and valence depression) across Pavlovian, Eysenckian, and Strelauvian approaches.

Chapter 5 presents selections of my research on anxiety and depressed mood as elements of the coherent and incoherent personality structures (described in Chapter 4) in the context of their effects on attentional processing. These effects were analyzed across two important questions: (a) How does the level of functional complexity reflected in coherent/incoherent personality structures affect quality of stimulation processing? And (b) how do functional interactions in coherent/ incoherent personality structures relate to the dynamics of attentional processes engaged in stimulation processing?

To answer these questions I utilized intercorrelational and interactional analyses.

- With reference to the quality and dynamics of attentional stimulation processing, no predictable, regular, or specific patterns of results for personality

---

[1] In this book the focus is on depressed mood. However, I use the terms "depression" and "depressed mood" interchangeably.

coherence and personality incoherence were shown within or across the temperament models studied here (except in very few situations).

- Regarding the quality of attentional stimulation processing, it was demonstrated that this is more frequently connected with personality structures characterized by lower integration levels (e.g., harmoniousness of temperament) than personality coherence/incoherence (this conclusion is valid for all of three models of temperament). In addition, it was evidenced that personality coherence or incoherence does not always mean strong or weak stimulation processing, respectively.
- In relation to the dynamics of attentional stimulation processing, it appeared that these dynamics originate from two types of interactions—synergistic (responsible for maintaining the attentional processes engaged in stimulation processing specific for types of mood rather than types of temperament) or antagonistic (evoking totally new attentional processes engaged in stimulation processing).

These results are discussed in light of the C-SAP. However, an important conclusion is that the theoretical advances presented in this book must be supported by related, systematic, and long-term studies. The studies presented in Chapter 5 represent only a modest exemplification of this theory.

Finally, Chapter 6 in Part III is concentrated around three major issues. First, it compares selected integrative approaches to personality and individual differences with the aim to outline the specificity of the C-SAP in the context of other theories. Second, it discusses the four main sins that I identify in the studies of anxiety and depression and argues that developments in the C-SAP model can help correct some of them. And finally, it characterizes three problems as top priorities in future research and theorizing: (a) continuation of empirical validation of the theory presented; (b) a neurophysiological perspective within the C-SAP; and (c) the applicative utility of the model.

# Part I

# A Complex–System Approach to Personality

# Introduction

## General view of a system-based approach to personality

To frame what links and organizes modern thinking about personality, four cumulative historical trends are usually considered. The first trend focuses on personality dynamics (e.g., Freud, Rogers, Jung, Adler, and Erikson); the second trend points to personality structure (e.g., Murray, Allport, Cattell, Eysenck, Gray, Zuckerman); the third trend describes the crisis when reactions against classic models produced a focus on individual differences (e.g., Mischel, Kelly, Rotter, and Cervone); and the fourth trend illustrates the cumulative and integrative resolution that addresses personality at multiple levels (e.g., McAdams, Mayer; see Campbell, 2008).

My own approach presented in Chapter 1, the Complex–System Approach to Personality (C-SAP), seeks to promote the development of integrative theorizing. The challenge is to formulate the framework that subsumes particular insights from earlier models while permitting both within-person and between-person comparisons. Therefore the central concern here is to explain from a global perspective that an individual is like all other individuals (general principles and dynamic processes that account for personality as an integrative and regulative hierarchical system: insights from the first trend), like some other individuals (taxonomy of between-person individual differences: insights from the second trend), and like no one else (coherent versus incoherent intraindividual structure: similarity with the first, second, and third trends; cf. Campbell, 2008; Murray, 1938). However, within this approach the main goal is to elucidate the origins of personality coherence versus incoherence, specify how they relate to personality dimensions and dynamic processes, and show how a particular structure of coherent/incoherent personality types corresponds to differing modes of adaptation and functional specialization (cf. Campbell, 2008).

The point of departure for formulating the C-SAP is the identification of universal principles, mechanisms, and processes (applicable to all individuals) that remain constant and give rise to explain basic, parallel personality characteristics: structure and dynamics, consistency and variability, and its two fundamental functions (regulation and integration). Thus, to meet this challenge, I employ the universal principles, mechanisms, and processes from the complex-system approaches to psychological phenomena (see Caprara & Cervone, 2000, for a review; cf. Thomas, Segal, & Hersen, 2006). I am presenting the C-SAP's meta-theoretical background in the form of four propositions: (a) personality is a complex system; (b) personality has a three-level organization; (c) personality develops and changes; and (d) personality reflects either coherent or incoherent structure.

As demonstrated in Chapter 1, the C-SAP's meta-theoretical background represents my "philosophy of personality" that I do not subject to empirical validation. I believe that answers to a number of questions or a presentation of the very specific and basic theoretical concepts must be forthcoming before a meta-view on personality can be developed. It is beneficial to consider the underlying assumptions of the basic concepts of personality since this allows us to better understand them; doing so may also inspire researchers and stimulate new scientific questions. But far more important is that it provides frames that permit us to formulate a cohesive theory to understand individuals. Still, personality psychology deals with a difficult task: to offer an integrated explanation of a person as a dynamic, complex whole living in a complex environment. One possibility to establish such a comprehensive view of personality is to combine a theorist's "meta-theoretical orientation" with his or her specific theoretical concepts. Thus what I propose is not to limit personality theory only to rigorous standards of empirical evidence (obtained through unbiased scientific investigation), but also to leave a place in this field for meta-analysis.

Thus, as described in Chapter 2, the basic concepts—the heart and soul of the C-SAP—are developed from a meta-theoretical analysis and compose an explanatory framework that provides an understanding of personality coherence versus incoherence. However, although personality coherence and incoherence are the targets of investigation here, other related concepts are presented. I introduce the System of Regulation and Integration Stimulation (SRIS) as a fundamental structure of personality architecture. The SRIS is seen as having a substantially important role in forming personality coherence/incoherence (functional consistency/ inconsistency over stimulation processing between temperament capacities and other personality traits related to stimulation processing). In addition, the foundations on which this theory rests are arousal and activation, temperament, and the attentional system (crucial for SRIS formation and a basic structure of personality). Also, a trait concept is broadened by analysis of their complexity and their dominant controlling functions over stimulation. And a theoretical analysis of the functional significance of personality coherence/ incoherence is undertaken.

In conclusion, in this part of the book the reader can find possible answers to the questions that represent basic issues in personality psychology.

- What is personality?
- How is personality organized?
- How does personality develop and change?

- What makes personality stable?
- What are personality coherence and incoherence and how are they studied?
- What is a trait and why is it useful in an analysis of personality coherence/incoherence?

However, personality psychology has more enduring questions that are not answered in this book—for example, the nature of the self and free will, and the extent to which conscious or unconscious motives explain individual behaviors. Moreover, the C-SAP does not focus on clinical issues associated with personality, the "organismic" side of personality, or developmental stages of personality.

# Chapter 1

## A Complex–System Approach to Personality: Related meta-theoretical issues

### 1.1.
### Personality as a complex system

The first proposition concerns personality as a complex system. It should be said that many psychologists have been influenced by the study of complexity in nonlinear, dynamic systems and have come to recognize the importance of nonlinear dynamics for their field (e.g., Barton, 1994; Carver, 2004; Carver & Scheier, 1998, 2002; Cervone, 1991, 1999, 2000; Eliasz, 1981; Matthews, 2009; Vallacher & Nowak, 1994, 1997). Substantial empirical evidence has been presented from both inside (e.g., Shoda & Mischel, 1998) and outside (e.g., Latané & L'Herrou, 1996; Matthews, 2009; Nowak & Vallacher, 1998) personality psychology that some psychological phenomena, including personality, result from the mutual relations among multiple elements of complex systems. It is worth noting that there is a striking resemblance between this complex-systems view incorporated into the different psychological branches and General System Theory (von Bertalanffy, 1950, 1968a, 1975). Thus, if personality can be perceived as a complex system of interacting elements, the relevant issue in this respect is to go into a more detailed description of the organization, structure, and dynamics of a system originally provided by General System Theory (von Bertalanffy, 1950) and subsequently developed by scholars from different disciplines (e.g., Allen & Hoekstra, 1984; King, 1997; Mayer, 1998, 2006, 2007a; Simon, 1973).

Starting with its definition, a system is seen as a high-level organization of a set of variables standing in interrelation among them and with the environment. In a system the focus is on the relationship between elements, rather than on the elements themselves. Additionally, a view of causality of events involves the feedback model of causality in which circular—rather than linear—processes are involved. What is defined initially as an effect becomes the cause of yet a later event; as demonstrated by von Bertalanffy (1968b), different causes can produce the same result (equifinality), whereas one cause may produce different results (equipotentiality).

A system is an organized wholeness that tends toward maintenance of a relatively stable and balanced internal and external environment through a series of interacting (e.g., physiological, psychological, and social) processes. The relatively stable structure of a system is featured by the reciprocal relations among its elements and by the properties of these interrelations. A living system may be analyzed in terms of its components, entities, or subsystems, or it may be viewed as part of a larger system (suprasystem). Thus a hierarchical system is a system of subsystems within a larger system, where the rank is canonical rather than optional. The hierarchical organization has two known nested forms: a scalar or compositional hierarchy, based on scale extension; and a specification or subsumptive hierarchy, based on descriptive complexity intension. These forms provide the model of organization, control, and development, respectively (e.g., Lemke, 2000; Mayer, 1993a, 1993b; Salthe, 1985, 1988, 1991, 1993; Simon, 1973). Each system has a measure of independence from the suprasystem of which is a part (e.g., a person from the environment, the temperament traits from personality), but only within certain limits—beyond which the system may be exposed to dysfunctionality.

A system's existence is guaranteed by its boundary, a region that contains and protects that part of the system and where the transfer of information and matter/energy is restricted relative to internal and external regions. Also, the individuality of each system is preserved by its boundary. Just as the boundary maintains a degree of autonomy for the system despite a general control by the suprasystem of which it is a part, so feedback loops adjusting the functioning of the system according to its performance maintain a general continuity of structure and function despite being "loose" enough to permit changing growth within permissible limits (cf. Fajkowska-Stanik, 2001; von Bertallanffy, 1950, 1968a, 1968b).

Incorporating these assumptions into the Complex–System Approach to Personality (C-SAP) posits personality as a complex, hierarchical system of interacting elements. As in other complex systems, these interacting elements tend to achieve relatively stable patterns of organization, which may not be entirely predictable. The behavior of complex systems is nonlinear. Rather than developing in a systematic, progressive manner, the system may shift immediately from one pattern or state to another. Moreover, a complex system tends to self-organize and its organization is a product of the interactions among its variables, which implies that there is no preexisting structure that determines the final form of the system (Caprara & Cervone, 2000). More precisely, the overall personality organization results from synergistic and diachronic interactions among multiple biological, psychological, and environmental subsystems, and their relatively distinct mechanisms and processes develop over time—as reciprocally interacting elements—into more complex and stable structures (cf. Caprara, 1996). The organization of personality is distributed across these subsystems, which operate with different degrees of interdependence versus independence (cf. Mayer, 1993b, 2007b). Regarding these premises, personality consists of a set of contrasts that have been often seen as incompatible—namely, structure versus dynamics, consistency versus variability. I argue that the assumption concerning the hierarchical organization of personality provides a promising integration across these contrasts.

Indeed, in terms of a hierarchical organization of personality, it seems essential to combine both forms—scalar and specification hierarchy—to identify how personality is an ordering of the parts that make up a system (i.e., "composed" of these parts) and how its parts are "subsumed" (i.e., classified from the general objects to the specific ones). Hence, with reference to the second and third propositions, I will argue that the compositional hierarchy can be used to support the utility of describing personality according to its components, the organization of its components, and control mechanisms; employing a subsumptive hierarchy allows us to explain personality changes over time and across situations. Finally, with regard to the fourth proposition, I would like to demonstrate that personality develops into an intraindividual, integrative system whose structure might be coherent or incoherent (see also Allport, 1937; Stern, 1935).

One needs to remember here that hierarchy is a conceptual construction, an analytical tool, and its use does not imply that personality itself is actually hierarchically organized. It does seem to be in many ways, but to suppose that this is the sole principle needed to understand personality would be naive. It is just one among many tools.

## 1.2.
## Personality organization

What are the definitional features of the compositional hierarchy? Generally, the compositional hierarchy (scalar or grading system) represents extensional complexity. In this form of hierarchy, subsystems of a system are organized into levels. Almost always, there are several criteria (running alone, in parallel, or divergent) by which upper levels reside above lower levels—namely, by virtue of (a) being the context; (b) providing constraint; (c) behaving more slowly at a lower frequency; (d) being populated by entities with greater integrity and higher bond strength; and (e) containing and being formed by lower levels (cf. Allen & Hoekstra, 1984; King, 1997; Lavelle et al., 2008). A subsystem is simultaneously a whole and a part of another whole, and this other whole exists at the next higher level of organization (Simon, 1973). Hence the temporal and spatial scales are inseparable from the consideration of a nested hierarchical system (cf. Allen & Star, 1982; Lavelle et al., 2008).

Guided by higher-level boundary conditions, the elements at one level emerge as a consequence of the interactions and relationships among elements at the next lower level. These emergent properties are the fundamental properties of hierarchically organized systems—functions that are not seen at the lower level. These level hierarchies are characterized by same-level causation and bidirectional, cross-level causation: upward causation, which may be seen as bottom-up; and downward causation, which may be seen as top-down (cf. King, 1997; von Bertalanffy, 1950, 1975). Some useful properties of the higher level may emerge naturally from lower-level behaviors, but not all of them; higher-level properties are also subject to selection pressures on heritable variation and the elaboration of complex functional adaptations. Thus, when postulating multiple levels of organization, we are not positing that the behaviors of all higher layers emerge automatically from the lowest layer.

When using the compositional hierarchy, the system can be described by a three-level triadic structure: a focal Level L, the next lower Level L-1, and the next higher Level L+1 (see Figure 1.1). Dynamics of the focal Level L may be explained by being dependent on the interactions at the next lower level (cf. O'Neil, de Angelis, Waide, & Allen, 1986). The levels are relatively distinct and nearly decomposable.

This three-level organization warrants stability because with it in place (a third level always anchoring relations between the other two) the focal level cannot be reduced either upward or downward by assimilation into a neighboring level; the system is implicitly synchronic (moments of different scale nest within each other). Here it is worth noting that this hierarchy might be used to explain how different phenomena manage to be as stable as they are (cf. Feibleman, 1954; Odum & Odum, 2000; Weiss, 1971). On a more elaborated level, the compositional hierarchy represents a single moment in space so its dynamics reflect homeostasis, not change. Large-scale moments "contain" many small-scale moments. It is often suggested that scalar levels fundamentally signal rate differences rather than component size differences. Because of the order-of-magnitude differences between levels in the scale hierarchy, dynamics at different levels do not directly interact or exchange energy, but transact by way of mutual constraint (i.e., via informational connections). Higher-scale dynamics are so slow with respect to the focal level that the current value of their momentary result appears relatively unchanging at the focal level. Cumulated results of lower-scale dynamics also appear relatively unchanging at the focal level, since it takes a very long time in lower-scale moments to effect a change detectable at the focal level. These points are the essence of constraints (cf. Aronson, 1984; Collier, 1989; Nicolis, 1986).

Looking at a system in Figure 1.1, there are two reasons behind what can be seen below. First, it is not possible to detect something if the entities of the system cannot do what is required of them to achieve the arrangement in the whole. These are the limits of physical possibility, coming from lower levels in the hierarchy. The second—and entirely separate—reason for what can be seen has to do with what is allowed by the upper-level constraints (cf. King, 1997). That is, focal Level L dynamics occur within the context of a higher-level system at Level L+1 and this context constrains the behavior of Level L elements; constraints on focal-level dynamics are thus found by reference to the next higher level. Moreover, because

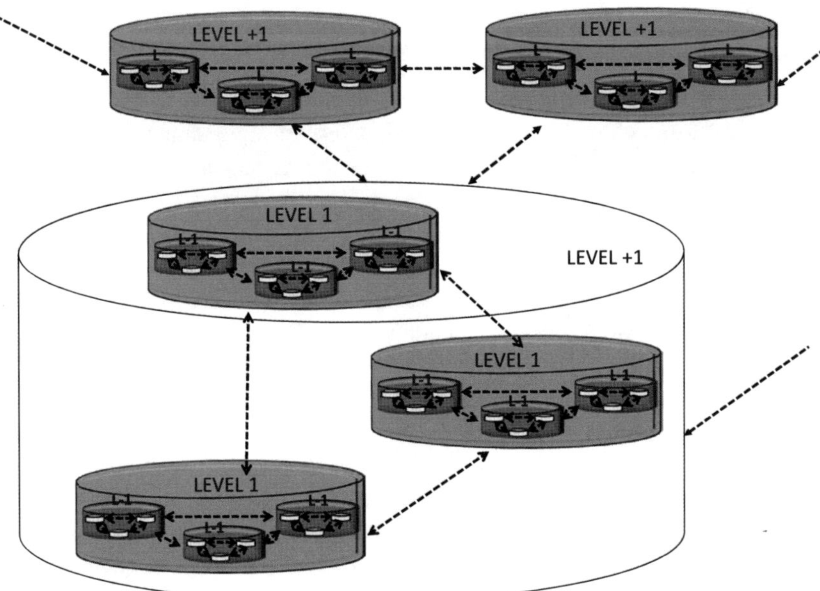


**Figure 1.1.** A hypothetical model of the compositional hierarchy. The cylinders represent the systems of a particular level of organization. Lines among all cylinders indicate dynamic interactions. Three cylinders, including one shown as bigger and transparent for clarity, represent systems at higher Level L+1. The Level L+1 systems interact as components of next higher Level L+2, not presented here. The next smaller cylinders symbolize the next lower level, which is the focal Level L1. Interactions among focal Level L1 systems, combined with the constraints of membership in Level L+2, arrange the Level L+1 systems. At the focal Level L1, the next smaller cylinders—depicted only in the biggest cylinder—illustrate the next lower Level L-1. Interactions among lower Level L-1 systems, combined with the constraints of membership in Level L+1, structure the Level L1 systems. The smallest cylinders are the L-2 components of the L-1 systems.

interactions among focal-level elements determine the dynamics of L+1 (as the parts or components of next level systems), the consequences or significance of focal-level behavior are also found by reference to the next higher level. It is worth noting that the dynamics of interaction among components of the focal Level L are independent of their internal structure and the dynamics of their own components. They interact as essentially "rigid entities." Their internal dynamics or behaviors are observed as the integrated properties of Level L-1. The focal Level L is isolated from dynamics below Level L-1; lower-level dynamics are filtered or buffered through Level L-1 by integration and might be ignored except for their determination of the stable L-1 properties (cf. King, 1997).

### *1.2.1. Three-level structure of personality*

This general description of the compositional hierarchy might be applied to a particular phenomenon like personality. Describing personality within the compositional hierarchy means that it assimilates the crucial features of this type of hierarchy. Thus I claim that the personality system is organized into three levels (subsystems): Level L-1 denotes Mechanisms and Processes; Level L represents Structures; and Level L+1 indicates Behaviors and Actions (see Figure 1.2).

It is assumed that Level L-1, representing Mechanisms and Processes, covers the personality components such as energetic capacities (e.g., physiological mechanisms of stimulation processing, mental energy, subjective arousal) and abilities (e.g., cognitive, social). Metaphorically, in the next upper level (Level L: Structures), these mechanisms and processes might be directly exploited by personality traits for particular purposes. For example, the Big Three trait extraversion suggests that an individual has personality components consisting of physiological mechanisms that indicate the tendency to seek out stimulation, and prosocial abilities that reflect seeking the company of others (cf. Eysenck, 1987). Thus the personality trait might be understood as the emergent property of a complex system capturing relatively consistent behavioral tendencies (Level L+1: Behaviors and Actions; cf. Carprara & Cervone, 2000) and the level of structures is classified from types or patterns of personalities (e.g., Type A personality; Friedman, 1996) to the traits (e.g., impatience, competitiveness, aggressiveness, restlessness).

It must be emphasized that there are several reasons explaining why certain personality components are identified at a particular level (capacities and abilities at Level L-1; traits, types, and patterns at Level L; and tendencies, strategies, and styles at Level L+1). Actually, there are three reasons why the upper levels of the personality system reside above the lower levels: they provide constraints (e.g., Level L+1 strategies may limit dynamics of a particular Level L structure of personality); they are populated by entities with greater integrity and higher bond strength (e.g., Level L-1 physiological mechanisms of stimulation-processing capacities seem to be less integrated entities than a Level L temperament type); and they contain and are formed by lower levels (e.g., Level L+1 styles have their roots in Level L1 traits). In addition, there are limits coming from lower levels L-1 and L; for example, Level L-1 biological mechanisms of low capacities of stimulation processing allow for a limited number of traits that may occur at the next higher Level L.

Following the above description of the three-level organization, it might be expected that personality tends to maintain a homeostasis and adaptation—as well as a general continuity of structure and function—to permit changes within permissible limits. In other words, these three levels are not reducible to each other (e.g., behavior tendencies to personality structures or psychological mechanisms) and the cumulated results of dynamics at the lower level are unchangeable at the higher level.

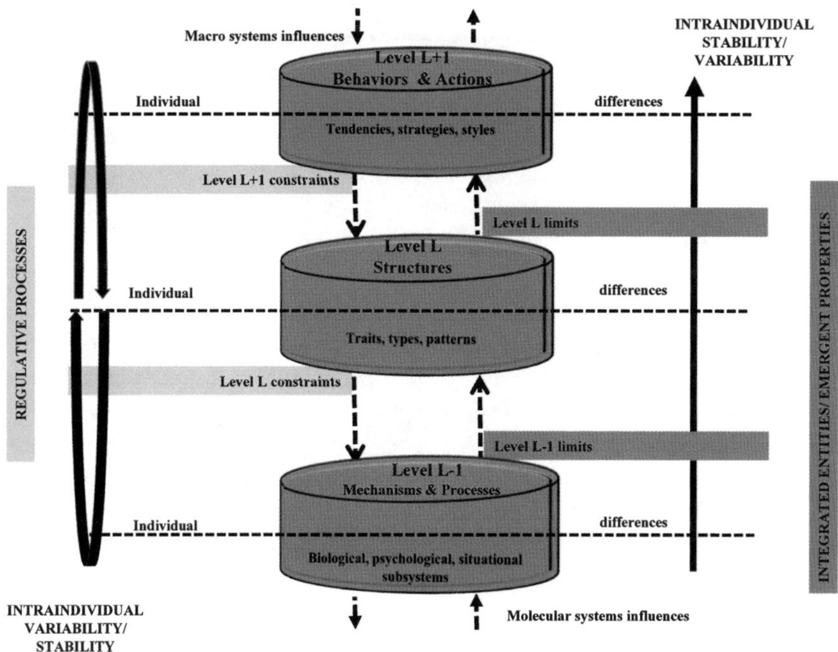



**Figure 1.2.** A hypothetical hierarchical organization of the personality system.

In addition to those identified across the three levels, there are components of control based on regulative and integrative mechanisms. The next section provides a more detailed picture of these personality components and their organizational principles.

### *1.2.2. Organizing mechanisms and emergent properties*

Which mechanisms organize personality structure? Addressing this point requires characterizing the variability that includes global stability or response of the system. Obviously, this characterization will not result from a one-to-one description and modeling of personalities (gene, trait, behavior), but rather from the correct identification of which components (and systems properties emerging from these components) are relevant for a given problem and the reconstruction of the mechanisms involved. Such a reconstruction allows us to use logical analysis as one of several possibilities (but except for, e.g., computational or mathematical tools) to subsume many of the insights and empirical evidence from earlier models. Generally, it can be achieved by defining:

- *Lower to upper functions (upward causation).* Unidirectional, bottom-up way to integrate parameters and/or mechanisms at a given level into effective and reduced descriptions at a higher level. It includes both intralevel/horizontal and interlevel/vertical couplings.
- *Upper to lower functions (downward causation).* Bidirectional, top-down feedbacks introduced to account for the strong interconnection between the levels, employed as regulative mechanisms (see Figure 1.2).

I submit that upward causation produces stability, which limits variability or allows for the optimal level of system variability. To say this in a more advanced manner, personality variability is the stability-framed scope of personality changes. The emergent properties originate from the constant dynamic interactions among the particular elements on a given level, after which they are interpolated into the *intra* or *inter* upper levels as integrated entities. The integration is based on three kinds of repeated and regular processes. The first process relates to interaction, understood as a changing sequence and hanging sequence of actions between elements, which modify their actions and reactions due to the actions by their interaction partner (or partners). The second process is intercorrelation, which is a mark of dependence, strength, and tendency of association between elements (cf. Fajkowska-Stanik, 2001). These two processes signify that dynamics at the same levels directly exchange energy/information, while the third process—transaction—informs us that dynamics at different levels indirectly exchange energy/information. Thus transaction reflects myriad ways in which elements of personality influence one another, multidirectional influences among various components, and interconnections via a network. Transaction mirrors action that is adapted to the situated environment/setting, and this action produces changes in the elements at the particular level of system that affect the status of the entire system, but also changes in the whole system that affect individual elements at the particular level of system. It implies that transactions involve interactions and intercorrelations, and together are associated with intralevel and interlevel emergent properties.

At the same time, regulative processes (downward causation) maintain stability and an optimum level of variability: they allow for a particular amount of variability without losing stability allied to homeostasis or adaptation to genetic and environmental changes (cf. Lavelle et al., 2008). Possible regulative mechanisms include mechanisms of negative and positive feedback loops. In other words, control, monitoring, modification, reinforcement, amplification, activation, or inhibition are achieved thanks to circular causation involving positive and negative feedbacks. Negative feedback tends to reduce or inhibit a process (upper-level constraints). Providing that the overall feedback of the system is negative, the system will tend to be stable. Positive feedback appears when an output is enhanced; this relates to the tendency to expand or promote process, resulting in amplification of the original signal instead of stabilizing the signal (cf. von Bertalanffy, 1968a, 1968b).

There are four important issues worthy of mention here.

*Intralevel and interlevel personality emergent properties*

It is not possible to separate the contribution of upward and downward causation in giving rise to emergent properties. In other words, they are products of both integrative and regulative processes. In addition, the integrative processes are activated, reduced, or inhibited since the final outcome is maintained by top-down causation. Moreover, the higher-level principles organize lower-level events into systemic self-sustaining or self-reproducing patterns of interactions. Thus, according to Figure 1.2, one can recognize the intralevel and interlevel personality properties that have emerged on the basis of upward and downward causations.

These Mechanisms and Processes (Level L-1), which resulted from the dynamic processes among biological, psychological, and situational subsystems, belong to the group of intralevel emergent properties. Hence the set of interlevel emergent properties originate from interactions among appropriate components of Level L-2 (for clarity not shown in Figure 1.2) and constitute three subsystems of Level L-1—namely, biological (involving, e.g., genetic, endocrinal, physiological, and neurobiochemical components), psychological (embracing, e.g., cognitive, affective, and motivational components), and situational (engaging, e.g., situational complexity and demands, the nature of object components). In other words, the three subsystems of personality mechanisms have their lower-level-related mechanisms and processes. Specifically, biological mechanisms are associated with, for example, physiological mechanisms of stimulation processing and cortical responsiveness to emotions; psychological mechanisms are linked to, for example, approach or avoidance mechanisms, signal information about self or others, and abstract reasoning; situational mechanisms are allied with, for example, relational mechanisms and information transmission processes.

The next group of intralevel emergent properties—namely, Level L structures—are seen as effects of interactions and intercorrelations between traits. Then traits as interlevel emergent properties arise from dynamic processes among given biological, psychological, and situational mechanisms and processes on Level L-1. Many central personality traits emerge (or draw their features) variously from those mechanisms and processes. So there exist such traits as emotional reactivity, perseveration (cf. Strelau, 2008), neuroticism, extraversion (cf. Eysenck, 1981), and other biologically based temperament traits. Also found are motivational traits like the need for achievement or need for aggression (cf. Murray, 1938); affective traits such as anxiety (cf. Spielberger, 1983) or fear or hostility (cf. Watson, 2000); cognitive traits like intelligence, creativity (cf. Sternberg, 2007), and attentional control (Derryberry & Reed, 2002); and situation-loaded traits such as agreeableness (Jensen-Campbell & Graziano, 2001) and communication apprehension (e.g., Boorom, Goolsby, & Romsey, 1998). This is not a complete picture of traits, because they emerge (and draw features from) expert knowledge structures with respect to the self and others (see Mayer, 2000).

Eventually, there is a class of intralevel emergent properties as behavioral tendencies and actions (Level L+1) that are transactional products of tendencies, strategies, and styles (reflecting, e.g., motives, plans, goals, defenses). The latter ones are interlevel emergent properties that materialize from the transactions among particular trait structures on Level L. Trait-like styles might be seen as relatively stable patterns of activity, behavior, or process running in the particular area; rather, they are involuntary mechanisms of controlling and modifying the relation between the present state and environment, while strategies are more intentional, situation, or task-specific and serve as the adaptive mechanisms aimed at reducing error in decision-making processes (cf. Grigorienko & Sternberg, 1997; Zhang & Sternberg, 2006). Thus we have the repressive coping styles more related to melancholic or sanguine temperament structures (cf. Fajkowska & Eysenck, 2008); the nonadaptive, cognitive strategies of emotion regulation (e.g., blame others, catastrophizing, rumination) positively connected with neuroticism (cf. Garnefski et al., 2002); and the task-oriented coping significantly related to extraversion and frustration tolerance in depressive individuals (e.g., Uehara, Sakado, Sakado, Sato, & Someya, 1999).

*Variability and stability of personality levels*

The second important issue is associated with the stability versus variability of the given personality levels. Variability and stability are analogous in certain respects to kinetic and potential energy, as Spielberger (1983) points out convincingly in his discussion of anxiety as a state and anxiety as a trait. Variability, like kinetic energy, refers to a palpable reaction or process taking place at a given time and level of intensity; it is completely frame-dependent (relative). Stability resembles a potential energy that is stored within a system as a result of the position or configuration of the different parts of that system, and exists when there is a force that tends to pull a system back toward some lower-energy position. The most popular example here is the motion of a roller coaster car. When the roller coaster car climbs a hill, it has potential energy. At the very top of the hill, it reaches its maximum potential energy. When the car speeds down the hill, the potential energy turns into kinetic, which is greatest at the bottom of the path.

This might help explain that the highest stability is expected at the top of the personality system L+1 (Behaviors and Actions), compared with its lower levels L (Structures) and L-1 (Mechanisms and Processes). Consequently, the highest variability might be observed at the lower levels of the personality system. This corresponds to the above description that the higher levels of the system consist of the most integrated entities, while the lower ones do not. It is typical for higher levels to have slow internal dynamics and weak interactions among their entities (Level L+1; Figure 1.2), whereas higher- or medium-frequency dynamics and strong or moderate interactions are observed among particular elements on the lower levels of personality systems (Level L; Level L-1; Figure 1.2). Obviously, this implies that Structure is moderately stable, and that Mechanisms and Processes is the least stable level of the personality system. Yet, in general, intraindividual stability is far more characteristic for one's behaviors and actions (Level L+1) than for one's structure of personality (Level L) or the biological, psychological, or situational mechanisms and processes that underlie this structure (Level L-1). Naturally, this issue is addressed to the particular levels of personality rather than the whole three-level system of personality, which inherently tends toward stability. The next section provides more support for these assumptions.

Thus two issues discussed here—namely, the contribution of upward and downward causation to the extraction of emergent properties and the stability versus variability of the particular personality levels—clarify why Figure 1.2 has intraindividual stability/variability on the top right and intraindividual variability/stability on the bottom left.

### Correspondence between levels of personality

This issue is addressed to the character of correspondence between personality levels. For instance, traditional approaches to the study of personality treat people's reports of their behavioral tendencies as an indicator of internal personality structures. In light of the C-SAP, there is no direct correspondence among levels—for example, between levels of overt actions and structures. That lack of direct correspondence between levels may be explained by equifinality and equipotentiality principles. In other words, interacting and transacting elements of the complex personality system tend to achieve stable patterns or structures of organization, but without prespecification of the exact final form. To provide an illustration of this, we can refer to an example of neuroticism as a trait-emergent property treated as the isolated subsystem of the three-level personality system or as one of the components of the focal level (L) of the three-level personality system.

Equifinality implies that there is no consistent explanation linking a set of intralevel causal dynamics to a given interlevel result. It seems to be problematic if only because individuals may engage in the same overt behaviors for different reasons (cf. Cervone, 2008). In the case of a neurotic individual, for example, we observe the tendency toward loss of control and nonadaptive coping (e.g., Clarke, 2004; Muris, de Jong, & Englelen, 2004). The neuroticisms encompass anxiety, so-called "worrisome thoughts," depressed mood, various psychosomatic disorders, overly emotional reactions, inappropriately strong responses to all sorts of stimuli, and irrational and rigid ways of reacting (Eysenck & Eysenck, 1985). Hence the diversity of the neuroticism trait inherently leaves open the possibility of equifinality: its different facets or interactions among them may affect impaired control and coping in a particular individual, whereas equipotentiality indicates that the particular intralevel casual dynamics may provide different interlevel results. The same facet of neuroticism or the same interaction among given facets may result, for instance, in loss of control (e.g., Clarke, 2004), cognitive failure (e.g., Wallace, 2004), rumination (e.g., Muris et al., 2004), or depression (e.g., Chioqueta & Stiles, 2005).

In summary, the specific behaviors outlined above arise from interactions and transactions among a complex neuroticism's multiple elements, no one of which directly corresponds to the behavior to be explained. Moreover, neuroticism as a component of Level L has its internal dynamics; it is observed as the integrated property on Level L-1 (Mechanisms and Processes) and it interacts, on Level L (Structures), as a stiff, autonomous entity with other "rigid" components of this level (e.g., extraversion, psychoticism; Eysenck, 1947/1998). The internal structures and dynamics of components of Level L are isolated from dynamics below Level L-1 and above Level L+1 (Behaviors and Actions), but the consequences or significance of the level of dynamics of structures are also found by reference to the level of behaviors and actions. In other words, if we treat failure control and coping as the emergent property of Level L+1 linked to neuroticism, we should take into account that it might be a product of the given interactions between components on the level of structures, including neuroticism. With regard to equifinality and equipotentiality principles, the tendency to exhibit these overt behaviors does not directly correspond to a particular component of Level L.

It is worth adding that differentiation of traits (Level L) from behavioral tendencies, styles, and strategies (Level L+1) corresponds to some theoretical propositions (e.g., Kreitler & Kreitler, 1990) and conflicts with others (e.g., Buss, 2012; Strelau, 2008).

*Mechanisms of control and personality*

As stated above, personality is governed by inner mechanisms of control (e.g., neurological versus psychosocial control; cognitive versus affective control) and distributed upward and downward across levels and subcomponents. These mechanisms act in concert or in conflict with its companion systems. Moreover, personality is viewed as having hierarchical mechanisms of control—for example, from automatic and unconscious to intentional and self-governed ones. Personality as a self-regulating system is equipped with the capacity to serve individual development and maintain the sense of stability and continuity across the life span (cf. Caprara & Cervone, 2000). However, personality is also organized according to outside control—other people, institutions, and situations. As the open system that exchanges energy, materials, or information with the environment, personality is seen as exquisitely sensitive to external factors; it is assumed that individual differences are elicited primarily in threatening (provoking self-protective reactions) and ambiguous situations (forming a response from an individual's unique abilities, dispositions, and motivations; cf. Mayer, 1993b). Obviously, the outside control of personality is typically only partial and usually interacts with the rest of personality. Not only do individuals respond differently to the environmental cues as proposed by early interactionism (e.g., Magnusson, 1988), but they actively construct and transform environments—which implies that individuals possess capacity to contribute actively to their experiences and development to attain a coherent sense of self.

Nevertheless, some extreme examples make it clear that personality might be substantially under outside mechanisms of control. For example, Eliasz (1981) provided results indicating the effects of environment on temperament properties. Lower temperament reactivity was observed in subjects living in prolonged, highly stimulating conditions compared with those living in less stimulating environments. In another longitudinal study, Klonowicz (2001) showed that changes in reactivity are synchronized with other personality characteristics (e.g., control beliefs in unemployment).

In sum, my attempt here has been to develop the second proposition concerning personality structure and to answer the question of why an individual is like all other individuals. The approach to that problem presented above posits the hypothetical existence of a three-level personality system composed of Mechanisms and Processes, Structures, and Behaviors and Actions. It is believed that intraindividual-limited stability is vertical; that is, it can be analyzed across levels in a particular three-level personality system. By contrast, individual differences are horizontal and can be studied between particular levels of personality across different individuals (Figure 1.2). This leads to a second question mentioned above—namely, in what way an individual is like other individuals. One solution to that puzzle is to explore the development and differentiation of a specific component of a given level of personality.

## 1.3.
## Personality development and change

The third proposition is addressed to personality development and change. Thus in the previous section I constructed personality stability by employing the compositional hierarchy of systems. Now I am going to consider how personality changes over time and across situations, employing the subsumptive hierarchy of systems.

A variety of theorists and researchers have viewed personality as relatively stable and believe that certain aspects of personality are relatively constant through the life span (e.g., temperament, intelligence). Presumably, some portions of personality remain much the same, but the other perspective is that personality follows rhythms, developmental stages, and self-actualization.

For example, Watson (2000) presented interesting findings with respect to the patterns of mood cyclicity. In sharp contrast to negative affect, positive affect showed a strong and systematic circadian rhythm. Positive mood levels are low at the beginning and end of the day and reach their peak at the midpoint between rising and retiring. Additionally, this pattern was highly generalizable across individual differences (e.g., morning and evening types) and different types of positive moods (e.g., joviality, attentiveness). Thus the emotion system appears stable; its state might change but its overall mood level and cyclicity will be consistent.

By far the most common perspectives on personality change over time are that it develops according to particular "normative" stages. For example, in his genetic epistemology, Piaget (1955, 1983) proposed four developmental stages of cognition: sensimotor (e.g., simple reflexes, circular reactions), preoperational (e.g., magical thinking), concrete operational (e.g., thinking with practical aids), and formal operational (e.g., abstract reasoning). And the final perspective concerning personality over time dealt with self-actualization, seen as the motive for realizing all one's capacities or potentialities (e.g., Goldstein, 1939/1995) or a level of development residing at the top of a hierarchy of needs (e.g., Maslow, 1954).

Thus, by following the guidance offered from the model of a specification hierarchy, we can understand the direction in which the particular level of personality or the component of this level have developed through time. In a subsumptive hierarchy, informational relations between levels are open ended, transitive, direct, and linked to the energy exchange—in contrast to a scalar hierarchy organization, where informational relations are generally indirect and transactional. There are functionally just two levels at work anywhere in the hierarchy and new levels may diverge from anywhere in the hierarchy, potentially giving rise to collections of coordinate classes (cf. King, 1997).

A subsumptive hierarchy is seen as a two-level basic form that offers a model of variability and development. Here the highest relevant level is always the one in focus, with the lower levels of the hierarchy providing cumulative initiating conditions simultaneously upon it. The two-level organization is unstable, allowing new levels to emerge at the top of the hierarchy, because without the anchoring provided by a third level, it can logically be reduced to a single level (cf. Figure 1.3). A subsumptive hierarchy constitutes levels as nested subclasses. Each level represents different integration. Higher levels transitively integrate dynamics and phenomena at lower levels and two levels are sufficient to explore integration (cf. Lavelle et al., 2008).

In light of a diachronic interpretation (the direction in which something has developed through time), a subsumptive hierarchy denotes stages of development, which is modeled as the accumulation of greater specification (via growth and/or differentiation). The order is then interpreted as having been generated by a chain of historical emergences, from the outermost to the innermost class. That is, the potentials arising within any class form a tree.

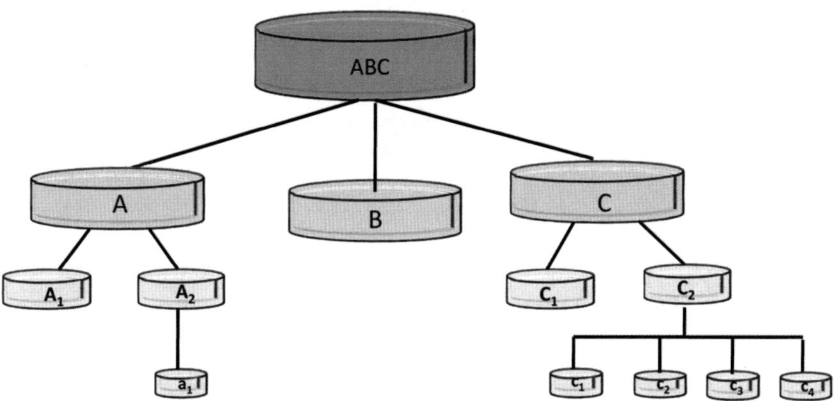


**Figure 1.3.** A hypothetical model of a subsumptive hierarchy. The highest ABC level contains a set of three lower-level classes: A, B, and C. In this picture class A involves two next lower-level subclasses $A_1$ and $A_2$, and the latest one is defined by $a_1$—the subclass on the lowest level. Class B is not developed. Class C is composed of two next lower-level subclasses $C_1$ and $C_2$. Subclass $C_2$ differentiates into four subclasses $c_1$, $c_2$, $c_3$, and $c_4$ on the lowest level.

For example, as presented Figure 1.4, the focus level of a particular personality system might be the coping strategies employed in stressful situations (Carver, Scheier, & Weintraub, 1989), located within Level L+1 (see Figure 1.2), with identified lower-level subclasses like active coping, planning, and suppression of competing activities.

However, these coping responses might be adaptive only in a specific class of situations (e.g., conflicts in the workplace), whereas they are not useful in other sets of situations (e.g., marital conflicts). Here the instability and growth of this two-level form may be caused by the situational factors by way of adding new subclasses of coping strategies. Additionally, individuals as active agents (Bandura, 1999) contribute to the shaping of their own repertoire of coping reactions. Consequently, new subclasses might emerge from the top of the hierarchy—for example, seeking instrumental or emotional social support or turning to religion, which may be more adequate for coping effectively with marital difficulties. Nonetheless, it is also possible that less adaptive forms of coping (e.g., focus on and venting of emotions, behavioral or mental disengagement) might emerge under sustained stress (cf. Carver, Scheier, & Weintraub, 1989).

In a subsumptive hierarchy, new levels would emerge from the current highest one, but also the lower levels make possible the emergence of a new realm in an epigenetic process involving finality. Let us consider the following example. The basic postulates in epigenetic theory are that behaviors are organized systems; that they become increasingly complex over time with cognitive, emotional, and social

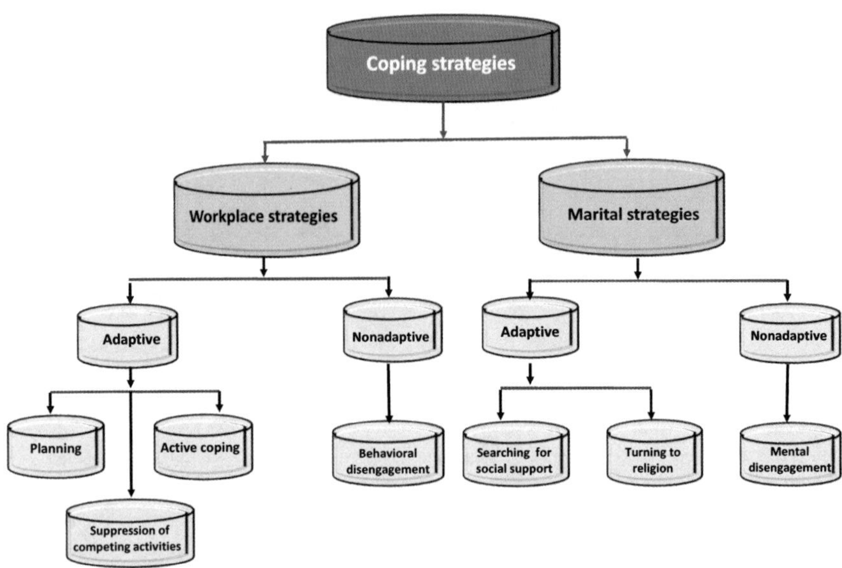



**Figure 1.4.** A hypothetical model of a subsumptive hierarchy showing how lower suprasystems emerge from the highest level. Two sets of lower-level strategies (workplace and marital ones) emerge from the highest level (coping strategies). Workplace strategies include adaptive and nonadaptive coping. Adaptive strategies include planning, active coping, and suppression of competing strategies; nonadaptive strategies include behavioral disengagement strategy. The marital adaptive strategies are composed of searching for social support strategies and turning to religion strategies; the marital nonadaptive strategy has only one class, mental disengagement strategy.

maturation; and that the organization of behavior at one point in time influences the organization at subsequent points in time (Rothbart & Ahadi, 1994; Willis, Sandy, & Yaeger, 2000). As applied to complex personality traits such as extraversion and neuroticism (see Figure 1.5), this suggests that these dimensions of temperament serve as the substrate from which more complex attributes or social behaviors develop (Level L or Level L+1; cf. Figure 1.2). And individual differences in extraversion and neuroticism can be regarded as arising from (a) variation within an underlying neural circuitry, which itself reflects gene-environment interaction; and (b) the individual's activity influencing his or her own environment or experiences, which in turn can alter gene expression and modify neural circuitry (cf. Canli, 2008).

Thus particular complex social behavior implies particular temperament traits; those traits imply particular biological mechanisms; and because this is a process of refinement, only a very narrow set of possibilities imply these complex social behaviors. In other words, biological mechanisms may give rise to many kinds of

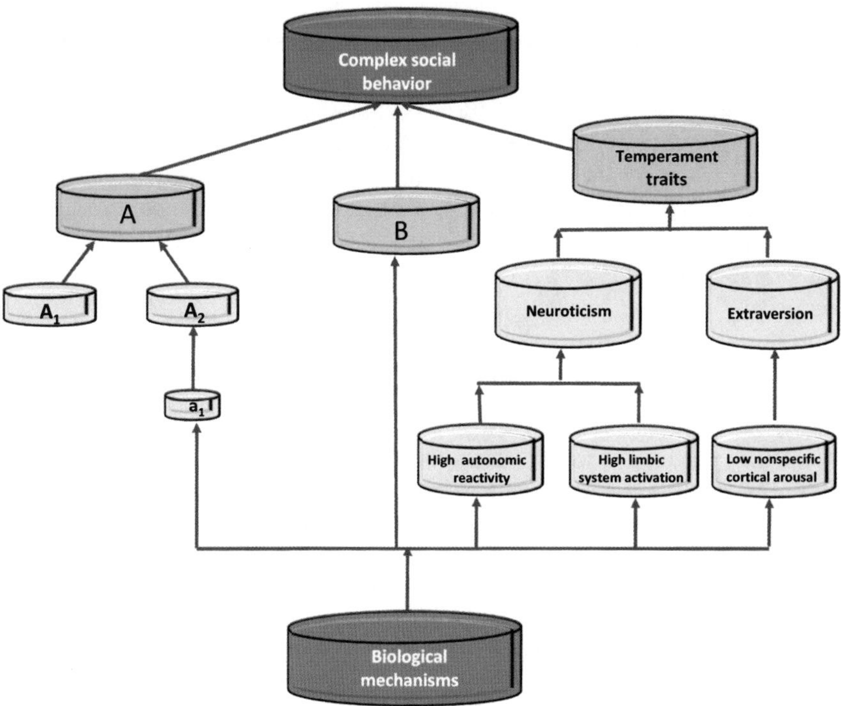


**Figure 1.5.** A hypothetical model of a subsumptive hierarchy, showing how higher supra-systems emerge from the lower level. The lowest level (biological mechanisms) gives rise to a set of higher-level classes, including subclasses of biological basis of temperament traits; then temperament traits participate in more complex social behavior. In this picture the classes $a_1$, $A_1$, $A_2$, A, and B symbolize other personality traits, which are not considered here for clarity.

suprasystems; temperament traits may give rise to fewer kinds of suprasystems; and complex social behaviors may give rise to even fewer kinds of suprasystems as the epigenetic system develops. However, levels in a specification hierarchy signify the qualitative differences in different realms of being, as in "traits realm" versus "biological mechanisms realm."

Hence it seems that a subsumptive hierarchy perspective allows us to understand how personality develops. Taken together, findings from the empirical studies designed around the question of what determines personality development suggest the interactions among three elements, resulting in between-person individual differences (e.g., Dickens & Flynn, 2001; Gray, 1982; Johnson, Vernon, & Feiler, 2008; Loehlin, 1992; Rothbart, Derryberry, & Posner, 1994). Accordingly, the psychological qualities of an individual reflect a continual process of interactions among biological factors—including genetic endowment—and the brain system, which partly determine one's dispositions, capacities, or abilities; the sociocultural environment, which facilitates or inhibits potential developmental pathways; and the activities of individuals, who causally contribute to their personal development by selecting their experiences and influencing the situations they encounter.

The questions of how individuals are unique, how they attain a coherent behavioral patterns and a coherent sense of self, and how personality develops into an integrative system that express itself in distinctive individual functioning remain perplexing. Thus in the next section I will demonstrate that these issues can be incorporated into the C-SAP.

## 1.4.
## Personality coherence and incoherence

The fourth proposition refers to personality coherence. It seems obvious that the main challenge for those focusing on the intraindividual personality system is to explain this system coherence. Vigorous interest in the coherent, holistic functioning of the individual is observed in the founders of the field like Stern, Allport, Rogers, Jung, Murray, Lewin, or Cattell, and continues in the present day in the work, for example, of Magnusson, Cervone, Shoda, McAdams (after Caprara & Cervone, 2000; see Funder, 2008), Eliasz (e.g., 1981), Mayer (e.g., 1993a), and Matthews (e.g., 2009). However, although the grand and standard theories of personality emphasize the consistency and coherence of personality and view the individual organism as an organized and complex wholeness, only a few of their adherents explain behavior in terms of coherence.

### *1.4.1. Personality coherence in selected present-day theories*

The investigation of cross-situational consistency in social behavior has been a major point of debate and serious disagreement (e.g., Block, 1993; Epstein, 1979; Funder, 1987; Magnusson, 1988; Mischel, 1968; Mischel & Peake, 1982). The trait-situation debate led interactionist psychologists to explain behavior and experiences as arising from the interactive effects of personal and situational factors, not from person factors or situation factors alone (e.g., Hettema, Leidelmeijer, & Greenen, 2000; Magnusson, 1999; Magnusson & Endler, 1977). That argument inherently required a psychology of situations explaining how different types of contexts contribute to the determination of behavior in interaction with the qualities of people, including personality coherence (cf. Caprara & Cervone, 2000). For example, Klirs and Revelle (1986) or Krahé (1990) demonstrated that responses cohere across situations according to the perceived similarity of the situations.

Alternative strategies of explaining coherence are provided by the social cognitive theories of personality. For example, according to Cervone and Shoda (1999a, 1999b), the phenomenon of personality coherence can be seen to incorporate three closely interrelated issues. The first major point is that personality processes and mechanisms function as interrelated and integrated systems. The second one emphasizes that coherence can be identified in overt psychological responses: across time and situations, individuals exhibit patterns of behavior that are qualitatively interconnected and consistent (cohere). And third, despite life transitions and positive or negative life episodes, individuals experience themselves as a whole, continuous being. Thus coherence embraces continuity in phenomenological experience.

Cervone (1997), however, suggests that the social cognitive and trait dispositional approaches are similar in that they both seek to explain the consistency and coherence of individual functioning—although these two personality frameworks exemplify two different strategies of scientific explanation, including cross-situational consistency in response (i.e., "top-down" and "bottom-up" strategies). The study of coherence has been dominated by top-down strategies of investigation and researchers have approached this issue by assessing the degree to which a group of subjects behaves consistently with respect to a high-level dispositional category (cf. Caprara & Cervone, 2000). In a top-down approach, one usually posits a high-level variable, such as a generalized tendency to behave in a particular manner. Then one specifies a set of lower-level situations and responses as valid indicators of a global construct. Having aggregated responses, one might assign a single score to each individual, which may be regarded as indicating the generalized tendency of the particular individual (cf. Cervone, 2004, 2008). According to Caprara and Cervone (2000), this strategy has significant drawbacks. First, by focusing on high-level dispositional tendencies, it provides little information about underlying causal mechanisms responsible for any observed cross-situational coherence. Moreover, explaining individual coherence in responses by the aggregate score may overlook the potentially unique patterns of high or low dispositional tendency that distinctively characterize the individual.

In the alternative bottom-up strategy, one may begin research by focusing on the mechanisms that may cause behaviors to cohere. Proposed by Cervone (2004; see also Cervone & Bartoszek, 2013), a knowledge-and-appraisal personality architecture (KAPA) model suggests that two mechanisms contribute to cross-situational coherence, self-schemas, and situational construals. Schematic self-knowledge drives consistent patterns of appraisal across a variety of encounters. Thus, to assess personality coherence, it is necessary to identify the content of schematic knowledge structures and the situations in which this knowledge is most likely to become activated. In studying self-efficacy appraisal, it was demonstrated that self-schemas drive appraisals that are already known to be strongly linked to emotional arousal, decision making, and motivation (cf. Bandura, 1997; Cervone, 1997; Shadel, Cervone, Niaura, & Abrams, 2004).

Subjects took part in a series of assessment sessions (cf. Cervone, 2008). An initial session was designed to identify enduring elements of self-knowledge, utilizing unstructured narratives in which subjects described their positive and negative attributes. The next session was dedicated to assessing situational knowledge, especially individuals' subjective beliefs about the relationships between personality attributes and social settings. In the categorization task, subjects indicated the social contexts that—in their perception—were most relevant to a given personality trait, including characteristics identified in the initial session. Thanks to this stage of the paradigm, it was possible to identify particular subsets of situations that were relevant to positive and negative self-schemas for each participant. Then subjects completed a multidomain self-efficacy questionnaire, which allowed the investigators to assess their confidence in being able to perform a variety of designated acts in designated contexts. Based on the information about participants' self-knowledge and situational beliefs, it was possible to identify clusters of schema-relevant situations in which subjects were predicted to display consistently high or low self-efficacy perceptions. Thus in this case the cross-situational consistency was predictable from the interaction between self-schemas and situational beliefs. Individuals did not express consistently high or low self-efficacy perceptions. To the contrary, both high and low self-appraisals were identified for each participant. Consistency in response was highly idiosyncratic.

Cervone (1999) treats top-down and bottom-up strategies for explaining personality coherence as totally irreconcilable. However, a middle ground between these two approaches in explaining intraindividual coherence is observed in studies on temperament, especially within the Transactional Model of Temperament proposed by Eliasz (cf. 1980, 1990, 2004). In this approach temperament is seen as a fundamental element of a system of regulation of stimulation and as a result of transactions between underlying biological mechanisms and environmental factors, and refers to formal aspects of behavior. Theoretical assumptions that relatively stable temperament may change under the impact of environmental factors and individual activity received empirical support. It is recorded that those changes may occur across time or may manifest themselves in intraindividual variability of behavioral dynamics (cf. Eliasz, 1981, 1985, 1993, 2001). Thus cross-situational variability and relative stability over time seem to be core features of temperament and correspond to the notion of "coherent stability" (Endler, 1977) or "behavioral signature" (Shoda, 1999). If so, the biological component of temperament is less susceptible to the influence of situations and this "averaged" profile of temperament reflects its biological or "context-free" element.

This primarily biological, relatively stable component of temperament may involve the top-down research strategy in explaining and predicting one's stability of behavior. Nevertheless, the trans-situational variability of temperament might be assigned to its environmental component or the influences of other personality traits, and this instability—which is produced by situational factors—instead requires bottom-up studies. A particularly advantageous feature of the work of Eliasz (for a review see Eliasz & Klonowicz, 2001) is that in exploring the relation between Type A and temperament reactivity (cf. Strelau, 2000), Eliasz introduced the internal incoherence between personality and temperament mechanisms resulting from the person-environment misfit (cf. Eliasz, 1988; Eliasz & Wrześniewski, 1991).

### 1.4.2. Three defining features of personality coherence/incoherence within the C-SAP

All these points have important implications for the concept of personality coherence versus incoherence within the C-SAP approach, where the idiographic/nomothetic dichotomy is seen as more a matter of levels of analysis and emphasis than incompatibility. In the process of analyzing personality coherence/incoherence, we should not forget Murray's and Eysenck's lessons about level of analysis and connections between them. It means that specific tendencies are not worlds apart with global or aggregated dimensions, but that the two serve different purposes and can be linked via the individual's experience in the specific situation (cf. Campbell, 2008). Consequently, defining key features of personality coherence versus incoherence are relevant to the assumption that internal dynamic processes are laid on relatively stable structures (e.g., sets of enduring attributes, traits), which in turn may modify these structures.

As reviewed in detail earlier in this chapter, two forms of complexity being modeled as hierarchical systems—extensional complexity as the compositional hierarchy, and intensional complexity as a subsumptive hierarchy—have referred to the description of personality as a complex system (cf. Salthe, 2006, 2009). Simply put, both may be applied to the elaboration of personality coherence/incoherence within the C-SAP framework. Thus the first defining feature is that personality coherence versus incoherence might be analyzed from the perspective of its structure and developmental patterns. In other words, it emerges as a high-ordered property in which a relatively stable, organized structure is formed by a specific set of internal mechanisms and expresses itself in the overt responses and behaviors. And there is good reason to expect that there may be relatively stable intra-individual patterns of coherence versus incoherence represented by their specific, underlying integrative and regulative mechanisms modified by individual historical encounters. "In both kinds of hierarchies, a higher level organizes, controls, regulates, guides, harnesses, and constrains, limits, etc., the lower levels" (Salthe, 2009, p. 89).

However, in the compositional hierarchy these constraints are nontransitive and limited to the next lower level, while in a subsumptive hierarchy upper-level constraints are transitive down through all the integrative levels below the level where they originate. In a related point, it seems reasonable to suggest that from the compositional hierarchy perspective, personality coherence versus incoherence might be analyzed between the specified entities from levels of Structures (L) and

Mechanisms and Processes (L-1) and between the specified entities from levels of Behaviors and Actions (L+1) and Structures (cf. Figure 1.2). Using a subsumptive hierarchy format, one may explore the developmental pattern of personality coherence versus incoherence and evaluate its uniqueness. This uniqueness of personality coherence versus incoherence accrues during development at all levels of personality organization, producing definable agents in many of them, but is greatly enhanced in functional importance in this complex system.

The compositional hierarchy might allow us to describe personality coherence between the levels of its organization (components) and identify the mechanisms of this coherence. In addition, it may enable us to explain the relative stability of this coherence. In other words, the compositional hierarchy permits us to identify the general mechanisms of personality coherence that might be reflected in a specific, relatively stable personality structure, which in turn may causally contribute to the patterns of cohere responses or behaviors. At the same time, a subsumptive hierarchy may serve as the framework to recognize the content of these mechanisms and structure and explain how they developed or evolved and how they reveal themselves over time and across situations. Together they provide information about the formal aspects or "compositional attractors" of personality coherence (e.g., physiological mechanisms, cognitive processes, trait structures) as well as about the content aspects or "individuation effects" of personality coherence (preserved, e.g., in genotype, historical information, individual information, and/or new information imposed by current encounters).

In summary, the compositional organization of coherent versus incoherent personality structure explains its relative stability and continuity, whereas a subsumptive arrangement points at its variability and dynamic changes resulting from the constant interactions among its elements, internal and external flow, and exchange of stimulation/energy and information.

In this approach a particular coherent/incoherent structure of personality exists in the particular form that it does because of the functions this structure serves for an individual. An implication and the second defining feature is that personality coherence/incoherence may be understood by reference to functional integration between different personality qualities. It means that there might be coherent as well as incoherent functional relations among distinct subsystems in personality. It inherently highlights a particular adaptive or maladaptive role of certain personality coherence/incoherence, and that functional integration between different personality qualities may be analyzed horizontally as located on the same level of the three-level personality organization—for example, between need for achievement and temperament structure (Level L) or vertically between two neighboring levels, such as personality structures (Level L) and behavioral units (Level L+1).

Here it is important to note that high-ordered personality coherence/incoherence is composed of particular entities, which may be recognized as lower-level but also complex, functionally integrated elements within the same personality quality. The single complex personality quality may be primarily biologically or environmentally determined, which in consequence determines its functional role. Thus from this perspective intraindividual personality coherence and incoherence is evidence of functional correspondence or conflict, respectively, between primarily biologically determined structures (e.g., neuroticism) and other, more environmentally determined personality structures (e.g., need for achievement).

This has an important theoretical implication. To be more specific, the third defining feature is that highly integrated personality coherence/incoherence reflects functional correspondence/conflict between the complex personality qualities that compose it. The challenge is to identify mechanisms of this functional correspondence and conflict.

## 1.5.
## Final remarks

Two issues should be noted to make the meta-theory of personality presented here more complete. The first relates to connections between personality coherence/incoherence and a system's funcunctionality/nonfunctionallity, while the second speaks to methodological matters.

### 1.5.1. Functional and nonfunctional personality system

Two meanings of complex-system functionality might be identified. A functional characteristic of a living complex system refers to the processes and structures that evolved in the system through a selection. Thus, along some chain of causation, one may explain the mechanisms on which the particular feature(s) occurred. But a functional characteristic is also known as an adaptation (cf. Dusenbery, 1992). Taken together, these two meanings of complex-system functionality may inform us about *why* and *for what* the particular structure of personality developed.

I believe that processes of morphogenesis and morphostasis and homeostatic mechanisms are involved in forming a functional or dysfunctional personality system. An adaptive system is an open system that is able to fit its behavior according to changes in its environment or in parts of the system itself. This is a suitability of system behaviors for achieving goals, reconfiguring themselves while minimizing loss of function (Dusenbery, 1992). Although an assumption that a functional complex system might be characterized by a high degree of adaptive capacity (to change and learn from experience), giving it resilience in the face of perturbation, some characteristics of a system are nonfunctional and may have lost their function over time due to changing conditions, or may simply be emergent phenomena arising as a side effect of functional systems (cf. von Bertalanffy, 1975, 1981). Thus functionality and nonfunctionality are the components of system stability and instability. On a more elaborated level, it means that some living systems may change their structure to adapt to environmental conditions by involving positive feedback—which denotes flexible structure, an openness to growth and change, and responsiveness to new stimulation (process of morphogenesis). Also, some systems may maintain their consistency through negative feedback in the face of environmental changes, which indicates a lack of change and stagnation of the structure (process of morphostasis; cf. Beavers, 1976).

A system maintains the balance to keep established equilibrium or to ensure a relatively stable environment or restore equilibrium when it is threatened in any way, and feedback loops may serve to maintain this balance. Each subsystem has its own set of functions, which can be performed only within the boundary formation that allows for subsystemic functional individuation-autonomy and appropriate degrees of interdependence. Boundaries, therefore, must serve to prevent undue interference in meeting subsystemic demands, and also must be permeable and sufficiently fluid to allow access and communication between subsystems and adaptability to developmental change. However, homeostatic mechanisms within a system may work for diffuse or rigid boundaries, leading in turn to systemic "overload" or difficulties for information flow between subsystems.

Thus all those processes and mechanisms described above should be considered to explain functional and nonfunctional complex systems. In conclusion, a functional complex system is an organization having (a) a relatively flexible and congruently interdependent structure of functions; (b) clearly individuated functions of its subsystems; and (c) a comparatively fluid exchange of information. By contrast, the nonfunctional complex system is an arrangement characterized by (a) a relatively rigid or disorganized, incongruently interdependent structure of functions; (b) not clearly discriminated functions of its subsystems; and (c) difficulties in information exchange—that is, overloading or insufficient flow of information.

The mechanism and processes outlined above may be applied to the examination of personality coherence and incoherence. Regarding the two points labeled (b) above, personality coherence versus incoherence is a synonym for functional or nonfunctional complex system, respectively. This indicates that in coherent personality the functions of its subsystems are clearly individuated, while in incoherent personality the functions of its subsystems are enmeshed.

Coherent and incoherent personality structure is also a living, open system: a set of interacting elements exchanges energy and information across its internal subsystems and with the external environment in order to live. The flow of energy and information is regulated to maintain the system's optimal energetic state; however, it happens that this energy and information exchange is a source of system dyfunctionality.

Functional/coherent as well as nonfunctional/incoherent personality structures emerge from the informational relations within a hierarchically organized complex system. As noted above, informational relations between compositional personality levels are intransitive. These three levels are screened from each other dynamically, and influence each other only indirectly via informational constraints. But signals moving from one level to another are transformed at boundaries between the levels. We can recall again the idea that scalar levels deliver stability to a system, via the screening effect if this is not the case—as when a signal from a higher level (e.g., L) occasionally or frequently transits to a much lower level (e.g., L-2) or, going the other way (that is, from L-2 to L), that level suffers damage or loses its function. Thus, for example, nonfunctional/incoherent personality structure may be a product of improperly transformed signals, or diffuse or rigid boundaries between levels.

A few sources of dysfunctional personality system states are emphasized within a subsumptive organization of personality. Involved here, as in all developments, is the process of senescence—a condition of information overload (information in this hierarchy is transitive across levels). As demonstrated by Salthe (1998, 2009), this leads to overconnectivity, which in turn results in functional underconnectivity, leading in its turn to inflexibility and habit-driven responses (loss of requisite variety) and ultimately to loss of adaptability (inability to produce interpretants of novel situations).

The question remains how does this coherent or incoherent personality structure affect overt behaviors?

### 1.5.2. Methodological issues

On conceptual grounds, however, it is not enough to talk about what "exactly" coherence of personality is. The real value of the construct also depends on how it might be operationalized, because the operationalization provides the referential meaning of the term. Hence the question of specific mechanisms and processes of personality coherence/incoherence may be critical to the design of investigations. (In turn, the evidence from the study on the mechanisms of personality coherence/incoherence may affect the meaning of that construct.) One possible approach to this question is to posit the existence of particular criteria by which the functional correspondence and functional conflicts among components of personality may be judged. Thus the attempt here is to identify the specific mechanisms and processes of control that put personality into coherent or incoherent structures, and to recognize the factors that affect the functional and dysfunctional personality system.

The other relevant point is how to measure and interpret data relating to a common personality coherence construct (cf. Caprara & Cervone, 2000). A coherence and continuity of personality can be appreciated by considering personality as a complex, hierarchically organized system and by examining personality organization combining measures of multiple response classes, across different situations and from a long-term perspective. One possibility is to combine measures of multiple response systems (e.g., physiological, affective, cognitive) but not interpret them as the functionally equivalent indicators of a particular differential construct or behavior (cf. Caprara & Cervone, 2000). Why is that? If personality is explained by reference to a complex system, the most important targets of investigation are the possible functional relations among subsystems. This can be achieved if the response clusters receive independent conceptual status and when they are analyzed separately. Such a line of deduction speaks not only to the possibility of analyzing personality coherence, but also to analyzing its incoherence (cf. Fajkowska, Krejtz, & Krejtz, 2009). However, it may be achieved by analysis of interactions and intercorrelations processes, not transactional ones. The latter reflect theoretical speculations that are difficult to operationalize.

## 1.6.
## Summing up

The investigation of coherence in social behavior has been a major point of debate and serious disagreement, and a number of theorists reject the notion that personality can be explained in terms of a fixed set of dispositional tendencies (e.g., Block, 1993; Epstein, 1979; Funder, 1987; Magnusson, 1988; Mischel, 1968; Mischel & Peake, 1982). Similarly, many scientists object to the complex-systems approach to study psychological phenomena. Debate has centered on a number of different points (see Fajkowska-Stanik, 2001). Some argue that a complex-systems approach consists of confusing generality and ambiguity, posing difficulty in operationalizating its abstract concepts for empirical studies. Others claim that it has no explanatory power, which means that it holds little potential for delineating relations among phenomena. Some maintain that this model fails the theoretical test of parsimony in that it includes phenomena that could simply be omitted from the explanation. Actually, the weakest points of the complex-systems approach have been identified and the C-SAP must confront them. I will return to this issue at a number of points in Part I and throughout the book.

However, the C-SAP might be an alternative scientific route to explain personality functioning, its organization and growth. Despite different theoretical backgrounds, the Complex–System Approach to Personality shares some basic common assumptions with the trait/disposition approach, social cognitive theories, and General System Theory (see Maruszewski, Fajkowska, & Eysenck, 2010). Referring to the latter, the converging elements between systems theory and the C-SAP concern those organized theoretical constructs adapted from it that can be used in the C-SAP to discuss personality and individual differences from a meta-theoretical perspective. In other words, a major advantage of this is that it informs the theoretical specificity of the C-SAP, which is reflected in a systemic approach to intraindividual variability and coherence and interindividual differences, and in a systemic analysis of person-environment relations.

The following chapters continue the discussion begun here. I maintain my focus on describing and explaining specific mechanisms and processes that potentially account for personality organization, dynamics, and coherence. I will view these issues through the lens of the meta-theoretical assumptions outlined above.

# Chapter 2

## Specifying the personality architecture within the Complex–System Approach to Personality: From related meta-theory to theory

### 2.1.
### System of Regulation and Integration Stimulation

The System of Regulation and Integration Stimulation (SRIS) is a fundamental element of personality architecture in the Complex–System Approach to Personality (C-SAP). Before embarking on a detailed discussion of the mechanisms and structure of the SRIS, clarification of terms and presentation of essential assumptions is necessary. Conceptually, the SRIS operates within the three levels of personality structure and functions as both an integrative and regulative stimulation system. Thus integration refers to the processes of accumulating elements of a system into one whole system (emergent property), whereas regulation is mandated by mechanisms for maintaining the existing state of things by preserving factors on which the system depends, within the appropriate ranges of variability (cf. Tomaszewski, 1967).

On a more elaborated level, the SRIS is seen as a hierarchically organized control system over organism activity and the level of arousal. Among different types of information, the SRIS receives feedback concerning the physiological state of organisms and adequacy or effectiveness of individual activity and performance. I believe that the SRIS controls reactionary and purposeful behaviors. Reactionary behaviors are connected with more automatic, linearlized control over one's need for stimulation, receptivity, and actions, whereas purposeful behaviors are rather linked to nonautomatic control over mental input. Thus I assume that predominantly temperament traits and attentional processes as subsystems of the SRIS control reactionary behaviors and are aimed at modulating the activity of organism. These regulators operate as devices, which have the function of managing or maintaining a designated characteristic or range of values in a system.

Thus I hypothesize that from the perspective of the subsumptive organization, the SRIS consists of the subclasses with (a) the physiological mechanisms of temperament traits, which determine one's need for stimulation, and attentional processes, which regulate the receptivity to signals (reception) and readiness to respond (action), related to emotional and motivational systems; (b) other internal stimulation-related elements—that is, personality characteristics, cognitive and affective mechanisms, and self-regulative processes; and also (c) external stimulation-related elements like environment with its subsystems (cf. Figure 2.1).

Temperament traits and attentional processes as functionally essential subclasses of the SRIS are based on the arousal and activation concepts,[1] which implies that they primarily refer to the energetic and effort mechanisms (cf. Sanders, 1998). In other words, they may be seen not only as the critical energetic "coordinators" but also as the "providers" of the energetic resources required by different types of individual activities reflected in reactions, mechanisms, or behaviors. A relevant assumption of the model is that active or controlled processes or activities are more energy- and resource-dependent than passive or automatic ones. Additionally, the differentiation in the stimulative value of situation or environment (e.g., high vs. low demands) affects the level of energy expenditure. Internal or external stimulation alert an organism and activate the appropriate subsystem(s)—for example, affective, motivational, or motor. Providing that the response of the activated system involves the energetic supply or resources, direct (via enhancing) or indirect (via facilitation) modulation of this response by variations of a range of temperament traits or attentional processes related to arousal and effort may be expected (Fajkowska & Eysenck, 2008). On the other hand, the control over purposeful behaviors mainly deals with other subsystems of the SRIS, which are personality components (e.g., traits), rather having integrative potentials.

The SRIS is also a hierarchically organized functional system. As mentioned above, it is assumed that the SRIS accounts for an effort allocation to attain and maintain (a) optimal level of system functioning by regulating the level of activation and arousal and (b) intraindividual coherence and behavioral integrity. As indicated in Chapter 1, the structural organization of coherent and incoherent personality types explains their relative stability and continuity, whereas changes in their variability and dynamics result from the constant interactions among their system elements—internal and external flow and exchange of stimulation/energy and information. Thus there is a good reason to expect that within this variability there may be stable and meaningful intraindividual patterns of consistency guaranteed by particular regulative and integrative mechanisms. Applying

---

[1] I define arousal and activation after Pribram and McGuinness (1975). Arousal is a phasic response to input; activation is a tonic readiness to respond. Both are basal energetic supply mechanisms, coordinated by the effort mechanisms. A detailed description of arousal and activation is presented in subsequent sections of this chapter.

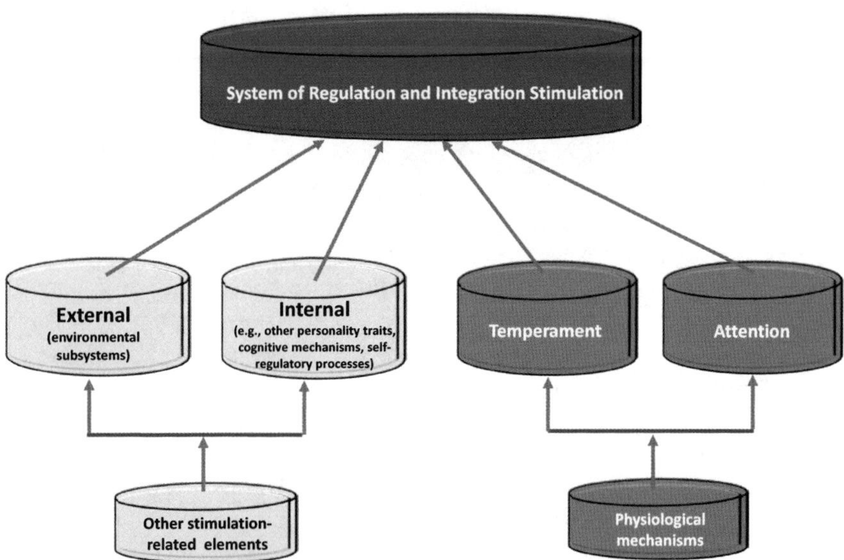


**Figure 2.1.** Subclasses of the System of Regulation and Integration Stimulation.

regulation and integration to the description of personality coherence/incoherence demands differentiation between levels of coherence versus incoherence. Theoretically, the compositional hierarchy of personality informs us that personality coherence/incoherence might be analyzed within the three levels studied separately as a degree of consistency of behaviors, a degree of consistency of structures, and a degree of consistency of mechanisms and processes. However, coherence/incoherence might be also considered as a degree of consistency across levels of behaviors and levels of mechanisms and structures.

Presuming that personality coherence/incoherence is an intrinsic attribute of the SRIS, two aspects of it should be noted. First, personality coherence/incoherence is an emergent property of interactions and transactions among one's need for stimulation—determined by the physiological mechanisms of temperament—and attentional processes, and other individual characteristics related to a self-providing stimulation and environmental properties related to an external-providing stimulation. (This refers to the integrative mechanisms of the personality system.) Second, the particular structure of coherent/incoherent personality corresponds to differing modes of adaptation and functional specialization. Each type of adaptation or function is consonant with a distinct attribute of the attentional system, involved in regulating stimulation and supporting adaptation (it refers to the regulative mechanisms of the personality system). This leads us to the question of how this intraindividual coherence versus incoherence is particularly formed within the SRIS.

The answer to this question should begin with the observation that the SRIS has an organization that controls its input and output of stimulation, but due to adaptation any part of it can be altered by a proposed "reorganization system" (part of the inherited, primary biologically rooted structure of the organism). Additionally, in this hierarchy of interacting control systems, different systems at one level can send conflicting goals to a higher-level system. When two systems are specifying different goals for the same higher-level variable, they are in conflict. For example, control by the SRIS over aggressive behaviors might be inefficient because low need for stimulation and attentional vigilance toward threat (lower level of control; see Figure 2.1) sends conflicting goals to the self-regulative processes—namely, avoiding a high dose of stimulation provided by aggressive behaviors and readiness to engage in aggressive responses, respectively. Thus sustained conflicts may be experienced by individuals as many forms of aggressive behaviors or inefficient performance.

Severe conflict destroys control by the affected system, here the self-regulative system, and may participate in personality incoherence. Higher-level control systems often may apply effective strategies to seek solutions that do not produce conflict or incoherence. If conflict persists and systematic "problem solving" by higher systems fails, the reorganization system (e.g., mechanisms of arousal and effort) may modify existing systems until they bypass the conflict or until they produce new reference signals/goals that are not in conflict at lower levels. It should be noted that this involves the basic trial-and-error learning mechanism, leading to the acquisition of more systematic kinds of learning processes. Any favorable outcome reduces or eliminates the error that is driving reorganization and slows or stops the process with a new organization or new means of controlling the behaviors in place.

This understanding of personality coherence versus incoherence suggests the integrated analysis of its processes and structures. The former address dynamic processing and explain "state status" of intraindividual coherence/incoherence, whereas the latter address enduring attributes and legitimize its "trait status." Moreover, personality coherence/incoherence and the SRIS are organized around specific, changeable processes and relatively stable traits. It is important to ask which processes and traits proposed within the SRIS help explain personality coherence and incoherence.

2.2.

## General view on the architecture of the SRIS

On one hand, the SRIS controls behaviors and the level of arousal and activation, and grants the adaptation by providing the optimal level of arousal and internal integrity; but on the other hand, the processes that it governs contribute to its structuralization. More specifically, it demonstrates that processes and structures cannot be dissociated, since dynamic functional relations between them drive the SRIS architecture. In other words, the SRIS architecture is located on the levels of processes and structures.

Theoretical analysis of personality composition, development, coherence (see Chapter 1), and the controlling and functional aspects of the SRIS lead us to the conclusion that processes and structures (traits) do not represent antagonistic concepts, but rather exist in harmony and are deeply interrelated constructs. Here processes correspond to the dynamic changes of personality (its subsystems—e.g., the SRIS) and contribute to the structures' formation, and at the same time are subjected to the structures (see levels L-1 and L1; Figure 1.2): the stronger the structure, the less flexible the process, and vice-versa (Smith, 1999). Traits, in turn, denote underlying, recurrent mechanisms that form a stable pattern and account for the stability of individual characteristics. Thus traits might be described as processes with a slow rate of change and might substitute for structures.

This understanding of trait includes the ongoing habituation (automatization) responsible for binding underlying mechanisms and processes in increasingly fixed paths; however, such relatively fixed patterns of process have their history and may be receptive to change (Smith, 1999). Traits (structures) have different degrees of permanence—for example, they are less stable in childhood than in adult life; they may gradually change under specific, persistent internal (e.g., physical illness) or external (e.g., pollution) factors; or their changes depend on their saturation with biological or environmental components. I believe that changes in traits depend on their complexity (how many functional components might be distinguished in them) and the specific dominating function that they play (how they typically control stimulation).

Specifically, I believe that within the SRIS arousal and activation might be considered as regulative and integrative processes. Involving intercorrelation and interaction mechanisms, integration refers to the processes of assembling the functional components of a system into one system and maintaining functioning of the subsystems as one system. Thus it produces a differentiated level of functional complexity in traits. Then I hypothesize that the regulative processes—with their key mechanisms of positive and negative feedbacks—eliminate or lessen extremes by moderating intensity and tempo, removing unsuitable contributors, and controlling consistency and accuracy. It seems probable that differentiated dominant controlling functions in traits originate from the regulative processes.

In closing, arousal and activation are regarded as processes contributing to the structuralization of the SRIS. Consequently, the integrative and regulative aspects of arousal and activation are associated with differentiated levels of functional complexity and differentiated dominant controlling functions in traits, respectively.

### 2.2.1. Level of processes

I consider below the physiological basis of arousal and activation and how they are connected with attentional and temperament mechanisms.

*Physiology of arousal and activation*

In early studies arousal was predominantly understood as a unitary concept and was defined as the energy expended by an organism in the process of controlling reactions, states, and behaviors (e.g., Duffy, 1957, 1962). During the 1950s this notion of a generalized drive state regulating and varying along a single dimension—that is, arousal—gained rapid acceptance due to studies on the relation between alertness and the state of the ascending pathways of the reticular formation in the brain (for a review see Sanders, 1998). Even the unidimensional arousal theory was seriously challenged by subsequent physiological and behavioral evidence (for a review see Sanders, 1998). Later theories proposed to limit arousal states to effort and arousal—and not further subdivide these states—in order to handle the entire range of effects associated with arousal variables (e.g., Humphreys, Revelle, Simon, & Gilliland, 1980; Revelle, Humphreys, Simon, & Gilliand, 1980). Now it is generally accepted that arousal is not a unitary concept, but that it comprises separate constructs that are regulated by different neural substrates, depending on environmental or task demands (e.g., de Brabander, Declerck, & Boone, 2002; Robbins, 1997).

In line with the theories postulating that arousal is not a unitary phenomenon, I suggest that it be seen as having two aspects when controlling and accumulating stimulation: (a) regulative over the sensory input and output, related to receptivity of stimulation, responsiveness to stimulation, intensity and tempo of response to signals, and readiness to response, connected with mechanisms of attention; and (b) integrative, responsible for the association together in time of a group of responses from different subsystems—which may be held to include, for example, alert response and a variety of emotional reactions connected with temperament mechanisms or (strictly speaking) with one's need for stimulation.

The question is how this energy expenditure can be evaluated. Arousal, on a physiological/bodily level, can be registered as changes in the nervous, cardiovascular, respiratory, and endocrine systems. However, cortical activity is a highly important constituent of arousal; it stems from the projection of the nervous impulses from the reticular formation (*formatio reticularis*). In other words, arousal involves activation of the reticular activating system in the brain stem, the autonomic nervous system (ANS), and the endocrine system, leading to increased heart rate and blood pressure and a condition of sensory alertness, mobility, and readiness to respond (see Carlson, 2001).

In addition, there are networks of E-cells—classified broadly as excitatory and causing an increase in firing rate—and I-cells, grouped as inhibitory and causing a decrease in firing rate (see Figure 2.2), as well as modulatory neurons that produce long-lasting effects not directly related to firing rate. Generally, a neuron affects other neurons by releasing a neurotransmitter, which binds to a chemical

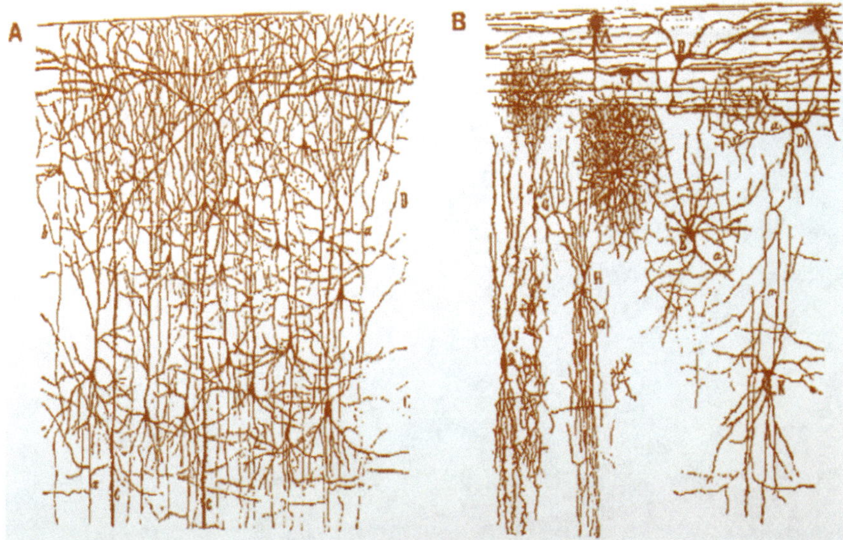

**Figure 2.2.** [A] Excitatory neurons: E-cells (approximately 85%; mainly the pyramidal and stellate cells). [B] Inhibitory neurons: I-cells (approximately 15%; mainly basket and chandelier cells). Compare Sheperd and Grillner (2010).

receptor. The effect upon the target neuron is determined by the type of receptor that is activated—excitatory, inhibitory, or modulatory (see Carlson, 2002). However, the distinction between excitatory and inhibitory neurotransmitters is not absolute; rather, it depends on the class of chemical receptors present in the target neuron. In principle, a single neuron that releases a single neurotransmitter can have excitatory effects on some targets, inhibitory effects on others, and modulatory effects on still others (see Carlson, 2002; Toates, 2001).

Nevertheless, it should be noted that the two most common neurotransmitters in the brain, glutamate and gamma aminobutyric acid (GABA), have actions that are largely consistent (see Carlson, 2002; Toates, 2001). Glutamate acts on several different types of receptors, but most of them have excitatory effects. Similarly, GABA reacts on several different types of receptors, but all of them have effects that are inhibitory. The cell membrane of the axon and soma contain voltage-gated ion channels, which allow the neuron to generate and propagate an electrical signal (an action potential). These signals are generated and propagated by charge-carrying ions including sodium ($Na^+$), potassium ($K^+$), chloride ($Cl^-$), and calcium ($Ca^{2+}$). Of course there are several stimuli that can activate a neuron, leading to electrical activity—for example, stretch, pressure, chemical transmitters, and changes in the electric potential across the cell membrane. Stimuli cause

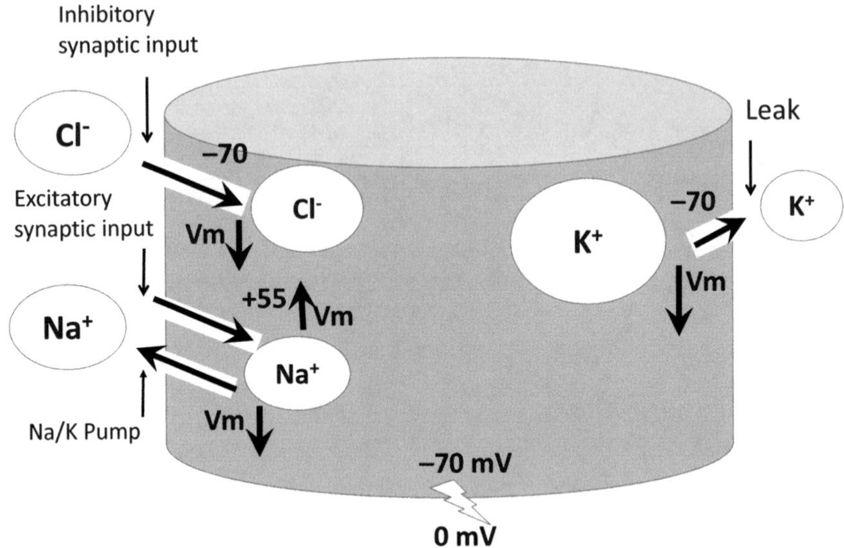


**Figure 2.3.** The chemical neurotransmission in the neurons of the CNS: excitatory and inhibitory potentials. Compare Carlson (2001, 2002) and Toates (2001).

specific ion channels within the cell membrane to open, leading to a flow of ions through the cell membrane and changing membrane potential (Figure 2.3; see also Carlson, 2002; Toates, 2001).

Although this functional specification of the cortex (cf. Brodmann areas) is widely accepted, one principle has remained unchanged across cortex cytoarchitecture. Namely, the excitatory neurons—through glutamate acid, their main neurotransmitter—open the $Na^+$ channels and carry signals across long or short distances. In other words, they serve as communication for the ingroup and outgroup neurons. One-directional general arousal means signal transmission, while two-directional general arousal reflects the completion of information or the reinforcement of weak signals. Thus inhibitory neurons, in order to avoid the negative effects of positive feedback, control the activation of excitatory neurons. They contribute to the GABA neurotransmitter, open the $Cl^-$ channels, and regulate the level of excitatory neurons (see Carlson, 2001, 2002; Toates, 2001).

Apart from cortical arousal, there is also the visceral one that is connected with the limbic system, hypothalamus, and autonomic nervous system. Eysenck (1967, 1970) described the hippocampus, amygdala, cingulum, septum, and hypothalamus as the "visceral brain" because these structures activate the cardiovascular, respiratory, endocrine, and digestive systems. And visceral arousal is caused by emotional stimuli.[2] Moreover, Eysenck (1967, 1970) referred to activation in terms of activity of the visceral brain and to arousal in regard to cortical activity. It is suggested that there is a wide range of physiological correlates of cortical arousal—for example, the spontaneous or evoked bioelectrical activity of the brain as recorded by the electroencephalogram (EEG) and autonomic arousal as measured by electrodermal activity, electromyographic activity, oculographic activity, pulse volume amplitude, or cardiovascular activity (see Krieger, Schröder, & Erhardt, 2003; Matthews & Deary, 2002; Strelau, 2000).

To conclude, arousal is related to the central (CNS) and autonomic nervous systems. There is a question about the relationship between arousal and autonomic or subcortical indices (e.g., Togo, Cherniack, & Natelson, 2006). Several studies have shown an inverse or positive correlation, respectively. Generally, it has been demonstrated that positive correlation is identified with low levels of the autonomic variables and that negative correlation is identified with higher levels (e.g., in studies on anxious and neurotic individuals; see Blowers, 1979; Claridge, 1967; Gruzelier, Lykken, & Venables, 1972; Hume & Claridge, 1965; Lykken & Maley, 1968; Venables, 1963).

However, there is a position on the relation between arousal and activation that differs from the Eysenckian view. Pribram and McGuinness (1975, 1980) proposed to treat activation as a tonic increment in neural activity connected with motor readiness, motivational system, and increased left-hemisphere activity, whereas arousal denotes a phasic increment in neural activity associated with perceptual receptivity, emotional system, and increased right-hemisphere activity. In other words, activation refers to relatively slow changes in base-level arousal (e.g., the daily cycle of sleep and wakefulness represent changes in activation). Stimulants (such as caffeine) or depressants (such as alcohol) also produce notable changes in activation that may last several hours (cf. Thayer, 1996). But arousal is stimulus related and more short lived; for example, when a door is unexpectedly slammed shut by the wind, we experience a systemic increase in arousal due to the release of epinephrine and norepinephrine. Depending on the stimulus, changes in phasic arousal may last from circa a dozen seconds to several minutes. I incorporate this description of the relation between arousal and activation into my theoretical approach and apply it to the attentional system and temperament when I portray them as associated on the level of physiological mechanisms.

---

[2] It is worth noting that for Eysenck (1967, 1981) emotions are the result of arousal, but for other researchers emotions are the cause of arousal (e.g., Gray, 1972, 1981, 1982, 1994; Watson & Tellegen, 1985; Zuckerman, 1979).

*Arousal and activation as components of*
*attentional and temperament mechanisms*

Arousal and activation might be considered as regulative and integrative components of a wide range of reactions, psychological mechanisms, and behaviors—particularly in regard to those connected with cognitive, affective, motivational, and (self-)regulative processes, and also with personality characteristics. With this in mind, my theoretical assumption is that arousal and activation are involved in regulative functions of attentional processes and in producing one's need for stimulation linked to a self-providing, appropriate dose of stimulation determined by the physiological mechanisms of temperament (see Eliasz, 1981; Fajkowska & Eysenck, 2008).

Admittedly, arousal and activation play a prominent role in perception and attention (e.g., maintaining alertness in dangerous or monotonous situations), in affect elicitation and sustainment or subjective experience of affective states (e.g., their intensity, valence, or potency), and in motivated behavior in subjects that is characterized by two basic parameters of direction (approach or avoidance) and intensity control action (e.g., Hebb, 1949; Schneirla, 1959). In humans the specific direction of behavior (i.e., approach, avoid) is no longer completely dictated by the eliciting stimulus; thus the basic motivational parameters of direction (toward, away) and intensity can be considered fundamental in organizing emotional behavior. Individual behavior is influenced by the intrinsically motivated desire to accomplish a specific level of stimulation (optimum stimulation level; Berlyne, 1960; Orth & Bourrian, 2005). Optimum stimulation level varies among individuals (Raju, 1980).

The external source of stimulation can cause the general activation of the cortex; however, the optimal cortical activation comprises an average level of activation. Hebb (1949), who formulated the optimal-level-of-stimulation theory and translated it into a behavioral-motivational construct, claimed that the optimal level of arousal is regulated by the interaction between sensory stimulation and the physiological characteristics of the reticular formation, including the cortex itself (see also Moruzzi & Magoun, 1949; Zuckerman 1994). Hebb (1955) distinguished two functions of sensory stimulation—namely, the cue function that guides behaviors and the arousal function that activates the whole behavioral system. The cue function cannot operate efficiently in the underaroused brain; the arousal function is absolutely necessary for the cue function. The relationship between the cue function and arousal, which prepares and energizes it, is not a simple linear one but has an inverted-U shape: cue function is inefficient at a low level of arousal, reaches a peak at some optimal level of stimulation, but declines beyond this optimal level where further arousal is associated with negative affectivity (see Zuckerman, 1994). Individuals are motivated to undertake the particular activity to reach an optimal level of arousal. If underaroused relative to this level, an increase in arousal is rewarding; if overaroused, a decrease in arousal is rewarding. In other words, individual activity regulates the optimal level of arousal or stimulation (see Hebb, 1949, 1955).

Individuals attempt to modify stimulation (increase too-low stimulation or decrease too-high stimulation) derived from the environment in the general direction toward the optimum level of stimulation. To be more precise, they seek balance between optimum and actual stimulation, and deviation between actual and optimal stimulation influences the intrinsic motivation to expose oneself to any environmental stimuli (Helm & Landschultze, 2009). When the optimal level of stimulation is not present, behavioral response or activity can serve as a homeostatic regulator such that its organisms will initiate stimulation seeking or stimulation avoidance (Zentall & Zentall, 1983).

On an individual basis, this preferred stimulation level is relatively constant over time: it is rooted in the physiological mechanisms of temperament and can be regarded as being a fairly constant individual trait variable—the need for stimulation (see Gray, 1964). Variations in levels of stimulation depend on one's need for stimulation but also on cognitive or attentional modulation. The effectiveness of attentional system functioning allows tolerating a wider range of stimulation (cf. Curtindale, Laurie-Rose, Bennett-Murphy, & Hull, 2007).

This well-known inverted-U curve, generalized from Yerkes and Dodson's (1908) learning study on mice to a general performance principle, served for some time as the leading theoretical interpretation about the relation between energy and cognitive factors in shaping performance, which is poor when arousal is too low or too high (see Sanders, 1998). Remarkably, this law relied on two major assumptions: that arousal refers to a one-dimensional, biological system and its level depends on the relation between internal biorhythms and external stimulation; and that properties of arousal and cognition are independent, with the exception of a general complexity factor (see Sanders, 1998). However, Easterbrook (1959) suggested that performance is supposed to decline when arousal is either too low or too high, but for different reasons and in different courses. Thus at a high level of arousal, insufficient but task-relevant information prevents adequate action; at a low level of arousal, distractibility and tendencies toward competing responses are disruptive for performance due to irrelevant cues. Even this statement has been widely debated (e.g., in the context of high anxiety related to high arousal and susceptibility to distractors; cf. Eysenck, 1982). Still, it offers an interesting perspective—namely, that low or high levels of arousal are not connected with one general pattern of performance, but to different forms of it.

Additionally, arousal can be considered as a result of any kind of stimulation or as the basal activity of particular neural structures without stimulation or prior to stimulation. Arousability—the degree to which an individual can be moved by stimulation—was first formulated by Gray (1964) within the theory that related behavioral differences in personality to underlying physiological activity (Eysenck,

1957). Based on the findings from his studies, which evaluated tolerance to sedative drugs and the duration of the so-called "Archimedes spiral aftereffect," Claridge (1967) proposed two functionally related mechanisms at the behavioral level that resemble those later proposed by Pribram and McGuiness's (1975; McGuiness & Pribram, 1980) model of activation and arousal: the tonic arousal system, which maintains an individual's gross ongoing level of arousal through internally and externally generated stimuli; and the arousal modulation system. The latter serves two functions: it controls the level of activity in the tonic arousal system and integrates the stimuli input to both systems by appropriate facilitation and suppression of incoming information. That is, it determines the extent to which an individual is to be aroused (see also Blowers, 1979).

It is assumed that under normal conditions a balance is maintained between these two systems. An efficient feedback loop is formed and when the tonic arousal level is high, it is bound in intensity by high-arousal modulation to dampen the tonic level and protect the nervous system from overstimulation. In other words, the modulating system actively facilitates the reception of relevant stimuli and suppresses irrelevant stimuli. Claridge (1967) claims that directional and attentional aspects are attached to the concept of the arousal modulation system, because it is involved in narrowing and widening attention under particular conditions of arousal. Thus arousability reflects the intensity of individual arousal on a behavioral level (Blowers, 1979).

### 2.2.2. Level of structures

I understand trait (structure) as a hierarchically organized system. I assume that it represents a complex inner mechanism, which indirectly determines the coherence of behaviors—that is, the relative inconsistency of behaviors across situations and relative consistency of behaviors across time (Eliasz, 1981; Eliasz & Klonowicz, 2001). This means that the trait might be interpreted through the relation *explanans-explanandum*. Following Eliasz (2004; see also section 1.2.2) this relation does not assume any direct correspondence between internal mechanisms (*explanans*) and behavior (*explanandum*). Eliasz posits two fundamental, relatively stable components of the trait, both of which can be derived from level L-1: the first is associated with dominance of biological determinacy in traits (it manifests itself in the trans-situational consistency of a behavior's dynamic), and the second is linked to dominance of environmental determinacy in traits (it manifests itself in the trans-situational inconsistency of a behavior's dynamic). Therefore traits are differentiated according to the level of saturation of these two components, which probably affects the specificity of relation between the trait and dynamics of a subject's activity (reaction, behavior) in particular areas of functioning, and depending on the context. On the other hand, traits are also emergent products of cognitive, affective, and motivational mechanisms (cf. Figure 1.2) and represent the contents that are related to them (cf. Kreitler & Kreitler, 1990).

Assuming that traits affect the dynamics and content of behavior across different classes of situations, and taking into account the constant flowing of information and stimulation into the subject, traits might be regarded as those having different functional complexity and controlling roles. As mentioned earlier, within the SRIS the integrative and regulative aspects of arousal and activation are associated with differentiated levels of functional complexity and differentiated dominant controlling functions in traits, respectively.

I realize that I am offering a different conceptualization of trait than that proposed by most researchers who examine personality structure (e.g., Strelau, 2008). These researchers claim that traits are generalized behavioral tendencies or behavioral dispositions. I consider this position as flawed in several respects. Traits and behaviors are located on different levels of the personality system (cf. Figure 1.2), which implies that transactional relations connect them and that there is no direct correspondence between them. Thus this point cannot support the claim that behavioral consistency over time and across situations is mostly "guaranteed" by traits. Moreover, behavioral tendencies (Level L+1) represent more integrated entities than traits (Level L), which means that they are more stable than traits. This implies that one cannot attribute the stability and continuity of behaviors to traits in the first place. Hence the stability and continuity of behaviors seems to be a transactional product of many elements—for example, different components of personality, situational/environmental conditions, and self-regulative processes. I hope that the following sections enhance my position.

*Functional complexity in traits*

When talking about differentiated levels of functional complexity in traits, the first challenge is to answer the question "What is complexity?" One possible way to define something as complex is to state that it is made up of several parts that are at the same time distinct and connected. Thus, intuitively, the degree of system complexity or component complexity depends on how many parts can be distinguished and the connections between them. Distinction corresponds to variety, heterogeneity, to the fact that different parts behave differently, and leads to "chaos and disorder"; connections correspond to constraints, redundancy, to the fact that different parts are not independent, and leads to order (Heylighen & Aerts, 1996). Thus complex entities are difficult to model and predict as being neither perfect disorder nor perfect order. However, traits as candidates for complex systems might be modeled through the concept of two components, biological and environmental. The simplest way to model order is to assume the relative invariance of the biological component of traits—from which one can predict the probability that the specific trait or component will be found at a particular position or will be activated in a particular context.

The complex nature of traits runs in spatial and temporal dimensions. As we have seen, spatial dimension means structural, componential differentiation.

Temporal dimension relates to the variety of a system's activities or functions. Spatial (componential) differentiation requires selection on the basis of relative fitness or adaptation, which produces structural integration by creating more and stronger linkages between different elements (cf. Heylighen & Aerts, 1996; Tran-Cao, Abran, & Lévesque, 2001). The law of requisite variety entails selection for functional differentiation: a larger repertoire of possible actions permits the system to survive in a larger variety of situations for the sake of adaptation and fitness. The integration of the sets of related activities into higher-order functions is required in order to minimize the difficulty of decision making and coordination between an increasing number of activities. The interaction between structural and functional complexity means that structural complexification seems to require a more complex group of functions to cope with it, and similarly that functional complexification seems to require a richer set of components and connections to implement it (cf. Heylighen & Aerts, 1996).

For example, as related to the arousal concept, extraversion is seen as a trait with slow and weak excitatory potential and rapid and strong—and slowly dissipated—reactive inhibition (Eysenck, 1947/1998). Additionally, it is the higher-order trait, structurally rich (e.g., it is composed of sociability, liveliness, activity, sensation seeking, and leadership), which might be characterized as functionally complex (cf. Eysenck, 1992). It was found to moderate cognitive performance, social interactions, or sexual activity (Eysenck & Eysenck, 1985). On the other hand, sensory sensitivity (the ability to react to sensory stimuli whose stimulating value is low; cf. Strelau, 2008), might be characterized as not complex in terms of adaptive functions. It operates as the energetic channel, contributing to a reduction of individual overstimulation (Zawadzki & Strelau, 1997). There is evidence that sensory sensitivity moderates the perception of auditory or visual stimuli. For example, Fajkowska, Krejtz, and Krejtz (2009) found that sensory sensitivity is connected with oculomotor control, the eye fixation time on emotional material.

*Dominant controlling functions in traits*

Structural and functional complexity requires control. Differentiated dominant controlling functions in traits are associated with the regulative aspect of arousal and activity might be approached in terms of reactivity, regulation, and self-regulation (cf. Derrybery & Rothbart, 1988, 1997; Rothbart, 1989a, 1989b; Rothbart & Ahadi, 1994). Thus traits with reactive dominant relate to the reception of flowing stimulation; they denote the readiness to activity (reaction, behavior), sensitivity, or (e.g., sensory) vigilance to stimuli and relate to the energy expenditure (in a particular time range), which is connected with reaction to stimuli or initiation of activity. Given such a description, anxiety (Spielberger, 1983), neuroticism (Eysenck, 1947/1998), or traits connected with BIS/BAS systems (Gray, 1994) might exemplify the traits with reactive dominant. For example, anxious individuals are hypervigilant to threatening material (e.g., Fajkowska & Krejtz, 2007) or social evaluation (e.g., Eysenck, 2006).

Traits with regulative dominant denote individual differences in energy expenditure, in a particular range of time, to direct and monitor the flowing stimulation adequately to the organism's capacities for stimulation processing. One example might be emotional reactivity (ER), a temperament trait formulated within the Regulative Theory of Temperament (RTT; Strelau, 2008). Despite the fact that the term "reactivity" is used in the name of this trait, its dominant function seems to be regulative. This trait informs us about the tendency to react intensively to emotion-generating stimuli, expressed in high emotional sensitivity and low emotional endurance. For example, ER is connected with the efficiency of processing emotional material; high ER reflects deficits in stimulation regulation and the increasing reactivity to emotional stimuli, which is coupled with attentional biases toward negative stimuli and worsened performance (e.g., Fajkowska & Krejtz, 2007; Fajkowska et al., 2009).

I assume that traits with reactive and regulative dominant represent traits associated with high or moderate dominance of biological determinacy and are connected to motivational, affective, and cognitive systems (Derrybery & Rothbart, 1988, 1997; Rothbart, 1989a, 1989b; Rothbart & Ahadi, 1994). Traits with self-regulative dominant, rather, are seen as being influenced by environmental determinacy and are attached to more complex personality mechanisms. This group of traits indicates individual ability to intentionally control stimulation; they signify effortful control and strategic reception and stimulation processing. They relate to the more complex personality, cognitive, executive, or affective mechanisms (cf. Lonigan, Vasey, Philips, & Hazen, 2004). For example, trait-like attentional control is one's ability to focus perceptual attention, switch attention between tasks, and flexibly control thought (see Derryberry, 2002). Supported by the anterior system, effortful attentional control is part of executive attention, is viewed as involved in the awareness of one's planned behaviors and subjective feelings of voluntary control of thoughts and feelings, and is believed to come into play when resolving conflicts (e.g., discrepant, ambiguous information), correcting errors, and planning new actions (see Eisenberg, Smith, Sadovsky, & Spinrad, 2004; Fajkowska & Derryberry, 2010; Rothbart, 1989a, 1989b; Rothbart, Derryberry, & Posner, 1994).

To conclude, one trait might be decomposed according to its level of complexity and controlling functions. However, it is worth mentioning that the functional complexity of traits affects their controlling functions, which leads to the fact that different controlling functions might coexist in one trait. For example, in neuroticism, a functionally and structurally complex trait (Eysenck & Eysenck, 1985), one might identify reactive and regulative aspects—although the reactive aspect seems to be the dominant one.

*Traits as subsystems*

As described above, traits are subsystems of higher systems (suprasystems)—that is, temperament and personality systems. However, temperament (Level L1) is seen as a subsystem of personality (cf. Strelau, 1998, 2006). This is revealed by several facts.

First, different sets of traits compose temperament and personality; formal, biologically rooted traits are connected with temperament and content, and more environmentally determined traits are associated with other-than-temperament personality traits (cf. Strelau, 2006). In other words, temperament refers mainly to formal characteristics of behaviors, to the style of behavior (intensity, energy, strength, speed, tempo, fluctuation, mobility), whereas other-than-temperament personality traits denote the content of behavior (the specificity of reactions, the relation of humans to themselves, to each other, toward the world, their motivation, preferences, desires, and other psychological phenomena). The content of behavior is a product of human activity under the impact of the specific human environment. Thus those personality traits that have been present since early childhood (e.g., emotional reactivity) belong to the domain of temperament, but personality traits that occur at a later period of development (e.g., need for achievement) are differently qualified (Strelau, 1983). Temperament comprises those personality traits that have a biological background. The dominance of biological determinacy in temperament traits makes them relatively stable and characterized by cross-situational consistency. The other-than-temperament personality traits, however, are products that emerged on the basis of the biological endowment regarded as a component of personality, but the dominance of environmental determinacy makes them prone to relative variability across situations and over time.

The second fact is associated with a different level of structural and functional complexity in temperament and other personality traits. It seems quite probable that temperament traits as formal traits are less structurally and functionally complex than other, content-saturated personality traits.

The third fact goes with the controlling aspects in temperament and personality traits. Temperament characteristics are rather reactive and regulative traits, whereas other personality traits have more self-regulative potentials—mechanisms that ensure the consistency of goal-directed activity, which might be described in the concepts of ego, self, superego, cognitive maps, value systems, program-oriented schemata, composition of traits, and dynamic hierarchical organization (cf. Strelau, 1983).

Fourth, the interactions and transactions among temperament traits and personality traits produce higher-order systems. This approach enables us to see traits as the subsystem of the higher structures: patterns and types—constructs embodying a larger grouping of internal mechanisms than traits. With respect to the dimensional representations of individual differences, the pattern and type approach (person-centered tradition) remains valid (Sava & Popa, 2011). It advocates the old tradition of global personality characteristics, which have substantial predictive power over longer periods of time (Block, 1971; Caspi, 1998; Schnabel, Asendorpf, & Ostendorf, 2002). The type models provide good predictive utility when the criteria applied have a status of quality variables (Zawadzki, Czarnota-Bojarska,

Strelau, & Sobolewski, 2004; Zawadzki & Strelau, 2003). Moreover, this approach is predominant in the study of health problems, including emotional difficulties (Denollet, 1997; de Fruyt & Denollet, 2002; Zawadzki, 2001, 2006; Zawadzki & Radzikowska, 2006), and can be compared with agent-based modeling in social psychology (Smith & Conrey, 2007).

Still, the predictive validity of the person-centered approaches (based on typologies and focused on the configuration of regularly observed traits; categorical) versus the variable-centered approaches (based on the covariations of traits in groups; dimensional) is widely debated (e.g, Asendorpf & Denissen, 2006; Chapman & Goldberg, 2011; Sava & Popa, 2011). From a practical perspective, the answer to the question of which approach has better predictive power depends on the type of outcome measured (cf. Asendorpf & Denissen, 2006). However, one good reason for using the type approach is that compared with dimensions, types are more integrated entities than traits (cf. Figure 1.2) and fluctuate significantly less across time—especially when they are studied as relatively stable, formal, and associated with dominance of biological determinancy in traits (like temperament types).

Thus the present analysis should examine the probable rules that explain how a content and formal structure of the patterns and types might be extracted. One possible—and for now general—explanation might be formulated within the SRIS.

### 2.3.
## The SRIS and personality coherence/incoherence

At this point it is useful to focus on two major elements of the SRIS based on the arousal and activation processes. These two elements—mechanisms of the attentional system and mechanisms of temperament—are believed to have a substantial role in forming personality coherence and incoherence. The attentional system (Level L-1), involved in response to stimulation input (e.g., reception, encoding, selecting, controlling) in readiness to respond to stimulation, may have the primary role of maintaining the optimal energetic conditions of organisms upon the arrival of signals and protecting the organism from overstimulation and understimulation. On the other hand, temperament traits (level L1) are assigned a particularly critical coordinating function between one's need for stimulation (general tendency to seeking or avoiding stimulation)—which is relatively stable and achieved in the learning processes—and other stimulation-related elements of the SRIS (e.g., other personality or environmental features).

### *2.3.1. Level of processes: Attentional mechanisms, processes, and personality coherence/incoherence*

There are two neuroanatomically and functionally different regulative control systems originally recognized by Pribram and McGuinness (1975) and subsequently elaborated by Tucker and Williamson (1984). Their scheme is reminiscent of earlier neuroanatomical models offered by Claridge (1967), Routtenberg (1968), and Gray (1971). Here the essential element is an explanation of the hemispheric specialization in attention, relying on the more fundamental specialization for motor readiness versus perceptual receptivity. Pribram and McGuinness consider three systems in the control of attention—namely, an arousal system as a phasic response to input, an activation system as a tonic readiness to respond, and finally the effort mechanisms as a coordinating and organizing principle. In other words, there are three energetic supply mechanisms. Two of these (activation and arousal) are basal and coupled with input and output stimulation-processing stages, respectively. The latter are coordinated and supervised by a third system, effort, which is linked to the stage of response to stimulation.

McGuinness and Pribram (1980), as well as Tucker and Williamson (1984), pointed out that activation differs from arousal with respect to (a) their associations with motivational and emotional systems; (b) perceptual receptivity and motor readiness; and (c) dynamics (de Brabander et al., 2002). Effort is supposed to coordinate the activity of arousal and promote the competence of the information-processing system and, as such, it comes close to the driving force behind reasoning and decision making (Sanders, 1983).

Activation as integral to motivationally directed motor action is regulated by dopaminergic neurons originating in the brainstem substantia nigra (with many connections to the frontal cortex) and operates in a tonic—or cumulative—fashion. Arousal, augmented by noradrenergic pathways originating in the locus coeruleus with widespread innervation in the limbic system and neocortex, produces a phasic increment in neural activity. The results obtained through experimental and brain imaging studies suggest a more left-lateralized dopaminergic pathway and a more right-lateralized norepinephrine pathway, and that the distribution of cortical activity related to visuomotor coordination also has separate control systems—with the perceptual system located more in the right cerebral hemisphere and the executive system more in the left cerebral hemisphere (for a review see de Brabander et al., 2002). Effort is a function of the limbic system in a circuit involving the cingulate cortex, hippocampus, septal nuclei, posterior hypothalamus, and anterior thalamic nucleus. The most important connections between arousal and effort are from the sensory cortex and amygdala to the hippocampus, and between effort and activation from the cingulate to the corpus striatum (cf. Sanders, 1983).

Thus one can assume that certain task design does not affect performance directly by influencing the activation and arousal systems proper, but more likely does so indirectly through its impact on motivational and emotional processes. From this, tonic motivational effects on activation or phasic emotional effects on arousal will possibly interact with particular task characteristics.

In accord with Pribram and McGuinness (1975), Sanders (1983, 1997, 1998) proposed three energetic supply systems activated upon arrival stimulation. A first resource type is related to motor adjustment, preparatory processes, and timing. These preparatory processes are close to Posner's (1978, 1980) attentional alertness; here the effect of time uncertainty is discussed in terms of receptivity to external signals. However, the interpretation of this effect by way of motor preparation, reflecting a general phasic readiness to respond, is confirmed by substantial physiological and behavioral evidence. It is further claimed that preparatory processes also depend on processes of tonic alertness (cf. Posner, 1978, 1980). Finally, interactions were observed between the effects of time uncertainty, sleep state, or time of day on reaction time (cf. Sanders, 1983).

The second resource type is related to signal quality, which is associated with the processes of features extraction required for identifying the signal. There is ample evidence that encoding processes run automatically on one hand, but that they demand energetic supply on the other (cf. Sanders, 1998). For example, the active feature extraction is involved in encoding unfamiliar, degraded signals or in separating relevant from irrelevant elements of percepts—which, for instance, may not be needed in the case of familiar signals. Thus these active processes refer to Posner's (1978, 1980) notion of selective attention.

Finally, a third kind of energetic supply is needed for adequate functioning of the response choice stage, which links perception and action and comes close to Posner's (1994) conscious processing (constituting his third component of attention). In other words, as indicated by Welford (1973) and Sanders (1983), the optimal energetic conditions include optimal stimulation (stimulus analysis), optimal pattering of events (readiness to respond), and optimal conflict (decision load).

There is another issue, which was touched upon at the beginning of this section. In order to be informed about the state of arousal and activation, effort-regulating mechanisms operate to sustain their appropriate functioning. Among different types of information, these regulative mechanisms receive feedback concerning the physiological state of organisms and adequacy or effectiveness of individual activity and performance. Individuals act efficiently in a state of optimal level of arousal and activation. Obviously, there are substantial differences among them in the level of stimulation, which enables accomplishing and maintaining an optimal level of arousal and activation. It is claimed that individuals learn how to attain their optimal level of arousal, which in turn forms their individual need for stimulation (Eliasz & Klonowicz, 2001), reflected in the temperament structure. Thus the optimal scope of stimulation and the relevant need for stimulation may change over time and across situations, which implies the internal differentiation of the optimal level of stimulation (Eliasz, 1981).

This brings us close to delineating a concept of dysfunctional activity or low level of performance. There is evidence that prolonged discrepancy between the desired state of stimulation and actual dose of stimulation produces a range of dysfunctional behaviors and inefficient performance (cf. Eliasz & Klonowicz, 2001; Klonowicz, 1973, 1987). On a behavioral level, this discrepancy activates corrective actions to regain the homeostasis at different levels of functioning: the individual may actively or passively reduce these inconsistencies (Eliasz, 1981). Coupling this energetic adjustment with the models derived from Pribram and McGuinness, and Sanders, effort allocation allows us to assume their covariance—to the extent that continuing high demands without sufficient success in maintaining or restoring an optimum level of stimulation are supposed to constitute the basis for different dysfunctional behaviors and inefficient performance. Altogether this would imply patterns of maladaptive functioning such as:

- *Overstimulation of the arousal system.* This may include sudden, intensive, prolonged, or demanding external and/or internal stimulation (e.g., sudden, unexpected, and threatening stimulation; dramatic cases of strong stimulation; prolonged worrisome thoughts; rumination). The major consequences of the overarousal may be a direct energetic overflow on the activation system, which in turn may provoke immediate action without cognitive control (cf. Sanders, 1983). In other words, the arousal and activation systems are fused and produce incompatible reactions or inadequate behaviors. It might happen, especially in the case of overstimulation, that processing stages and effort are bypassed when the rise in arousal triggers a signal to the activation system, which in turn enhances response readiness and response execution. This effect is known as immediate arousal (Sanders, 1983; van Molen & Keuss, 1981) and might be harmful and may produce incompatible choice reactions—for example, reducing reaction time in the case of simple reactions or prolonging it in the case of choice reactions. However, it is hypothesized that uncoupling the arousal and activation systems through effort allows avoiding negative immediate arousal influence (cf. Sanders, 1980).
- *Understimulation of the arousal system.* This might be considered as the perceptual habituation and reduced readiness to respond. For example, effects on the discriminability index $(d')$ or decision-making strategy $(\beta)$[3] might be observed in vigilance tests. However, underarousal affects $d'$ while the effects on $\beta$ refer to underactivation (cf. Sanders, 1983).

It is worth noting that if arousal and activation systems are on the optimum level and underarousal or overarousal are not present, the effort allocation does not have the status of "a-specific processing capacity" or "compensatory factor of

---

[3] Signal Detection Theory includes two parameters (among others): the discriminability index $(d')$, which is the distance between the signal and noise distributions and reflects sensitivity to the signal; and the strategy of decision making $(\beta)$, which includes a proportion of false alarms for all incorrect responses (a high $\beta$ index shows an impulsive strategy for making decisions; a low $\beta$ index shows a careful strategy for making decisions). For more discussion see Balakrishnan and MacDonald (2001) and Green and Swets (1974).

cognitive performance" and its role is to keep the energetic supply at the optimum. In other words, when this optimum is realized, the performance measures are reliable indicators of mental functioning. However, if conditions affect the energetic state and turn it into being underaroused or overaroused, performance depends on the amount of effort invested. The consequence is that performance measures indicate that "a-specific processing capacity" or "compensatory factor of cognitive performance" are engaged in computational processing.

One relevant issue in this respect concerns the assumption of relative independence of the arousal, activation, and effort systems. The main argument is that emotional and motivational variables are strongly related to triggering the arousal and activation systems, respectively, whereas effort only plays a role in nonoptimal conditions (overaroused or underaroused) if energy supply through arousal or activation deviates from the optimum. In other words, it is advocated that effort might affect energetic supply correction of arousal and activation, and affect behaviors and performance (cf. Sanders, 1983). However, this restoration to the optimum does not mean that one can simply avoid maladaptive behaviors or that performance can always be improved by allocation of extra effort. Sometimes effort fails or is continually loaded and we observe a low level of performance or inadequate behavior. It is obvious from the perspective of the SRIS that other factors also affect the final outcomes. Consequently, it is not possible to exclude the influence of other-than-energy-related personality traits, self-regulative processes, or environmental factors on the quality of a person's activity. This issue will be discussed in detail in the next sections.

Another important theoretical problem is whether effort allocation is reflexive and automatic or more voluntary and flexible. The next assumption here is that effort operates as the automatic and voluntary energetic supply and still is a more secondary energy provider, controlling the more primary or basal types of energy supply—namely, arousal and activation—in order to maintain the optimal level of stimulation. The automatic effort allocation is seen as more organismic, somatic, and stimuli driven and runs for a relatively short period of time. It resembles the arousal and activation systems, which are based on the deduction that those systems reflect the gain level of the affective, motivational, or motor amplifiers (Blum, Geiwitz, & Stewart, 1967). Whereas voluntary effort allocation is more related to cognition and reflects the gain level of the cognitive amplifier (Blum et al., 1967), it also seems to be more connected with cognitive control and self-regulative processes, which implies its longer-term functioning.

Differentiation between tonic and phasic activation is also important from the perspective of temperament mechanisms (Strelau, 2006). Theories of temperament based on the concepts of arousal and activation attempt to identify the relations between particular temperament traits and physiological markers related to tonic and phasic arousal (Strelau, 2008). Usually, physiological indices of temperament are measured in response to a specific provocation—such as experimental manipulation or discrete situational conditions—and refer to phasic activation. It is also possible to test physiological markers of temperament measured at resting or baseline conditions, which denotes tonic activation (Strelau, 2000). Such relationships suggest that the functional properties of the underlying brain systems give rise to the claim that physiological mechanisms of the attentional systems are associated with physiological mechanisms of temperament when integrating and regulating stimulation.

### 2.3.2. Level of structures: Temperament traits and personality coherence/incoherence

After discussing the attentional processes involved in forming personality coherence and incoherence, I focus on the components located at a higher level of the personality system—temperament traits and types. I consider these as essential in forming personality coherence/incoherence from the structure level.

#### Harmonious and disharmonious types of temperament

It is evident from the previous theoretical discussion that the analysis of intraindividual architecture of personality should be aimed at mutual, relatively stable relations among traits—or, more precisely, at types and patterns composed of traits. I assume that within the temperament subsystem the internal linkages among traits are based on their physiological mechanisms connected with stimulation regulation and integration. The strength of these linkages seems to be pretty high, and the final outcomes relatively stable.

On a more elaborated level, some researchers assume that temperament traits have different adaptive functions, but that all are based on the same biological mechanisms responsible for regulating the level of arousal (e.g., Strelau, 2008). And individual differences in the reactivity of these mechanisms affect the tendency toward chronically elevated or suppressed level of arousal (arousability) and high or low need for stimulation. Based on the concepts of augmentation/reduction of stimulation, it might be stated that individuals who have temperament traits typically associated with a high level of arousability have stimulation-augmenting mechanisms. Stimulation (sensory, motor, cognitive, or affective) of a given intensity leads to a higher level of arousal than that implied by intensity of stimulation. Individuals who have temperament traits typically associated with a low level of arousability present stimulation-reducing mechanisms; stimulation of the same intensity leads to a lower level of arousal than that implied by intensity of stimulation (Strelau, 2008).

Thus the particular configuration of temperament traits is involved in the process of maintaining the optimal level of stimulation and effective stimulation regulation. However, the regulation of stimulation might be also ineffective (Eliasz, 1992; Zawadzki & Strelau, 1997). In other words, depending on the configuration of traits, stimulation regulation may have different levels of effectiveness. Effective stimulation regulation reflects the fitness between the amount of the flowing stimulation and individual stimulation-processing capacities (SPC), which affect the formulation of harmonious types of temperaments (HTT). Hence both types of individuals—with high stimulation-processing capacities and with low stimulation-processing capacities—might be distinguished within harmonious structures. However, different ways of maintaining effective stimulation regulation and the optimal level of stimulation may be identified in high-SPC and low-SPC individuals—that is, seeking or avoiding stimulation, respectively (cf. Zawadzki & Strelau, 1997).

Ineffective stimulation regulation is connected with the quantity of stimulation, being beyond the optimal level of stimulation. Relations among temperament traits change adequately to the primary functions of these traits, which results in disharmonious types of temperament. For example, a high (nonoptimal) level of stimulation in individuals with low SPC may be associated with a tendency toward reducing arousal, but without a tendency toward avoiding stimulation; a low (nonoptimal) level of stimulation in individuals with high SPC may be associated with a tendency toward reducing arousal, coupled with a tendency toward avoiding stimulation (cf. Zawadzki & Strelau, 1997).

There are several arousal-related theories of temperament. They propose the structures of temperament, which resemble the four temperaments according to the Hippocrates–Galen typology. However, these theories emphasize different aspects of functioning through which the optimal level of arousal might be achieved: control of the nervous system, affective activity and social tendencies, energetic and temporal characteristic of behaviors, and self-regulation. These aspects seem to play a key role in adaptation. Thus the next step is to describe these structures, which are an essential part of the SRIS.

*Structure of the four temperaments and optimal*
*stimulation level in different theoretical perspectives*

Generally, neurobiologically based theories of temperament draw on the fundamental assumptions endorsed by the Pavlovian notion of nervous system types and arousal mechanisms. Indeed, a revolutionary advance in the study of the biological bases of individual differences was initiated through his work (cf. Eysenck, 1987; Simonov & Ershov, 1991). Starting with applications of nervous types to the conditioned reflexes of dogs, Pavlov extended his theory to human personality and concluded that types of nervous system activity are comparable to the temperament types described by Hippocrates and Galen, with specific aspects of emotionality characterizing each type.

Pavlov's approach to CNS types has gained increased popularity, especially among biologically oriented personality researchers (e.g., Claridge, 1985; Eliasz, 1981; Eysenck, 1972; Gray, 1964; Strelau, 1983; Zuckerman, 1991), because the Pavlovian typology offers the most accurate basis for a physiological interpretation of the Hippocrates–Galen types of temperament, and the constructs of strength of the CNS and protective inhibition are closely related to the concept of arousal to which most of these scholars refer. This reference has been especially visible in two theories of personality and temperament; namely, Eysenck's (e.g., 1967, 1970, 1981, 1991, 1994) and Strelau's (e.g., 1969, 1974, 1983, 1994, 2001, 2008) models share some theoretical foundations with Pavlovian and neo-Pavlovian approaches to temperament and the concept of arousal. According to Eysenck, the interaction of the ascending reticular formation with frontal neocortical areas determines the strength properties of the central nervous system, and it relates to extraversion and introversion. Later Gray (1981) revised the Eysenckian conception, adding the hippocampus and septal area to the neuroanatomical scheme and linking a strong nervous system to extraversion and a weak nervous system to introversion. Strelau's Regulative Theory of Temperament and its modification proposed by Eliasz (1981), which directly refer to Pavlov's theory of CNS properties and their adaptive role, also postulated stable individual differences in arousal—which resembles strength of excitation understood as a trait in accordance with Pavlov's suggestions.

Obviously, in Eysenck's and Strelau's theories the Pavlovian concepts have been extended, reformulated, and supplemented with psychological interpretation. Consequently, this resulted in formulating three specific models of temperament. The most important theoretical divergences among Pavlov's, Eysenck's, and Strelau's approaches lie in the different set of features composing the structure of temperament. For that reason these structures reflect different underpinnings of behavior.


*Optimal stimulation level achieved by nervous system control*

Based on the so-called "nervism paradigm," according to which any behavior is governed and regulated by the central nervous system, Pavlov assumed that particular properties of the nervous processes are responsible for the observed individual differences in conditioning (cf. Pavlov, 1928; Strelau, Angleitner, & Newberry, 1999). Pavlov proposed—as the basic properties of the CNS—strength of excitation (SE) and strength of inhibition (SI), and a balance (BA) between these two types of processes and mobility of the nervous processes (MO). Depending on the configuration of these properties, Pavlov distinguished different types of nervous system, which are the physiological foundations of temperament (cf. Strelau, 1983, 2008). In other words, for Pavlov temperament is a psychological manifestation of the type of nervous system.

Thus strength of the nervous processes of excitation is seen as a trait (not a state) that refers to the working capacity of cortical cells. SE manifests itself in the ability to withstand strong excitation (whether prolonged or short lived) without slipping into protective (transmariginal, unconditioned, inherited) inhibition—estimated by recording the organism's responses to strong, prolonged, or recurrent stimulation. Protective inhibition guards the nervous system from stimulation that exceeds its working capacity. The appearance of transmariginal inhibition under strong, prolonged, or recurrent stimulation is a main index of SE and might be registered as (a) a decrease in intensity (amplitude) of reactions; (b) lack of changes in intensity of reactions; (c) disappearance of reactions in spite of increasing intensity of stimuli; or (d) disturbances of behavior (mostly emotional) resulting from excessive stimulation. Individuals with protective inhibition to low-intensity or duration stimuli are considered as having a weak CNS, whereas individuals with a strong CNS have the capacity to react adequately to high-intensity or/and long-duration stimuli without slipping into protective inhibition. Hence strong personality types have a higher CNS working capacity (endurance) compared with weak ones. Since people are confronted in their everyday lives with high-intensity stimuli, Pavlov considered SE to be the most important property of the nervous system (cf. Strelau et al., 1999).

Although rather succinctly stated by Pavlov, strength of the nervous processes of inhibition is defined as a trait representing the capacity to maintain a conditioned inhibition. It reveals itself in the ability to maintain a state of conditioned inhibition—to stop or delay behavior when needed and to refrain from behaviors when required. SI is opposed to unconditioned inhibition (one of whose specific forms is protective inhibition) and manifests itself in the effectiveness of one's functioning with respect to all possible forms of conditioned inhibition that are learned and acquired (i.e., extinction, delay, differentiation; cf. Strelau, 2008). Strength of inhibition was usually assessed to determine the balance between strength of excitation and strength of inhibition. The effectiveness of these two processes depends on endogenous differences in strength, and this differential inherently maintains the equilibrium between SE and SI. In some occurrences the excitatory and inhibitory processes are equal, whereas in others the excitatory processes are strong and the inhibitory processes are weak (Strelau, 1983).

Hence, according to Pavlov, the balance of the nervous processes is the ratio of SE to SI, which implies that it has a status of a secondary trait. Regarding its functional meaning, BA is the ability to inhibit particular excitations—when required—in order to evoke other reactions appropriate to the environmental demands (cf. Strelau et al. 1999).

And finally the last property proposed by Pavlov, mobility of the nervous processes, reveals itself as the ability to react quickly and adequately to changes in the environment—or, to be more precise, as the ability to prioritize impulses according to external conditions (excitation before inhibition and vice-versa; cf. Pavlov, 1928). It does not refer to the speed with which nervous processes are initiated and terminated but to the speed with which the changes in these processes occur. This ability was usually measured by the alteration method, which consists of tools measuring the speed of developing adequate—positive or negative—conditioned reflexes to changes in the signal value of conditioned stimuli (cf. Strelau, 1983).

Different configurations of the aforementioned properties of nervous processes resulted in distinctions among the four temperaments, as shown in Table 2.1.

**Table 2.1.** Three arousal-related typologies of temperament

| Type of temperament | Pavlovian Typology<br>*Optimal stimulation level achieved by nervous system control* | Eysenckian Typology<br>*Optimal stimulation level achieved by content (emotional and social) aspects of behavior* | Regulative Theory of Temperament<br>*Optimal stimulation level achieved by formal (energetic and temporal) aspects of behavior* |
|---|---|---|---|
| Harmonious sanguine | **Strong, mobile, and balanced type of NS**<br>(high SE; high SI; high MO; BA between SE:SI) | **Emotionally stable extravert**<br>(high E; low N) | **High stimulation-processing capacities & effective stimulation regulation**<br>(very high EN; low ER; very high AC; high SS; high BR; low PE) |
| Harmonious melancholic | **Weak type of NS**<br>(low SE; low SI) | **Neurotic introvert**<br>(low E; high N) | **Low stimulation-processing capacities & effective stimulation regulation**<br>(very low EN; very high ER; low AC; low SS; low BR; high PE) |
| Disharmonious phlegmatic | **Strong, slow, and balanced type of NS**<br>(high SE; high SI; low MO; BA between SE:SI) | **Emotionally stable introvert**<br>(low E; low N) | **High stimulation-processing capacities & ineffective stimulation regulation**<br>(very high EN; low ER; low AC; low/moderate SS; low/moderate BR; low/moderate PE) |
| Disharmonious choleric | **Strong, unbalanced type of NS**<br>(high SE; moderate/low SI; Unbalance: SE > SI) | **Neurotic extravert**<br>(high E; high N) | **Low stimulation-processing capacities & ineffective stimulation regulation**<br>(very low EN; very high ER; very high AC; high/moderate SS; high/moderate BR; high/moderate PE) |

*Note.* NS = nervous system; SE = strength of excitation; SI = strength of inhibition; MO = mobility; BA = balance; E = extraversion; N = neuroticism; EN = endurance; ER = emotional reactivity; AC = activity; SS = sensory sensitivity; BR = briskness; PE = perseveration.

Individual differences related to these properties systematically ally with differences in behavior that are classified as sanguine, melancholic, phlegmatic, or choleric, respectively. Accordingly, a Sanguine Type is associated with a strong nervous system, whereas a Melancholic Type is coupled with a weak nervous system characterized by inhibition. Moreover, the strong nervous system is also linked to mobility, which underscores the adaptive capabilities of an individual (the speed at which a person can adopt specific appropriate responses to environmental stimulation). Consequently, Pavlov distinguished between the mobile type of nervous system (sanguine temperament) and the slow type of nervous system (phlegmatic temperament). Pavlovian classification recognizes in both the sanguine and phlegmatic types strong excitatory processes that are balanced by strong inhibitory processes. The unbalanced type comes in one form only (choleric temperament) and is seen as a dominance of excitation over inhibition (see Table 2.1). Harmonious types of temperament—sanguine and melancholic—are built on the consistency between levels of SE and MO, while disharmonious types of temperament—phlegmatic and choleric—emerge from the inconsistency between levels of SE and MO. It is worth mentioning that Strelau (2008) claims that these properties, which differ also in intensity, allow for the identification of many more temperament types than Pavlov suggested.

Using the parameters of strength, balance, and mobility, Pavlov extended his theory by incorporating a higher order of central nervous system functioning: the association between micro activity and overt behavior lies in the reciprocal interaction of macro structures, representing functionally distinct regions of the brain. Pavlov, for example, connected the functional specialization of the neocortical and subcortical areas with the intellectual and artist type, respectively (cf. Cassimjee, 2003).

Such followers of Pavlov as Nebylitsyn (e.g., 1972) and Teplov (e.g., 1985) adapted his theory and suggested that characterizations of the nervous system based on the Hippocrates–Galen types revert to characterizations based on properties of the nervous system (cf. Cassimjee, 2003; Simonov, 1987). One important conclusion emerges from their studies: the strength of nervous system functioning is similar to the concept of arousal (e.g., a strong nervous system requires more intense arousal than a weak nervous system because the latter is far more quickly aroused). The biological mechanism of arousal is viewed as one of the essential factors mediating temperament. The Pavlovian idea of arousal is associated with the excitatory mechanisms of the central nervous system, which involve excitatory process, intensity of stimulus, and transmariginal inhibition. Intensity of stimuli determines intensity of excitation and at a set point excitation converts into transmariginal inhibition (cf. Eysenck, 1970).

Researchers argue here that as identified by Pavlov, three fundamental properties (strength, balance, mobility) of two processes of the central nervous system (excitation, inhibition) determine individual differences in temperament and indicate the control processes of behavior. The ability to withstand intense and persistent stimulation without exhibiting protective inhibition, the ability to evoke and preserve a state of conditioned inhibition, and the response capabilities of the central nervous system to continuous alterations in the environment (cf. Simonov & Ershov, 1991; Strelau & Zawadzki, 1997) seem to be highly desirable for the control of behavior. These abilities explain to a certain extent why some activities and actions are enhanced, changed, refrained from, or delayed when required. Ample evidence has been collected that shows the importance of these abilities in moderating behavior under demanding, stressful, or highly stimulating natural or experimental conditions (e.g., Eliasz, 1981; Klonowicz, 1985, 1992; Marszał-Wiśniewska & Fajkowska, 2005; Merlin, 1986; Strelau, 1983, 1995; Zawadzki, 1992).

One might predict that a central nervous system in which strong excitatory processes are balanced by strong inhibitory processes would play an essential role in performance, professional, or school activities in which control (continuing, delaying, or ceasing of behavior) is demanded. For example, pilots, firemen, professional sportsman, and steelworkers have higher strength of excitation compared with the normative population (cf. Eliasz, 1981; Strelau, 1983; Zawadzki 1992). It has also been demonstrated that performance under situations demanding high-speed switching from one activity to another is associated with high mobility (e.g., Zawadzki, 1992), and that individual differences in concentration of attention depend on the strength of the nervous system (cf. Yermolayeva-Tomina, 1964). Moreover, it has been shown that utilized emotional material SE is connected with effectiveness of attentional processing and that SI is connected with attentional control and strategic processing, while MO is connected with all these attentional functions (Marszał-Wiśniewska & Fajkowska, 2005).

Eysenck's (e.g., 1967, 1970, 1981) view of temperament as an affective trait is inherent in his thesis that personality arises from the interaction of four components—that is, the cognitive (intelligence), conative (character), somatic (constitution), and temperament (affective) ones. This means that temperament reflects the emotional underpinnings of behavior. However, it might be claimed that the Eysenckian structure of temperament also comprises the traits that express the social aspects of behavior. The idea of temperament as an emotive or social component of personality has been challenged by theories espousing the behavioral connotation of temperament, where the "how" or "content-free" notion of behavior is the basis of temperament. In Strelau's model temperament is also considered as a formal characteristic of behavior (similar to the Pavlovian conception). Here the structural characteristics of temperament reveal themselves in behaviors as the capacity and effectiveness of stimulation processing (e.g., Strelau, 1983, 2001, 2008). The following two sections outline Eysenck's and Strelau's understandings of temperament in more detail.

*Optimal stimulation level achieved by content
(emotional and social) aspects of behavior*

Eysenck's model (e.g., 1967, 1987, 1994) is recognized as a biologically based explanation of individual differences in personality and temperament. He identified three personality factors—psychoticism, extraversion, and neuroticism (PEN)—and believed that they have strong biological roots in which hormones, arousal, and visceral brain activation actuate these three dimensions, respectively.[4] In his model the state-trait distinction allows for differentiation between a relatively permanent disposition (trait) and a transitory intrinsic condition (state). And the essential element of his structural model is a hierarchical taxonomy of temperament containing four levels of behavioral organization (cf. Eysenck, 1947/1998).

- Level 1: simple behaviors or reactions that occur at a single moment.
- Level 2: habits or recurring behaviors and reactions.
- Level 3: traits or factors (i.e., interrelated sets of habits).
- Level 4: orthogonal superfactors—that is, psychoticism, extraversion, and neuroticism (interrelated sets of traits). This hierarchy represents a trait (e.g., hostility: Level 3) and a type (e.g., psychoticism: Level 4).

There is similarity between the Pavlovian concept of strength of the nervous system and the Eysenckian view of activation and arousal (e.g., Newberry et al., 1997), with extraversion associated with arousal and neuroticism connected with activation (Eysenck, 1970).

The biological mechanisms underlying the extraversion dimension are linked to the activity level of the cortico-reticular loop, a part of the ascending reticular activating system responsible for attenional processes and arousal and regulated by the brainstem and some areas of the thalamus (cf. Cassimjee, 2003; Eysenck & Eysenck, 1985; Strelau, 2001; Woodruff-Pak, 1997). The oscillations in rhythmic arousal patterns are controlled by subcortical structures, whereas the frontal cortical parts govern the inhibitory control of the reticular system. Eysenck (1970) claimed that neural impulses are transmitted to projection areas in the cortex and the reticular system. When the arousal information is sent from the reticular formation to the cortex, the latter mandates the reticular formation to continue with the excitatory impulses or switch to inhibition. This activity of the cortico-reticular loop, which Eysenck (1970) referred to as cortical arousal, explains the differences between extraverted and introverted subjects.

The position on the excitation-inhibition continuum determines the optimal level of arousal and designates whether an individual is an extravert or introvert.

---

[4] It is worth noting that for Eysenck and Gray "personality" and "temperament" are interchangeable terms (cf. Strelau & Angleitner, 1991).

Generally, introverted individuals have a higher level of arousal than extraverted ones, because introversion is a "product" of the fast functioning of the ascending reticular activating system. That is why introverts are able to tolerate less intense arousal than extraverts, who begin with a higher threshold. The neocortex of introverted subjects exerts more inhibition on the subcortex, which explains more inhibited overt behavior in them than in extraverted subjects (see also Revelle, 1997). Therefore the opposite characteristic is typical for extraverts: individuals in whom excitatory potential is generated slowly and weakly, and in whom the reactive inhibition is generated rapidly and strongly and is dissipated slowly, are predisposed to develop extraverted patterns of behavior (cf. Strelau, 1998). Drugs can shift a person's position on the extraversion-introversion dimension: stimulant drugs are introverting, depressant drugs are extraverting (Eysenck, 1967, 1981).

In sum, a great variety of experimental laboratory investigations (e.g., Eaves, Eysenck, & Martin, 1988; Eysenck, 1967, 1972, 1981) have shown that (a) the constitutional aspect of extraversion is related to greater susceptibility to inhibition and chronically lower arousal; (b) less efficient conditioning and tranquilizers increase inhibition, decrease excitation, and reveal extraverted patterns of behavior; (c) the previous description of extraverts encourages us to characterize the constitutional aspects of introversion as lower susceptibility to inhibition and chronically higher arousal; and (d) stimulant drugs decrease inhibition, increase excitation, and reveal introverted patterns of behavior. The descriptive, phenotypic differences in extraversion and introversion, which were usually measured in terms of questionnaires such as the Eysenck Personality Questionnaire or Eysenck Personality Questionnaire–Revised (cf. Eysenck & Eysenck, 1985), emphasized that typical extraverts are sociable, like parties, have many friends, need to have people with whom to talk, and do not like reading or studying by themselves; they tend to be aggressive, lose their temper quickly, do not keep their feelings under tight control, and are not always reasonable people. Typical introverts—on the other hand— are quiet and retiring, introspective, fond of books rather than people, reserved and distant, tend to plan ahead, do not like excitement, keep their feelings under control, seldom behave in an aggressive way, and do not lose their temper easily (Eysenck & Eysenck, 1985).

It should be noted that there has been some disagreement on the relation between arousal and extraversion; probably part of the disagreement can be explained by the inconsistent operationalization of the arousal construct (cf. Fahrenberg, 1987). For example, when EEG signals were recorded, it was demonstrated that low cortical arousal was not associated with extraversion but with high psychoticism (cf. O'Gorman & Lloyd, 1987). Moreover, the high psychoticism scorers presented physiological hyporesponsiveness, which indicated a low arousal level (Robinson & Zahn, 1985). Furthermore, the extraversion-arousal relationship cannot be reduced to the scope of the theory, which deals exclusively with cortical arousal. Several investigations have provided results that suggested the contribution of dopaminergic activity and subcortical arousal to individual differences in the extraversion dimension (e.g., Pivik, Stelmack, & Bylsma, 1988).

The activities of the visceral brain (sympathetic nervous system), which comprises the hippocampus, amygdala, striatum, septum, and hypothalamus, mediate the level of neuroticism. These structures bind with neuroticism in an information pathway that determines when the visceral brain sends messages to the reticular formation and arouses the cortex by the ascending reticular activating system. Eysenck (1991) referred to the mechanism of the activity of the visceral brain as activation and postulated that the high neuroticism scorers display greater activation levels and lower excitation thresholds in the visceral brain. He assumed that the ascending activating system arousal (cortical) does not affect limbic system activation (autonomic), but that the limbic system activation produces an increase in reticular and cortical arousal (Eysenck, 1967, 1970). In other words, the activation loop causes arousal, whereas the arousal loop bypasses the activation loop.

Serotonin activity has been linked to temperament traits—such as impulsivity and aggression—that are contained in the psychoticism dimension (Eysenck, 1970, 1992). Eysenck (1992) found that low MAO (enzyme-degrading serotonin) concentrations were associated with one's vulnerability to aggressive and impulsive behavior.

In addition to biological mechanisms, there are also neurocognitive mechanisms connected with the extraversion and neuroticism dimensions. A major dimension of personality, which has received considerable attention in research on event-related potentials (ERPs), is that of extraversion (Stelmack, 1990; Zuckerman, 1991). Research indicates that introverts—compared with extraverts—reveal early attentional vigilance toward incoming stimuli, indexed by higher amplitudes of early somatosensory components (N1–P2 ERP; de Pascalis, Strelau, & Zawadzki, 1999). However, most studies on ERPs and personality dimensions have focused mainly on the positive component P3, which is believed to denote the magnitude of attentional resources allocated to a task. Some studies revealed higher P3 amplitude in introverts than extraverts, suggesting that introverts are experiencing greater levels of attentional demand (Stelmack & Houlihan, 1995). However, as Zuckerman (1991) noticed, failure to replicate effects even across similar studies is a cause for concern. Additionally, the relationship between the neuroticism-emotional stability dimension and the amplitude of P3 component was not found (Strelau, 2009b). The study of Fajkowska, Zagórska, Strelau, and Jaśkowski (2012) proposed a temporal distributional approach to ERP analysis in an attentionally demanding task as an optimal design for capturing some of the dynamism and complexity of attentional processing of facial stimuli among sanguines, melancholics, phlegmatics, and cholerics. Among others, the authors found a specific association between attentional control (P3, N2) and emotional stimulation and four temperaments formed along the extraversion and neuroticism dimensions.

The dimensional (rather than categorical) model of temperament enables individuals to have some degree of extraversion or neuroticism on a colinear continuum. For example, by coupling the extraversion and neuroticism dimensions, one can identify the sanguine with the stable extrovert, the phlegmatic with the stable introvert, the choleric with the unstable extrovert, and the melancholic with the unstable introvert. As shown in Table 2.1 (see also Strelau, 1998), a negative relation between extraversion and neuroticism indicates the harmonious types of temperament (sanguine and melancholic) and a positive relation between extraversion and neuroticism implies the disharmonious types of temperament (phlegmatic and choleric).

*Optimal stimulation level achieved by formal (energetic and temporal)*
*aspects of behavior: The Regulative Theory of Temperament*

The Regulative Theory of Temperament begins with the conceptualization of temperament not as the content of behaviors and reactions, but rather as a reflection of relatively stable formal aspects of behaviors and reactions. In other words, dual levels embracing the energetic and temporal features mediate temperment's effects on the form of behavioral output. These features manifest themselves from early childhood and have their counterpart in the animal world. Despite the fact that temperament is primarily determined by innate neurobiochemical mechanisms, it is subjected to gradual changes due to maturation and individual-specific interactions between the genotype and the environment (see Strelau, 1983, 2000, 2001, 2008).

The energy system allows individuals to exchange energy with the environment, learn from these exchanges, and ultimately interact efficiently with the environment to conserve energy. This process operates in a systemic way and involves exchange, transmission, feedback, and control mechanisms (Cassimjee, 2003). Applying this paradigm to individual differences in temperament, the energy system is perceived as the structure embracing acquisition, expression, storage, and monitoring elements. Energy acquisition might be slow or quick or frequent or rare, might originate from a few or many sources, and its differentials are observable in behaviors. The expression system is characterized by high or low motor displays that require intense or mild energy conversion and output. Next the efficient or inefficient storage systems are able to either store and distribute energy to appropriate behaviors or waste energy output, respectively. Each of these systems works toward efficiency with a monitoring system; nevertheless, depending on individual differences in temperament, the control system would focus on different things and maintain differential thresholds (see Cassimjee, 2003). For instance, although both extraverts and introverts have an efficient expression and acquisition system, the latter functions at a low threshold and the former at a high one; the monitoring system of extraverts is biased toward expression (high output) and the monitoring system of the introverts toward acquisition (low output). Thus the interaction of these four energy level systems is responsible for differences in behaviors (Cassimjee, 2003).

It is postulated that the neuroendocrine system, the ascending reticular formation, and the frontal cortex are three anatomical systems that determine the energetic features of temperament (cf. Strelau, 1987). Therefore energetic characteristics of reactions and behaviors are responsible for individual differences in physiological mechanisms responsible for the energy level of the organism (i.e., for the accumulation and release of stored-up energy; Zawadzki & Strelau, 1997). Within the RTT there are four factors indexing energetic temperament traits: emotional reactivity (ER), the tendency to react intensively to emotion-generating stimuli, expressed in high emotional sensitivity and low emotional endurance; sensory sensitivity (SS), the ability to react to sensory stimuli whose stimulating value is low; endurance (EN), the ability to react adequately in situations requiring prolonged or highly stimulating activity or under conditions of intensive external stimulation; and activity (AC), the tendency to undertake highly stimulating behaviors or behaviors providing intensive external stimulation (Strelau, 2006, 2008; Zawadzki & Strelau, 1997).

The temporal characteristics of behavior indicate the group of characteristics of the dynamics of reaction over time (Zawadzki & Strelau, 1997). Two factors are proposed for the temporal traits of temperament: perseveration (PE), the tendency to continue and repeat behavior and experience an emotional state after termination of stimuli or situations evoking this behavior or state; and briskness (BR), the tendency to react quickly, keep a high tempo in performing activities, and shift easily in response to changes in surroundings from one behavior or reaction to another (Strelau, 2008; Zawadzki & Strelau, 1997).

In comparison with the research on energetic aspects, the temporal dimensions are underscored by limited scrutiny. However, Strelau and Zawadzki (1995) outline three reasons for the separation of energetic and temporal features in the structure of temperament. First, intensity of behavior and speed of reaction underlie separate functions. Second, the biophysiological substrates of temporal and energetic elements are distinct. According to Strelau and Zawadzki (1995), temporal traits are explained by recourse to tempo of reaction, termination, course of the neural process, and interaction between these activities. Netter (1991) suggests that the actions of dopamine in different parts of the brain might be involved in temporal processes. The arousal-orienting mechanisms appear to contribute to the energetic aspects of behavior. The traits of sensory sensitivity, endurance, and activity appear to be linked to processes of the cortical-reticular system, and emotional reactivity appears to be mediated by the actions of the limbic system and the ANS (cf. Cassimjee, 2003; Strelau, 2008).

Third, temperament is characterized on the level of primary traits and the dual structure allows for the specificity of these characteristics to be emphasized. In contrast to personality, temperament in the RTT pertains solely to aspects that modify and regulate behavior, as well as to the way behavior expresses itself.

Temperament manages these processes by regulating reaction levels proportionate to exogenous stimulative and endogenous activity values. The stable individual differences observed in the organization of more goal-directed, flexible, and adaptive future-directed activity have their origins in a person's individual style of behavior—situation dependent, stereotyped, bound-to-the present reactivity (Cassimjee, 2003; Klonowicz, 1987). High reactivity (high sensitivity and low endurance) and low reactivity (low sensitivity and high endurance) are governed by physiological mechanisms underlying stimulation processing. Moreover, reactivity controls the level of arousal by operating as a filter for environmental stimuli that have arousal potentials (Eliasz, 1988).

Thus reactivity as a temperament dimension influences the acquisition, storage, expression, and control of an individual's energy level. Activity is appropriate to the goal-directed behavior or reaction, which is characterized by a specific stimuli value—the amount and range of the behavior undertaken. According to Strelau and Zawadzki (1995), activity can be related to behavior associated with motor features, as well as with many features manifested in social situations. The stimulation for activity may emerge from a number of external (e.g. events, tasks, or environment) and internal (e.g., behavior, emotions, thoughts, and individual reactions) sources.

A person's optimal level of arousal and level of reactivity determine the regulation of activity. Individuals with a high level of reactivity and low need for stimulation (a low optimum scope of arousal) are less likely to be active than individuals with a low level of reactivity and high need for stimulation (a high optimum scope of arousal). Accordingly, complex biophysiological processes that augment stimulation typify individuals with high reactivity; by contrast, processes that repress stimulation characterize persons with low reactivity (Strelau, 2008). As a consequence of these differences in activity levels that arise from the expression system, high reactives have control systems that monitor input sources, and low reactives have control systems that monitor output on account of their tendency to increased activity and energy expansion (Cassimjee, 2003; Strelau, 1994).

Although the biological mechanisms underlying individual differences in temperament are postulated within the RTT, there are only a few studies that investigate this issue. However, there is an interesting line of studies exploring the connections between neurocognitive mechanisms and RTT temperament traits. For example, de Pascalis et al. (1999) indicate that individuals with low levels of trait EN exhibit higher P3 amplitudes than high-EN subjects, which may be interpreted as greater effort investment for these subjects. Moreover, research investigating a range of ERP components at various points in time and brain locations between low and high scorers on six RTT temperament traits revealed that individuals low in trait ER exhibit vigilance to facial affect indexed by enhanced P1 and N170, and extended processing of facial affect manifested by larger LPC potential (Zagórska, Fajkowska, Strelau, & Jaśkowski, 2010). Additionally, low-AC scorers displayed better top-down attentional control over threatening material (higher N2/NoGo amplitudes). And finally, Fajkowska et al. (2012) investigated both behavioral and cortical (ERPs) patterns of response reflecting functioning of attention in four temperament structures and showed the specific connections between effortful attention allocation and four temperaments formulated within the RTT.

Moving from mechanisms of RTT temperament traits to temperament types (see Table 2.1), one can notice that temperament structure—which resembles the Sanguine Type—is composed of very high levels of endurance and activity, high levels of sensory sensitivity and briskness, and low levels of emotional reactivity and perseveration. The typical configuration for the Melancholic Type indicates very low levels of endurance and activity, low levels of sensory sensitivity and briskness, and high levels of emotional reactivity and perseveration. The Phlegmatic Type is characterized by a very high level of endurance, a very low level of emotional reactivity, a low level of activity, and average or low levels of sensory sensitivity, briskness, and perseveration. A temperament with a low level of endurance, very high levels of emotional reactivity and activity, and average or high levels of sensory sensitivity, briskness, and perseveration represents the Choleric Type. The fitness between AC and individual stimulation-processing capacities (relation between level of EN and level of ER) reflects harmonious types of temperaments, while lack of fitness between AC and individual stimulation-processing capacities (relation between level of EN and level of ER) indicates disharmonious types of temperament (sanguine and melancholic and choleric and phlegmatic, respectively).

*Optimal stimulation level achieved by formal (energetic) aspects of behavior: The Transactional Model of Temperament*

The Transactional Model of Temperament proposed by Eliasz (TMT; e.g., 1981, 2001) modified the RTT in several respects. Temperament is regarded here as one of the essential elements of the system of stimulation regulation (cf. Eliasz, 1981), which is similar to my formulation of the System of Regulation and Integration Stimulation. Traits, which form the structure of temperament, are the principal constituents of a complex mechanism that maintains an optimum stimulation and activation (cf. Eliasz, 1981). Maintaining optimum stimulation and activation depends on the presence of mutual relations among temperament traits. In addition, findings from many studies point to circular relationships among physiological mechanisms of temperament and stimulative value of environmental factors that affect the appearance of behaviors addressed toward attaining or maintaining optimum stimulation and activation (cf. Eliasz, 1985, 1988, 1990, 2001; Eliasz & Klonowicz, 2001). There are grounds to believe that a regulative role of temperament is directly connected with one's need for stimulation, a state of arousal defined as optimal (Eliasz & Klonowicz, 2001). However, this regulation is also possible from the level of personality mechanisms associated with affective, motivational, cognitive, social, or self systems (Eliasz, 1981).

Temperament has two components. One, which has a primarily biological background, is cross-situationally consistent and in this sense is "free" from environmental impact—although under its effect it may undergo gradual changes over time. Those changes may be caused not only by phenomena associated with maturation, aging, or traumatic events, but also by ecological variables or the stress of unemployment (cf. Eliasz, 2001; Eliasz & Klonowicz, 2001). Eliasz (2001) postulates that as a substantially context-free dimension having a primarily biological determinancy, this component may be evaluated within a top-down approach. The second component of temperament, which results from biological factors and specific impact of the environment, affects differentiation of cross-situational dynamics while maintaining their relative stability over time. Thus this component informs us about effects of the environment and individual experience, while the structure (or profile of temperament) indicates its biological background. It implies that the valid assessment of temperament also requires us to adopt a bottom-up approach in relation to certain categories of situations.

Within the TMT (Eliasz, 1981, 1990, 2001), the structure of temperament is reduced to two formal, energetic traits: reactivity and activity, both terms borrowed from Strelau's approach (cf. Strelau, 1985, 2000, 2008). Reactivity means the individual-specific tendency to react with a given intensity (magnitude) and determines the organism's sensitivity (sensory or emotional) and efficiency (endurance). Sensitivity is measured mainly in terms of the sensitivity threshold, whereas endurance is expressed in reactions and behavioral responses to intensive or prolonged stimuli. Thus the higher one's reactivity, the higher one's sensitivity to weak stimuli, and at the same time the lower one's resistance to strong stimuli; the lower one's reactivity, the lower one's sensitivity to weak stimuli, and at the same time the higher one's resistance to strong stimuli. Activity determines the number and range of activities of a given stimulating value that the individual undertakes, has the status of a regulator in need of stimulation, and is determined by individual levels of reactivity.

The advantage of the Transactional Model of Temperament is its attempt to bridge the idiographic (bottom-up) and nomothetic (top-down) approaches (cf. Caprara & Cervone, 2000; Cervone, 1999; Kitcher, 1985). On this basis the TMT deals with the problem of cross-situational consistency of temperament and other personality traits. However, there are several drawbacks to this model. For instance, sufficient empirical validation—especially of those parts of the model that postulate the biological background of reactivity and activity—is lacking and the temporal aspect of temperament traits is neglected. Additionally, temperament structure is limited to two traits. As presented above, the theoretical analysis and empirical studies conducted within Pavlov's, Eysenck's, and Strelau's theories clearly showed that the structure of temperament is more complex than that postulated by the TMT. However, the TMT provides "binding material" for these three theories, because it highlights the connections between temperament and other personality traits and environmental conditions. Thus only within the TMT is it possible to formulate the adequate definition of intraindividual coherence/incoherence.

*Optimal level of stimulation achieved by self-regulative aspects of behavior*

Based on previous conceptions, I would like to suggest a systemic view of temperament that differs from the conventional thinking of Pavlov, Eysenck, Strelau, or Eliasz (that temperament is a reflection of dimensions or traits) and proposes to understand temperament as an emergent property. However, here the emergent property grows out of nonlinear interactions between processes (state-like elements, resembling the dominance of environmental determinany in traits) within particular structures (trait-like elements, resembling the dominance of biological determinany in traits). Consequently, central to understanding this approach is the conception that temperament is both a state-like (based on the dynamic, situational, and environmental determinants) and trait-like (based on the relatively stable genetic, psychophysiological, and neuropsychological constituents) phenomenon.

Temperament as state-like is seen as a self-organizing system that might be explained within the subsumptive hierarchy framework. This view allows us to perceive state-like temperament as a developing system and explain why temperament shows a large amount of variability across time and situations. Temperament, by sharing the status of a state, would also share its inherent attributes. Essential in the definition of a state is that it is derived from circular interactions among many subprocesses and is an immediate and evolving process. Additionally, states on a biological level determine the probabilities of neural system activation, and on a psychological level they determine the possibilities of certain dispositions in thought, affect, and behavior (cf. Cassimjee, 2003).

Temperament as trait-like is a compositional hierarchical system having its structure or content (as in all theories of temperament described above). The stability of temperament arises from its structure. Components of temperament are psychological constructs reflecting genetic determinants, the activity of distributed neural and physiological systems, and the influence of environmental factors. The structure of temperament reflects its functions and determines its potentialities and constraints.

Thus four important implications arise from a systemic view of temperament. The first relates to the idea that temperament is a modular, distributed, and hierarchically organized system (cf. Grigsby & Stevens, 2000). The second relates to the notion that temperament is a functional system that comprises both structural and functional components, and thus function and structure to some extent are synonymous. The third is related to the belief of self-organizing or self-regulating systems (e.g., genetic, neurophysiological, perceptual, or behavioral). Since temperament arises from the interactions of such systems, the optimal level of arousal cannot account for the self-regulative mechanisms of temperament; hence the arousability concept should be expanded by considering the self-regulative nature of these systems (as demonstrated in section 2.2; see also Cassimjee, 2003). Fourth, because these systems act in either opposing or facilitatory ways with each other, features of temperament—which are emerging properties of these interactions—are not likely to be purely orthogonal in their relations to one another (cf. Cassimjee, 2003).

In comparison with the theories discussed above, similarities between the systemic approach to temperament and the RTT and TMT lie in the conceptualization of temperament as the structure of formal (content-free) dispositions. Additionally, it shares with the Pavlovian, Eysenckian, and Strelauvian typologies a strong relationship with neurophysiological descriptions of concepts, and resembles Eliasz's model in postulating two components of temperament (environmental or state-like and biological or trait-like). The systemic approach to temperament differs from the behavioral emphasis inherent in the RTT and from the content-saturated dispositions immanent in PEN.

The systemic view of temperament implies that hierarchical relationships exist between different subsystems and components of temperament, and that multilevel functional relations are involved in both the structure of temperament and its connections with other personality traits and environmental elements.

### 2.3.3. Functional categories of coherent/incoherent personality structures

Intraindividual architecture is also composed of other-than-temperament traits. This means that clusters or constellations of temperament types are linked to other personality attributes, which results in the emergence of a new quality—intraindividual coherence or incoherence. In the literature on temperament, we can find some attempts to provide definitions of intraindividual personality coherence or incoherence. The most suitable to my theoretical approach postulates that intraindividual coherence between temperament capacities and other personality traits means intraindividual consistency between temperament traits associated with one's need for stimulation, and other individual differences related to a self-providing dose of stimulation adequate to one's need for stimulation determined by physiological mechanisms of temperament (cf. Eliasz 1985, 1995, 2001; Strelau, 2006). Analogously, intraindividual incoherence between temperament capacities and other personality traits means intraindividual inconsistency between temperament traits associated with one's need for stimulation, and other individual differences related to a self-providing dose of stimulation not adequate to one's need for stimulation determined by physiological mechanisms of temperament.

However, I propose to reformulate this understanding of personality coherence and incoherence by introducing into this definition the aspect of relations in dominant controlling functions over stimulation among temperament types and other personality traits/types. Thus I claim that intraindividual personality coherence/incoherence is built upon functional consistency/inconsistency over stimulation processing between temperament and other personality traits related to stimulation processing. The dominant controlling function over stimulation in temperament type is a foundation for judging about personality coherence and incoherence. Based on the theories of temperament presented in the previous section, it might be assumed that regulative dominant controlling functions over stimulation is recognized in sanguines and phlegmatics, while the reactive one is recognized in melancholics and phlegmatics.

Hence the harmonious and disharmonious types of temperament are the basis for talking about intrapersonal coherence/incoherence. Theoretically, there are four possibilities.

- *Coherent Type of personality based on the harmonious type of temperament.* For example, high stimulation-processing capacities, coupled with maintaining the optimal stimulation level by seeking stimulation (it resembles the regulative Sanguine Type), may correspond with a (self-regulative) high need for achievement, considered as a need connected with a self-providing high dose of environmentally determined stimulation (cf. Eliasz, 1981).
- *Incoherent Type of personality based on the harmonious type of temperament.* For example, low stimulation-processing capacities, coupled with maintaining the optimal stimulation level by avoiding stimulation (it resembles the reactive Melancholic Type), may conflict with one's (self-regulative) high need for achievement (cf. Eliasz, 1981).
- *Coherent Type of personality based on the disharmonious type of temperament.* For example, one's (self-regulative) high need for achievement (cf. Eliasz, 1981) may be consistent with his or her low (nonoptimal) level of stimulation and high stimulation-processing capacities (it resembles the regulative Phlegmatic Type).
- *Incoherent Type of personality based on the disharmonious type of temperament.* For example, one's (self-regulative) high need for achievement (cf. Eliasz, 1981) may be inconsistent with his or her high (nonoptimal) level of stimulation and low stimulation-processing capacities (it resembles the reactive Choleric Type).

The problem that may be noted in this context is how to theoretically analyze the functional significance of personality coherence/incoherence. To meet this challenge, the following categories according to which this functional significance may be examined are proposed.

*Correlational relations between components of
coherent/incoherent types of personalities*

Functional distinctness between temperament and other personality traits in their controlling functions leads to a relatively high level of functional complexity (i.e., personality incoherence). A particular temperament type $T_T$ co-occurs with a particular effect $E_1$ (e.g., reaction, behavior, emotional state, cognitive function, or motive), while a particular level of personality trait $P^T$ co-occurs with a particular effect $E_2$ since they are connected with different aspects of controlling functions in a particular situational arrangement $S$. If they coexist within a certain personality system, they produce incoherent structure. As an example, consider the quality of performance under stressful conditions ($S$) in the Incoherent Type of personality built upon a high need for achievement ($P^{high\ need\ Ach}$) and the HTT with low SPC ($T_{HTT+\ low\ SPC}$). A high need for achievement, as connected with a high self-providing dose of stimulation, is in conflict with low SPC (see Eliasz, 1981). It is difficult to predict how this structure is related to the outcome of general performance and quality of functioning. However, it is likely that the Incoherent Type (considered rather as dysfunctional) may be connected with ineffective control over stimulation and poor performance, specifically under stressful conditions.

After decomposing this Incoherent Type of personality ($INPT_{HHT+\ low\ SPC}{}^{high\ need\ Ach}$) according to the dominant functions in their elements, it is clearly seen that harmonious temperament structures (resembling the Melancholic Type) are connected with a reactive aspect of stimulation control by avoiding stimulation (see Strelau, 2008), whereas the high need for achievement attached to this structure of temperament plays different (self-regulative) controlling functions. This promotes conflict in controlling functions between this temperament and the need for achievement, resulting in relative functional complexity in the analyzed personality constellation and potentially worsening one's performance.

Functional overlapping between temperament and other personality traits in their controlling functions leads to a relatively low level of functional complexity (i.e., personality coherence). A particular temperament type $T_T$ or a particular level of personality trait $P^T$ alternatively co-occurs with a particular effect $E$ (e.g., reaction, behavior, emotional state, cognitive function, or motive) since they perform a similar controlling function in a particular situational arrangement ($S$). If they coexist within a certain personality system, they produce coherent structure. Hypothetically, one may expect that in the coherent personality type $CPT_{HHT+\ low\ SPC}{}^{high\ anxiety}$ (in which there is no conflict between two sources of stimulation) the level of anxiety and stimulation-processing capacities would be associated with good academic performance.

Decomposing this personality constellation implies that good academic achievement may be accomplished or predicted on the way of elevated reactivity associated with low SPC or high anxiety (good academic performance is connected with anxiety; e.g., Moutafi, Furnham, & Tsaousis, 2006) when they interact with external stressors (e.g., exams, deadlines, public speeches). This probably leads to improved academic performance by several behaviors (such as attending classes, preparing for exams, and completing assignments) and avoiding negative outcomes or evaluations. Accordingly, both high trait anxiety and low SPC seem to operate as traits with a reactive dominant controlling function in the analyzed context, which indicates the functional simplicity in these personality constellations and improvement of performance.

Generally, correlational relations between controlling functions in focal traits inform us first about functional simplicity (coherence) or complexity (incoherence) of the personality system, and second about its relation to quality of stimulation processing—that is, whether it worsens or improves general performance. In other words, it tells us about improving/worsening the quality of stimulation processing on the basis of comparing the quality of processing identified in coherent/incoherent personality structures with (for example) elevated anxiety, with the quality of processing identified in particular coherent/incoherent personality structures with (for example) low anxiety. However, it should be underscored that a simple connection is not expected between personality coherence and incoherence and improvement or deterioration of quality of stimulation processing, respectively.

*Interactive relations between dominant controlling functions of temperament and other personality traits in coherent/incoherent types of personality*

Generally, in the same situational arrangement $S$, a particular effect $E$ (e.g., reaction, behavior, emotional state, cognitive function, or motive) is a result of the interaction between a particular temperament type $T_T$ and a particular level of personality trait $P^T$. In terms of general adaptiveness, there can be additive, synergistic, or antagonistic types of functional interactions (*per analogiam* to widely known types of chemical interactions). This would provide an indication of the dynamics of effects on stimulation processing and fluctuation of processes engaged in stimulation processing. Put another way, the interaction between elements composing a particular personality structure may modify the effects on stimulation processing and type of process involved in stimulation processing. Matching the category of interaction—additive, synergistic, or antagonistic—with the interaction between a particular temperament type and a particular personality trait/type is possible with reference to patterns of stimulation processing, when the latter are examined independently.

Additive functional interaction ("=") means that the effect of two "elements" is equal to the sum of the effect of the two "elements" taken separately, which is usually due to the two "elements" acting on the final outcome in the same way. In other words, they have the same dominant controlling function over stimulation (e.g., reactive x reactive; regulative x regulative). This indicates that processes and mechanisms involved in a certain aspect of structure of coherent/incoherent personality do not intensify a final outcome, or do not change the patterns of stimulation processing typical for each focal trait/type. In that sense the description presented above of the Coherent Type of personality—harmonious temperament and anxiety—may suggest that, in certain situations (e.g., academic performance), the joint impact of (reactive) high anxiety and (reactive) low SPC produces an equal effect to the sum of the effect of the two taken separately.

Synergistic functional interaction ("+") means that the effect of two "elements" that process stimulation in the same (e.g., regulative x regulative) or in a different (e.g., reactive x regulative) manner taken together is greater than the sum of their separate effect, or that a typical pattern of stimulation processing is maintained for one of them. Taking into consideration the example of $INPT_{HHT+\ low\ SPC}^{\ high\ need\ Ach}$ it may be observed that under specific conditions the interaction between a (self-regulative) high need for achievement and a (reactive) low SPC may maintain the effect typical for the first trait.

Antagonistic functional interaction ("-") means that the interaction between two "elements" that produce the same (e.g., reactive x reactive) or different (e.g., reactive x regulative) ways of stimulation processing affects a quite new pattern of stimulation processing, not identified even in one of them or lessening the sum of the effect of the two elements taken independently of each other. This is because the second element increases the "excretion" of the first, or even directly blocks its actions. For example, in $INPT_{HHT+\ high\ SPC}^{\ high\ anxiety}$ the tendencies to seek stimulation as connected with (regulative) high SPC may be blocked by a (reactive) high anxiety, which generally leads to a decline in academic performance.

It is now clear that beyond temperament traits other self-providing stimulation traits of personality form the structure of the SRIS. Thus, from the perspective of personality coherence/incoherence, the reciprocal relations between temperament mechanisms and stimulative properties of other attributes of personality, cognitive, affective, and motivational processes, and environment are most important in the dynamic structure of the SRIS. These reciprocal relations impact differentiation in functions of emerged coherent or incoherent suprasystems, since the basic function of the SRIS reveals itself in the individual's effort to attain and maintain an optimal level of arousal and activation influencing the efficiency of performance, development, general adaptation, and well-being (see Eliasz, 1981, 2004; Eliasz & Klonowicz, 2001).

### *2.3.4. Environmental factors and personality coherence/incoherence*

It seems probable that specific types of correlational and interactional relations between temperament traits and other personality traits may co-occur under specific conditions. Thus it might be reasonable to broaden the set of situational arrangements $(S_1, S_2 \ldots S_n)$ in the analyzed context. For example, in situational arrangements $S_1$ and $S_2$ the coexistence of a particular temperament type $T_T$ and a particular level of personality trait $P^T$ may present itself in the form of an antagonistic interaction in situation $S_1$ or in a form of an additive interaction in situation $S_2$. This reasoning leads us to the next element of the structure of the SRIS—namely, the environmental factor. The presence of an environmental system is seen in the formation of personality coherence/incoherence and in determining the functional specification of a particular coherent/incoherent personality structure.

Person-environment fit theory (Brandstätter, 1994; Holland, 1985; Jahoda, 1961; Pervin, 1976) proposes that if individuals are to feel and perform well, their motives, skills, or capacities correspond to the gratifications and demands of their environment. The functioning of an individual in his or her natural environment is a continuous, dynamic process of mutual exchange of information: a person influences his or her environment and at the same time is under the influence of that environment (Eliasz, 1992). Thus behaviors or experiences arise from the interactive effects of personal and situational factors, and are the result of continuous processes of multidirectional feedback between the individual and the situations he or she encounters; here the individual is seen as an active agent.

Each situation or behavior, in spite of the content, has its own stimulative value and may also be a source of stimulation. All individuals tend to fulfill their need for stimulation by undertaking actions that lead to gaining or maintaining optimum stimulation, but that are not in conflict with individual desires, needs, aspirations, or social expectations (Eliasz, 1981, 1990). In ontological development the preferences of situations or forms of activity of particular (low or high) stimulative value enhance the relatively stable tendencies specific to each individual. This might participate in forming and maintain personality coherence. However, it is also the case that there is no correspondence between one's need for stimulation and the environmental demands or stimulative value of a situation. This might be labeled the "person-environment misfit" and may relate to personality incoherence. There is considerable empirical evidence showing that the person-environment misfit promotes the emergence of many personal disturbances or maladaptive behaviors (cf. Eliasz, 1981, 2004; Eliasz & Klonowicz, 2001).

Thus intraindividual mechanisms and person-situation transactions cannot be understood simply by locating personality coherence versus incoherence within the system of linear dimensions. They require studies of the biological, cognitive, affective, and environmental processes that contribute to individual personality structure. However, since this is not the main focus of this book, I would like to leave this topic in the present form.

## 2.4.
## Summing up

An overarching goal of this chapter has been to identify a system of the main variables—processual, structural, and content—that are explanatory. This system of variables rests on a set of explicit principles that, in combination, produce a relatively comprehensive C-SAP model of intraindividual personality architecture. In this model the System of Regulation and Integration Stimulation may be applied to explain the phenomenon that is central to the psychology of personality—namely, personality coherence versus incoherence.

My presentation of the SRIS model in light of personality coherence/incoherence has highlighted two major themes. One is the structure and processes of the SRIS, which are seen as basic for forming personality coherence/incoherence. It is not possible to gain a full understanding of personality coherence/incoherence unless one makes explicit the diverse theoretical assumptions that have guided investigations in this area. A second main theme is that personality coherence and incoherence have the potential to contribute to the explanation of different adaptive and maladaptive behaviors.

The C-SAP model is not sufficient for capturing all aspects of intraindividual personality structure and functioning; like other models, it can be improved. For example, it says little about the role of genetics in the explanation of personality consistency. However, in general, the C-SAP emphasizes the fundamental role of the SRIS, which is based on arousal and activation processes rather than genetic foundations of action. Furthermore, a complete account of personality coherence/incoherence clearly requires more coverage of environmental factors than is found in this chapter. Without input into the system, detailed descriptions of the environmental mechanisms underlying personality coherence/incoherence can generate an incomplete picture of these phenomena. Obviously, the area of personality coherence/incoherence will have taken an important step forward when research routinely assesses both genetic and environmental variables.

Nonetheless, Part I has focused on the internal processes of personality coherence/incoherence, while Part II pays special attention to research on closely related constructs like affective phenomena (e.g., anxiety and depression). I am especially interested in anxiety and depression as relatively common phenomena that impose significant costs on individuals and their relatives or families. I am dedicated to the task of trying to better understand the dynamics and causes of these moods with the assistance of the C-SAP model. Thus the second part of the book attempts to exemplify some of the theoretical assumptions presented here in the context of anxiety and depression.

# Part II

## Anxiety and Depression in the Complex–System Approach to Personality

# Introduction

## Introducing anxiety and depression: The complex phenomena

The theoretical chapters presented in Part I suggest that human functioning can be studied at a number of levels, from a molecular level to the level of gross behavior, as well as examining how sets of neurons, traits, or behaviors operate at a "system" level. Affective functioning, including anxiety and depression, seems to be an ideal candidate for such an integrated, multiple-levels-of-analysis approach.

Two widely endorsed approaches to the analysis of affect and affective phenomena—discrete and dimensional ones—promote focusing primarily on a single level of analysis (e.g., activity of particular brain structure, expressive reaction, subjective experience), and then generalizing the results from this particular level of analysis to all levels (see Fox, 2008).

The discrete emotion approach (e.g., Dolan, 2002; Ekman, 1992; LeDoux, 1996; Panksepp, 2000) postulates that some emotions are crucial for adapting to common and significant life events and evolved to help individuals deal easily with these universal situations (Fox, 2008). Thus basic emotions would be expected to have key expressive signals that are likely to elicit them. Discrete emotion theorists often focus on the neural (cortical-subcortical neural circuits with an emphasis on the subcortical structures) or physiological underpinnings of emotions or moods. In investigating the fundamental nature of emotion reaction times to prototypical stimuli (e.g., angry, happy, or sad expressions), recognition of prototypical facial expressions, autonomic nervous system specificity to particular emotions, and activation of specific neural circuits are typically utilized. Here the focus is on the neural and cognitive aspects of affect (Fox, 2008).

The focus of a dimensional view of affect is often on how the world is experienced along broad dimensions, rather than discrete categories of different emotions, and much of the research in this tradition employs self-report data as the primary evidence (e.g., Feldman Barrett, 2006; Russell & Lemay, 2000; Watson, 2000). Research on a number of different emotion components (subjective report, physiological response, neural activity, cortical-subcortical neural circuits with an emphasis on the cortical structures activity) has revolved around the notion that affect can be described along two broad dimensions—arousal and valence

(Russell, 1983, 1991), approach and avoidance (Davidson, 1994), or positive affect and negative affect (Watson & Tellegen, 1985).

A clear implication of the research focused on the exploration of a single level of analysis leads to an incomplete view of a particular affective phenomenon. The discrete emotion and dimensional approaches can be seen as complementary; both are necessary to explain the totality of different affective phenomena, including anxiety and depression. Thus a key challenge is to examine these different research traditions and determine whether the empirical evidence from both sides can be integrated in a reasonable way to provide a comprehensive understanding of affect in normal and clinical populations (Fox, 2008).

In my view, adopting a consistent terminology and then providing a unifying framework of how discrete and dimensional approaches to affect might be integrated within the C-SAP seems to be promising for a more valid understanding of the broad range of affective phenomena with anxiety and depression.

Thus, according to Fox (2008), a careful definition of different elements of affect—emotions, moods, feelings, emotion schemas—allows for combining data from both aforementioned approaches to provide a comprehensive overview of affective functioning. It seems probable that emotion scientists can agree to use the term "emotion" to refer to brief and intense reactions to significant situations and stimuli, involving the coordination of several subsystems—for example, neural, physiological, and behavioral—or a set of components such as bodily response, feeling state, and cognitive appraisal (cf. Fox, 2008; Scherer, 2001). For many emotion researchers, basic emotions are few in number and given to us by nature (Fox, 2008).

However, basic emotions can be differentiated from nonbasic emotions through emotion schemas. Emotions schemas can integrate the components of basic emotions with complex appraisals and cognitive biases, and these complex emotion-cognitive interactions then form part of more general regulatory and motivational systems (e.g., Ellsworth & Scherer, 2003; Izard, 2007), whereas the notion of mood can indicate more enduring and less intense states that can be associated with emotions but can also represent a broader range of subjective states (e.g., Fox, 2008; Watson, 2000). In other words, moods can be seen as a type of objectless core affect (e.g., Russell, 2003) or as an emotion that is extended over time (e.g., Damasio, 1999). The function of moods is different from emotions in that the former allow for interpreting how individuals are doing in life in a more general way (Fox, 2008; Prinz, 2004). Moods rather directly relate to regulatory, motivational, and cognitive systems, while emotions relate to behavioral output. Feelings denote the conscious representation of both emotions and moods, while affect is an overarching concept that encompasses all affective reactions and experiences, emotions, feelings, and moods (e.g., Watson, 2000).

Having this terminology, we can apply the compositional hierarchy framework to study the organization of affective phenomena, which allows us to distinguish three levels of analysis (cf. Figures 1.1 and 1.2).

- *Mechanisms and processes of emotion systems.* These systems integrate the biological, psychological, and situational components appropriate to this level. Basic emotions or affect programs are activated rapidly (also dissipated rapidly) and automatically upon the perception of an emotion-related stimulus (stimuli); these emotion systems are adaptive and produce a relatively narrow range of responses (see Fox, 2008). The basic emotions might be seen as interlevel emergent properties originating from the interactions among mechanisms and processes of a particular emotion system. Its structure is composed of markers of activated physiological and nervous systems, expressive behaviors, subjective feeling states, and cognitive processes and its function is to facilitate the rapid coordination of the body's various processes including motor systems, energy levels, physiological reactions, and cognitive processes (e.g., Öhman & Mineka, 2001; Tooby et al., 2000). Hence when one sees a wolf in the forest (a dangerous situation), various physiological changes occur (e.g., activation of the brain's autonomic systems) that allow for a rapid shift of attention toward potential danger (the wolf) and an adequate response to it. On this level of analysis, it is possible to identify the mechanisms and processes contributing to the formation of anxiety and depression.
- *Structures of emotion systems.* The activation of primary mechanisms and processes of emotion systems potentially leads to the synchronization of the particular components into more complex structures of emotions, associated with specific feeling states. Interlevel structures composing a core background mood emerge from interactions between emotions and feelings (Fox, 2008), which is equivalent to core affect (e.g., Feldman Barret, Mesquita, Ochsner, & Gross, 2007; Russell, 2003) or (state/trait) mood (e.g., Davidson, 2000; Prinz, 2004). The key point here is that the changes in this core background affect are consciously perceived (cf. Fox, 2008). One can observe the changes in intensity (arousal) or how pleasant or unpleasant it feels (valence). In other words, the discrete emotion systems cannot directly reach one's conscious awareness. However, one may report subjective emotional experience on arousal or valence as emergent properties from lower, separate, discrete emotion systems. Thus on this level of analysis we can identify structures, subtypes of anxiety, and depression.
- *Behavioral tendencies evolving from emotion systems.* A discrete and dimensional interpretation of emotional functioning might then develop through the recruitment of other structures involved in temperament/personality traits and motivational or cognitive processes. In dynamic system terms, the self-organizing emotion system shows increased connectivity among the various subcomponents or subsystems that are reciprocally activated in real time. This can lead to a range of enduring behavioral strategies or styles associated with temperament/personality structures, motivational tendencies, or cognitive beliefs. Thus over time these enduring behaviors representing emotion systems might become very stable strategies, and can be seen (for example) in approach motivation or

specific cognitive biases. This level of analysis allows for recognizing the behavioral tendencies in different types of anxiety and depression.

The implication of the three-level analysis discussed above is that both "normal" (e.g., sad mood) and disordered (e.g., social anxiety or clinical depression) states remain complex and multidimensional phenomena. This occurs because anxiety and depression structures include not only specific discrete aspects, but also specific dimensional aspects of affectivity associated with specific behavioral tendencies.

There are currently many competing models of anxiety and depression, each entailing different antecedent stimulus conditions, latent mediating processes, and outcomes (cf., Barlow, 2002; Levens & Gotlib, 2009). These conceptual distinctions expand the variability of measurement and assessment procedures, which further poses a problem for the operationalization of those phenomena and—in consequence—the implications of empirical findings for validating theories (cf. Corr & Fajkowska, 2011; Dunn, Dalgleish, Ogilvie, Lawrence & Cusock, 2004). However, there are indications that certain core elements of anxiety and depression are achieving some measure of consensus. One way to achieve this consensus is through a closer integration of these three levels of analysis in the case of anxiety and depression, and to view them as disorders of mood rather than disorders of emotions (Fox, 2008).

The chapters in Part I provide evidence that the most important element in personality structure, as described within the Complex–System Approach to Personality (C-SAP), is the System of Regulation and Integration Stimulation (SRIS). The SRIS controls behaviors and the level of arousal and activation and supports the adaptation by providing the optimal level of arousal and internal integrity. Temperament structure and attentional processes, as based on the arousal and activation mechanisms, are crucial elements of the SRIS. However, within the SRIS it is possible to locate other internal characteristics (e.g., anxiety and depression) that potentially contribute to stimulation processing. According to the logic of the C-SAP, anxiety and depression are complex (multidimensional) disorders of mood. I understand them both as traits (structures) that are hierarchically organized and connected with states (anxiety state or depression state). This understanding is based on the assumption that state is a result of interaction between the trait and the environment/situation (e.g., Endler, 1983). It implies that they (traits and states) have the same compositional structure, but that what differentiates them is the proportion and intensity of their particular components.

Chapter 3 presents three ways that mood traits, as elements of the SRIS, participate in stimulation processing. They represent direct and indirect modulators of stimulation processing. As indirect modulators, mood traits—together with temperament—operate from the level of structure when processing stimulation. Mood traits may moderate stimulation processing by interacting with temperament; in addition, they may mediate stimulation processing. This means that temperament may modulate mood traits, and mood traits in turn may affect stimulation processing. The attention system, as one of two basic elements of the SRIS, operates from the level of process. It is associated with stimulation reception, and through its interrelations with temperament or moods is linked with the readiness to respond to stimulation.

However it is sorted out, the theoretical and empirical evidence discussed in Chapter 3 provides important data contributing to the development of a view of anxiety and depression as complex elements of the SRIS directly influencing stimulation processing. With the help of the compositional hierarchy rationality, indicating structural differentiation of particular phenomenon, it is demonstrated that as complex heterogeneous phenomena, anxiety (arousal x apprehension) and depression (valence [in]sensitivity x anhedonia) produce specific attentional patterns of stimulation processing.

On the basis of the subsumptive hierarchy organization, indicating functional differentiation of particular phenomenon, the recognition of these specific patterns allowed for establishing the exact controlling functions of each subtype within the SRIS. I claim that the reactive nature of control over stimulation is more typical for the Arousal Type of anxiety and Valence Type of depression, while the regulative one seems to be more specific for the Apprehension Type of anxiety and Anhedonic Type of depression.

Chapter 4 is addressed to constructing theoretical links between four temperament types (regulative sanguine and phlegmatic, and reactive melancholic and choleric) and mood subtypes (regulative apprehension anxiety and anhedonic depression, and reactive arousal anxiety and valence depression). Thus coherent and incoherent personality structures are built into the three arousal-related theoretical approaches to temperament—Pavlovian, Eysenckian, and Strelauvian. This is grounded on the assumption that a joining between a particular structure of temperament and a particular type of anxiety or depression may produce intra-individual coherence or incoherence on the basis of the compatibility or conflict between their controlling functions, respectively.

Chapter 5 presents some empirical evidence on the indirect influences of anxiety and depression subtypes on stimulation processing. Given these indirect influences, in the context of personality coherence/incoherence (an intrinsic attribute of the SRIS), intercorrelational and interactional analyses are utilized. Intercorrelational analysis informs us how functional complexity (incoherence: distinct controlling functions in focal traits; e.g., reactive in arousal anxiety and regulative in sanguine temperament) or simplicity (coherence: overlapping controlling function in focal traits; e.g., regulative in anhedonic depression and regulative in phlegmatic temperament) influence the quality of stimulation processing—in other words, whether it worsens or improves stimulation processing—whereas functional interactions analysis enables us to assess the dynamics of attentional effects and fluctuation of attentional processes engaged in stimulation processing. This is possible with three types of functional interactions—additive, synergistic, and antagonistic.

Thus the results obtained provide answers to two questions: (a) How does the level of functional complexity reflected in coherent/incoherent personality structures affect quality of stimulation processing? And (b) how do functional interactions in coherent/incoherent personality structures relate to the dynamics of attentional processes engaged in stimulation processing?

# Chapter 3

# Anxiety and depression within the System of Regulation and Integration Stimulation

3.1.

## General characteristics of anxiety and depression

We can gain a better understanding of the role of anxiety and depression in stimulation processing within the System of Regulation and Integration Stimulation (SRIS) if we begin this discussion by focusing on the general characteristics of these two phenomena.

### 3.1.1. Prevalence and comorbidity of anxiety and depression

Anxiety- and depression-related disorders are relatively common, occurring in around 20% of the population (Fox, 2008). The National Comorbidity Survey Replication (NCS-R; Kessler, 2001–2004) conducted in the United States found that the lifetime risk of any anxiety disorder is 25% for men and 36% for women. The risk for any depressive disorder is 17% for men and 25% for women (cf. Kessler, 2001–2004). It was also found that lifetime specific phobias and social fears are quite common in both men (9% and 11%, respectively) and women (13% and 16%, respectively), compared with other anxiety disorders—for example, generalized anxiety disorder (GAD), 4–7%; panic disorders, 3–6% (cf. Kessler, 2001–2004; Stein et al., 2010). In addition, the fact is that lifetime major depressive disorder (MDD) is also more common in men (13%) and women (20%) than other mood disorders (e.g., bipolar disorders, 4% for both sexes; dysthymia, 2% for men, 3% for women). Another interesting finding is that anxiety and mood disorders appear to decrease in later life (cf. Kessler, 2001–2004; Kessler et al., 2010a, 2010b). Studies disagree on the prevalence of anxiety and depression in the elderly, but most data suggest that there is a reduction in this age group. However, affective disorders—especially depressive disorders—are more prevalent in urban than rural populations and in groups with higher socioeconomic levels (cf. APA, 2000; WHO, 1992).

The European Study of the Epidemiology of Mental Disorders (ESEMeD; cf. Alonso et al., 2008) found that the prevalence of mood disorders is between

93

9.9% and 21% of the general adult (18+) population of Belgium, the Netherlands, Germany, France, Spain, and Italy. By comparison, the Central Statistical Office (GUS; 2007, 2011) reported across two studies that the prevalence of anxiety and depressive disorders is 7% of the general adult (15+) population of Poland. This implies that approximately nine million adults in these Western European countries reported a lifetime history of mood disorder. Among the mood disorders, MDD was more common than others (e.g., dysthymia.) In the same study, it was demonstrated that about 44% of respondents met the criteria for any anxiety disorder.

Another important fact is the high degree of comorbidity that occurs between anxiety disorders and depression. Gorman (1996) reported that almost 90% of individuals with anxiety disorders suffered at least one clinical depression episode during their lifetime. According to studies conducted in the United Kingdom (*Adult Psychiatric Morbidity in England, 2007*; McManus, Meltzer, Brugha, Bebbington, & Jenkins, 2009), it was estimated that common mental disorders comprising different types of depression and anxiety—which cause marked emotional distress and interfere with daily function but do not usually affect insight or cognition—are present in 84% of the total sample and are more frequent in women than in men.

On the basis of both theoretical and empirical evidence, it appears that negative affect is a nonspecific dimension for anxiety and depressive disorders (Watson, 2000). Gotlib and MacLeod (1997), for example, inquire whether these emotional disorders share symptoms that are unrelated to cognitive functioning or, alternatively, share a common pattern of dysfunctional cognitive processing. The critical issue here is the severity of depression (i.e., mild versus clinically depressed individuals) and type of anxiety disorder (Watson, 2000). One study, for instance, indicates that depressed mood (subclinical depression) is strongly associated with anxiety and worry, but relatively weakly with features typical for clinical depression like introversion, self-blaming, or self-focusing (Parker & Roy, 2002).


### 3.1.2. Diagnostic categories relating to anxiety and depression

There have been attempts to provide classification systems for mental disorders, including mood disorders. The best-known examples are the World Health Organization's *International Statistical Classification of Diseases and Related Problems* (ICD-10; 1992) and the American Psychiatric Association's *Diagnostic and Statistical Manual of Mental Disorders Text Revision* (DSM-IV-TR; 2000). Both ICD-10 and DSM-IV-TR provide a strictly categorical classification scheme, assuming that there are distinct and separate categories of emotional disorders with specific causes and treatments. However, it might be more accurate to assume that people experience a variety of symptoms to varying extents (cf. Fox, 2008; also the discussion regarding discrete and dimensional approaches to emotion presented in the introduction to Part II). Nonetheless, the diagnostic categories proposed by the DSM-IV-TR or ICD-10 are widely used for assessing and treating mental disorders. Additionally, they define disorders by observable symptoms rather than features believed to caused each disorder, and each diagnostic category differentiates between those characteristics that are considered essential and those that are not (see Fox, 2008).

Thus anxiety is associated with feelings of uneasy suspense, the tense anticipation of a threatening but obscure events (Rachman, 2004), and feelings of apprehension and worry whose sources are ill-defined and largely unknown (Himmelhoch, Levin, & Gershon, 2001); specific physical signs and somatic symptoms accompany anxiety (Corr, 2008; Gray, 1982; Kasturagi et al., 1999; Schwerdtfeger, 2004). Fear and anxiety share some common features but fear tends to have a specific, usually identifiable focus and to be more intense and episodic (Rachman, 2004). Excessive anxiety is an essential feature of many psychological disorders. The DSM-IV-TR (APA, 2000) recognizes:

- Generalized anxiety disorder: persistent, uncontrollable worry and anxiety present for at least six months.
- Panic disorder: repeated episodes of intense fear of rapid onset.
- Panic disorders with agoraphobia: unexpected panic attack in open space.
- Social phobia: intense, persistent anxiety about social situations, especially if exposed to the scrutiny of others.
- Specific phobia: extremely intense, persistent, circumscribed fear of a specific object or place.
- Obsessive-compulsive disorder (OCD): characterized by persistent obsessions such as intrusive anxious thoughts, as well as compulsions like repeated actions and rituals.
- Post-traumatic stress disorder (PTSD): triggered by a specific event such as a natural disaster or war, consists of reexperiencing a traumatic event, avoidance of situations or thoughts related to the triggering event, increased arousal, intense anger, anxiety, depression, and guilt.
- Separation anxiety: the feeling of excessive and inappropriate levels of anxiety over being separated from a person or place, childhood anxiety disorders.

The risk factors that may leave people more vulnerable to developing anxiety disorders are low levels of gamma aminobutyric acid (a neurotransmitter that reduces activity in the central nervous system), disrupted functioning of the amygdala, and life stresses (cf. APA, 2000). The genetic contribution to anxiety has long been established (Eysenck, 1992; Eysenck & Eysenck, 1985), although the identification of which genes are involved has proved more elusive (e.g., Deary et al., 1999; Hariri & Weinberger, 2003). Some studies (e.g., Hariri & Holmes, 2006) have proved promising, although all studies face the difficult challenge of replication.

The term "depression" covers a wide range of emotional states that differ in severity from normal, everyday moods of sadness to clinical episodes with increased risk of suicide. According to the DSM-IV-R (APA, 2000), there are two main depressive symptoms (depressed mood and anhedonia), at least one of which must be present to determine diagnosis of a major depressive episode. Major depressive disorder is characterized by the presence of a severely depressed mood that persists for at least two weeks. The episodes might be isolated or recurrent and are categorized as mild (few symptoms in excess of minimum criteria), moderate, or severe (marked impact on social or occupational functioning). Of course an episode with psychotic features (psychotic depression) is considered the most severe. Depressive disorders without mania are referred to as unipolar, because mood remains at one emotional state or "pole." They require one or more periods of clinically significant depression without a history of either manic or hypomanic episodes and are characterized by at least a two-week period of sad, depressed mood or a loss of pleasure and interest in usual activities, as well as a number of other symptoms—such as difficulties in sleeping, changes in activity level, weight loss or gain, fatigue, feelings of guilt or worthlessness, and recurring thoughts of suicide or death. Bipolar depression is a condition in which subjects alternate between experiences of both severe depression and mania (i.e., a mood state involving elation, intense activity, talkativeness, and unjustifiably high self-esteem). The DSM-IV-TR recognizes five subtypes of MDD.

- Melancholic depression (loss of pleasure in most or all activities, a failure of reactivity to pleasurable stimuli, excessive weight loss, guilt).
- Atypical depression (mood reactivity/paradoxical anhedonia and positivity, increased appetite, social impairment).
- Catatonic depression (rare and severe disturbances in motor behavior).
- Postpartum depression (experience by women after giving birth).
- Seasonal affective disorder (depressive episodes come on in the autumn or winter and resolve themselves in the spring).

It should be added that depressed mood or subclinical depression, which is the main focus of this book, is clearly within the range of normal human emotional experience. It seems to be quantitatively and qualitatively distinct from clinical depressive disorders.

It is understood that biological (e.g., increased volume of the lateral ventricles and adrenal gland and smaller volumes of the basal ganglia, thalamus, hippocampus, and frontal lobe), psychological (e.g., negative emotionality, low self-esteem), and social (e.g., stressful life events, the lack of social support) factors play a role in causing depression (cf. APA, 2000). The diathesis-stress approach indicates that depression results when a preexisting vulnerability, or diathesis, is activated by stressful life events. The preexisting vulnerability can be either genetic (e.g., actions of norepinephrine, dopamine; one or two short alleles of the 5-HTT gene, which encodes the serotonin transporter protein and is thus active in the serotonin nerve pathways), implying an interaction between nature and nurture, or schemas— resulting from views of the world learned in childhood (e.g., physical, emotional, sexual abuse; cf. APA, 2000; Delgado et al., 1994; Garlow & Nemeroff, 2003).

To summarize, many mechanisms and processes are involved in the activation and experience of anxiety or depression; it is a process rather than a categorical event that occurs or does not occur. Sometimes essentially quantitative and continuous diagnostic items fill this process. It is assumed that people vary in their proneness to experience anxiety or depression and become vulnerable when they encounter a triggering situation. Thus the risk factors that make individuals more vulnerable to developing anxiety or depression are specific patterns of neural activity, genetic make-up, temperament or personality traits, cognitive processes and biases, and stressful environmental or life events. The interactive quality of these factors points to the crucial fact that both predisposition and stressful environmental events are necessary for a disorder to develop (Fox, 2008).

How does this process work? It is based on systemic, circular causality. There is substantial evidence that stressful life events are associated with subsequent emotional disorders, including anxiety and depression. (This causal link between contextual influences and anxiety disorders is perhaps most obvious in PTSD.) However, these stressful environmental events (e.g., child abuse, parental divorce) primarily induce disorder only in those with a particular genotype—for example, the s-allele carrier on the serotonin transporter (cf. Fox, 2008). As we know, both genetic and environmental factors contribute to temperament structure (e.g., neuroticism, emotional reactivity); on the other hand, temperament can affect the type of environment experienced and that is why the type of genes are more likely to be expressed (Fox, 2008; Strelau, 2008). These factors can modify specific neural circuits (e.g., cortico-limbic connections), which in turn can determine the nature of somatic response to stressful life events (e.g., functioning of the hypothalamic-pituitary-adrenal axis). Then the possession of specific cognitive biases or patterns of neural or autonomic reactivity to negativity influence the experience of life in anxious and depressed individuals (Fox, 2008).

## 3.2.
## Anxiety, depression, and stimulation processing within the SRIS

The impact of everyday events and situations on one's functioning can vary in consistent ways due to individual differences in one's need for stimulation and how people process stimulation. The previous chapters provide empirical and theoretical evidence that the structure of temperament and attentional processes, as based on the arousal and activation mechanisms, are crucial elements of the System of Regulation and Integration Stimulation. It is important to keep in mind that within the SRIS it is possible to locate other internal characteristics that potentially contribute to stimulation processing. Thus we might expect that mood traits may be associated with stimulation processing, which will be particularly obvious when individuals encounter emotionally loaded stimulation. More precisely, anxiety-related and depression-related moods might contribute to stimulation processing via the fact that as dimensional emotional phenomena, they relate to arousal, activation, and activity in different neurobiological and physiological systems (cf. Fox, 2008, for a review). Thus if the biological mechanisms of arousal and activation bind temperament traits, mood traits, and attentional processes, a strong interrelation would be expected between them in response to emotional stimuli. However, there is the important question of how these mood traits modulate the patterns of stimulation processing within the SRIS. This issue refers to the influence of formal or operational aspects of mood traits on stimulation processing.

Anxiety and depression may represent direct or indirect modulators (moderators and mediators) in stimulation processing within the SRIS (Figure 3.1). First, the effects of stimulation processing may be modulated directly by variations of a range of anxiety-related and depression-related moods. Also, as crucial elements of the SRIS, enduring temperament traits (or types) may of course operate in a more direct manner in terms of amplifying or attenuating stimulation (see Figure 3.1A). Some findings from the research in which temperament and moods are studied together indicate that temperament activation and its direct influence on stimulation processing depend on the complexity of the situation, while mood disorders activation and their direct influence on stimulation processing relate more to the content of the stimulation (e.g., Fajkowska & Krejtz, 2006, 2007; Fajkowska & Marszał-Wiśniewska, 2006; see also Strelau, 2008). However, here the focus is on the influences of mood traits on stimulation processing.

Both moods and temperament operate from the structure level when processing stimulation, whereas attention operates from the process level. The attention system is associated with stimulation reception, and through its interrelations with temperament or moods the attention system is linked to readiness to respond to stimulation (see Figure 3.1). Thus it seems appropriate to study interactions or intercorrelations between temperament traits (types) and moods (mood types), as components from the same structure level, and observe how they relate to the attentional patterns of response while processing stimulation (see Figures 3.1B and 3.1C).

According to Figure 3.1B, moods (mood types) work as moderators. Moderators are essentially third variables that represent conditions under which some independent variable (here temperament) becomes maximally efficient or potent (cf. Coan & Allen, 2004). Thus, second, mood (mood types) may interact with temperament traits (types), which may specifically relate to attentional processes and affect the outcome of stimulation processing. The specificity of influence of interaction between temperament and moods on attentional stimulation processing is clearly demonstrated in a few studies (e.g., Fajkowska & Krejtz, 2007; Fajkowska & Marszał-Wiśniewska, 2006). Mediators, by contrast, are third variables that

[A] Temperament and moods (anxiety and depression) as direct modulators of stimulation processing in the SRIS

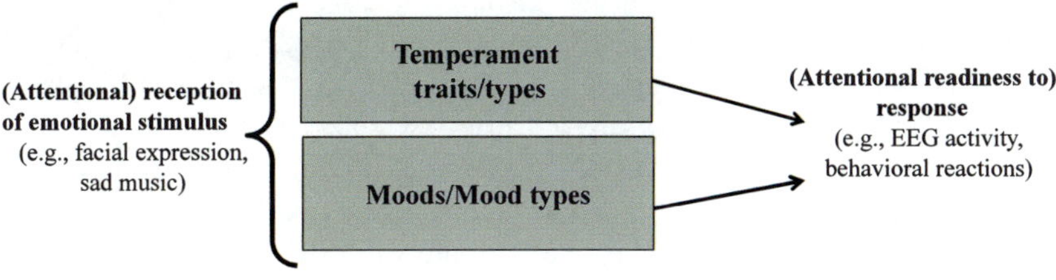



[B] Moods (anxiety and depression) as moderators of stimulation processing in the SRIS

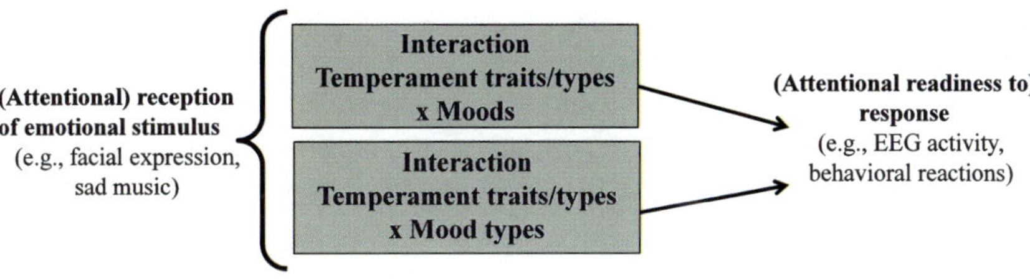



[C] Moods (anxiety and depression) as mediators of stimulation processing in the SRIS

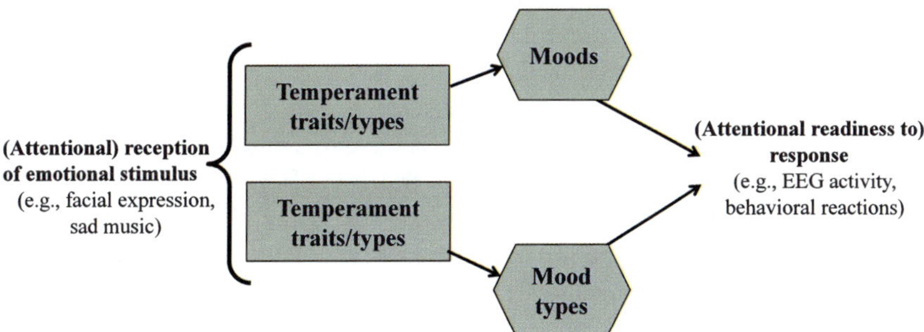



**Figure 3.1.** How moods and mood subtypes influence stimulation processing. (For clarity mutual interactions between attention system and traits are not presented in this figure.)

represent the mechanisms through which—or partially through which—the effect of a particular independent variable (here temperament) is made manifest (cf. Coan & Allen, 2004). Hence, third, temperament traits (types) may modulate moods (mood types), which may in turn affect the attentional response to emotional stimulation (Figure 3.1C). Some research documents these kinds of intercorrelations between temperament and mood disorders (e.g., Fajkowska & Eysenck, 2008; Marszał-Wiśniewska & Fajkowska, 2005).

The modulating role of mood disorders leads us to the second important point: what is the role of these mood traits in modulating patterns of stimulation processing within the SRIS? This question refers to the functional (rather than formal) aspects of the influence of mood traits on stimulation processing within the SRIS. The role of anxiety and depression in direct modulation of stimulation processing is associated with specific patterns of stimulation processing formed by dominant controlling functions in them. The role of anxiety and depression in indirect modulation of stimulation processing is associated with intercorrelational and interactional relations among dominant controlling functions in them and in temperament types. The former means that indirect modulation is connected with a level of functional complexity—personality coherence and incoherence reflected in overlapping or distinctness of controlling functions in focal traits, respectively. It informs us about the quality of processing. The latter denotes functional interactions among dominant controlling functions of anxiety, depression, and temperament types, and allows for assessing the intensity of attentional effects and fluctuation of attentional processes engaged in stimulation processing. I return to the indirect modulation issue later, in Chapters 4 and 5.

Current categorizations of anxiety and depression offered by the DSM-IV-TR (APA, 2000) do not reveal consistent patterns of stimulation processing (especially on the attentional level) in the proposed anxiety and depression subtypes. To the contrary, the DSM-IV-TR classification leads to discrepancies in the findings. In addressing these discrepancies, I suggest an alternative grouping of these two moods. On the basis of the compositional hierarchy—indicating structural differentiation of affective phenomena—and the analysis of direct modulation of stimulation processing in anxiety and depression, their subtypes may be identified. In the next section, which presents subtypes of anxiety and depression, I review the empirical and theoretical discussions that have been particularly influential in establishing the most important processes that contribute to the formation of anxiety and depression subtypes. This allows for a detailed explanation of the functional role of the distinguished subtypes in attentional stimulation processing within the SRIS. In this context I have examined this issue according to the following points.

- *Bridges to subtypes of anxiety and depression: Inconsistencies in results on neurocognitive factors contributing to anxiety and depression.* With reference to the subtypes of anxiety and depression, one issue should be clarified. Interesting lines of research on the structures of affective space emerged from the dimensional approach to emotions (e.g., Russell, 1980; Thayer, 1985, 1996; Watson, 2000; Watson & Tellegen, 1985). However, the specificity of anxiety and depression is best understood by the view suggesting that positive affect (PA) and negative affect (NA) represent separate and unrelated dimensions of experience within which the specificity of anxiety and depression are best captured (Watson, 2000; Watson & Tellegen, 1985). Negative affect is a nonspecific dimension and is common to anxiety and depression; therefore it is primarily responsible for the observed comorbidity between them. Positive affect shows far greater specificity when related to anxiety and depression. More precisely, although low levels of PA have been identified in different affective disorders (e.g., social phobia), anhedonia and low PA seem to play a particularly important role in mood disorders—especially melancholic depression—and low PA is a risk factor for depression and social phobia. A specific factor for anxiety is defined by symptoms of somatic arousal (Watson, 2000). Instead, to address the issue of differentiating subtypes of anxiety and depression, I will rely on the implications from cognitive and neurocognitive studies. With all due respect to the proposed tripartiate model (Clark & Watson, 1991; Mineka, Rafaeli, & Yovel, 2003), including the explanation of the comorbidity that occurs between anxiety and depression and accounts for the clear distinctions that manifest themselves in different types of emotional disorders, there is still insufficient explanation of how other (e.g., cognitive, neuronal) mechanisms contribute to the formation of anxiety and depression, and how other arousal-related personality characteristics and arousal-related processes might be involved in the development and maintenance of these emotional disorders. Consistent with this statement, affective elements identified and perfectly documented in the tripartiate model will be omitted from the structure of subtypes of anxiety and depression proposed within the Complex–System Approach to Personality (C-SAP). In other words, the neurobiological, cognitive, and motivational processes and mechanisms will be emphasized.

- *Crucial processes and mechanisms contributing to the formation of anxiety and depression subtypes.* Consequently, the appropriate point of departure for the identification of anxiety and depression subtypes is recognition of relevant processes and mechanisms that potentially contribute to their structural formation. I argue that specific cognitive (e.g., impairment in working memory, attentional control) and somatic processes and mechanisms are key in contributing to the formation of anxiety subtypes, while specific cognitive (e.g., selective recall of negativity, valence insensitivity) and motivational (e.g., anhedonia, lack of approach behavior) mechanisms are essential in the development of depression subtypes.

- *Building components of anxiety and depression subtypes.* In accordance with systemic logic, the repetitive interactions among cognitive processes and the repetitive interactions among somatic mechanisms lead to the more integrated cognitive and somatic components, from which in turn emerge more somatic-related arousal and more cognitive-related apprehension. These two elements are basic in building anxiety subtypes. In the case of depression, the recurring interactions among cognitive processes and the repetitive interactions among motivational processes lead to more integrated components: more cognitive-related valence (in)sensitivity and more motivation-related anhedonia. Thus dynamic interactions between these two components produce the subtypes of depression.

- *Specific effects of anxiety and depression subtypes on stimulation processing within the SRIS.* The crucial issue of the emerged subtypes of anxiety and depression is how they function in stimulation processing . From the SRIS perspective, the most interesting question is the indirect influences of these mood traits on stimulation processing (see Figures 3.1B, 3.1C). However, in the next section I will selectively review the studies investigating direct influences of mood traits on stimulation processing (see Figure 3.1A). The logic behind this is that the set of specific patterns of stimulation processing depending on variation in mood traits (types) should be identified. With this knowledge the next step becomes more feasible: studying the influence of coherent/incoherent personality structures (built upon anxiety types and depression types, respectively, and temperament types) on stimulation processing. The findings on this topic will be presented in Chapter 5.

3.3.

## Subtypes of anxiety and depression as elements of the SRIS

The neuropsychological models of emotion (Heller, 1993a, 1993b; Robinson & Compton, 2006) serve here as a guide to decomposing two complex disorders of mood—anxiety and depression—according to valence and arousal dimensions. This primary "mood trait disintegration" is necessary in light of their later "integration" (structuralization). Why is that? It is believed that this helps identify the basic processes forming the structures of anxiety and depression.

According to available findings, the arousal dimension seems to be more frequently connected with somatic processes related to motivational and emotional mechanisms, while the valence dimension shows more stable relations with cognitive processes (cf. Davidson, 2000; Heller, 1990; section 2.2.1). If both anxiety and depression might be described on the valence and arousal dimensions, the typical processes attached to these dimensions might also describe these mood traits. Differentiated levels and proportions of arousal and valence sensitivity contribute to the structure and formation of both moods. This explains different subtypes of these mood traits and their interference and priming effects on patterns of stimulation processing.

What do we usually mean by the arousal[1] and valence dimensions? Although various theoretical models have used different terms to refer to the arousal dimension (e.g., *activation, energy, activity*), these terms cover the same underlying

---

[1] The reader can find a comprehensive answer to the question "What is arousal?" in section 2.2.1.

construct. It is the amount of energy we feel that we have available, ranging (for example) from drowsiness, relaxation, and alertness to excitation. Some scholars argue that this subjective experience of arousal may be represented by a factual physiological state at a given time (e.g., Russell & Feldman Barrett, 1999). There is evidence that fluctuations in the experience of arousal appear over the course of the day, situation, lifestyle, health or other individual differences (cf., Thayer, 1996; Watson, 2000). The term "valence" denotes hedonic tone, positive and negative affect, pleasant or unpleasant feelings, and approach or avoidance (cf. Davidson, 2000; Watson, 2000). Generally, evidence from both self-report and physiological studies suggests the strong interrelation between the arousal and valence dimensions. However, self-report studies emphasize that valence and arousal emerge as important elements of one's subjective experience, while physiological and brain imaging studies reveal that valence and arousal are coded across autonomic and brain systems (for a review see Fox, 2008).

Self-report studies demonstrate that an individual's affective experience is described primarily in terms of two dimensions—arousal and valence—rather than several discrete emotions. A typical research methodology is to obtain self-report data about how moods, emotions, and feelings are consciously experienced. Subjects may be asked to characterize their affective experience by selecting representative adjectives (e.g., Watson, 2000); then these data should cluster around the valence or arousal dimension and self-reports of affective experience may be projected into the geometric space by means of statistical techniques (cf. Russell & Feldman Barrett, 1999). There are three prominent models building structures of affective space on self-report studies. The first one represents two independent dimensions of arousal (tension vs. energy; Thayer, 1985, 1989, 1996); the second one corresponds to two unrelated dimensions of valence (PA vs. NA; Watson, 2000, 2005; Watson & Tellegen, 1985); and the third one, embracing both valence and activation and every affective experience, is a combination of these two dimensions (Russell, 1980, 1983, 1991). Despite differences, it has been argued that all these models implicitly or explicitly incorporate the notion of arousal and valence, which are blended in describing the affective space (cf. Fox, 2008).

The findings from physiological measures demonstrated that activity in facial muscles and variation in heart rate show specific patterns of responses for the valence dimension, whereas measures of skin conductance and the startle reflex are indicative of arousal (e.g., Dillon & LaBar, 2005; Lang, 1995, 2000; Lang, Greenwald, Bradley, & Hamm, 1993). Generally, it was shown that prefrontal cortical regions—ventromedial prefrontal cortex and dorsolateral prefrontal cortex (DLPFC)—might contribute to emotional valence processing (Dolcos, LaBar, & Cabeza, 2004; Grimm et al., 2006; Small et al., 2003); however, in studies that looked at both valence and arousal, increased cortical activity (EEG studies; Lang, Bradley, & Cuthbert, 1997) and involvement of amygdala (fMRI studies; Anderson et al., 2004; Dolcos et al., 2004) are associated with increased arousal. As the amygdala and associated regions (e.g., insula, basal ganglia) respond to increases in intensity (Anderson et al., 2003; Lewis, Critchley, Rothstein, & Dolan, 2007), the orbitofrontal cortex (OFC) reacts to variations in valence (Small et al., 2003).

However, Lewis et al. (2007) reported more complex relations between OFC activity and negative and positive valence. It was found that increasing positive valence was linked to the enhanced activity in the right lateral OFC and anterior insula, whereas increasing negative valence was associated primarily with elevated activity in the posterior insula, anterior cingulate cortex, right OFC, and left medial OFC. On one hand, this pattern of functional dissociation of brain activity supports the dimensional models of emotions (e.g., orthogonal positive and negative dimensions; Watson & Tellegen, 1985); but on the other hand, it suggests that the brain might be activated by the concomitance of valence and arousal, which indicates that these two dimensions may be integrated in one representation (see Fox, 2008). The left medial OFC and striatum, for example, were activated by interactions between valence and arousal in response to negative words. Fox (2008) concludes that this valence-specific brain reactivity to arousal supports the view that the content of emotion is associated with specific responses to arousal. It is in line with the model proposed by Wintston, Gottfried, Kilner, and Dolan (2005), which shows that valence increases from most neutral to most intense (positive or negative), which in turn forms the U-shaped relationship between intensity/arousal and valence.

Turning to the neuropsychological model developed by Heller (1986, 1990, 1993a, 1993b), it is clear that Heller attempts to integrate the dimensional theory of emotion with neuropsychological data on cognitive, emotional, and autonomic functioning during different affective states. Thus, based on theoretical work by numerous authors (e.g., Heilman, Schwartz, & Watson, 1978; Levy, Heller, Banich, & Burton, 1983; Tucker, 1981), the arousal dimension (or activation dimension; Larsen & Diener, 1992) is seen as dependent on right parieto-temporal regions of the brain. More activity in this region is associated with higher self-reported arousal, whereas less activity is connected with lower self-reported arousal. Generally, this suggests a special role for the (posterior) right hemisphere in emotion-related arousal functions. Benefiting from EEG, blood flow, and lesion studies, Heller's model postulates that the valence dimension (pleasant, unpleasant) is dependent on functions of the anterior regions. When the left frontal region is active relative to the right, affective valence is pleasant; when the right frontal region is active relative to the left, affective valence is unpleasant. The connection of valence with asymmetric activity of the anterior regions has been comprehensively studied (cf. Davidson, 1992a, 1992b, 2000; Heller, 1990).

Anterior and posterior asymmetries have been extensively reported for both depression and anxiety, but the magnitude and direction of these asymmetries has been variable (Heller & Nitschke, 1998). The inconsistencies in the depression and anxiety literatures may be due to significant differences in regional brain activity that covary strongly with dispositional characteristics or attentional functions associated with emotional functioning. Anterior and posterior asymmetries in cortical activity and their effects on lateral attention are often, but not always, reported in depression and anxiety (e.g., de Brabander, Declerck, & Boone, 2002; Engels et al., 2007; Heller & Nitschke, 1998; Posner & Petersen, 1990; Pribram & McGuinness, 1975; Tucker & Williamson, 1984). However, relatively few studies on regional differences in brain function for temperament characteristics—such as extraversion or neuroticism—point to the possible significance of temperament in understanding regional brain activity in mood disorders (see Canli et al., 2001; Fox, 2008; Heller & Nitschke, 1998).

Thus a promising avenue for clarifying the discrepancies reported in the literature for both anxiety and depression is the identification of their subtypes with reference to the arousal and valence dimensions. This is also promising from the perspective of better understanding the specificity of the role of mood traits in stimulation processing within the SRIS.

### 3.3.1. Processes and mechanisms forming subtypes of anxiety

Demonstration of the specific anxiety subtypes is essential in this section. The extraction of them is based on systemic logic and is adequate to the four points proposed in section 3.2.

*Bridge to subtypes of anxiety: Inconsistences in results*
*on neurocognitive factors contributing to anxiety*

Anxiety has been an increasingly popular focus of research in recent decades. However, these studies are plagued by inconsistencies. Generally, there are two lines of conflicting evidence regarding anxiety.

The first line of research looks at disagreements in how neural mechanisms of cognitive processes operate in anxiety in relation to hemispheric lateralization (e.g., Compton, Heller, Banich, Palmieri, & Miller, 2000; Crost, Pauls, & Wacker, 2008; Engels et al., 2007; Heller, Nitschke, Etienne, & Miller, 1997), event-related potentials (ERPs; e.g., Fajkowska, Eysenck, Zagórska, & Jaśkowski, 2011; Kline, Allen, & Schwartz, 1998), and activation in the anterior cingulate cortex and prefrontal cortex (e.g., Bishop, Duncan, Brett, & Lawrence, 2004; Dennis & Chen, 2009).

With respect to arousal and valence dimensions, the most informative findings from the perspective of forming anxiety subtypes are those on hemispheric lateralization. Generally, a subset of this research suggests an asymmetry in favor of right-hemisphere activation in various regions—frontal, lateral prefrontal, precentral frontal, anterior temporal, parietal, occipital, and parahippocampal (cf. Heller & Nitschke, 1998). Nevertheless, heightened right-hemisphere activity has been reported when subjects were classified according to state anxiety, panic disorder patients after inducing a panic attack, GAD patients during an anxiety-stimulating task, or social phobia patients prior to making a public speech (cf. Heller & Nitschke, 1998, for a review). But heightened left-hemisphere activity has been found in various cortical and subcortical regions (orbital frontal, inferior frontal, anterior cingulate, caudate, putamen, and thalamus) when subjects were classified according to trait anxiety, as obsessive-compulsive disorder patients, or as GAD patients, and categorized as "worriers" on the basis of self-reports when asked to "worry about a specific topic of personal concern" (cf. Heller & Nitschke, 1998, for a review). Thus some findings for anxiety indicate increased right-hemisphere activation—which corresponds to the arousal dimension—whereas others indicate increased left-hemisphere activation, which corresponds to the valence dimension. Indeed, it may be the case that they could co-occur, which could account for the findings of bilateral increases or no asymmetries (Heller & Nitschke, 1998).

Second, anxiety theorists have spent several decades disagreeing among themselves about the nature of the effects of individual differences in trait and state anxiety on cognitive performance. However, there is plentiful evidence that anxiety (whether regarded as trait or state) is responsible for performance impairments on many cognitive tasks. Moreover, there have been numerous attempts to provide a theoretical explanation for the cognitive biases specific to anxious individuals in stimulation processing. For example, apart from evidence that anxiety might boost the early allocation of attention toward threat, there are also results reflecting a difficulty in attentional disengagement from threat processing in highly anxious participants (e.g., Derryberry & Reed, 2002; Fajkowska, Krejtz, & Krejtz, 2009; Fox, Russo, & Dutton, 2002). There is also evidence suggesting an avoidance attentional bias for threat stimuli in anxiety (e.g., Brosschot, de Ruiter, & Kindt, 1999; Dawkins & Furnham, 1989; Eysenck, 1997; Fajkowska & Eysenck, 2008; Fox, 1993; Newman & McKinney, 2002). In addition, there have been numerous attempts to provide empirical data on the adverse effects of anxiety on attentional control. Generally, it is claimed that in the presence of threat-related stimuli, anxiety impairs the efficiency of inhibition and shifting functions and performance effectiveness (the quality of performance; e.g., Eysenck & Derakshan, 2011). However, there are conditions in which these trends do not appear (e.g., Fajkowska et al., 2011).

In spite of the nature of cognitive biases, anxiety is associated with enhanced processing of negative—especially aversive—stimuli. However, these attentional biases toward negative valence are more automatic in high-arousal situations, particularly when a social or physical threat is induced and more deliberate when worrisome thoughts, as a compensatory strategy to compensate for performance deficits, might be activated by anxious individuals (e.g., Eysenck, 1982; Eysenck & Fajkowska, 2009; Fajkowska & Krejtz, 2006; Fox et al., 2002; Mogg, Bradley, Williams, & Mathews, 1993).

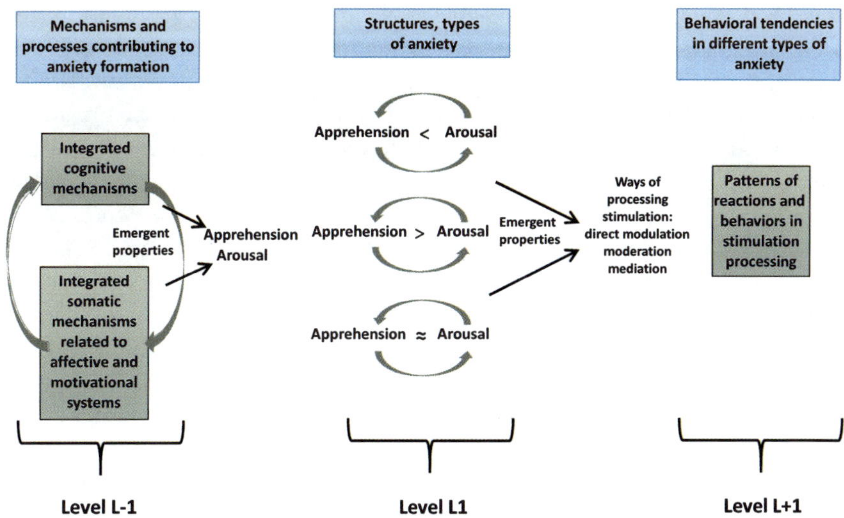


**Figure 3.2.** The organization of anxiety subtypes according to the three-level compositional hierarchy.

Nevertheless, despite these theoretical disagreements, there are indications that certain core elements of anxiety are achieving some measure of consensus. One possible theoretical attempt to account for (a) divergent and convergent results in anxiety studies, and (b) understanding how anxiety influences the patterns of reactions and behaviors in stimulation processing, is to distinguish the anxiety subtypes. Figure 3.2 presents the hierarchical three-level structure of complex anxiety phenomena useful in decomposing anxiety into subtypes.

*Crucial processes and mechanisms contributing*
*to the formation of anxiety subtypes*

Anxiety is not a monolithic construct. The starting point for the identification of anxiety types is to point to relevant processes and mechanisms that contribute to structures of anxiety types. As reviewed earlier, studies that examine neurophysiological aspects of anxiety with reference to arousal and valence dimensions suggest that anxiety is associated with greater activity in the left hemisphere compared with the right hemisphere, which appears to be more robust for the cognitive aspect of anxiety, worrisome thoughts, and anxious apprehension. However, greater right-hemisphere activity may relate to the affective, motivational, or arousal aspect of anxiety (cf., Wilt, Oehlberg, & Revelle, 2011). In keeping with this information, it might be argued that somatic (related to affective and motivational systems) and cognitive processes are key for anxiety structuralization (see Figure 3.2, Level L-1).

With reference to somatic mechanisms, from an evolutionary perspective the neural substrates mediating anxiety are assumed to have developed to promote survival in the face of danger and threat (Panksepp, 1998). It is suggested that several cortico-limbic neural structures (amygdala, septo-hippocampal circuit, insula, interior and medial hypothalamus, cingulum), operating in a parallel and synergic manner, form the substrates of normal anxiety and the various anxiety disorders (Corr & Fajkowska, 2011; Gray, 1982; Gray & McNaughton, 2000; Zeidner, 2008). Also, although it is not universally endorsed, arousal theory continues to be used to account for some features of anxiety and, especially, its effects on performance (e.g., Matthews, Davies, Westerman, & Stammers, 2004). Accordingly, the somatic mechanisms relate to affective and motivational systems in such a way that anxiety, a physiologically hyperaroused affective phenomenon (cf. Watson, 2000), modulates the degree to which a class of emotional stimuli draws attention. Anxiety is associated with an increase in influence of the stimulus-driven attentional system, especially in the presence of negative stimulation. However, under more demanding tasks or clear task goals, anxiety is associated with an increased level of motivation. More specifically, anxiety accounts for producing attempts to override the influence of the stimulus-driven attentional system by making extensive use of compensatory strategies (e.g., intentional effort, volitional attentional control) to perform efficiently (cf. Eysenck & Derakshan, 2011; Hayes, MacLeod, & Hammond, 2009).

Regarding cognitive mechanisms, a central feature of anxiety disorders is the presence of worrisome thoughts. It seems that one of the consequences of worry is to maintain cognitive sensitivity to threat-related stimulation (cf. Fox, 2008). This is reflected in the adverse effects of worry on cognitive performance, especially in the presence of the negative valence material.

Consistent with this view are numerous laboratory-based studies demonstrating the processing mechanisms contributing to bias in selective attention (e.g., Fajkowska & Eysenck, 2008; Fox, 1994), impairment of working memory and attentional control (for a review see Eysenck, Derakshan, Santos, & Calvo, 2007), and reduction in on-task effort (e.g., Humphreys & Revelle, 1984). The biasing effects of anxiety on encoding, processing, and rehearsal are generally robust; however, further studies are needed to detail the influence of anxiety on more complex cognitive processes (e.g., judgment, decision making, problem solving, categorization, or reasoning). Furthermore, studies of real-world situations find that specific types of anxiety (e.g., social, math, exam, or sport performance) interfere with appropriate competence, and by so doing influence many behaviors of widespread significance (for a review see Zeidner, 2008).

*Building components of anxiety subtypes*

Thus the repetitive interactions among cognitive mechanisms (e.g., connected with attentional and working memory systems) and the repetitive interactions among somatic mechanisms (related to affective and motivational systems) lead to more integrated cognitive and somatic components, from which in turn emerge two essential components composing anxiety types: somatic-related arousal and cognitive-related apprehension. In other words, these two interlevel emergent properties originate from bidirectional interactions between the cognitive and somatic components of Level L-1 (see Figure 3.2). This explains the fact that by interacting with each other, different levels of arousal and apprehension build different types of anxiety at the higher-level L (see Figure 3.2). As Figure 3.2 demonstrates, there are three subtypes of anxiety that to some extent capitalize on prior neuropsychological models of emotion (cf. Heller, 1993a, 1993b).

Thus, as we know from the literature, two types of anxiety—anxious apprehension and anxious arousal—associated with different patterns of brain and behavioral activity are distinguished (Heller & Nitschke, 1998). Anxious apprehension is primarily characterized by worry and verbal rumination, typically about future events (Barlow, 1991; Heller et al., 1997), while anxious arousal is described by Watson et al. (1995; see also Watson, 2000) as being distinguished by symptoms of physiological hyperarousal and somatic tension. Although Heller et al. (1997) state that the two kinds of anxiety are not mutually exclusive, their approach seems to be categorical. They claim that extreme degrees of anxious apprehension (e.g., being worried or fearful about the future) may prompt experiences of anxious arousal (e.g., somatic symptoms and exaggerated physiological responses to stressful events). Rather, I maintain that the relation between apprehension and arousal elements is continuous.

Hence, in accord with the theoretical line of reasoning presented above, we can distinguish three types of anxiety presented in Figure 3.2: when the proportion between degree of apprehension and degree of arousal (a) is in favor of arousal (the Arousal Type: apprehension < arousal; Type A < a); (b) is in favor of apprehension (the Apprehension Type: apprehension > arousal; Type A > a); or (c) when there is a balance between apprehension and arousal (the Balanced Type: apprehension ≈ arousal; Type A ≈ a). Panic attacks, high-stress states, and state anxiety as defined by self-report, behavioral, or physiological response systems would be covered by the Arousal Type (cf. Heller & Nitschke, 1998). It seems more probable that the Apprehension Type would be characteristic of obsessive-compulsiveness, generalized anxiety states, and trait anxiety as identified by self-reports of anxious apprehension and worry on various questionnaires (cf. Heller & Nitschke, 1998). Theoretically, the Balanced Type might be identified among all the categories of anxiety mentioned above (e.g., OCD, GAD); however, repressors are good candidates for this type (cf. Fajkowska et al., 2011). This idea will be developed later in this section.

Now the most important question pertains to the specific role played by different types of anxiety in stimulation processing within the SRIS. In the next section, I will selectively review the studies investigating direct influences of this mood on stimulation processing.

*Specific effects of anxiety subtypes on stimulation processing within the SRIS*

Within the SRIS, moods—together with temperament—operate from the structure level in stimulation processing, whereas the attention system operates from the process level. As we know, the attention system is associated with stimulation reception and is linked to the readiness to respond to stimulation through its interrelations with temperament or moods (cf. Figure 3.1). Thus if we analyze a direct influence of anxiety on stimulation processing, I suggest that key features constituting the anxiety types—arousal and apprehension (worries)—trigger specific attentional functions, which in turn produce different (behavioral, autonomic, cortical) patterns of responses to stimulation and different strategies of stimulation processing. Hence attentional biases are considered here as patterns of stimulation processing in anxiety.

More specifically, while interacting with their environment, individuals automatically or consciously process perceived information or stimulation relevant to their general well-being (Applehans & Luecken, 2006; Öhman, 1997). If the environment provides significant information or demanding stimulation for anxious individuals, which usually relates to threat, this implies a series of affective, motivational, cognitive, physiological, and neural responses. In the case of anxiety types, the character of this reactivity depends on their dominating component. I argue that a predominance of somatic tension in the Arousal Type or worrisome thoughts in the Apprehension Type—or a balance between these components in the Balanced Type—specifically determines the manner of stimulation processing (direct or indirect), as well as patterns of response to stimulation across different response systems (see Level L+1, Figure 3.2).

*Arousal Type*

The Arousal Type (Type A < a) is characterized by somatic tension and physiological hyperarousal. Threats that reflect perceived immediate danger are rather more likely than events in the distant future to trigger anxious arousal (Nitschke, Heller, & Miller, 2000). Perceptual and interpretive processes can influence the hypothalamic control centers involved in triggering physiological activity (Lovallo & Gerin, 2003). Thus when one faces a potential threat, physiological responses motivate and enable one to respond by mobilizing stored energy, increasing cardiac output, sweating, shortening of breath, affecting digestive and immune functions, and activating the hypothalamic-pituitary-adrenocortical axis (Applehans & Luecken, 2006; Nitschke, Heller, Palmieri, & Miller, 1999; Saplosky, 1992). The experience of negative emotional arousal may initiate regulative strategies in an attempt to adjust the level of arousal to its optimal level.

The current results suggest that two strategies are activated when one encounters threat. In clinically anxious individuals, elevated arousal might be associated with attentional vigilance toward threat; by contrast, in nonclinical populations with a high level of anxiety, elevated arousal is associated with attentional avoidance of threat (Applehans & Luecken, 2006). Vigilance toward threat serves to perpetuate anxiety and is connected with physiological arousal, which in turn maintains anxiety (e.g., Beck & Clark, 1997; Mathews & MacLeod, 2002), whereas avoidance strategy may serve as a regulative strategy, allowing one to regulate one's arousal and activate a protective strategy against pathological forms of anxiety (Derryberry & Reed, 2002). For example, in a study evaluating the interaction of anxiety and attentional biases in the regulation of cortisol responses to social threat stimuli (a dot-probe task), it was shown that anxiety (nonclinical participants) was associated with avoidance of threat cues. In addition, attentional avoidance predicted decreased cortisol responses at higher levels of anxiety and elevated cortisol responses at lower levels of anxiety (Applehans & Luecken, 2006). This implies that clinical anxiety disorders with a dominating arousal component may result from the loss of the protective biases (avoidance) that buffer vulnerable individuals from threat-induced arousal, rather than from a predisposition toward vigilance (cf. Applehans & Luecken, 2006).

However, there is evidence suggesting that the perceived intensity of a threatening stimulation may influence this cognitive strategy. That is, stimulation perceived to be minimally threatening or highly threatening elicits attentional vigilance, whereas stimuli perceived to be moderately threatening elicit avoidance (cf. Wilson & MacLeod, 2003). It is reasoned that this might be due to differences in appraisals of threat intensity (cf. Wilson & MacLeod, 2003); however, it is also possible that it is associated with the specific structure of temperament.

Thus vigilant and avoidant reactions to threatening stimuli are indicators of two fundamental attentional strategies of coping with aversive stimuli (Calvo & Eysenck, 2000; Heim-Dreger, Kohlmann, Eschenbeck, & Burkhardt, 2006; Hock & Krohne, 2004). In addition, in a study by Fisher et al. (2010), event-related brain potentials were registered while participants reporting features of anxiety (and depression) completed an emotional Stroop task. Individuals also reported their ability to attend to, understand, and reinterpret emotional situations and events. Among the results of this study was that lower anxious apprehension and greater reported emotional clarity were related to slower processing of negative stimuli indexed by ERPs, whereas higher anxious arousal and reported attention to emotion were associated with ERPs—evidence of early attention to all stimuli regardless of emotional content.

Moreover, later attentional disengagement with stimuli was also associated with anxious arousal and clarity of emotions. This pattern of behavior is consistent with previous empirical and clinical evidence. For example, individuals with GAD tend to worry about the future (e.g., Dugas et al., 1998), while people who experience anxious arousal symptoms tend to react to a perceived threat and then have difficulty disengaging from it (e.g., Fox, Russo, Bowles, & Dutton, 2001).

Numerous studies employing EEG, ERP, and hemodynamic (PET, fMRI) methods demonstrated increased right-hemisphere activity in anxious arousal (Engels et al., 2007; Heller, Etienne, & Miller, 1995; Heller & Nitschke, 1998; Heller et al., 1997; Nitschke et al., 2000; Mathersul, Williams, Hopkinson, & Kemp, 2008), in patients with panic disorder or panic symptoms (Reiman, Raichle, Butler, Herscovitch, & Robins, 1984; Swedo et al., 1989) and nonpatients in high-stress situations (Tucker, Roth, Arneson, & Buckingham, 1977). The right hemisphere is involved in vigilance and autonomic arousal (Compton et al., 2003; Heller et al., 1997) and the right-hemisphere temporoparietal cortex and inferior frontal cortex are involved in detecting salient stimuli that are behaviorally relevant (Corbetta & Shulman, 2002; Engels et al., 2007). For example, the aim of the study by Mathersul et al. (2008) was to investigate the relationship between nonclinical anxiety, depression, and lateralized frontal and temporoparietal activity by grouping participants on the basis of both negative mood and alpha EEG. Findings (among others) support the valence-arousal model that anxiety subtypes are characterized by opposing frontal asymmetry profiles.

To summarize, in the case of the Arousal Type of anxiety, physiological arousal dominates over other elements. Thus it may be concluded that the typical patterns of stimulation processing in these types are associated with (a) attentional vigilance (usually in clinical anxiety) to threat and attentional avoidance (usually in the nonpatient group) of threat; (b) elevated autonomic reactivity in the presence of threat; and (c) right-hemisphere involvement in processing threatening stimuli.

*Apprehension Type*

The term "chronic worry" in the Apprehension Type (Type A > a) refers to a relatively uncontrollable stream of negative thoughts and images related to events that may occur in the future with uncertain and/or unpredictable outcomes (cf. Borkovec, Ray, & Stober, 1998; Laguna, Ham, Hope, & Bell, 2004). The adverse effects of worry on cognitive performance, given that worrisome thoughts are internal, distracting, threat-related stimuli, are reduced attentional control and related processing efficiency (cf. Eysenck, 2006). On one hand worrisome thoughts are very difficult to ignore, but on the other they serve a motivational function, in that they lead the individual to make use of compensatory strategies. For example, the content of persistent worrisome thoughts may include personal and emotional threats to the self, physical health, competence at work, or general world problems. Although worry is defined as a cardinal feature of GAD and OCD (Sanderson & Barlow, 1990), it is also a common experience in healthy populations, occurring as short-term thoughts and images (Borkovec, 1994). Nonetheless, the question about the function of chronic worry remains. This primarily verbal activity is seen as a method of cognitive, attentional avoidance of perceived threat by avoiding emotional imagery (Laguna et al., 2004).

Moreover, many psychophysiological studies reveal that unlike other anxious states (e.g., those with a dominating arousal component), worrisome thoughts are not associated with a greater response of the autonomic system (e.g., cardiovascular arousal, heart rates); by contrast, they are associated with autonomic rigidity and vagal tone (e.g., Hoehn-Saric, MacLeod, & Zimmerli, 1989; Thayer, Friedman, & Borkovec, 1996). Preliminary findings examining brain activity (EEG) in individuals with GAD demonstrated that worriers engage less in imagery processes and influence on the frontal lobe, have less executive control over mental activities when worrying, and are connected with a delay in accessing the limbic system and emotional processing (Borkovec et al., 1998). In addition, self-report data showed that individuals with GAD utilized worries as distractors from emotional topics (e.g., Borkovec & Roemer, 1995). Thus, if chronic worriers apply worrisome thoughts as a strategy to avoid emotional arousal, they may actively inhibit emotional processing and maintain pathological worrying.

This conclusion receives empirical support from studies that describe worrying as characterized by reduced concreteness (Borkovec et al. 1998; Stober, 1998); it means that imagery associated with worrying might be less accessible. In fact, initially worrying might provide positive effects; however, in long-term perspective it forms continuous threat associations and inabilities of learning new patterns of reactions (Laguna et al., 2004). However, it was observed that although normal individuals with a high level of worry avoided listening to the worry script due to the discomfort associated with the worry images, they did not have less physiological arousal (indicative by skin conductance and constant skin temperature) than low worriers (Laguna et al., 2004). The last outcome is supported by other findings showing that in addition to worry, physical symptoms often accompany anxious apprehension—including restlessness, fatigue, and muscle tension (Nitschke et al., 1999).

Additionally, the left hemisphere has been implicated in studies of obsessive-compulsive disorder (e.g., Baxter et al., 1987; Swedo et al., 1989), generalized anxiety disorder (e.g., Wu et al., 1991; for a review see Nitschke & Heller, 2002), and trait anxiety (Tucker, Antes, Stenslie, & Barnhardt, 1978), and emerges as particularly salient in anxious apprehension. Compared with a control group, psychometrically defined anxious apprehension participants exhibited an EEG asymmetry in favor of the left hemisphere during a resting condition (Heller et al., 1997). Similarly, worrying about an unprepared speech task was associated with greater left frontal EEG activity than fearing a more impending stressor (Hofmann et al., 2005).

These findings linking the left hemisphere to anxiety disorders that feature worry and anxious apprehension are consistent with its specialization for language. Thus anxiety-related impairments in various tasks could reflect ruminative activity in left-hemisphere verbal-processing circuits. Indeed, behavioral and fMRI responses to threat stimuli in an emotional Stroop task examined in nonpatient groups reporting anxious apprehension and anxious arousal showed that the anxious apprehension group (trait anxious) exhibited more left-hemisphere activity in the inferior frontal gyrus (closely approximating Broca's area), the middle and temporal gyrus, and the inferior parietal lobule. In addition, the left inferior frontal gyrus region was identified in the anxious apprehension group as more active for negative than neutral words (Engels et al., 2007). Thus the left inferior frontal regions are involved in maintenance of verbal information (Fletcher & Henson, 2001; Wagner, 1999), accessing word meaning, holding language-related information online, and verbal rehearsal—consistent with the ruminative style of cognition that characterizes anxious apprehension.

These patterns of brain activity associated with anxious apprehension implement the distinctive or specific computations associated with this state. In other words, worry may affect attention and working memory by drawing from a limited pool of resources (Eysenck, 2006; Eysenck & Calvo, 1992), by interfering with performance due to competition with or distraction from attention to task-relevant information (Nitschke et al., 2000), or by interfering with optimum performance in a variety of circumstances—particularly those that require or would benefit from high levels of selective attention (see Eysenck, 1997).

Taken together, these findings may suggest that more enduring and intensive worrying affects physiological arousal less in the Apprehension Type. Accordingly, the typical patterns of stimulation processing in this type are associated with (a) reduced attentional control and related impaired effectiveness of stimulation processing and avoidance of threatening stimuli (in clinical and nonclinical groups and trait anxiety); (b) reduction in autonomic reactivity; (c) impairment/inhibition of emotional processing, both on an attentional and physiological level; and (d) left-hemisphere involvement in stimulation processing.

*Balanced Type*

I argue that a good representative of the Balanced Type of anxiety is repressive coping. The Balanced Type denotes a relatively harmonized composition of arousal and apprehension components. Theoretically, it seems possible to identify this balanced structure among different (clinical and nonclinical) categories of anxiety; however, the available literature does not discuss this issue. As a consequence, I will limit myself to describing repressive coping in this context (cf. Fajkowska et al., 2011).

Repressors report high levels of defensiveness (social desirability) and low levels of anxiety but show high levels of physiological and behavioral reactivity, indicative of anxiety (e.g., Derakshan, Feldman, Campbell, & Lipp, 2003; Weinberger, 1990). The arousal component of anxiety is represented in repressors by the fact that they have higher autonomic arousal than nonanxious individuals (e.g., Asendorpf & Scherer, 1983; Derakshan & Eysenck, 2001; Newton & Contrada, 1992) and greater right frontal and parietal involvement than both high- and low-anxious subjects when processing negative stimulation (e.g., Vendemia, 2006). But the apprehension component (i.e., worrisome thoughts) is represented in repressors primarily when they encounter self-relevant threats—for example, self-evaluative or socially threatening stimuli or situations or threats to physical well-being (cf. Mendolia & Baker, 2008; Newman & McKinney, 2002)—and when they anticipate negative events. The latter is also associated with increased left anterior and frontal activity (cf. Vendemia, 2006).

Repressors are very vigilant to self-relevant threats and they exhibit attentional (and interpretive) biases. This vigilance produces behavioral and physiological reactions indicative of the arousal component of anxiety (which is obtained by psychophysiological and behavioral measures). However, repressors also utilize various avoidant attentional biases (as well as interpretive and memory avoidant biases); these cognitive biases are instrumental in producing low levels of experienced anxiety, which is obtained by self-report measures (cf. Derakshan, Eysenck, & Myers, 2007).

However, in an experiment conducted by Fajkowska et al. (2011), repressors exhibited attentional vigilance toward threatening social stimuli but did not reveal threat avoidance. They were also receptive to nonthreatening faces. On a more elaborated level, in this study a range of ERP components responsive to facial stimuli and indexing the rapid attentional engagement (P1, N170), and increased (N400) and sustained (LPC) attention allocation and attentional control (N2), was investigated among low-anxious individuals, high-anxious individuals, repressors, and defensive high-anxious individuals. Participants completed the Emotional Go/ NoGo task while EEG signals were recorded. They were instructed to respond to threatening, sad, or friendly faces (respectively) but not to any other facial expression. Among other findings, it was revealed that the sequence of processing emotional material in repressors was associated with (posterior and anterior, right-lateralized) early vigilance to threatening faces, when they presented enhanced responsivity to threatening faces and happy faces in several right prefrontal areas. Moreover, repressors exhibited posterior inhibitory control over negativity (threatening and sad faces).

These results indicate that attentional vigilance toward threatening information in repressors is associated with a posterior attentional system and may develop on the basis of the arousal component, and together with an anterior attentional system is probably associated with the apprehension component. Also, the arousal component in repressors may be responsible for the enhanced responsivity to more arousing emotions like threatening and happy faces, and for more automatic control over negativity. The lack of avoidance patterns of responding in repressors might be explained by the fact that this experiment did not activate the self-relevant information.

The question is which typical patterns of stimulation processing we should expect in the Balanced Type. With caution, I try to make a final conclusion; however, the validity of this generalization is limited since it is based only on the functioning of the repressive coping group. Thus it seems possible that typical patterns of stimulation processing in the Balanced Type comprise specific patterns of both nonbalanced types—that is, the apprehension and arousal types—and that their activation is situation-dependent (e.g., related to the presence of self-relevant information or social evaluation).

### 3.3.2. Processes and mechanisms forming subtypes of depression

The complexity of unipolar depressive disorders, including depressed mood as its mildest form, makes it unlikely that a single set of factors can adequately explain the full range of phenomena associated with them. Thus when examining unipolar depressive disorders, one must explore biological, cognitive, affective, motivational, and personality factors to understand the etiology, dynamic, maintenance, and treatment of this group of affective disorders. However, these factors associated with investigations on unipolar depression are confounded when depression is studied as a uniform construct, and when depression is not separated from the effects of anxiety types.

*Bridge to subtypes of depression: Inconsistencies in results*
*on neurocognitive factors contributing to depression*

With respect to the arousal and valence dimensions, this section has discussed selected research on neuropsychological classes of variables that appear to be important for construing depression subtypes. On one hand, the number of consistencies across this research—which I am going to document—suggests some commonality; but on the other hand, the inconsistencies could be due in part to the heterogeneity of depressive disorders. Also worthy of note is whether studies of clinical depression, psychometrically defined depression, and sad mood are addressing the same phenomenon.

Generally, it is believed that depression-related disorders are characterized by significant disruptions to neural circuits underlying emotional and motivational systems (Ressler & Mayberg, 2007; Robinson, Meier, Tamir, Wilkowski, & Ode, 2009). However, it is very difficult to determine the causal direction of this relationship. In other words, it is not clear whether a specific pattern of brain activity is a result of experiencing depression, or whether this pattern might be a causal factor in the occurrence of depressive disorders (cf. Fox, 2008).

The most plausible hypothesis is that particular forms of frontal asymmetries might constitute a risk factor for depressive disorders. Although anterior asymmetries have often been reported in depression, and a large body of research does suggest that (resting) prefrontal asymmetry may serve as a risk factor for the development of depression, the more common finding of higher left than right activation is not invariably found (e.g., Davidson, Pizzagalli, Nitschke, & Putnam, 2002; Henriques & Davidson, 1991; Shankman, Klein, Tenke, & Bruder, 2007). In addition, although anterior asymmetries have often been reported in clinical depression, psychometrically defined depression, and sad mood, the more common finding of higher left than right activation is not consistently obtained (e.g., Fisher et al., 2010). For example, increased activation of the left prefrontal cortex (EEG)—in contrast to normal control—has been observed in depressed individuals when reward is anticipated (Shankman et al., 2007). In another study Davidson, Larson, and Abercrombie (1995) reported that the severity of depression in melancholic subjects (with anhedonia) was predicted by the extent to which activation was decreased in the left lateral prefrontal region, while among nonmelancholics (without anhedonia) the severity of depression was predicted by the extent to which activation was increased in the right medial prefrontal area.

The implications emerge for the relationship between pleasant/unpleasant affect in depression and anterior regions of the brain. It seems probable that melancholic depression is characterized by decreased pleasant affect, whereas depression without melancholic features may be better characterized by increased unpleasant affect. In other words, it might be more accurate to link the left anterior region to the activated pleasant affect (i.e., positive valence) and the right anterior region to the activated unpleasant affect (i.e., negative valence), which in fact is in accord with a dimensional model of emotion (cf. Heller & Nitschke, 1998).

Experimental studies utilizing neuroimaging methods and different cognitive tasks to identify cortical and subcortical structures potentially involved in depression more vigorously suggested bilateral lateralization in depression when processing stimulation (e.g., Mathersul et al., 2008). In a PET study using a perceptual asymmetry task, Bench et al. (1992) reported less activity in the left dorsolateral prefrontal cortex compared with nondepressed controls. Other studies have reported decreased activity in the left dorsolateral prefrontal cortex in patients with major depression; the degree of this activity decreases as negative symptoms become more severe (e.g., Galynker et al. 1998). Recent fMRI findings indicate that both depressed and nondepressed participants showed a leftward lateralization of DLPFC activity for positive stimuli (Herrington et al., cited in Fisher et al., 2010). Moreover, the depressed group was also characterized by a pattern of less left- and more right-lateralized DLPFC activity to negative versus neutral stimuli, which was consistent with previous resting EEG studies (see Davidson et al., 2002). These findings support the hypothesis that depression is associated with a deficit in a left-lateralized positive affectivity circuit and might be partly associated with a deficit in a motivational, approach-based appetitive system (e.g., Davidson, 2000).

The neurocognitive studies reviewed above indicate that depressive disorders are associated with responsivity to valence of stimulation, which is reflected across different systems: neural, which has been already described; and cognitive and motivational, which are described below.

Regarding the motivational system, other studies showed that depression was associated with smaller slow-wave amplitude to positive stimuli than to negative and neutral stimuli, and with equivalent slow-wave responses to both positive and negative stimuli (Deveney & Deldin, 2004; Shestyuk, Deldin, Brand, & Deveney,

2005), which implies that depressed individuals do not engage in such elaborate processing of negative stimuli as healthy people. However, the association between slow wave and depression was observed in studies utilizing working memory tasks, but not in studies using an emotion-word Stroop task among melancholic individuals (Fisher et al. 2010). Depressed individuals are hypothesized to lack approach motivation (Robinson et al., 2009) and thus might not engage in elaborate processing unless required by task demands (e.g., remembering the stimuli for an upcoming recall or recognition session).

These results correspond with the view that depressed people often do not voluntarily initiate general controlled procedures that imply impairments in motivation (cf. Ellis & Moore, 2000; Hertel, 1997). Deficits in motivation explain deficits in memory and cognitive (attentional) control (cf. Hertel, 1994). A motivational account posits that depressed individuals could possess cognitive resources to perform tasks efficiently, but that they are insufficiently motivated to do so (cf. Hartlage Alloy, Vazquez, & Dykman, 1993). Although there can be no doubt that motivational deficits may be present in depressed individuals, this explanation appears insufficient to account for all cognitive deficits in depressed individuals.

To complete this picture, it should be noted that it has also been suggested that depression (and depressed mood) are associated with biases in attention, memory, and judgment (cf. Fox, 2008). In a number of studies, depressed individuals have been found either to attend more strongly to negative than positive stimuli, or to fail in avoiding negative stimuli demonstrated by nondepressed subjects (e.g., Gotlib, Krasnoperova, Yue, & Joorman, 2004; Gotlib & MacLeod, 1997). Depressed

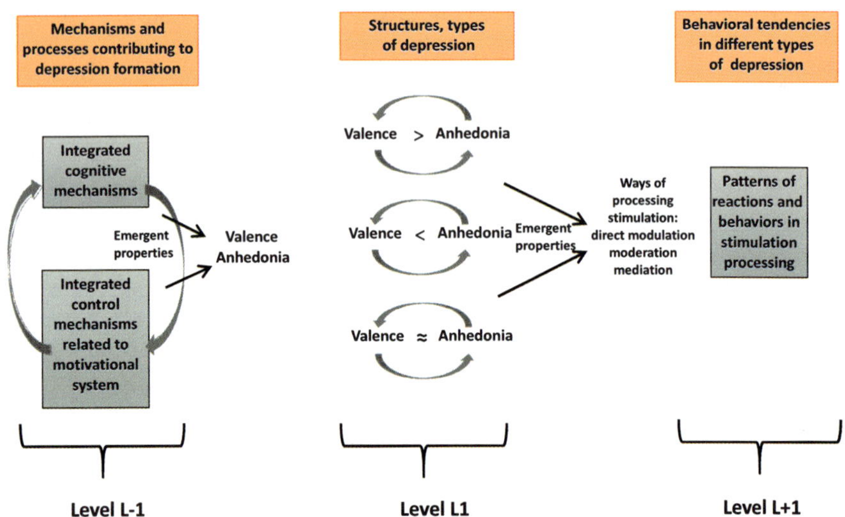


**Figure 3.3.** The organization of depression subtypes according to the three-level compositional hierarchy.

individuals have also been found to recall negative memories and material more quickly than positive memories and material, and they have been found to make more negative judgments concerning both hypothetical and real-life events (see Gotlib, Gilboa, & Sommerfeld, 2000, for a review).

In conclusion, concerning stimulation processing, although there are a number of consistencies in the neurophysiological and psychological literature, these inconsistencies could in part be due to the heterogeneity among the samples studied. Therefore it is understandable that decomposing depression into subtypes can potentially have an important impact on eliminating vagueness from results in this area. Figure 3.3 illustrates the organization of depression subtypes according to the three-level compositional hierarchy.

*Crucial processes and mechanisms contributing*
*to the formation of depression subtypes*

I postulate that depression, like anxiety, is a complex phenomenon. With reference to the studies reviewed above, I would like to draw attention to two central themes in the phenomenology of depression. The first is connected with the emphasis on the valence oversensitivity or undersensitivity in cognitive systems (e.g., Davidson et al., 1995) and negative emotional experience (e.g., Beck, Rush, Shaw, & Emery, 1979); the second is connected with impaired control, a loss of pleasure and interest in previously enjoyable activities (anhedonia), reduction in response to reward-related stimuli, and a lack of positive reinforcement (e.g., Sloan, Strauss, & Wisner, 2001), coupled with a deficit in approach behavior (e.g., Henriques & Davidson, 2000). Rather, it seems that impairments of sensitivity to valence of cognitive systems are associated with increased activity in the right medial prefrontal area, while deficits in control and the motivational system correspond to decreased activity in the left prefrontal area (e.g., Davidson et al., 1995, 2002). Accordingly, I argue that cognitive and motivational processes are crucial in the formation of the structure of depression subtypes (cf. Figure 3.3, Level L-1).

According to the research results presented in the previous discussion of studies examining valence reception, it is important to note that depressive disorders and depressed mood have been found to be associated with biases in attention, memory, judgment, and interpretation (Gotlib et al., 2000). However, the question is toward which valence—positive, negative, or both—depressed people are biased.

The nature of attentional biases in depression, when it is obtained in studies, is unclear. There have been several failures to find evidence for attentional biases in depression (e.g., MacLeod, Mathews, & Tata, 1986; Mogg et al., 1993). However, there is growing evidence that depressed participants selectively attend to negative information when that information is presented for a relatively long time (e.g., Gotlib et al., 2004; Joorman & Gotlib, 2007). In addition, attentional biases seem more likely to emerge when stimuli with particular relevance to depression are used (e.g., Gotlib & Cane, 1987) and in tasks involving multiple stimuli (e.g., the deployment-of-attention task; McCabe & Gotlib, 1995), contrary to a single-stimulus task such as the Stroop task.

The selective recall of negative material is a central characteristic of clinical depression (e.g., Mineka et al., 2003; Williams, Watts, MacLeod, & Mathews, 1997). Depressed individuals tend to remember negative information, especially when it is encoded in a self-referential way (e.g., Bellew & Hill, 1990; Matt, Vazquez, & Campbell, 1992). Further, there is extensive evidence that clinical depression is associated with explicit and implicit memory biases for negative information (Williams et al., 1997). There is also evidence that retrieval in depressed people tends to be very general (overgeneral memory effects) compared with retrieval in nondepressed people, despite valence of material (Williams, 2004).

Generally, under free-recall instructions depressed subjects recalled signifi-cantly more negatively valenced than positively valenced words, whereas the opposite pattern was observed in nondepressed controls (e.g., Denny & Hunt, 1992). Other studies extended these patterns in several aspects. For example, the study examining differential brain activity in depressed individuals (MDD) associ-ated with encoding of emotional stimuli varying in valence and arousal showed that memory biases for negative words were observed for arousal words, which was not reflected in ERP amplitudes (Deldin, Naidu, Shestyuk, & Casas, 2009). Lev-ens and Gotlib (2009) provided findings indicating that valence-specific deficits in working memory may contribute to the inability of depressed participants to regulate emotions, and that positive insensitivity might contribute to maintenance of depression. Specifically, it has been found that depressed individuals were impaired in selecting task-relevant positive stimuli compared with nondepressed controls, whereas the performance of the two groups was comparable for selecting task-relevant neutral and negative stimuli.

Another class of cognitive biases frequently observed in depression is asso-ciated with the reduced anticipation of positive future events (e.g., MacLeod & Cropley, 1995), as well as negative interpretive bias (Lawson, MacLeod, & Ham-mond, 2002).

It is clearly demonstrated that depressed individuals consistently display deficits in processing and responding to positive hedonic stimuli on self-report, behavioral, and psychophysiological measures (e.g., Dichter & Tomarken, 2008; Dichter, Tomarken, Shelton, & Sutton, 2004; Henriques & Davidson, 2000; Sloan et al., 2001). Nonetheless, the results concerning responses to negative affec-tive stimuli are more ambiguous. There are some interesting findings concern-ing arousal and valence ratings of emotional visual stimuli in depression (e.g., Dunn, Dalgleish, Ogilvie, Lawrence, & Cusack, 2004; Sloan et al., 2001). For example, Dunn et al. (2004) found clear group differences (depressed subjects versus never-depressed controls) in response to positive—but not negative—visual stimuli. Depressed individuals (MDD) presented reduced responsiveness to posi-tive—but not negative—stimuli and elevated sadness reports to positive stimuli.

Other studies have found augmented responses to negative stimuli in depressed individuals (e.g., Watkins, Vache, Verney, Mathews, & Muller, 1996), whereas others have not or have found inconsistencies in results across dependent measures (e.g., Yee & Miller, 1988).

An interesting line of studies represents work indicating that depressed individuals are less responsive than nondepressed individuals to variations in the affective valence of eliciting stimuli (Rottenberg, 2007; Rottenberg, Kasch, Gross, & Gotlib, 2002). Investigators argue that depression is associated with broad emotion-context insensitivity, which is based on the concept that depression is a syndrome characterized by disengagement and a bias against action (e.g., Nesse, 2000). To some extent this finding received support from a study conducted by Dichter and Tomarken (2008). They examined an affective startle modulation by unipolar depressed and nondepressed individuals assessed during the anticipation and viewing of emotional pictures. Overall these data add to the literature documenting responsiveness to valence in depression that unipolar depression is associated with relative insensitivity to variations in affective content.

I argue that this relative insensitivity to variations in affective content in depression seems to be a more ecologically valid finding than biases to negative and/or positive valence. Why is that? These findings on valence insensitivity address the issue about the impaired cognitive initiative in depressed individuals (cf. Hertel, 1994). This position focuses on the use of cognitive (control) strategies that might be employed by depressed subjects to remediate cognitive deficits. Depressed people are usually motivated or mobilized to perform well when undertaking cognitive tasks. Naturally, depressed-mood individuals are simply less energized to perform (well) in (effortful) tasks and are disengaged from their actions. Moreover, emotional stimulation utilized in these tasks is usually limited to a narrow emotional context, while real life provides a broad emotional context.

The conclusion is that the ecologically correct cognitive valence insensitivity in depression corresponds to motivational deficits associated with these disorders. In some circumstances the effects of asymmetrical moods on motivation has been reported (cf. Isen, 2000). Specifically, there is evidence that people who are feeling happy are motivated to maintain this state or that people with positive affect show more intrinsic motivation. This evidence implies that people in a positive mood exhibit cognitive initiatives to perform well.

In recent years there has been a growing interest in applying models of emotion and motivation stemming from (neurobiological) basic research to the study of depression. Some of these models propose higher-order dimensions reflecting the operation of biologically rooted systems that organize and activate responses to rewarding, appetitive, or otherwise positive hedonic stimuli and to aversive, threatening, or otherwise negative hedonic stimuli (e.g., Carver & White, 1994; Dichter & Tomarken, 2008; Tomarken, Shelton, & Hollon, 2007). In light of these models, unipolar depression is characterized by a combination of hypoactivation in a biologically based approach system that mediates responses to the appetitive stimuli, and hyperactvation of a protective-defensive withdrawal system that mediates responses to aversive, stressful, or threatening stimuli (e.g., Fowles, 1988).

*Building components of depression subtypes*

In congruence with the theoretical assumptions of the C-SAP, the recurring interactions among cognitive mechanisms and the repetitive interactions among motivational mechanisms lead to more integrated components, from which in turn emerge more cognitive-related valence (in)sensitivity and more motivation-related anhedonia. In other words, these two interlevel emergent properties originate from bidirectional interactions between cognitive and motivational components of Level L-1 (see Figure 3.3) and have a dimensional character. Further, dynamic interactions between the higher-ordered components anhedonia and valence (in)sensitivity produce three subtypes of depression (see Figure 3.3, Level L1). Similarly, anxiety and the proposed subtypes of depression were inspired by the neupsychological model of emotion (Heller & Nitschke, 1998).

Thus, in spite of the fact that the current version of the DSM precisely divides unipolar depression into subtypes (APA, 2000), according to Heller and Nitschke (1998) the most useful distinction in psychophysiological and psychological research on depression has been the comparison of melancholic and nonmelancholic depression. The key feature of melancholic depression is anhedonia, which is the inability to experience pleasure; more precisely, it is most strongly characterized by a loss of pleasure in all activities and a lack of responsivity to pleasurable stimulation. This suggests that we should expect that leading deficits in this type are associated with the motivational system, whereas lack of anhedonia is typical for nonmelancholic depression. Also, a dominance of cognitive valence insensitivity in stimulation processing is specific to this type of depression.

Both types of depression, however, share many symptoms such as sadness, depressed mood, difficulties in eating and sleeping, low self-esteem, inability to concentrate, psychomotor retardation, fatigue, indecisiveness, feelings of guilt, and recurring thoughts about death. Despite current controversy over whether melancholic depression is qualitatively different from nonmelancholic depression (e.g., the question is whether the primary distinction is one of severity; cf. Zimmerman, Coryell, & Pfohl, 1986), psychological, neuropsychological, and neurophysiological studies have been consistent in demonstrating differences between melancholic and nonmelancholic depression (cf. Heller & Nitschke, 1998). For example, Davidson et al. (1995) reported that the severity of depression in melancholic subjects was predicted by the extent to which activation was decreased in the left lateral prefrontal region. By contrast, the severity of depression among nonmelancholics was predicted by the extent to which activation was increased in the right medial prefrontal area. In addition, it has been demonstrated that nonmelancholic depression corresponds to a higher degree of personality dysfunction compared with melancholia (e.g., Rubino, Zanasi, Robone, & Siracusano, 2009) and different cognitive patterns of stimulation processing (e.g., Schock, Schwenzer, Strum, & Mathiak, 2011; Withall, Harris, & Cumming, 2009).

Thus, in terms of types of depression, my proposal is that they relate to valence (in)sensitivity and anhedonia components, which constitute (a) type where degree of valence (in)sensitivity dominates degree of anhedonia (Valence Type: valence (in)sensitivity > anhedonia; Type V > Anh); (b) type where degree of valence (in) sensitivity is dominated by degree of anhedonia (Anhedonic Type: valence (in)sensitivity < anhedonia; Type V < Anh); and (c) type with structure resting on a relative equilibrium, balanced between anhedonia and valence (in)sensitivity components (Balanced Type: valence (in)sensitivity ≈ anhedonia; Type V ≈ Anh).

All these types might be present in both nonclinical (depressed mood) and clinical forms of depression. The Valence Type embraces nonmelancholic subtypes of MDD, while the Anhedonic Type covers the melancholic subtype of MDD suggested by DSM-IV-TR (APA, 2000). The Valence Type is treated here as an exogenous and state-like type, and as primarily connected with a biased cognitive system on account of the content or valence of stimulation. The Anhedonic Type is relevant to an endogenous and trait-like type (cf. Rubino et al., 2009) and is primarily connected with impaired control and motivational deficits in stimulation processing. The Balanced Type emerges from theoretical speculation rather than from analyzing the results of the relevant literature. It is a matter for future research to elucidate more clearly the circumstances in which this type may be obtained.

Here a central issue of the emerged subtypes of depression is how they function in processing stimulation within the SRIS. In the next section, I will rely on the empirical evidence to analyze the direct influence of extracted subtypes of depression on stimulation processing (cf. Figure 3.1A). Similar to what has been done in the case of anxiety, I will present selected studies on stimulation processing in depression in the context of attention as the crucial element of the SRIS. However, the number of studies on depression and attentional processing is quite small compared with the number of studies on anxiety and attentional processing. Thus it is important to point out that the conclusions I will draw from the results of these studies must be taken as preliminary.

*Specific effects of depression subtypes on*
*stimulation processing within the SRIS*

Examining the direct influence of depression on stimulation processing within the SRIS indicates that key features constituting depression types—anhedonia and valence (in)sensitivity—prompt specific attentional functions, which in turn produce different (behavioral, autonomic, cortical) patterns of responses to stimulation and different strategies for stimulation processing. As we learned from the sections on anxiety types, attenional biases are regarded here as patterns of stimulation processing. Put another way, I believe that a predominance of valence (in)sensitivity or anhedonia in the Valence Type or Anhedonic Type (respectively), or a balance between these components in the Balanced Type, specifically determines the manner of stimulation processing (direct or indirect), as well as patterns of response to stimulation across different response systems in (see Figure 3.3., Level L+1).

*Valence Type*

The specificity of the Valence Type (Type V > Anh) is that a degree of valence (in)sensitivity dominates a degree of anhedonia. There is evidence that the hyperactive right hemisphere is involved in processing negative emotions and elevated anxiety in nonmelancholic depressed individuals (Valence Type). Additionally, the right hemisphere mediates attentional vigilance and arousal, accounting for the tendency of depressed individuals to avoid external stimulation and focus attention inward (Hecht, 2010). Along this line it has been observed that right-hemisphere involvement—particularly posterior regions—in (depressed) people induced sad moods in both laboratory and ecological contexts (see Heller & Nitschke, 1997).

Indeed, one possible method to explore an influence of the Valance Type on attentional processing is to utilize sadness-inducing mood tasks. However, some authors argue that attentional biases may be not a marker of state depression, but might represent more enduring, trait-like characteristics of depression (cf. Fox, 2008). In general, however, few studies examine mood induction and attentional functioning in depressed individuals. Those that are available suggest that the nature of attentional biases in depression, when it is obtained, is unclear—involving selective attentional processing of negative information on one hand, and attentional allocation to positive, neutral, and negative content stimulation on the other (see Gotlib et al., 2000, for a review). It might be argued that the lack of content specificity in depression supports the idea of predominating valence insensitivity in the Valence Type. This valence-independent attentional processing, meaning a generalized pattern of reaction that is unrelated to an elicitor's affective valence, may represent an avoidance strategy. Depressed individuals perform the task in a "self-protective," "energy-conserving" manner, essentially avoiding attending to negative stimuli (see Gotlib et al., 2000, for a review; also Watson, 2000).

Moreover, an analysis of the subtypes of nonmelancholic depression (Valence Types) revealed elevated anxiety, tenseness, hostility, more fragile inner self, and social avoidance (cf. Parker et al., 1999; Sato et al., 2003; Tembler and Schüssler, 2009). This reaction seems to be quite adaptive from an evolutionary viewpoint. Valence-depressed people should attentionally avoid processing arousal-loaded stimulation (such as negativity or social material) as being not physiologically prepared to effectively cope with this type of stimulation. It has been suggested that a central feature of MDD, including the Valence Type, is a dysregulation in physiological arousal and brain areas implicated in processing arousal characteristics of information (Nitschke, Heller, Imig, McDonald, & Miller, 2001).

To conclude, it appears that specific patterns of stimulation processing in the Valence Type of depression correspond to (a) attentional avoidance reflected in valence (in)sensitivity to emotional and social material, and (b) increased right-hemisphere activity in stimulation processing.

### Anhedonic Type

In the Anhedonic Type (Type V < Anh), the degree of valence (in)sensitivity is dominated by degree of anhedonia. This type is characterized by a loss of pleasure in all—or in almost all—activities and deficits in one's motivational system. Therefore it seems likely that it reflects a dysfunctional dopaminergic system, which indicates a failure in delivering sufficient pleasure or reward following approach behaviors. It is no surprise that anhedonic individuals lose interest in pursuing goal-directed activities and show a marked reduction in motivated behaviors (cf. Watson, 2000). There is one more important characteristic of this type that has not been mentioned before—namely, extremely low positive affect (cf. Watson, 2000).

Anhedonia and very low positive affect are associated with hypoactivation in the same brain region (e.g., Heller, 1993b), as well as a hypoactivation of the left prefrontal area (Tomarken & Keener, 1998). The latter also appears to be associated with stable individual differences in temperament (see Watson, 2000, for a review).

Along these lines, a PET study of melancholic depression reported less activity in the left dorsolateral prefrontal cortex compared with nondepressed controls (Bench et al., 1992; cf. also Bruder, 1995). In a related vein, in anhedonic depressed subjects the left hemisphere was specifically involved in decreased processing of pleasurable experiences, indecisiveness (Hecht, 2010), and reduced attentional alertness (Schock et al., 2011).

The Mood and Anxiety Symptom Questionnaire (MASQ; Watson & Clark, 1991) is usually used to assess the Anhedonic Type of depression. The MASQ Anhedonic Depression Subscale displays good convergent validity with the Beck Depression Inventory (BDI; cf. Beck, Hammen, Hollon, Ingram, & Kendall, 1987). Thus it might be assumed that studies utilizing the BDI evaluate the Anhedonic Type of depression.

There are few studies that have addressed the Anhedonic Type of depression (evaluated on the BDI measure) in attentional information processing. With regard to executive control skills, these studies demonstrated the impaired selective attention involving a top-down process of focusing attention and inhibitory control (cf. Egeland et al., 2003; see also Withall et al., 2009, where the BDI was not utilized). Anhedonic depressed individuals showed a decrement in sustained vigilance and inability to sustain effort and were weakened on all chronometric tests (Egeland et al., 2003).

Consistent with previous findings (e.g., Gotlib & McLeod, 1997; Krasnoparova, Neubauer, & Gotlib, 1999; Westra & Kuiper, 1997) and the so-called "trait congruence hypothesis" (Bargh, Lombardi, & Higgins, 1988), researchers have explored whether depression is connected with attentional biases toward negative—and especially sad—stimuli. Generally, anhedonic depressed individuals have been found as showing a careful strategy of processing facial happiness (lower beta index and fewer false alarms toward happiness obtained in the signal detection task) and displaying inaccuracy in the detection of facial threat (Marszał-Wiśniewska & Fajkowska, 2005). The similar basic patterns have been observed in the next studies designed using the face-in-the-crowd procedure. It has been demonstrated, among other results, that depressed (compared with nondepressed) individuals were slowest in detecting happiness (Fajkowska & Marszał-Wiśniewska, 2006; for a review see Bourke, Douglas, & Porter, 2010). Taken together, these studies suggest slower or inaccurate responding to positive and negative stimulation in anhedonic depressed individuals, which we might treat as reduced attentional vigilance and impaired sustain effort in processing facial affect (despite its valence).

In summary, on the basis of both theoretical and empirical evidence, it appears that specific patterns of stimulation processing in the Anhedonic Type of depression are matched with (a) impaired attentional control over positive as well as negative material and (b) decreased left-hemisphere activity in stimulation processing.

*Balanced Type*

As mentioned before, I have conceptualized the Balanced Type of depression, but the answer to the question about specific patterns of stimulation processing in this type should be left for future research.

3.4.

## Functional complexity and specific dominant controlling functions of anxiety and depression subtypes

Previous sections addressed the role of anxiety and depression subtypes in directly modulating stimulation processing. Thus far, however, I have ignored the important question that had been posed earlier: what is the functional role of these mood subtypes in modulating patterns of stimulation processing within the SRIS? When the question about the functional aspects of traits in stimulation processing arises in the C-SAP model, it generally refers to a level of functional complexity and specific dominant controlling functions of traits in stimulation processing.

The literature reviewed earlier provided theoretical and empirical evidence that anxiety and depression are good candidates to be accorded the status of complex traits. Both are higher-ordered, multilevel traits consisting of interacting, integrated specific components. I postulate that apprehension and arousal, and valence (in)sensitivity and anhedonia in anxiety and depression (respectively), are relatively stable structural components. Importantly, the relative invariance of a presence of these components within the structure of anxiety and depression is dictated by their biological origin (cf. neurocognitive data). However, I assume that the level of intensity of these components appears to be more contextual since it is modeled by other elements of the SRIS: temperament traits, attentional processes, and environmental factors.

The spatial dimension (componental, structural) of anxiety and depression influences their temporal dimension. This implies the variety of activities or functions of anxiety and depression subtypes within the SRIS, which manifests itself when one is confronted with stimulation processing. In other ways anxiety and depression subtypes exert different control functions over stimulation, and the nature of their controlling functions is primarily determined by the dominating component in their structure.

As far as the controlling functions of traits are concerned, we know from Chapter 2 that there are traits with reactive or regulative dominant. The reactive dominant in traits relates to the reception of flowing stimulation, readiness to activity (reaction, behavior), sensitivity or vigilance to stimuli, fast avoidance of stimulation, and relation to energy expenditure (within a particular time range); the latter, in turn, is connected with reaction to stimuli or initiation of activity. The regulative dominant in traits denotes individual differences in energy expenditure within a particular range of time, to control (direct and monitor) the flowing stimulation adequately to the organism's capacities for processing stimulation. Thus I postulate that two different components of anxiety and depression have different controlling dominant. In consequence, it differentiates the functional role of particular subtypes.

Decomposing anxiety according to its controlling functions, we have the arousal component, which seems to correspond to reactive dominant. This assumption is based on findings demonstrating that arousal anxiety is associated with lower-level reactive attentional biases at the early stages of processing (vigilance) and with upper-level attentional biases (avoidance) at the later stages of processing (e.g., Fischer et al., 2010; Onnis, Dadds, & Bryant, 2011). On the other hand, the apprehension component is linked to regulative dominant. This conclusion is formulated from the data on the regulative role of chronic worrying (e.g., Laguna et al., 2004). Worrisome thoughts or apprehension are associated with impaired attentional control and avoidance to regulate the level of arousal.

As seen in Figure 3.4A, (a) the Arousal Type of anxiety (Type A < a) is associated with reactive control over stimulation; (b) the Apprehension Type of anxiety type (Type A > a) is a type having regulative control over stimulation; and finally (c) the relatively Balanced Type of anxiety (Type A ≈ a) is characterized by functional balance between reactive and regulative control over stimulation.

Fragmentation of depression in relation to its controlling functions allows for obtaining the valence (in)sensitivity component with reactive dominant; this reasoning comes from the data on nonmelancholic depression, which suggests that valence (in)sensitivity to affective stimulation represents an attentional avoiding strategy that protects depressed individuals against arousal characteristics of information (e.g., Beck et al., 1979; Watson, 2000). I argue that the anhedonia

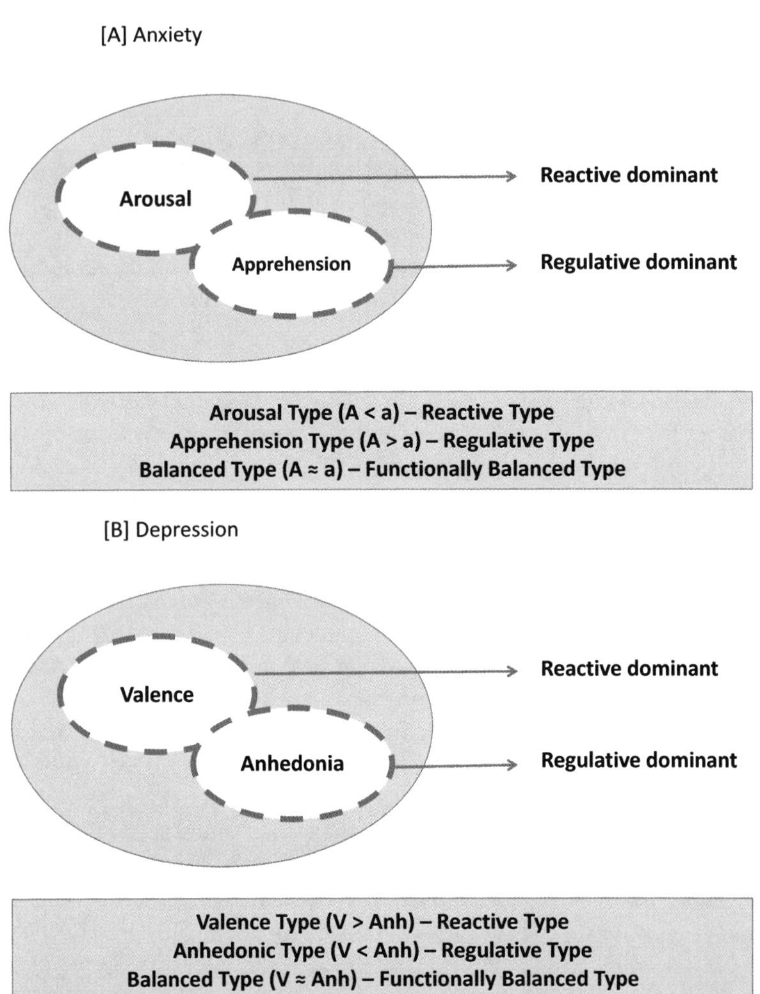



**Figure 3.4.** Reactive and regulative controlling functions in subtypes of [A] anxiety and [B] depression.

component is associated with regulative dominant; this reasoning comes from the data on melancholic depression that implies impaired attentional control (e.g., reduced sustained vigilance, ineffectiveness) over negative and positive information, which relates to motivational deficits recognized in this type of depression (e.g., Sloan et al., 2001; Watson, 2000). Accordingly, (a) the Valence Type of depression (Type V > Anh) is associated with reactive control over stimulation processing; (b) the Anhedonic Type of depression (Type V < Anh) may be defined by regulative control over stimulation processing; and (c) in the Balanced Type of depression (Type V ≈ Anh), the functional balance between two controlling tendencies—namely, reactive and regulative ones—is emphasized (see Figure 3.4B).

It is worth noting that traits with reactive and regulative dominant represent individual characteristics being associated with high or moderate dominance of biological determinacy (Derrybery & Rothbart, 1988, 1997; Rothbart, 1989a, 1989b; Rothbart & Ahadi, 1994). This suggests that the presence of elevated levels of anxiety and depression within the SRIS has rather enduring effects on patterns of stimulation processing. Obviously, these patterns should be considered in light of mutual relations between subtypes of these emotional disorders and temperament types—specifically, in light of personality coherence and incoherence, which will be discussed later in this book.

3.5.

## Toward distinctive and overlapping functions of anxiety and depression subtypes within the SRIS

The central finding in this area of study is that anxiety and depression are correlated with each other. To put it simply, people who experience significant levels of one affective disorder are also likely to report comparable amounts of the other (cf. Watson & Kendall, 1989; section 3.1). This leads us to the question "What is behind this correlation between anxiety and depression?" One possible explanation relates to poor discriminant validity of measures, which produces some correlations between these two phenomena. Logically, however, assessment problems are insufficient to explain that fact. Perhaps there are some more basic explanations for their co-occurrence. On a more elaborated level, both phenomena are associated with negative affect conditions involving substantial levels of subjective distress (e.g., Watson, 2000); stressful life events (Naragon-Gainey & Watson, 2011); and impaired cognitive processes involving (for example) negative (automatic) thoughts, a negative self-view, self-focused attention, negativistic information processing, biased attentional and memory functioning, and biased judgement and interpretation. Finally, they share a common biological/genetic diathesis (for a review Fox, 2008; Watson & Kendall, 1989).

In spite of a set of common (nonspecific) features, anxiety and depression are clearly not identical phenomena. Differences between them are best viewed through their complex, heterogeneous nature (subtypes) and the structural components related to their controlling functions. In addition, it seems to be a good approach to examine anxiety and depression concurrently on several levels. This is a promising avenue to better understand some specificity in their cognitive, affective, and behavioral content and is possible to achieve within the C-SAP.

Consistent with my earlier statement, differentiation should be improved by reducing the importance of overlapping features, and by giving greater weight to distinctive aspects of these affective phenomena. Thus, according to the theoretical analysis and findings presented above, we have two groups of anxiety and depressive disorders that are parallel in their controlling functions. Both the Arousal Type of anxiety and the Valence Type of depression represent the reactive character of control over stimulation processing within the SRIS, related to increased right-hemisphere activity (see Figure 3.5). However, they are connected with distinct patterns of behavioral responses: the Arousal Type of anxiety is associated with attentional vigilance and avoidance in threat processing, while the Valence Type of depression is associated with attentional avoidance of affect processing. Rather, the presented patterns of reaction to emotional material— differentiated in the Arousal Type and the Valence Type—are associated with maladaptive behaviors. Vulnerability to arousal anxiety may reside in maladaptive interaction between initial and subsequent information processing of threat, and this may trigger the vigilant-avoidant pattern of biases, maintaining anxiety (Onnis et al., 2011). It is likely that the attentional avoidance of aroused, loaded, emotional material in the Valence Type of depression simply exposes individuals with the Valence Type of depression to consuming an inadequate amount of resources (e.g., energetic, cognitive).

Further, the Apprehension Type of anxiety and Anhedonic Type of depression reflect regulative control over stimulation processing (cf. Figure 3.5). Again, they are associated with specific neural patterns of activity—namely, the Apprehension

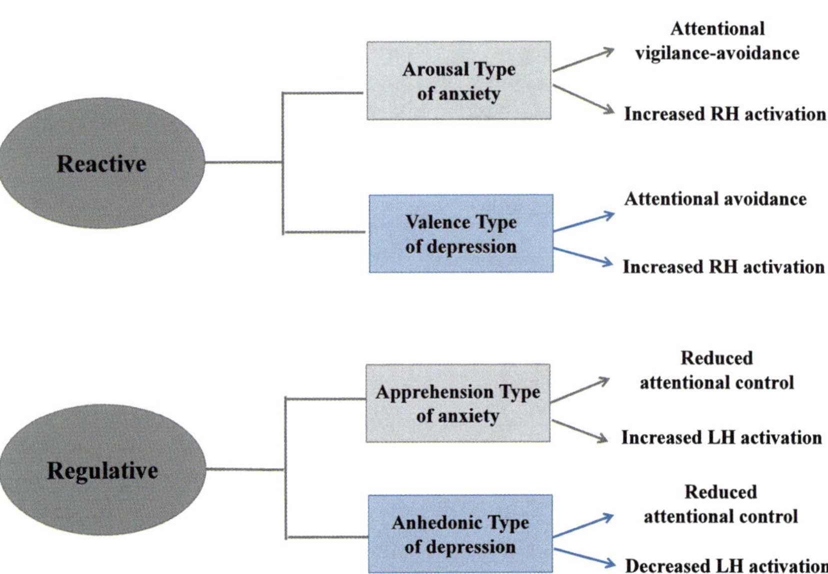


**Figure 3.5.** Common and differentiating functions of anxiety and depression within the SRIS. RH = right hemisphere; LH = left hemisphere. Because of insufficient data, the Balanced Type of both anxiety and depression was omitted from the analysis.

Type of anxiety with increased left frontal hemisphere activity, and the Anhedonic Type of depression with decreased left-hemisphere activity. In addition, apprehension anxiety represents impaired attentional control over threatening material, whereas anhedonic depression represents impaired attentional control over affective material. Both the Apprehension Type of anxiety and Anhedonic Type of depression might be viewed as having reduced levels of adaptive behaviors (Foa, Rothbaum, & Kozak, 1989), which are associated with lower levels of general activity and autonomic arousal. Speculatively, both might be seen as the evolutionary adaptive response of energy conservation (e.g., Nesse, 2000) through an inhibition/avoidance of threat processing (Apprehension Type of anxiety) or emotional material processing (Anhedonic Type of depression).

It is worth noting that reactive functions of mood traits are linked to attentional vigilance and avoidance, but that their regulative functions are connected with attentional control over stimulation processing.

### 3.6.
## Summing up

The evidence discussed here provides important data that have contributed to the development of a view of anxiety and depression as elements of the SRIS. In order to facilitate the understanding of the specific contribution of these two phenomena to stimulation processing, it was pivotal to identify their subtypes. As complex heterogeneous phenomena, anxiety (apprehension x arousal) and depression (valence [in]sensitivity x anhedonia) produce specific attentional patterns of stimulation processing. The recognition of these patterns allowed us to establish the exact controlling functions of each subtype.

The data discussed in this chapter clearly have significant implications for further theorizing on anxiety and depression subtypes. To meet this challenge, the next chapters address the indirect influences of anxiety and depression subtypes on stimulation processing. Interactions and interrelations between subtypes of mood disorders and temperament types operationalize personality coherence/incoherence. Now we know that the expectation that mood subtypes, as elements of coherent or incoherent personality structures that intensify or lessen temperament sensitivity to stimulation, is oversimplified and should be confronted with reactive or regulative controlling functions over stimulation—in particular, anxiety and depression subtypes.

# Chapter 4

## Anxiety and depression within the structure of coherent and incoherent types of personalities

4.1.

### Structures of coherent/incoherent types of personalities: Theoretical links between the four temperament types and anxiety and depression subtypes

A link between personality and mental health has been hypothesized since the time of the ancient Greeks. The doctrine of the four humors attributed to Hippocrates and Galen (cf. Strelau, 2008) is the most popular example of these early theories. Generally, this theory described four temperament types (sanguine, melancholic, phlegmatic, and choleric) and posited that they determine vulnerability to physical and mental illnesses (cf. Kotov, Gamez, Schmidt, & Watson, 2010). Personality and temperament psychology have continued to expand this tradition since the earliest days of the discipline. For example, Pavlov (1927) and his school, Eysenck (1947/1998; Eysenck & Eysenck, 1991), and Strelau (1969, 1983, 2008) continued to advocate the four-humor doctrine, which they reframed in terms of neuronal responses rather than humors (cf. Kotov et al., 2010). Interest in this topic continues to this day (e.g., Fajkowska & Eysenck, 2008; Fajkowska, Zagórska, Strelau, & Jaśkowski, 2012; Watson, 2000).

The study of the associations between temperament and affective disorders is of much interest in this book. Indeed, the research promises to improve the prognostic abilities and might help elucidate the etiology of affective disorders through the identification of shared mechanisms. Moreover, the Complex–System Approach to Personality (C-SAP) offers the tools to investigate these issues with better precision. A few developments within the C-SAP in particular have made such research possible: the formulation of personality coherence versus incoherence, with temperament determining one's need for stimulation as its basis; the classification of anxiety and depression subtypes, with specific reference to their controlling functions over stimulation; and the postulated analysis of functional intercorrelations and functional interactions among elements composing the coherent/incoherent personality types, and their associations with quality and dynamics of stimulation processing.

133

Thus my goal in the next two chapters is to extend this body of knowledge by (a) constructing theoretical links between the four temperament types and anxiety and depression subtypes, allowing for building the structures of personality coherence/ incoherence (Chapter 4), and (b) presenting some empirical evidence showing how the associations between temperament and affective traits relate to attentional stimulation processing (Chapter 5).

With reference to the goal formulated for this chapter, it is worth remembering that mechanisms of temperament are assigned a particularly critical function in coordinating between the relatively stable need for stimulation (general tendency to seek or avoid stimulation) achieved through the learning processes and other stimulation-related elements of the System of Regulation and Integration Stimulation (SRIS; here anxiety and depression). Thus the coherence between temperament capacities and anxiety/depression is understood as intraindividual consistency between temperament traits associated with one's need for stimulation and anxiety/depression, related to a self-providing dose of stimulation and adequate to one's need for stimulation determined by physiological mechanisms of temperament. By contrast, intraindividual incoherence between temperament capacities and anxiety/depression means intraindividual inconsistency between temperament traits associated with one's need for stimulation and anxiety/depression, related to a self-providing dose of stimulation and not adequate to one's need for stimulation determined by physiological mechanisms of temperament.

The question is in what way anxiety and depression are stimulation-related elements of the SRIS. One reasonable answer is that both phenomena might be described as the characteristics having reactive and regulative functions when confronted with stimulation (see Chapter 3). Reactive nature is more typical for the Arousal Type of anxiety and Valence Type of depression; it is connected with increased activity of the right hemisphere. But regulative nature seems to be more specific for the Apprehension Type of anxiety and Anhedonic Type of depression. In this case it is on account of increased left-hemisphere activity in the former and decreased left-hemisphere activity in the latter (cf. Figure 3.5). Logically, the Arousal Type of anxiety and Valence Type of depression are associated with a lower level of self-providing (more strategic) and a higher level of self-avoiding (more automatic) dose of stimulation than the Apprehension Type of anxiety and Anhedonic Type of depression. By contrast, both the Apprehension Type of anxiety and Anhedonic Type of depression might be linked to a higher level of self-providing (more strategic) and a lower level of self-avoiding (more automatic) dose of stimulation than the Arousal Type of anxiety and Valence Type of depression. However, the question is how these types relate to effectiveness of stimulation processing.

I stated that different structures of temperament also represent different controlling functions over stimulation. Thus it is assumed that the harmonious melancholic and disharmonious choleric types are more reactive (avoiding stimulation) than regulative (seeking stimulation) types of temperament, while the harmonious sanguine and disharmonious phlegmatic types seem to be more regulative (seeking stimulation) than reactive (avoiding stimulation) types of temperament (cf. Chapter 2).

In consequence, a "meeting" between a particular structure of temperament and a particular type of anxiety or depression may produce intraindividual coherence or incoherence on the basis of the compatibility or conflict between their controlling functions—in other words, between the need for stimulation determined by the structure of temperament and dose of stimulation provided by anxiety or depression. However, the SRIS has an organization that controls the input and output of stimulation, and due to adaptation any part of it can be altered by a "reorganization system," part of the inherited, primary biologically rooted structure of the organism (here temperament).

The structural level of personality coherence/incoherence should be reflected in the functional level of personality coherence/incoherence. This leads to the conclusion that personality coherence is composed of traits consistent in their controlling functions over stimulation (functional simplicity), and personality incoherence constitutes traits inconsistent in their controlling functions over stimulation (functional complexity). Theoretically, the following structures are proposed.

- Coherent types of personality based on the harmonious type of temperament: regulative Sanguine Type with high-apprehension anxiety and -anhedonic depression (both regulative types); reactive Melancholic Type with high level of arousal anxiety or valence depression (both reactive types).
- Incoherent types of personality based on the harmonious type of temperament: regulative Sanguine Type with high level of arousal anxiety or valence depression (both reactive types); reactive Melancholic Type with high level of apprehension anxiety or anhedonic depression (both regulative types).
- Coherent types of personality based on the disharmonious type of temperament: regulative Phlegmatic Type with high-apprehension anxiety and -anhedonic depression (both regulative types); reactive Choleric Type with high level of arousal anxiety or valence depression (both reactive types).
- Incoherent types of personality based on the disharmonious type of temperament: regulative Phlegmatic Type with high level of arousal anxiety or valence depression (both reactive types); reactive Choleric Type with high level of apprehension anxiety or anhedonic depression (both regulative types).

4.2.

## How optimal stimulation level binds anxiety and temperament

Much of Chapter 3 was addressed to the issue of the role of anxiety and depression subtypes within the SRIS. Using a direct modulation term, I explained how anxiety and depression subtypes might directly affect the patterns of stimulation

processing (see Figure 3.1). However, indirect influences are particularly important when anxiety or depression are analyzed as part of coherent or incoherent
types of personalities.

Generally, it is advocated that hyperarousal (i.e., an overreactive arousal system)
of the autonomic nervous system is considered to be specific to anxiety (Watson,
2000). The degree of autonomic arousal heightened by anxiety is not the same
thing as temperament arousability: the latter relates to a broader range of stimuli,
whereas the former is a more specific type of reactivity (cf. Fox, 2008). In general,
anxiety coupled with a particular temperament structure may modulate temperament reactivity to specific stimulation and employ specific somatic and cognitive
processes. This might be true for both arousal anxiety and apprehension anxiety.
In other words, the reactive Arousal Type of anxiety may intensify temperament
sensitivity or insensitivity to stimulation, which is primarily reflected in different
somatic symptoms, while the regulative Apprehension Type of anxiety may influence temperament monitoring over stimulation, which is primarily reflected in
cognitive control (see Figure 3.2).

In the context of stimulation processing, individuals differ in their need for
stimulation, but they do not differ in their general tendency to keep the optimum
level of stimulation/arousal determined by the physiological mechanisms of temperament. Within three models of temperament closely related to the concept of
arousal (cf. Pavlov's, Eysenck's, and Strelau's approaches), this optimum level of
stimulation may be achieved thanks to different aspects of individual activity. However, regardless of the specific theoretical approach, the sanguine and melancholic
temperament types enhance keeping their habitual level of stimulation in optimal scope of stimulation thanks to effective stimulation processing, whereas the
phlegmatic and choleric types of temperament contribute to retaining habitually
low or high (respectively) nonoptimal levels of stimulation because of ineffective stimulation processing (cf. Strelau, 2008). That is why the Sanguine Type
and Melancholic Type are considered to be harmonious structures of temperament, while the Phlegmatic Type and Choleric Type are seen as disharmonious (cf.
Zawadzki & Strelau, 1997; Chapter 2).

Thus, if need for stimulation reflected in the particular structure of temperament is challenged by a specific anxiety type, this may specifically affect the patterns of stimulation processing. Some studies suggest that the trait constellation in
the sanguine and phlegmatic types, indicating high stimulation-processing capacities, does not contribute etiologically to development of long-lasting trait anxiety
disorders. By contrast, the structure of traits in the Melancholic Type and Choleric
Type—indicating low stimulation-processing capacities—predispose etiologically to occurrence of trait anxiety (cf. Fajkowska & Eysenck, 2008; Strelau, 2008;
Zawadzki & Strelau, 1997). But obviously the situation is more complicated. In
light of the functional relations between focal traits composing incoherent/inco-
herent personality structures, one can expect that both types of anxiety—that is,
arousal and apprehension—might be empirically identified in all temperament

types. This is on account of the occasional or persistent environmental (situational) influences that lead to the emergence of state-like or trait-like affective disorders, respectively (e.g., Eliasz, 1981).

Taking these statements into consideration, it seems probable that we can identify an Incoherent Type of personality based on the regulative Sanguine Type (harmonious low-arousal type oriented to seeking stimulation to keep an optimal level of stimulation) and high anxiety denoting instead reactive state anxiety—which is here a synonym for the Arousal Type of anxiety—and a Coherent Type of personality based on the regulative Sanguine Type and high regulative trait anxiety, which is here a synonym for the Apprehension Type of anxiety. Also, we can identify an Incoherent Type of personality based on the regulative Phlegmatic Type (disharmonious low-arousal type with tendency not to seek stimulation to keep an optimal level of stimulation) and reactive high anxiety signifying instead state anxiety (Arousal Type of anxiety), and a Coherent Type of personality built on the regulative Phlegmatic Type and regulative high anxiety signifying instead trait anxiety (Apprehension Type of anxiety). However, when coupled with a low level of arousal or apprehension anxiety, the sanguine and phlegmatic types—which do not incline etiologically to anxiety—can be considered as coherent types of personality. In these cases the analysis of consistency/inconsistency between controlling functions over stimulation in focal types seems to be inadequate. This analysis would be adequate only for high levels of both types of anxiety, revealing their dominant functions of controlling stimulation.

In addition, we can also distinguish an Incoherent Type of personality built on the reactive Melancholic Type (harmonious high-arousal type oriented to avoiding stimulation to keep optimal level of stimulation) and regulative high anxiety implying trait anxiety (Apprehension Type of anxiety), and a Coherent Type of personality built on the reactive Melancholic Type and reactive high anxiety implying state anxiety (Arousal Type of anxiety).

Then we can differentiate an Incoherent Type of personality composed of the reactive Choleric Type (disharmonious high-arousal type without tendency to avoiding stimulation to keep optimal level of stimulation) and regulative high trait anxiety (Apprehension Type of anxiety), and a Coherent Type of personality composed of the reactive Choleric Type and reactive high state anxiety (Arousal Type of anxiety). In addition, when coupled with a low level of arousal anxiety (indicating lack of somatic tension and physiological hyperarousal in the presence of emotional and social stimulation), the melancholic and choleric types—which do incline etiologically to anxiety—can be considered as incoherent types of personality; but when they are matched to a low level of apprehension anxiety (indicating no reduction in autonomic reactivity to emotional and social stimulation), they can seen as coherent types of personality. Here too the examination of consistency/inconsistency between controlling functions over stimulation in focal types seems to be insufficient.

Functional simplicity (coherence) or complexity (incoherence) probably confronts the tendency to maintain an optimal level of arousal determined by a particular temperament type.

Obviously, the conceptual issues stated above involved in building structures of coherent and incoherent personalities must be supported with empirical data from more detailed investigations, with correlational and distributional analysis that demonstrate the distribution of a specific anxiety type in a particular temperament type defined within Pavlovian, Eysenckian, and Strelauvian theories. Each of these three arousal-related theories of temperament indicates different areas of an organism's activity in maintaining the optimal level of arousal (stimulation). Thus sustaining the optimal level of arousal depends on (a) nervous system control (Pavlov); (b) content (emotional and social) characteristics of activity (Eysenck); and (c) formal (energetic and temporal) characteristics of activity (Strelau). It is interesting how this differentiation relates to the type of stimulation being processed and to maintaining/impairing a temperamentally determined optimal level of arousal, when a particular type of anxiety/depression is included in the analysis.

### 4.2.1. Coherent/incoherent personality structures composed of strength of excitation, strength of inhibition, mobility, balance, and subtypes of anxiety

As identified by Pavlov, three fundamental properties (strength, balance, mobility) of two processes of central nervous system (excitation, inhibition) determine individual differences in temperament and are considered here as the control processes of the nervous system over stimulation. The ability to withstand intense and persistent stimulation without exhibiting protective inhibition (strength of excitation; SE), the ability to evoke and preserve a state of conditioned inhibition (strength of inhibition; SI), and the response capabilities of the central nervous system to continuous alterations in the environment (mobility; MO) seem to be highly desirable for the control of stimulation or behavior (cf. Simonov & Ershov, 1991; Strelau & Zawadzki, 1998).

Strelau, Angleitner, and Newberry (1999) present a detailed description of relations among Pavlovian temperament traits. They also employed the Pavlovian Temperament Survey (PTS). It is noteworthy that according to the results obtained on American, German, and Polish samples, all traits are positively correlated; however, the moderate correlation describes relations between SE and MO, but much lower correlations are reported for SE and SI, and SI and MO. These findings indicate that as measured by Strelau et al.'s questionnaire, Pavlovian traits are less independent than expected.

The findings on the relationship between anxiety and Pavlovian properties of the nervous system are ambiguous. In line with Pavlov's predictions, Strelau (1983) reported consistent negative correlations between anxiety measured by the State–Trait Anxiety Inventory (STAI; Spielberger, 1983) and SE. In addition, anxiety was also found as negatively related to SI, but to a much lesser extent, and only a few studies demonstrated a negative association with MO (e.g., Daum, Hehl, & Schugens, 1988; Strelau et al., 1999). This evidence suggests that anxiety may be identified in melancholics (low SE, low SI), cholerics (low or moderate SI), and phlegmatics (low MO). But these correlational data make it difficult to draw any conclusions for sanguines in this respect. To some extent the distributional data solve this problem.

To present the general trends of typical anxiety subtypes in the four temperament types built of Pavlovian traits SE, SI, and MO (PTS; Strelau & Zawadzki, 1998), a distributional analysis of anxiety as a state and anxiety as a trait (STAI; Spielberger, 1983; Wrześniewski & Sosnowski, 1996) was conducted ($N = 138$, 105 females, $M = 25.5$ years, $SD = 8.03$).

It appeared that distributions of state (arousal) anxiety and trait (apprehension) anxiety in sanguines ($n = 40$) are normal distributions ($p > 0.05$, $p > 0.05$,[1] respectively).

The distributions of state (arousal) anxiety and trait (apprehension) anxiety in melancholics ($n = 60$) are significantly different from a normal distribution ($p < 0.001$, skewness: 0.89, confidence interval from –0.43 to 0.43, kurtosis: –0.16, confidence interval from –0.83 to 0.83; $p < 0.05$, skewness: –0.27, confidence interval from –0.43 to 0.43, kurtosis: –1.03, confidence interval from –0.83 to 0.83). The findings suggest that low-arousal anxiety is more frequent in melancholics than high-arousal anxiety (positively skewed data). By contrast, high-trait (apprehension) anxiety scores for melancholics indicate that high-trait anxiety is more frequent in melancholics than low-trait anxiety (negatively skewed data).

For phlegmatics ($n = 19$) the state (arousal) anxiety and trait (apprehension) anxiety distributions are not normal ($p < 0.001$, skewness: 0.75, confidence interval from –0.72 to 0.72, kurtosis: –1.71, confidence interval from –1.40 to 1.40; $p < 0.001$, skewness: –0.78, confidence interval from –0.72 to 0.72, kurtosis: –1.71, confidence interval from –1.40 to 1.40, respectively). The findings imply more frequent low than high state anxiety and more frequent high than low trait anxiety in phlegmatics.

Finally, in cholerics ($n = 19$) one can more regularly observe both low-arousal anxiety and low-apprehension anxiety than high degrees of these two dimensions (not normal distributions, $p < 0.001$, skewness value: 0.85, confidence interval from –0.72 to 0.72, kurtosis: –1.71, confidence interval from –1.40 to 1.40; $p < 0.05$, skewness: 0.61, confidence interval from –0.72 to 0.72, kurtosis: –1.71, confidence interval from –1.40 to 1.40).

This distributional information can account for the existence of low and high results on state and trait anxiety in the four temperament types. However, all distributional data presented in this book are based on a small number of participants and the conclusions drawn from them should be treated cautiously—even though, together with correlational data, they help in the design of the coherent/incoherent types of personalities based on the Pavlovian properties of the nervous system

---

[1] Shapiro–Wilk test.

and subtypes of anxiety. Table 4.1 presents hypothetical constellations of coherent (*CPT*) and incoherent (*INPT*) types of personalities.

As we know from Chapter 2, the effectiveness of stimulation processing depends on the constellation between SE (signifying one's need for stimulation) and MO (signifying one's activity). According to Table 4.1, the harmonious types of temperament—sanguine and melancholic—are built on the agreement between levels of SE and MO (however, in the case of melancholics, mobility and balance are viewed as less important in the definition of this type). Thus it might be assumed that compatibility between a high level of SE (high need for stimulation) and high level of MO (high activity) in sanguines and a low level of SE (low need for stimulation) and low level of MO (low level of activity) in melancholics promotes effective control of the nervous system over stimulation and maintains the optimal level of arousal in these types. The regulative harmonious sanguine temperament, indicating a strong, mobile, and balanced type of nervous system coupled with (1) lack of arousal anxiety, (2) lack of apprehension anxiety, or (3) regulative high-apprehension anxiety reflects a Coherent Type of personality, while coupled with (4) reactive high-arousal anxiety denotes an Incoherent Type of personality. The reactive harmonious melancholic temperament, representing a weak type of nervous system with (5) reactive high-arousal anxiety or (6) low-apprehension anxiety results in a Coherent Type of personality, but accompanied by (7) regulative high-apprehension anxiety or (8) lack of arousal anxiety marks an incoherent personality structure.

In analyzing the relation among Pavlovian properties of the nervous system, one can also identify disharmonious types of temperament—phlegmatic and choleric. The key feature of these types is a conflict between levels of SE and MO: high level of SE (high need for stimulation) and low level of MO (low activity) in phlegmatics, and high SE (high level of stimulation, higher than low or moderate SI, which results in unbalance) and high MO (high activity) in cholerics (MO is not mentioned in the table as having less significance in the structure of this type of temperament than unbalance between SE and SI). Hence both the phlegmatic and choleric types of temperament are connected with ineffective control of the nervous system over stimulation and with nonoptimal level of arousal. The regulative disharmonious phlegmatic temperament, designating a strong, slow, and balanced type of nervous system, coupled with (9) lack of arousal anxiety or (10) lack of apprehension anxiety, or (11) regulative high-apprehension anxiety represents intraindividual coherence, while married with (12) reactive high-arousal anxiety results in intraindividual incoherence. The reactive disharmonious choleric temperament, signifying a strong, unbalanced type of nervous system, joined with (13) reactive high-arousal anxiety or (14) low-apprehension anxiety produces a Coherent Type of personality, but combined with (15) regulative high-apprehension anxiety or (16) lack of arousal anxiety results in an incoherent personality structure (see Table 4.1).

**Table 4.1.** Coherent and incoherent types of personalities: Strength of excitation, strength of inhibition, mobility, balance, and anxiety

**Coherent versus incoherent types of personalities based on harmonious structures of temperament**

**(1)** $CPT_{\textit{Sanguine: strong, mobile, balanced type of NS}}^{\textit{low-arousal anxiety}}$
Low-arousal anxiety + high SE, high SI, high MO, and BA between SE:SI (regulative type)

**(5)** $CPT_{\textit{Melancholic: weak type of NS}}^{\textit{high-arousal anxiety}}$
High-arousal anxiety (reactive type) + low SE and low SI (reactive type)

**(2)** $CPT_{\textit{Sanguine: strong, mobile, balanced type of NS}}^{\textit{low-apprehension anxiety}}$
Low-apprehension anxiety + high SE, high SI, high MO, and BA between SE:SI (regulative type)

**(6)** $CPT_{\textit{Melancholic: weak type of NS}}^{\textit{low-apprehension anxiety}}$
Low-apprehension anxiety + low SE and low SI (reactive type)

**(3)** $CPT_{\textit{Sanguine: strong, mobile, balanced type of NS}}^{\textit{high-apprehension anxiety}}$
High-apprehension anxiety (regulative type) + high SE, high SI, high MO, and BA between SE:SI (regulative type)

**(7)** $INPT_{\textit{Melancholic: weak type of NS}}^{\textit{high-apprehension anxiety}}$
High-apprehension anxiety (regulative type) + low SE and low SI (reactive type)

**(4)** $INPT_{\textit{Sanguine: strong, mobile, balanced type of NS}}^{\textit{high-arousal anxiety}}$
High-arousal anxiety (reactive type) + high SE, high SI, high MO, and BA between SE:SI (regulative type)

**(8)** $INPT_{\textit{Melancholic: weak type of NS}}^{\textit{low-arousal anxiety}}$
Low-arousal anxiety + low SE and low SI (reactive type)

**Coherent versus incoherent types of personalities based on disharmonious structures of temperament**

**(9)** $CPT_{\textit{Phlegmatic: strong, slow, balanced type of NS}}^{\textit{low-arousal anxiety}}$
Low-arousal anxiety + high SE, high SI, low MO, BA between SE:SI (regulative type)

**(13)** $CPT_{\textit{Choleric: strong, unbalanced type of NS}}^{\textit{high-arousal anxiety}}$
High-arousal anxiety (reactive type) + high SE, moderate or low SI, Unbalance: SE > SI (reactive type)

**(10)** $CPT_{\textit{Phlegmatic: strong, slow, balanced type of NS}}^{\textit{low-apprehension anxiety}}$
Low-apprehension anxiety + high SE, high SI, low MO, and BA between SE:SI (regulative type)

**(14)** $CPT_{\textit{Choleric: strong, unbalanced type of NS}}^{\textit{low-apprehension anxiety}}$
Low-apprehension anxiety + high SE, moderate or low SI, Unbalance: SE > SI (reactive type)

**(11)** $CPT_{\textit{Phlegmatic: strong, slow, balanced type of NS}}^{\textit{high-apprehension anxiety}}$
High-apprehension anxiety (regulative type) + high SE, high SI, low MO, and BA between SE:SI (regulative type)

**(15)** $INPT_{\textit{Choleric: strong, unbalanced type of NS}}^{\textit{high-apprehension anxiety}}$
High-apprehension anxiety (regulative type) + high SE, moderate or low SI, Unbalance: SE > SI (reactive type)

**(12)** $INPT_{\textit{Phlegmatic: strong, slow, balanced type of NS}}^{\textit{high-arousal anxiety}}$
High-arousal anxiety (reactive type) + high SE, high SI, low MO, and BA between SE:SI (regulative type)

**(16)** $INPT_{\textit{Choleric: strong, unbalanced type of NS}}^{\textit{low-arousal anxiety}}$
Low-arousal anxiety + high SE, moderate or low SI, Unbalance: SE > SI (reactive type)

*Note.* NS = nervous system; SE = strength of excitation; SI = strength of inhibition; MO = mobility; BA = balance.

Here I would like to present the attempts of "translating" the coherent and incoherent types of personalities based on anxiety and the Pavlovian properties of nervous system into Eysenckian and Strelauvian terms. The well-established correlation coefficients among these traits provide a good basis for this "translation." It is also warranted by the fact that all these approaches are based on the arousal concept and all postulate the similarities between their basic temperament dimensions and the Hippocrates–Galen typology (cf. Chapter 2). However, they differ in the aspect of behaviors through which the optimal level of arousal is generated, which seems to be most interesting from a theoretical point of view. More precisely, the variations in areas of an organism's activity in maintaining the optimal level of stimulation identified across these three theories may lead to differentiation in the functional significance of the temperament traits/types postulated by these theories.

With the use of questionnaires, results obtained showed that extraversion positively correlates with SE and MO, while neuroticism negatively correlates with SE, SI, and MO (cf. Strelau et al., 1999; see also Brzozowski & Drwal, 1995; Daum et al., 1988; Strelau & Zawadzki, 1998; Zawadzki & Strelau, 2010). It was found that strength of excitation relates positively to EN, BR, and AC and negatively to PE and ER; similary, mobility is positively associated with BR, EN, and AC and negatively associated with PE and ER, but strength of inhibition positively correlates only with EN (cf. Strelau et al., 1999). These results are confirmed by findings on the relation between Eysenckian dimensions and traits distinguised by Strelau. Hence extraversion positively relates to AC, BR, and EN and negatively to ER and PE, while neuroticism is highly and positively correlated with ER and PE and negatively with EN and BR (cf. Zawadzki & Strelau, 1997).

### *4.2.2. Coherent/incoherent personality structures composed of extraversion, neuroticism, and subtypes of anxiety*

Turning to relations among dimensions in the Eysenckian model, studies showed that the association between extraversion and neuroticism measured by the Eysenck Personality Questionnaire–Revised (EPQ-R) is negative (Brzozowski & Drwal, 1995; Eysenck & Eysenck, 1994; data collected by Fajkowska, Zagórska, & Jaśkowski, 2008–2011).

Neuroticism and extraversion account for most of the variance in affective disorders, which is evidenced by cross-sectional and longitudinal studies (cf. Levenson, Aldwin, Bossé, & Spiro, 1988; Watson, 2000). For example, neurotic introverts may report symptoms of anxiety and depression, whereas neurotic extraverts may exhibit hostility (Claridge, 1985). Recent studies, however, have shown very high correlations among various measures of psychological symptoms, personality characteristics of neuroticism, and negative affect, suggesting the presence of an underlying general trait termed negative affectivity (e.g., Kotov et al., 2010; Watson, 2000). Neuroticism measured by Eysenck's questionnaire correlates very highly with trait measures of anxiety (Levenson et al., 1988).

The objective of the study by Mehrabian and O'Reilly (1980), which was designed within an emotion-based approach to personality and social psychological phenomena, was to categorize personality measures with reference to three basic dimensions of temperament—pleasure-displeasure, arousal-nonarousal, and dominance-submissiveness. The grouping procedure showed that neuroticism (Eysenck & Eysenck, 1968) and anxiety (Spielberger, Gorsuch, & Lushene, 1970) related to the same cluster of traits and revealed a similar constellation of temperament attributes: high arousability, displeasure, and submissiveness. Additionally, both neuroticism and anxiety are connected with harm avoidance (lack of enjoyment connected with exciting activities, especially if danger is involved) and defensiveness (suspicion that people mean harm or general antagonism). Interestingly, social phobia and agoraphobia correlate negatively with extraversion (e.g., Ball, 2005; Kotov et al., 2010).

The review of data from other sources (Brzozowski & Drwal, 1995; Wrześniewski & Sosnowski, 1996; data collected by Fajkowska, Zagórska, & Jaśkowski, 2008–2011) showed relatively similar correlations for trait and state anxiety (STAI; Spielberger, 1983; Wrześniewski & Sosnowski, 1996) and extraversion and neuroticism dimensions (EPQ-R; Brzozowski & Drwal, 1995; Eysenck & Eysenck, 1994). A moderate negative correlation with extraversion and a moderate and high positive correlation with neuroticism is usually obtained for both state and trait anxiety. Apparently, the three temperament types are connected with an increased level of (state and trait) anxiety: melancholics (low extraversion, high neuroticism), cholerics (high neuroticism), and phlegmatics (low extraversion). The occurrence of both types of anxiety in sanguines is more visible but with distributional rather than correlational data.

The frequency distribution of state and trait anxiety (STAI; Spielberger, 1983; Wrześniewski & Sosnowski, 1996) in the four temperament types (EPQ-R; Brzozowski & Drwal, 1995; Eysenck & Eysenck, 1994) was analyzed on a total of 258 individuals (208 females, $M = 25.14$ years, $SD = 7.07$).

The lower scores on state anxiety characterize most sanguines ($n = 138$); the distribution of state (arousal) anxiety is significantly different from a normal distribution ($p < 0.001$, skewness: 1.09, confidence interval from −0.21 to 0.21, kurtosis: 2.42, confidence interval from −0.41 to 0.41). By contrast, the distribution of trait (apprehension) anxiety seems to be normal ($p > 0.05$).

The state (arousal) anxiety scores for melancholics ($n = 34$) indicate that their distribution is not normal ($p < 0.01$) and denotes that low-arousal anxiety is less frequent than high-arousal anxiety in melancholics (skewness: 0.88, confidence interval from −0.40 to 0.40, kurtosis: 0.69, confidence interval from −0.79 to

0.79). But the trait (apprehension) anxiety scores for melancholics indicate normal distribution ($p > 0.05$).

For phlegmatics ($n = 44$) the state (arousal) anxiety distribution is not normal ($p < 0.001$) and implies higher frequency of lower results on state anxiety in this temperament type (skewness: 1.11, confidence interval from –0.35 to 0.35, kurtosis: 1.41, confidence interval from –0.70 to 0.70). The trait (apprehension) anxiety distribution in phlegmatics seems to be normal ($p > 0.05$).

The state (arousal) anxiety distribution in cholerics ($n = 42$) is normal ($p > 0.05$). But the distribution of trait (apprehension) anxiety in cholerics is significantly different from a normal distribution ($p < 0.001$) and signifies that lower scores on trait anxiety are more frequent in cholerics than higher ones (skewness: 0.71, confidence interval from –0.36 to –0.36, kurtosis: –0.14, confidence interval from –0.72 to 0.72).

These results suggest that low and high levels of arousal and apprehension anxiety may be observed in the four temperament types. Thus the correlational analysis and the data on distribution of state and trait anxiety among the four temperament types, coupled with the previously pronounced theoretical predictions, allow for constructing the constellations of coherent and incoherent types of personalities, composed of anxiety subtypes and temperament properties in Eysenckian theory (see Table 4.2).

It might be claimed that the Eysenckian structure of temperament comprises the traits that reflect the emotional underpinnings of behavior (neuroticism-emotional stability) and express the social aspects of behavior (extraversion-introversion). This suggests that optimum stimulation may be achieved through the emotional and interpersonal aspects of functioning.

As we know, effective stimulation processing is connected with harmonious types of temperament, while ineffective stimulation processing is associated with disharmonious ones. According to Eysenckian theory, the negative relation between extraversion and neurosticism indicates the harmonious type of temperament (cf. Strelau, 1998). For example, there is an agreement between high extraversion (seeking stimulation or arousal in social exchanges) and low neuroticism (low emotional excitability, low anxiety, and low tension). In other words, low neuroticism does promote the approach tendencies toward stimulation expressed by high extraversion, which encourages keeping optimal levels of stimulation (see Sanguine Type, Table 4.2).

The regulative harmonious sanguine temperament, indicating emotional stability and extraversion boosted by low anxiety, signifying lack of (1) arousal and (2) apprehension anxiety or (3) regulative high-apprehension anxiety, results in a Coherent Type of personality, but combines with (4) reactive high-arousal anxiety resulting in an incoherent personality structure. In addition, there is also consensus between low extraversion—avoiding stimulation or arousal potentially emerging from social interactions—and high neuroticism (high emotional excitability, high anxiety, and high tension). In sum, high neuroticism does promote the withdrawal

**Table 4.2.** Coherent and incoherent types of personalities: Extraversion, neuroticism, and anxiety

### Coherent versus incoherent types of personalities based on harmonious structures of temperament

**(1)** $CPT_{Sanguine:\ emotionally\ stable\ extravert}^{low\text{-}arousal\ anxiety}$
Low-arousal anxiety + high E and low N (regulative type)
*Repressors?*

**(5)** $CPT_{Melancholic:\ emotionally\ unstable\ introvert}^{high\text{-}arousal\ anxiety}$
High-arousal anxiety (reactive type) + low E and high N (reactive type)

**(2)** $CPT_{Sanguine:\ emotionally\ stable\ extravert}^{low\text{-}apprehension\ anxiety}$
Low-apprehension anxiety + high E and low N (regulative type)
*Repressors?*

**(6)** $CPT_{Melancholic:\ emotionally\ unstable\ introvert}^{low\text{-}apprehension\ anxiety}$
Low-apprehension anxiety + low E and high N (reactive type)

**(3)** $CPT_{Sanguine:\ emotionally\ stable\ extravert}^{high\text{-}apprehension\ anxiety}$
High-apprehension anxiety (regulative type) + high E and low N (regulative type)

**(7)** $INPT_{Melancholic:\ emotionally\ unstable\ introvert}^{high\text{-}apprehension\ anxiety}$
High-apprehension anxiety (regulative type) + low E and high N (reactive type)

**(4)** $INPT_{Sanguine:\ emotionally\ stable\ extravert}^{high\text{-}arousal\ anxiety}$
High-arousal anxiety (reactive type) + high E and low N (regulative type)

**(8)** $INPT_{Melancholic:\ emotionally\ unstable\ introvert}^{low\text{-}arousal\ anxiety}$
Low-arousal anxiety + low E and high N (reactive type)
*Repressors?*

### Coherent versus incoherent types of personalities based on disharmonious structures of temperament

**(9)** $CPT_{Phlegmatic:\ emotionally\ stable\ introvert}^{low\text{-}arousal\ anxiety}$
Low-arousal anxiety + low E and low N (regulative type)
*Repressors?*

**(13)** $CPT_{Choleric:\ emotionally\ unstable\ extravert}^{high\text{-}arousal\ anxiety}$
High-arousal anxiety (reactive type) + high E and high N (reactive type)

**(10)** $CPT_{Phlegmatic:\ emotionally\ stable\ introvert}^{low\text{-}apprehension\ anxiety}$
Low-apprehension anxiety + low E and low N (regulative type)
*Repressors?*

**(14)** $CPT_{Choleric:\ emotionally\ unstable\ extravert}^{low\text{-}apprehension\ anxiety}$
Low-apprehension anxiety + high E and high N (reactive type)

**(11)** $CPT_{Phlegmatic:\ emotionally\ stable\ introvert}^{high\text{-}apprehension\ anxiety}$
High-apprehension anxiety (regulative type) + low E and low N (regulative type)

**(15)** $INPT_{Choleric:\ emotionally\ unstable\ extravert}^{high\text{-}apprehension\ anxiety}$
High-apprehension anxiety (regulative type) + high E and high N (reactive type)

**(12)** $INPT_{Phlegmatic:\ emotionally\ stable\ introvert}^{high\text{-}arousal\ anxiety}$
High-arousal anxiety (reactive type) + low E and low N (regulative type)

**(16)** $INPT_{Choleric:\ emotionally\ unstable\ extravert}^{low\text{-}arousal\ anxiety}$
Low-arousal anxiety + high E and high N (reactive type)
*Repressors?*

*Note.* E = extraversion; N = neuroticism.

tendencies toward stimulation expressed by low extraversion, which in turn allows for keeping an optimum level of arousal (see Melancholic Type, Table 4.2). Thus personality structure based on the reactive harmonious melancholic temperament, indicating emotional instability and introversion and (5) reactive high-arousal anxiety or (6) low-apprehension anxiety, reflects a coherent personality structure, but associated with (7) regulative high-apprehension anxiety or (8) lack of arousal anxiety denotes incoherent types of personality.

By contrast, a positive relation between extraversion and neuroticism reflects the disharmonious type of temperament and ineffective stimulation processing (cf. Strelau, 1998; Zawadzki & Strelau, 1997). For example, the arrangement low extraversion (avoiding stimulation or arousal in social exchanges) and low neuroticism (low emotional excitability, low anxiety, and low tension) does not allow for an optimal level of arousal. In other words, low extraversion and low neuroticism promote a nonoptimal level of arousal in the Phlegmatic Type (see Table 4.2). The regulative disharmonious phlegmatic temperament, indicating emotional stability and introversion occurring with lack of (9) arousal and (10) apprehension anxiety, or (11) regulative high-apprehension anxiety, characterizes a coherent structure of personality, but when combined with (12) reactive high-arousal anxiety results in an Incoherent Type of personality.

Moreover, high extraversion—seeking stimulation or arousal potentially emerging from social interactions—and high neuroticism (high emotional excitability, high anxiety, and high tension) maintain a nonoptimal level of stimulation in the Choleric Type (see Table 4.2). Thus the reactive disharmonious choleric temperament, indicating emotional instability and extraversion linked to (13) reactive high-arousal anxiety or (14) low-apprehension anxiety, indicates a coherent personality type, but associated with (15) regulative high-apprehension anxiety or (16) lack of arousal anxiety characterizes incoherent personality structures.

One more point deserves a brief explanation. I postulated that in Eysenckian theory the social aspect of functioning is one of the two the most important aspects involved in achieving the optimum of arousal (stimulation). This is a good reason to consider repressiveness in anxious people (cf. Asendorpf & Scherer, 1983; Weinberger, Schwartz, & Davidson, 1979). A key characteristic of repressors is dissociation between self-reports indicative of low anxiety and responses across other different systems (e.g., behavioral, physiological) that point to high anxiety. The repressiveness (repressive coping composed of low anxiety and high defensiveness) in anxious individuals corresponds to social threat.

Decades of research has shown that repressive coping styles may serve a protective function (see Coifman, Bonanno, Ray, & Gross, 2007, for a review; Derakshan, Eysenck, & Myers, 2007; Fox, 2008) and specifically influence stimulation processing (e.g., Fajkowska & Eysenck, 2008). To illustrate, a series of studies has shown that repressive coping is associated with an automatic tendency to avoid threatening stimulation (e.g., Derakshan, Myers, Hansen, & O'Leary, 2004; Myers,

Vetere, & Derakshan, 2004). As Table 4.2 shows, low anxiety indicating repressive coping (signifying the Balanced Type; see Chapter 3) or truly low anxiety are both identified in coherent sanguine and phlegmatic types, and incoherent melancholic and choleric types. With reference to the efficiency of controlling stimulation, a repressive style of coping may operate differently than true anxiety as a part of a coherent or incoherent personality type. Some of these issues are empirically validated and demonstrated in the next sections.

### 4.2.3. Coherent/incoherent personality structures composed of endurance, emotional reactivity, activity, sensory sensitivity, perseveration, briskness, and subtypes of anxiety

The relationships regarding energetic and temporal traits postulated by the Regulative Theory of Temperament (RTT) were documented by Zawadzki and Strelau (1997). Thus, according to these data, emotional reactivity positively correlates with perseveration and negatively with briskness, activity, and endurance; activity negatively relates to emotional reactivity and positively to endurance; endurance is positively associated with briskness and activity and negatively with perseveration and emotional reactivity; and sensory sensitivity is positively correlated with briskness. Regarding temporal traits, briskness is associated positively with endurance and sensory sensitivity and negatively with perseveration and emotional reactivity, while perseveration relates positively to emotional reactivity and negatively to briskness and endurance.

It was demonstrated within the Regulative Theory of Temperament that anxiety, understood as a trait (Spielberger, 1983), is positively correlated with ER and PE and is negatively associated with BR (Zawadzki & Strelau, 1997). In addition, Zawadzki and Strelau (1997) identified a factor, which they label emotionality/endurance, as the most appropriate since it incorporated emotional reactivity and perseveration (Formal Characteristics of Behavior–Temperament Inventory), neuroticism (EPQ-R and NEO Five-Factor Inventory), distress, anger, fear (Emotionality–Accessibility–Sociability Temperament Survey), and the approach-withrawal dimension (Revised Dimensions of Temperament Survey). The rationale behind the results obtained might be that the mechanisms of activation (Gray, 1964; Strelau, 1998), including anxiety, are what hold these constructs of affectivity together (cf. Strelau, 2008, 2009a, 2009b).

The data from my and my colleagues' studies (e.g., Fajkowska & Krejtz, 2007; data collected by Fajkowska, Zagórska, & Jaśkowski, 2008–2011) reveal relatively similar correlations for trait and state anxiety (STAI; Spielberger, 1983; Wrześniewski & Sosnowski, 1996) and RTT temperament traits (FCB-TI; Zawadzki & Strelau, 1997). Thus trait anxiety negatively correlates with AC, BR, EN, and SS and positively with ER and PE. Similarly, state anxiety is negatively associated with AC, BR, and EN and positively with ER and PE.

Thus the correlational data gathered revealed once again that elevated state and trait anxiety might be identified in melancholics (high ER, high PE, low EN, AC, BR, SS), cholerics (high ER, low EN, moderate or high PE, BR, SS), and phlegmatics (low AC, moderate or low PE, BR, SS). However, the issue is more complicated in the case of sanguines. Among other information, distributional analysis provides useful data on how state and trait anxiety occur in this type of temperament.

A total of 260 subjects (210 females, $M = 25.15$ years, $SD = 7.08$) completed the STAI (Spielberger, 1983; Wrześniewski & Sosnowski, 1996) and FCB-TI (Zawadzki & Strelau, 1997) to obtain a precise picture of the distribution of state and trait anxiety in the four temperament types defined within the RTT. Thus the distributions of state (arousal) anxiety in sanguines ($n = 62$) are significantly different from a normal distribution ($p < 0.01$), and lower scores on state anxiety—rather than higher ones—characterize most sanguines (skewness: 0.93, confidence interval from –0.44 to 0.44, kurtosis: 0.13, confidence interval from –0.85 to 0.85). The trait (apprehension) anxiety scores for sanguines indicate that their distribution is normal ($p > 0.05$).

The state (arousal) anxiety and trait (apprehension) anxiety scores for melancholics ($n = 70$) indicate that their distributions are not normal ($p < 0.01$, $p < 0.001$, respectively). Evidence suggests that most melancholics are characterized by lower—rather than higher—scores on state and trait anxiety (skewness: 0.86, confidence interval from –0.41 to 0.40, kurtosis: 0.03, confidence interval from –0.81 to 0.81; skewness: 0.67, confidence interval from –0.41 to 0.40, kurtosis: 1.17, confidence interval from –0.81 to 0.80, respectively).

For phlegmatics ($n = 58$) the state (arousal) anxiety distribution is normal ($p > 0.05$) but the trait (apprehension) anxiety distribution seems to be not normal ($p < 0.05$). Data suggest that most phlegmatics are high in trait anxiety (skewness: –0.63, confidence interval from –0.46 to 0.46, kurtosis: –0.45, confidence interval from –0.89 to 0.89).

The state (arousal) anxiety distribution in cholerics ($n = 70$) is normal ($p > 0.05$). The distribution of trait (apprehension) anxiety in cholerics is significantly different from a normal distribution ($p < 0.001$) and denotes that among cholerics lower scores on trait anxiety are more frequent than higher scores (skewness: 1.05, confidence interval from –0.41 to 0.41, kurtosis: 0.51, confidence interval from –0.81 to 0.81).

In conclusion, both low and high arousal and apprehension anxiety can be observed in the four temperaments. Table 4.3 presents suggested coherent and incoherent types of personalities constructed on the anxiety subtypes and temperament types postulated by Strelau in his Regulative Theory of Temperament. As in the case of previous propositions, this one also emerged from the correlational and distributional data and theoretical predictions.

Biological mechanisms of emotional reactivity and activity with the limbic system and the autonomic nervous system (ANS), and cortical structures and brainstem reticular formation, respectively, are closely associated with one's level of stimulation (Stralau, 2008). Suffice it to say that depending on the configuration of energetic traits, stimulation regulation may have different levels of effectiveness. For example, if high stimulation-processing capacities (high EN and low ER) are accompanied by high AC, we have effective stimulation regulation. But if stimulus-processing potential is low (low EN and high ER) and AC is high, stimulation processing will not be effective (Strelau, 2008; Zawadzki & Strelau, 1997). However, as indicated by Zawadzki and Strelau (1997), temporal traits also contribute to the process of stimulation processing: they can either increase or decrease stimulation input (the main function of BR) or discharge level of arousal to a lesser or greater extent (the main function of PE).

Effective stimulation regulation reflects the fitness between the amount of the flowing stimulation (e.g., through AC) and individual stimulation-processing capacities (EN, ER), which affect the formulation of harmonious (i.e., sanguine and melancholic) types of temperaments (Table 4.3). Hence both types of individuals—with high and low stimulation-processing capacities (SPC; sanguine and melancholic, respectively)—might be distinguished within the harmonious structures. However, different ways of effective stimulation regulation and maintaining the optimal level of stimulation may be identified in low-SPC and high-SPC individuals—that is, avoiding (because of low EN and high ER) or seeking (because of high EN and low ER) stimulation, respectively (cf. Zawadzki & Strelau, 1997). Thus the regulative harmonious sanguine temperament, indicating high stimulation-processing capacities accompanied by low anxiety signifying lack of (1) arousal and (2) apprehension anxiety or (3) regulative high-apprehension anxiety, results in coherent types of personality, but boosted by (4) reactive high-arousal anxiety characterizes an incoherent structure of personality. If the reactive harmonious melancholic temperament, indicating low stimulation-processing capacities, co-occurs with (5) reactive high-arousal anxiety or (6) low-apprehension anxiety, we have a coherent personality system; but when it appears with (7) regulative high-apprehension anxiety or (8) lack of arousal anxiety, we observe incoherent structures of personalities.

Ineffective stimulation regulation is associated with the quantity of stimulation, being beyond the optimal level of stimulation. Relations among temperament traits change commensurately with the primary functions of these traits, which result in disharmonious types of temperament. For example, low (nonoptimal) level of stimulation in individuals with high stimulation-processing capacities (phlegmatic) may be associated with a tendency to reduce arousal, coupled with a tendency to avoid stimulation; or high (nonoptimal) level of stimulation in individuals with low stimulation-processing capacities (choleric) may be associated with a tendency to reduce arousal but without a tendency to avoid stimulation (cf. Zawadzki & Strelau, 1997). Hence a Coherent Type of personality originates from low anxiety—that is, lack of (9) arousal and (10) apprehension anxiety or (11)

**Table 4.3.** Coherent and incoherent types of personalities: Endurance, emotional reactivity, activity, sensory sensitivity, perseveration, briskness, and anxiety

|  |
| --- |
| **Coherent versus incoherent types of personalities based on harmonious structures of temperament** |

**(1)** $CPT_{Sanguine:\ high\ SPC\ +\ high\ AC}^{low\text{-}arousal\ anxiety}$
Low-arousal anxiety + low ER, low PE, high BR, and high EN, SS, AC (regulative type)

**(5)** $CPT_{Melancholic:\ low\ SPC\ +\ low\ AC}^{high\text{-}arousal\ anxiety}$
High-arousal anxiety (reactive type) + high ER, high PE, low BR, and low EN, SS, AC (reactive type)

**(2)** $CPT_{Sanguine:\ high\ SPC\ +\ high\ AC}^{low\text{-}apprehension\ anxiety}$
Low-apprehension anxiety + low ER, low PE, high BR, and high EN, SS, AC (regulative type)

**(6)** $CPT_{Melancholic:\ low\ SPC\ +\ low\ AC}^{low\text{-}apprehension\ anxiety}$
Low-apprehension anxiety + high ER, high PE, low BR, and low EN, SS, AC (reactive type)

**(3)** $CPT_{Sanguine:\ high\ SPC\ +\ high\ AC}^{high\text{-}apprehension\ anxiety}$
High-apprehension anxiety (regulative type) + low ER, low PE, high BR, and high EN, SS, AC (regulative type)

**(7)** $INPT_{Melancholic:\ low\ SPC\ +\ low\ AC}^{high\text{-}apprehension\ anxiety}$
High-apprehension anxiety (regulative type) + high ER, high PE, low BR, and low EN, SS, AC (reactive type)

**(4)** $INPT_{Sanguine:\ high\ SPC\ +\ high\ AC}^{high\text{-}arousal\ anxiety}$
High-arousal anxiety (reactive type) + low ER, low PE, high BR, and high EN, SS, AC (regulative type)

**(8)** $INPT_{Melancholic:\ low\ SPC\ +\ low\ AC}^{low\text{-}arousal\ anxiety}$
Low-arousal anxiety + high ER, high PE, low BR, and low EN, SS, AC (reactive type)

|  |
| --- |
| **Examples of coherent versus incoherent types of personalities based on disharmonious structures of temperament** |

**(9)** $CPT_{Phlegmatic:\ high\ SPC\ +\ low\ AC}^{low\text{-}arousal\ anxiety}$
Low-arousal anxiety + high EN, low ER, low AC, and moderate or low SS, PE, BR (regulative type)

**(13)** $CPT_{Choleric:\ low\ SPC\ +\ high\ AC}^{high\text{-}arousal\ anxiety}$
High-arousal anxiety (reactive type) + low EN, high ER, high AC, and moderate or high SS, PE, BR (reactive type)

**(10)** $CPT_{Phlegmatic:\ high\ SPC\ +\ low\ AC}^{low\text{-}apprehension\ anxiety}$
Low-apprehension anxiety + high EN, low ER, low AC, and moderate or low SS, PE, BR (regulative type)

**(14)** $CPT_{Choleric:\ low\ SPC\ +\ high\ AC}^{low\text{-}apprehension\ anxiety}$
Low-apprehension anxiety + low EN, high ER, high AC, and moderate or high SS, PE, BR (reactive type)

**(11)** $CPT_{Phlegmatic:\ high\ SPC\ +\ low\ AC}^{high\text{-}apprehension\ anxiety}$
High-apprehension anxiety (regulative type) + high EN, low ER, low AC, and moderate or low SS, PE, BR (regulative type)

**(15)** $INPT_{Choleric:\ low\ SPC\ +\ high\ AC}^{high\text{-}apprehension\ anxiety}$
High-apprehension anxiety (regulative type) + low EN, high ER, high AC, and moderate or high SS, PE, BR (reactive type)

**(12)** $INPT_{Phlegmatic:\ high\ SPC\ +\ low\ AC}^{high\text{-}arousal\ anxiety}$
High-arousal anxiety (reactive type) + high EN, low ER, low AC, and moderate or low SS, PE, BR (regulative type)

**(16)** $INPT_{Choleric:\ low\ SPC\ +\ high\ AC}^{low\text{-}arousal\ anxiety}$
Low-arousal anxiety + low EN, high ER, high AC, and moderate or high SS, PE, BR (reactive type)

*Note.* SPC = stimulation-processing capacities; AC = activity; ER = emotional reactivity; PE = perseveration; BR = briskness; EN = endurance; SS = sensory sensitivity.

regulative high-apprehension anxiety and the regulative disharmonious phlegmatic temperament, indicating high stimulation-processing capacities, whereas an Incoherent Type of personality is based on (12) reactive high-arousal anxiety and the regulative phlegmatic temperament. In the case of the reactive disharmonious choleric temperament, indicating low stimulation-processing capacities, a Coherent Type of personality comprises (13) reactive high-arousal anxiety and (14) low-apprehension anxiety, whereas an Incoherent Type of personality is composed of the reactive Choleric Type and (15) regulative high-apprehension anxiety or (16) low-arousal anxiety.

However, one issue should be explained at this point. Predictions concerning coherent and incoherent personality types, based on the relation between anxiety and disharmonious structures of temperament, seem to be complicated. This is because PE and BR may achieve a moderate level. They may also remain inconsistent between themselves and/or inconsistent with the level of ER. For example, in the phlegmatic case low ER, moderate PE, and low BR may predispose to a moderate (not high or low) anxiety, whereas in the choleric case high ER, moderate PE, and high BR may be associated with a moderate (not high or low) level of anxiety. This clarifies why only examples of coherent versus incoherent types of personalities within disharmonious types of temperament are presented here (cf. Table 4.3).

Analogically, the following compositions emerged within the Pavlovian, Eysenckian, and RTT models (cf. Tables 4.1–4.3).

- The reactive Arousal Type, combined with the regulative sanguine and phlegmatic types, results in incoherent structures of personality.
- The reactive Arousal Type, attached to the reactive melancholic and choleric types, produces coherent structures of personality.
- The regulative Apprehension Type, joined with the regulative sanguine and phlegmatic temperaments, results in coherent systems of personality.
- The regulative Apprehension Type, joined with the reactive melancholic and choleric temperaments, builds incoherent structures of personalities.
- Lack of both anxieties—together with sanguine and phlegmatic temperaments—represent coherent structures of personality, whereas lack of arousal or apprehension anxiety—together with melancholic and choleric temperaments—form incoherent or coherent structures of personality, respectively.

### 4.3.
## How optimal stimulation level binds depression and temperament

As anxiety is associated with hyperarousal (Watson, 2000), thus is depression connected with hypoarousal (e.g., Mehrabian & O'Reilly, 1980). Also, depression (in)sensitivity to a specific stimulation is more narrow than temperament (un) responsiveness to stimulation. The combination of a particular (reactive or regulative) type of depression and a particular (reactive or regulative) type of temperament may specifically affect the responsiveness to stimulation. However, a more important question for now is how they are grouped together considering their functional roles in stimulation processing.

As stated above, the trait constellation in the sanguine and phlegmatic types—indicating high stimulation-processing capacities—does not contribute etiologically to the development of a long-lasting trait like "moodiness" (cf. Eysenck & Fajkowska, 2009; Watson, 2000). However, under permanent environmental influences, it may happen that both temperament structures may be connected with trait-like emotional disorders (cf. Eliasz, 1981). Bearing in mind the functional consistency between temperament types and subtypes of depression, this seems more probable. Thus the combination of the regulative harmonious low-arousal Sanguine Type (oriented to seeking stimulation to maintain an optimal level of stimulation) or regulative disharmonious low-arousal Phlegmatic Type (with a tendency to not providing stimulation to maintain an optimal level of stimulation) and a high level of regulative anhedonic depression may result in coherent types of personalities. Consequently, it seems probable that coherent types of personality based on the Sanguine Type or Phlegmatic Type and high-anhedonic depression denote state-like depression. And it appears that incoherence of personality occurs when these two regulative temperament types are combined with reactive valence depression.

In addition, when coupled with a low level of valence or anhedonic depression, the sanguine and phlegmatic temperaments—which are not etiologically linked to depression—can be considered as coherent types of personality. Logically, the exploration of the consistency/inconsistency between controlling functions over stimulation in these constellations of types looks inaccurate because the dominant controlling functions in both types of depression can be observed on their elevated levels.

By contrast, the structure of traits in the Melancholic Type and Choleric Type—indicating low stimulation-processing capacities—predisposes etiologically to the occurrence of trait-like affective disorders (cf. Eysenck & Fajkowska, 2009; Watson, 2000). Thus it seems more probable that state-like emotional disorders, resulting from interaction between the trait and the environment, may be associated with these temperament types. Again, according to the principle of functional consistency between focal traits, they may occur together as coherent types of personalities. Hence the reactive harmonious high-arousal Melancholic Type (oriented to avoiding stimulation to maintain an optimal level of stimulation) or the reactive disharmonious high-arousal Choleric Type (without a tendency to avoiding stimulation to maintain an optimal level of stimulation) and the high level of reactive valence depression produce coherent types of personality. But incoherence of personality is possible when regulative anhedonic depression is attached to these two reactive types of temperament.

Moreover, when coupled with a low level of valence depression (signifying here physiological capacity to cope effectively with emotional and social stimulation), the melancholic and choleric types—which are etiologically disposed to depression— can be considered as incoherent types of personality; but when matched to a low level of anhedonic depression (indicating here an unregulated physiological alertness to emotional and social stimulation), they can be considered as coherent types of personality. Thus, again, the evaluation of the consistency/inconsistency between controlling functions over stimulation in these focal types seems to be insufficient.

To construct the coherent and incoherent types of personalities built on depression subtypes and the Pavlovian, Eysenckian, and RTT models, I am going to utilize the correlational data reported in section 4.2, distributional analysis, and theoretical assumptions. Because depression frequently co-occurs with other psychiatric disorders, especially anxiety disorders (cf. Angold, Costello, & Erkanli, 1999; Hankin, Gibb, Abela, & Flory, 2010), this may also be taking into account the evidence on the relation between anxiety (STAI) and depression (Beck Depression Inventory, BDI; Beck et al., 1987; Parnowski & Jernajczyk, 1977). Thus depression (BDI) relates positively to anxiety as a state and a trait (Fajkowska & Krejtz, 2007; Fajkowska & Marszał-Wiśniewska, 2009).

However, the thing to note is that most empirical evidence relates to anhedonic depression. The theoretical framework is the foundation for building coherent/ incoherent personality types, with valence depression included among them.

### 4.3.1. Coherent/incoherent personality structures composed of strength of excitation, strength of inhibition, mobility, balance, and subtypes of depression

Correlational and between-group design studies on depression and Pavlovian properties of temperament are only useful to some extent in building coherent/incoherent personality types. Nonclinical depression (BDI) relates negatively to Pavlovian temperament dimensions SE, SI, and MO. Results obtained for clinically depressed individuals demonstrated that both SE and MO are significantly lower in clinically depressed individuals than in nondepressed individuals. What is more, analysis showed that SI is positively associated with clinical depression (data collected by Fajkowska & Marszał-Wiśniewska, 2004–2007, and Fajkowska, Zagórska & Jaśkowski, 2008–2011). According to these data, it is more probable that nonclinical depression occurs in melancholic (low SE and SI) and choleric (moderate or low SI) types, but also under specific circumstances in phlegmatic (low MO) and sanguine types (see Table 4.4).

The degree of normality in a set of scores of (anhedonic) depression (BDI; Beck et al., 1987; Parnowski & Jernajczyk, 1977), and in the four temperament types defined within the Pavlovian approach (PTS; Strelau & Zawadzki, 1998), was assessed on 136 subjects (100 females, $M = 25.5$ years, $SD = 7.66$).

The distribution of (anhedonic) depression in sanguines ($n = 40$) is significantly different from a normal distribution ($p < 0.001$), and the data suggest that

**Table 4.4.** Coherent and incoherent types of personalities: Strength of excitation, strength of inhibition, mobility, balance, and depression

### Coherent versus incoherent types of personalities based on harmonious structures of temperament

| | |
|---|---|
| **(1)** $CPT_{\text{Sanguine: strong, mobile, balanced type of NS}}^{\text{low-valence depression}}$<br>Low-valence depression + high SE, high SI, high MO, and BA between SE:SI (regulative type) | **(5)** $CPT_{\text{Melancholic: weak type of NS}}^{\text{high-valence depression}}$<br>High-valence depression (reactive type) + low SE and low SI (reactive type) |
| **(2)** $CPT_{\text{Sanguine: strong, mobile, balanced type of NS}}^{\text{low-anhedonic depression}}$<br>Low-anhedonic depression + high SE, high SI, high MO, and BA between SE:SI (regulative type) | **(6)** $CPT_{\text{Melancholic: weak type of NS}}^{\text{low-anhedonic depression}}$<br>Low-anhedonic depression + low SE and low SI (reactive type) |
| **(3)** $CPT_{\text{Sanguine: strong, mobile, balanced type of NS}}^{\text{high-anhedonic depression}}$<br>High-anhedonic depression (regulative type) + high SE, high SI, high MO, and BA between SE:SI (regulative type) | **(7)** $INPT_{\text{Melancholic: weak type of NS}}^{\text{high-anhedonic depression}}$<br>High-anhedonic depression (regulative type) + low SE and low SI (reactive type) |
| **(4)** $INPT_{\text{Sanguine: strong, mobile, balanced type of NS}}^{\text{high-valence depression}}$<br>High-valence depression (reactive type) + high SE, high SI, high MO, and BA between SE:SI (regulative type) | **(8)** $INPT_{\text{Melancholic: weak type of NS}}^{\text{low-valence depression}}$<br>Low-valence depression + low SE and low SI (reactive type) |

### Coherent versus incoherent types of personalities based on disharmonious structures of temperament

| | |
|---|---|
| **(9)** $CPT_{\text{Phlegmatic: strong, slow, balanced type of NS}}^{\text{low-valence depression}}$<br>Low-valence depression + high SE, high SI, low MO, and BA between SE:SI (regulative type) | **(13)** $CPT_{\text{Choleric: strong, unbalanced type of NS}}^{\text{high-valence depression}}$<br>High-valence depression (reactive type) + high SE, moderate or low SI, Unbalance: SE > SI (reactive type) |
| **(10)** $CPT_{\text{Phlegmatic: strong, slow, balanced type of NS}}^{\text{low-anhedonic depression}}$<br>Low-anhedonic depression + high SE, high SI, low MO, and BA between SE:SI (regulative type) | **(14)** $CPT_{\text{Choleric: strong, unbalanced type of NS}}^{\text{low-anhedonic depression}}$<br>Low-anhedonic depression + high SE, moderate or low SI, Unbalance: SE > SI (reactive type) |
| **(11)** $CPT_{\text{Phlegmatic: strong, slow, balanced type of NS}}^{\text{high-anhedonic depression}}$<br>High-anhedonic depression (regulative type) + high SE, high SI, low MO, and BA between SE:SI (regulative type) | **(15)** $INPT_{\text{Choleric: strong, unbalanced type of NS}}^{\text{high-anhedonic depression}}$<br>High-anhedonic depression (regulative type) + high SE, moderate or low SI, Unbalance: SE > SI (reactive type) |
| **(12)** $INPT_{\text{Phlegmatic: strong, slow, balanced type of NS}}^{\text{high-valence depression}}$<br>High-valence depression (reactive type) + high SE, high SI, low MO, and BA between SE:SI (regulative type) | **(16)** $INPT_{\text{Choleric: strong, unbalanced type of NS}}^{\text{low-valence depression}}$<br>Low-valence depression + high SE, moderate or low SI, Unbalance: SE > SI (reactive type) |

*Note.* NS = nervous system; SE = strength of excitation; SI = strength of inhibition; MO = mobility; BA = balance.

the majority of sanguines are rather low on depression (skeweness: 2.05 confidence interval from –0.51 to 0.51, kurtosis: 4.77, confidence interval from –0.99 to 0.99). Similarly, the (anhedonic) depression distributions in melancholics ($n = 58$), phlegmatics ($n = 19$), and cholerics ($n = 19$) are not normal ($p < 0.001$, $p < 0.05$, $p < 0.001$, respectively). There are more frequencies at the left end of distribution, implying more lower than higher scores on depression in melancholics (skewness: 0.81, confidence interval from –0.43 to 0.43, kurtosis: 0.05, confidence interval from 0.83 to 0.83), phlegmatics (skewness: 0.21, confidence interval from –0.72 to 0.72, kurtosis: –1.71, confidence interval from –1.14 to 1.14), and cholerics (skeweness: 0.79, confidence interval from –0.72 to 0.72, kurtosis: –1.71, confidence interval from –1.40 to 1.14).

Low- and high-anhedonic depression was identified in the four temperaments. However, the results imply that low-anhedonic depression is more typical than high-anhedonic depression for all temperament types.

As shown in Table 4.4, types of personality based on the regulative harmonious sanguine temperament, indicating a strong, mobile, and balanced type of nervous system and low depression, signifying lack of (1) valence and (2) anhedonic depression or (3) regulative high-anhedonic depression, mark coherent structures, but combined with (4) reactive high-valence depression produce an incoherent personality type.

The reactive harmonious melancholic temperament, indicating a weak type of nervous system and (5) reactive high-valence depression or (6) low-anhedonic depression, comprises a Coherent Type of personality, while with (7) regulative high-anhedonic depression or (8) low-valence depression makes up incoherent personality systems.

The regulative disharmonious phlegmatic temperament, indicating a strong, slow, and balanced type of nervous system with lack of (9) valence and (10) anhedonic depression or (11) regulative high-anhedonic depression, builds a Coherent Type of personality, but with (12) reactive high-valence depression produces an incoherent structure. In the case of the reactive disharmonious choleric temperament, indicating a strong, unbalanced type of nervous system with (13) reactive high-valence depression or (14) low-anhedonic depression, forms a Coherent Type of personality, but with (15) regulative high-anhedonic depression or (16) lack of valence depression constitutes incoherent structures of personality.

### *4.3.2. Coherent/incoherent personality structures composed of extraversion, neuroticism, and subtypes of depression*

As mentioned above (section 4.2.2), the studies of Mehrabian and O'Reilly (1980) demonstrated that depression and extraversion are related and belong to the same cluster. However, they are located at opposite poles. Extraversion is mostly associated with the ability to become emotionally aroused as an important aspect of positive social exchanges, whereas depression is linked to dimensions of displeasure, unarousability, and submissiveness (cf. also Strelau, 2008; Zawadzki, 2001). Kotov et al. (2010) also provided evidence that extraversion contributes to depression, but its effect is more important for chronic forms of this illness. In Mehrabian and O'Reilly's studies it was shown that extraversion is not specific to major depressive disorder (including single episodes and chronicle illnesses); on the other hand, dysthymic disorder, representing long-lasting depression, is strongly and negatively correlated with this trait, so extraversion clearly plays and important role in some forms of depression. (Major depressive disorder also had a relatively small elevation on neuroticism.) If one moves beyond the broad higher-order trait and analyzes the specific facets of extraversion related to depression, it is found that depressive symptoms correlated strongly only with low positive emotionality (Naragon-Gainey, Watson, & Markon, 2009).

Generally, in most studies low extraversion and high neuroticism are found in clinical and nonclinical depression (cf. Brown, Chorpita, & Barlow, 1998; Kotov et al., 2010; Watson, Wiese, Vaidya, & Tellegen, 1999). According to my and my colleagues' data on depression (measured by the BDI; Beck et al., 1987; Parnowski & Jernajczyk, 1977), depression relates negatively to extraversion and positively to neuroticism (data collected by Fajkowska & Marszał-Wiśniewska, 2004–2007, and Fajkowska, Zagórska & Jaśkowski, 2008–2011).

These outcomes suggest that one can predict the elevated level of depression attached to melancholics (low extraversion and high neuroticism), cholerics (high neuroticism), and phlegmatics (low extraversion), but that it is difficult to predict the level of depression in sanguines.

The distributional analysis ($N = 250$, 200 females, $M = 25.18$, $SD = 7.09$) does not resolve this problem. Moreover, it suggests that a low level of anhedonic depression (measured by the BDI; Beck et al., 1987; Parnowski & Jernajczyk, 1977) is  more representative for all four temperament types (assessed by the EPQ-R; Brzozowski & Drwal, 1995; Eysenck & Eysenck, 1994) than a high level of anhedonic depression.

The distribution of (anhedonic) depression in sanguines ($n = 130$) is significantly different from a normal distribution ($p < 0.001$). The data obtained suggest that the majority of sanguines are rather low on depression, but only a few of them are high depression scorers (skeweness: 1.43, confidence interval from –0.21 to 0.21, kurtosis: 2.34, confidence interval from –0.41 to 0.41). Also, the (anhedonic) depression distributions in melancholics ($n = 34$), phlegmatics ($n = 44$), and cholerics ($n = 42$) are not normal ($p < 0.001$, $p < 0.001$, $p < 0.001$, respectively). This translates into a higher frequency of low results than high results on depression in melancholics (skewness: 0.97, confidence interval from –0.40 to 0.40, kurtosis: 0.61, confidence from interval –0.79 to 0.79), phlegmatics (skewness: 0.42, confidence interval from –0.36 to 0.36, kurtosis: –0.94, confidence interval from –0.70 to 0.70), and cholerics (skewness: 0.74, confidence interval from –0.36 to 0.36, kurtosis: –0.59; confidence interval from –0.72 to 0.72).

Following this evidence and theoretical assumptions addressed to the functional relations in focal traits, I propose the below-demonstrated types of personality coherence and incoherence based on the Eysenckian traits of temperament and depression (Table 4.5). On a more elaborated level, Table 4.5 presents types of personality based on the regulative harmonious sanguine temperament, representing emotional stability and extraversion, and (1) low-valence and (2) low-anhedonic depression

**Table 4.5.** Coherent and incoherent types of personalities: Extraversion, neuroticism, and depression

### Coherent versus incoherent types of personalities based on harmonious structures of temperament

**(1)** $CPT_{\text{Sanguine: emotionally stable extravert}}^{\text{low-valence depression}}$
Low-valence depression + high E and low N (regulative type)

**(5)** $CPT_{\text{Melancholic: emotionally unstable introvert}}^{\text{high-valence depression}}$
High-valence depression (reactive type) + low E and high N (reactive type)

**(2)** $CPT_{\text{Sanguine: emotionally stable extravert}}^{\text{low-anhedonic depression}}$
Low-anhedonic depression + high E and low N (regulative type)

**(6)** $CPT_{\text{Melancholic: emotionally unstable introvert}}^{\text{low-anhedonic depression}}$
Low-anhedonic depression + low E and high N (reactive type)

**(3)** $CPT_{\text{Sanguine: emotionally stable extravert}}^{\text{high-anhedonic depression}}$
High-anhedonic depression (regulative type) + high E and low N (regulative type)

**(7)** $INPT_{\text{Melancholic: emotionally unstable introvert}}^{\text{high-anhedonic depression}}$
High-anhedonic depression (regulative type) + low E and high N (reactive type)

**(4)** $INPT_{\text{Sanguine: emotionally stable extravert}}^{\text{high-valence depression}}$
High-valence depression (reactive type) + high E and low N (regulative type)

**(8)** $INPT_{\text{Melancholic: emotionally unstable introvert}}^{\text{low-valence depression}}$
Low-valence depression + low E and high N (reactive type)

### Coherent versus incoherent types of personalities based on disharmonious structures of temperament

**(9)** $CPT_{\text{Phlegmatic: emotionally stable introvert}}^{\text{low-valence depression}}$
Low-valence depression + low E and low N (regulative type)

**(13)** $CPT_{\text{Choleric: emotionally unstable extravert}}^{\text{high-valence depression}}$
High-valence depression (reactive type) + high E and high N (reactive type)

**(10)** $CPT_{\text{Phlegmatic: emotionally stable introvert}}^{\text{low-anhedonic depression}}$
Low-anhedonic depression + low E and low N (regulative type)

**(14)** $CPT_{\text{Choleric: emotionally unstable extravert}}^{\text{low-anhedonic depression}}$
Low-anhedonic depression + high E and high N (reactive type)

**(11)** $CPT_{\text{Phlegmatic: emotionally stable introvert}}^{\text{high-anhedonic depression}}$
High-anhedonic depression (regulative type) + low E and low N (regulative type)

**(15)** $INPT_{\text{Choleric: emotionally unstable extravert}}^{\text{high-anhedonic depression}}$
High-anhedonic depression (regulative type) + high E and high N (reactive type)

**(12)** $INPT_{\text{Phlegmatic: emotionally stable introvert}}^{\text{high-valence depression}}$
High-valence depression (reactive type) + low E and low N (regulative type)

**(16)** $INPT_{\text{Choleric: emotionally unstable extravert}}^{\text{low-valence depression}}$
Low-valence depression + high E and high N (reactive type)

*Note.* E = extraversion; N = neuroticism.

or (3) regulative high-anhedonic depression, which indicates coherent personality systems, but associated with (4) reactive high-valence depression results in an incoherent structure. The reactive harmonious melancholic temperament, indicating emotional instability and introversion, added to (5) reactive high-valence depression or (6) low-anhedonic depression composes a Coherent Type of personality, while added to (7) regulative high-anhedonic depression or to (8) lack of valence depression makes up an Incoherent Type of personality.

The regulative disharmonious phlegmatic temperament, indicating emotional stability and introversion with (9) low-valence and (10) low-anhedonic depression, or (11) regulative high-anhedonic depression, comprises the coherent type of personality, but attached to (12) reactive high-valence depression arranges an incoherent structure. In the case of the reactive disharmonious choleric temperament, indicating emotional instability and extraversion with (13) reactive high-valence depression or (14) low-anhedonic depression, forms a Coherent Type of personality, but with (15) regulative high-anhedonic depression or (16) low-valence depression constitutes an incoherent structure of personality.

### *4.3.3. Coherent/incoherent personality structures composed of endurance, emotional reactivity, activity, sensory sensitivity, perseveration, briskness, and subtypes of depression*

The analysis of relations among temperament traits formulated within the RTT and endogenic depression showed that depression correlates positively with ER and PE and negatively with EN, BR, SS, and AC (Habrat, 1997). Depressiveness assessed by means of Zawadzki's (2001) Personality Pattern Inventory correlated positvely with ER and negatively with AC (see also Strelau, 2008). Evidence from our studies (data collected by Fajkowska, Zagórska, & Jaśkowski, 2008–2011) confirmed that depression (BDI) is negatively correlated with EN, BR, and SS and positively correlated with ER and PE. However, measured by the BDI, depression is not significantly connected with AC. In essence, one can anticipate the increased depression in melancholics (high ER, high PE, low EN, BR, SS, AC), cholerics (high ER, low EN, high PE, moderate BR and SS), and phlegmatics (low AC, moderate PE, BR, SS). Again, with these data it is difficult to predict the level of depression in sanguines.

Using distributional data ($N = 114$, 98 females, $M = 24.75$, $SD = 6.21$), it appears that a low level of depression can be obtained more frequently across all four temperaments, although a high level of depression is also registered. The distribution of (anhedonic) depression in sanguines ($n = 28$), melancholics ($n = 30$), phlegmatics ($n = 26$), and cholerics ($n = 30$) is significantly different from a normal distribution ($p < 0.001$, $p < 0.001$, $p < 0.001$, $p < 0.001$, respectively). The findings revealed that those not normal distributions point to higher frequency of lower scores on depression in sanguines (skewness: 2.05, confidence interval from –0.44 to 0.44, kurtosis: 4.77, confidence interval from –0.86 to 0.86), melancholics (skewness: 1.17, confidence interval from –0.41 to 0.40, kurtosis: 0.52, confidence from interval –0.81 to 0.81), phlegmatics (skewness: 0.89, confidence interval from –0.46 to 0.46, kurtosis: –0.35, confidence interval from –0.89 to 0.89), and cholerics (skewness: 0.74, confidence interval from –0.41 to 0.41, kurtosis: 1.85, confidence interval from –0.81 to 0.81).

The content of Table 4.6 is based on the data and theoretical analysis reported here.

Table 4.6 illustrates types of personality grounded on regulative harmonious sanguine temperament, indicating high stimulation-processing capacities and (1) low-valence and (2) low-anhedonic depression or (3) regulative high-anhedonic depression indicating coherent personalities, but is associated with (4) reactive high-valence depression effects in an incoherent structure. The reactive harmonious melancholic temperament, indicating low stimulation-processing capacities and (5) reactive high-valence depression or (6) low-anhedonic depression, composes a Coherent Type of personality, while added to (7) regulative high-anhedonic depression or (8) low-valence depression establishes an Incoherent Type of personality.

The regulative disharmonious phlegmatic temperament, indicating high stimulation-processing capacities with (9) low-valence and (10) low-anhedonic depression or (11) regulative high-anhedonic depression, builds a Coherent Type of personality, but with (12) reactive high-valence depression produces an incoherent system. The reactive disharmonious choleric temperament, indicating low stimulation-processing capacities and (13) reactive high-valence depression or (14) low-anhedonic depression, is used as a basis for a Coherent Type of personality, but forms an incoherent structure of personality when regulative high-anhedonic depression or (15) regulative high-anhedonic depression or (16) low-valence depression are utilized.

There is a parallel between anxiety and depression in respect to the disharmonious types of temperament formulated within the RTT approach. Predictions concerning coherent and incoherent personality types based on the relation between depression and disharmonious structures of temperament seem to be complicated. This is because PE, BR, and SS may achieve a moderate level. They may also remain inconsistent between themselves and/or inconsistent with the level of ER, EN, and AC. For example, in the phlegmatic case high EN, low ER and AC, plus moderate PE, BR, and SS may predispose to a moderate (not high or low) level of depression, whereas in the choleric case low EN, high ER and AC, plus moderate PE, BR, and SS may be associated with a moderate (not high or low) level of depression. This clarifies why only examples of coherent versus incoherent types of personalities within disharmonious types of temperament are presented here (cf. Table 4.6).

Taken together, the following personalities compositions emerged within the Pavlovian, Eysenckian, and RTT models (cf. Tables 4.4–4.6).

- The reactive Valence Type, combined with regulative sanguine and phlegmatic temperaments, results in incoherent structures of personality.
- The reactive Valence Type, attached to reactive melancholic and choleric temperaments, produces coherent structures of personalities.

**Table 4.6.** Coherent and incoherent types of personalities: Endurance, emotional reactivity, activity, sensory sensitivity, perseveration, briskness, and depression

### Coherent versus incoherent types of personalities based on harmonious structures of temperament

**(1)** $CPT_{\textit{Sanguine: high SPC + high AC}}^{\textit{low-valence depression}}$
Low-valence depression + low ER, low PE, high BR, and high EN, SS, AC (regulative type)

**(5)** $CPT_{\textit{Melancholic: low SPC + low AC}}^{\textit{high-valence depression}}$
High-valence depression (reactive type) + high ER, high PE, low BR, and low EN, SS, AC (reactive type)

**(2)** $CPT_{\textit{Sanguine: high SPC + high AC}}^{\textit{low-anhedonic depression}}$
Low-anhedonic depression + low ER, low PE, high BR, and high EN, SS, AC (regulative type)

**(6)** $CPT_{\textit{Melancholic: low SPC + low AC}}^{\textit{low-anhedonic depression}}$
Low-anhedonic depression + high ER, high PE, low BR, and low EN, SS, AC (reactive type)

**(3)** $CPT_{\textit{Sanguine: high SPC + high AC}}^{\textit{high-anhedonic depression}}$
High-anhedonic depression (regulative type) + low ER, low PE, high BR, and high EN, SS, AC (regulative type)

**(7)** $INPT_{\textit{Melancholic: low SPC + low AC}}^{\textit{high-anhedonic depression}}$
High-anhedonic depression (regulative type) + high ER, high PE, low BR, and low EN, SS, AC (reactive type)

**(4)** $INPT_{\textit{Sanguine: high SPC + high AC}}^{\textit{high-valence depression}}$
High-valence depression (reactive type) + low ER, low PE, high BR, and high EN, SS, AC (regulative type)

**(8)** $INPT_{\textit{Melancholic: low SPC + low AC}}^{\textit{low-valence depression}}$
Low-valence depression + high ER, high PE, low BR, and low EN, SS, AC (reactive type)

### Examples of coherent versus incoherent types of personalities based on disharmonious structures of temperament

**(9)** $CPT_{\textit{Phlegmatic: high SPC + low AC}}^{\textit{low-valence depression}}$
Low-valence depression + high EN, low ER, low AC, and moderate or low SS, PE, BR (regulative type)

**(13)** $CPT_{\textit{Choleric: low SPC + high AC}}^{\textit{high-valence depression}}$
High-valence depression (reactive type) + low EN, high ER, high AC, and moderate or high SS, PE, BR (reactive type)

**(10)** $CPT_{\textit{Phlegmatic: high SPC + low AC}}^{\textit{low-anhedonic depression}}$
Low-anhedonic depression + high EN, low ER, low AC, and moderate or low SS, PE, BR (regulative type)

**(14)** $CPT_{\textit{Choleric: low SPC + high AC}}^{\textit{low-anhedonic depression}}$
Low-anhedonic depression + low EN, high ER, high AC, and moderate or high SS, PE, BR (reactive type)

**(11)** $CPT_{\textit{Phlegmatic: high SPC + low AC}}^{\textit{high-anhedonic depression}}$
High-anhedonic depression (regulative type) + high EN, low ER, low AC, and moderate or low SS, PE, BR (regulative type)

**(15)** $INPT_{\textit{Choleric: low SPC + high AC}}^{\textit{high-anhedonic depression}}$
High-anhedonic depression (regulative type) + low EN, high ER, high AC, and moderate or high SS, PE, BR (reactive type)

**(12)** $INPT_{\textit{Phlegmatic: high SPC + low AC}}^{\textit{high-valence depression}}$
High-valence depression (reactive type) + high EN, low ER, low AC, and moderate or low SS, PE, BR (regulative type)

**(16)** $INPT_{\textit{Choleric: low SPC + high AC}}^{\textit{low-valence depression}}$
Low-valence depression + low EN, high ER, high AC, and moderate or high SS, PE, BR (reactive type)

*Note.* SPC = stimulation-processing capacities; AC = activity; ER = emotional reactivity; PE = perseveration; BR = briskness; EN = endurance; SS = sensory sensitivity.

- The regulative Anhedonic Type, joined with regulative sanguine and phlegmatic temperaments, results in coherent systems of personality.
- The regulative Anhedonic Type, added to reactive melancholic and choleric temperaments, builds incoherent structures of personalities.
- Lack of depression—together with sanguine and phlegmatic temperaments—represent coherent structures of personalities, whereas lack of valence or anhedonic depression—together with melancholic and choleric temperaments—form incoherent or coherent structures of personalities, respectively.

## 4.4
## Summing up

This chapter presented the particular coherent and incoherent types of personality built upon the four temperament types (formulated across Pavlovian, Eysenckian, and Strelauvian approaches) and subtypes of anxiety and depression. These theoretical assumptions were necessary to achieve the second goal of this part of the book: to provide (in Chapter 5) some empirical evidence on how associations between temperament and affective disorders relate to attentional stimulation processing. Thus, regarding the goal of the next chapter, from the perspective of personality coherence/incoherence the reciprocal relations between reactive or regulative controlling functions of temperament types and anxiety/depression types are important in the dynamic structure of the SRIS.

These reciprocal relations have an effect on functional specification of emerged coherent or incoherent suprasystems. Coherent/incoherent structures of personality relate to one's effort to attain and maintain an optimal level of arousal and activation, which in turn affects (for example) the efficiency of performance, development, general adaptation, and well-being (see Eliasz, 1981, 2004). The particular functional significance of a particular coherent/incoherent personality structure may reveal itself, for instance, during cognitive performance—specifically, when attentional stimulation processing is activated. Attentional system is a crucial element of the SRIS associated with stimulation reception and readiness to reaction. Thus it might be hypothesized that reactive and regulative functions of personality traits/types analyzed through "correlational" and "interactive" ways account for the variance in attentional performance in a particular structure of personality coherence/incoherence.

It should be emphasized that the studies included in the next chapter are preliminary and should be viewed as a modest attempt to empirically validate some of the theoretical assumptions presented here. I am aware that reported findings need to be replicated and that further analysis should be long-term and systematic.

# Chapter 5

## Coherent/incoherent personality structures and attentional stimulation processing

### 5.1.
### Attentional processes and coherent/incoherent personalities built upon temperament, anxiety, and depression

As stated several times in this book, both temperament mechanisms and attentional processes are crucial elements of the System of Regulation and Integration Stimulation (SRIS). Temperament and attentional mechanisms relate to arousal and activation concepts. In addition, attention operates in a specific manner in terms of highlighting or amplifying the more important sources of information in a given situation, and temperament is designed to adjust this information to one's need for stimulation. Various forms of arousal can serve to alert organisms to particular information.

It is also evident that anxiety and depression are associated with arousal and activation processes. Given that most studies have demonstrated that anxiety is connected with hyperarousal and depression with hypoarousal, it would appear that both might be considered as critical components of the SRIS. These components determine the SRIS's responsiveness to specific stimulation. In consequence, the behavioral output originates from the dynamic interplay between a particular structure of temperament and structure of anxiety/depression and attentional functions. To date, however, the information presented here has been largely dedicated to stimulation processing in relation to associations between temperament types and anxiety/depression subtypes composing personality coherence/incoherence, but not particularly to the role of attentional processes in stimulation processing. This led us to the question of how specific attentional functions are engaged in stimulation control.

Indeed, this issue has been described in section 2.3.1. Briefly, I proposed after Pribram and McGuinnis (1975) three systems in the control of attention—namely, an arousal system as a phasic response to input; an activation system as a tonic readiness to respond; and finally effort-related mechanisms as a coordinating and organizing principle. More precisely, we have three energetic supply mechanisms, two of which are basal (activation and arousal) and coupled with (respectively) an input- and output-processing stimulation stage; these are coordinated and supervised by a third system—effort—that is linked to the stage of response to stimulation. On this ground Sanders (1983, 1997, 1998) proposed three energetic supply systems that are activated upon arrival stimulation.

- Energetic supply related to motor adjustment, preparatory processes—close to Posner's (1978, 1980) attentional alertness, depending on the processes of tonic alertness—and timing (time uncertainty, interpreted by the way of motor preparation reflecting a general phasic readiness to respond).
- Energetic supply related to signal quality and linked to the processes of features extraction as required for identifying the signal, these active processes refer to Posner's (1978, 1980) notion of selective attention.
- Energetic supply needed for adequate functioning of the response choice stage, which links perception and action and comes close to Posner's (1994) conscious processing and constitutes his third component of attention—effortful attentional control (cf. Sanders, 1983; Welford, 1973).

In other words, "active" and "passive" attentional processes control the optimal energetic conditions. It is important to note that William James (1890) distinguished between "active" and "passive" modes of attention. Attention is active when controlled in a top-down way by the individual's goals, whereas it is passive when controlled in a bottom-up way by external stimuli. Posner and his colleagues have described a top-down, anterior attentional system that functions in relation to more reactive, bottom-up, posterior attentional and vigilance systems and regulates automatic pathways throughout the cortex (Posner & Petersen, 1990; Posner & Rothbart, 1998). The anterior system—associated with the left hemisphere, anterior cingulate cortex, and limbic and frontal motivational systems—is viewed as an executive system that carries out more voluntary attentional functions (e.g., inhibition of dominant response tendencies and conceptual associations). Additionally, this system is responsible for more voluntary and flexible attentional control, shifting, and focusing, while the posterior system (connected with the right hemisphere and parietal lobe) is often reflexive and responds in a fairly automatic way when attention is oriented to stimuli or environmental events (Derryberry, 2002; Fajkowska & Derryberry, 2010).

In order to be informed about the state of arousal and activation, the effort (attentional and temperament) regulative mechanisms operate to sustain their appropriate functioning. Among different types of information, these regulative mechanisms receive feedback concerning the adequacy or effectiveness of individual activity and performance. Individuals act efficiently in an optimal state of arousal and activation. The prolonged discrepancy between the desired state of stimulation and actual dose of stimulation produces a range of dysfunctional behaviors and inefficient performance (cf. Eliasz & Klonowicz, 2001; Klonowicz, 1987). However, effort might affect energetic supply, correction of arousal and activation, behaviors, and performance (cf. Sanders, 1983). The emotional and motivational variables are strongly related to triggering the arousal and activation systems respectively, whereas effort only plays a role in less-than-optimal conditions (overarousal or underarousal) if energy supply through arousal or activation deviated from the optimum. Nevertheless, this restoration of the optimum does not mean that one can simply avoid maladaptive behaviors or that performance can always be improved by allocation of extra effort. Sometimes effort fails or is continually loaded and we observe a low level of performance or inadequate behavior.

To sum up, temperament and attention interact in stimulation processing and in determining the adequacy of reactions and behaviors. Activated upon the arrival of stimulation, the anterior or posterior attentional systems engage attentional orienting and selectiveness or effortful attentional control, respectively. On the other hand, it should also be kept in mind that anxiety and depression are factors that are involved in controlling and processing stimulation. High levels of anxiety or depression may modulate temperament reactivity to stimulation, which may be especially observable as intensifying temperament reactivity to stimulation or blocking temperament sensitivity to stimulation. For example, reactive arousal anxiety associated with particular temperament types may affect somatic symptoms and—connected with them—early attentional vigilance and later attentional avoidance toward stimulation. By contrast, regulative apprehension anxiety coupled with specific temperament types may influence patterns of attentional control over stimulation connected with protecting a particular temperament structure against elevation of somatic arousal.

Thus a particular type of anxiety and depression and a particular temperament structure composing relatively stable incoherent or coherent types of personalities guide the attentional processes toward a specific type of stimulation. According to the trait congruency hypothesis, personality traits should predispose people to preferentially process information that is congruent with these traits (e.g., Bargh, Lombardi, & Higgins, 1988; Fox, 2008). On the other hand, it is important to keep in mind that the relationship between personality structure and attentional processes is bidirectional. This means that personality traits might induce an attentional bias toward specific information, and conversely that a preexisting attentional bias (e.g., the tendency to selectively process either positive or negative information) may result in maintaining or forming particular personality traits.

To better understand these relations, we should refer to the SRIS as a hierarchical controlling system. Personality coherence/incoherence along with the SRIS are organized around specific, changeable processes and relatively stable traits. In a hierarchy of interacting control systems, different systems at one level can send conflicting goals to one lower system. When two systems are specifying different goals for the same lower-level variable, they are in conflict. For example, control by the SRIS over attentional hypersensitivity to negativity might be inefficient because high stimulation-processing capacities (SPC) and high-valence depression send conflicting goals to the attentional system—respectively seeking or avoiding a high dose of stimulation determined by negative material. Thus sustained conflicts may be experienced by individuals as many forms of inadequacy or inefficient performance. Severe conflict destroys control by the affected system—here the attentional system—and may contribute to personality incoherence. If the conflict persists and systematic problem solving by higher systems fails, the reorganization system (e.g., mechanisms of arousal and effort) may modify existing systems until they bypass the conflict or produce new reference signals/goals that are not in conflict at lower levels (cf. Chapter 2, section 2.1).

To illustrate these theoretical predictions, some empirical evidence is provided in the next two sections. The common theme running through the studies presented is that a functional significance of personality coherence/incoherence, built upon temperament types and anxiety/depression types, will be analyzed within the context of attentional performance.

5.2.
## How attentional stimulation processing relates to coherent/incoherent personality types built upon temperament and anxiety

Various studies have demonstrated that anxiety, when not divided into a construct of subtypes, is connected with excessive attentional vigilance to threat (e.g., Coan & Allen, 2003; Fox, Russo, & Georgiou, 2005; Hock & Krohne, 2004), avoidance of threat processing, or difficulties in disengaging attentional resources from threat (e.g., Derryberry & Reed, 2002; Fajkowska & Eysenck, 2009; Fajkowska & Krejtz, 2006; Fajkowska, Krejtz, & Krejtz, 2009; Fox, Russo, & Dutton, 2002). Generally, researchers claim that high anxiety goes with impaired attentional control—especially the inhibition and switching functions—in the presence of threat-related distractors and reduced cognitive control resources to support task-focused processing (e.g., Broomfield & Turpin, 2005; Compton, 2003; Derryberry & Reed, 2002; Fox, 1994; Savostyanov et al., 2009). This implies the overactivity of a bottom-up attentional system and an impaired top-down attentional system in the presence of threat in anxious individuals.

When presenting results of studies examining the direct associations between anxiety subtypes and attentional biases, I illustrated how some of these attentional biases are divided into anxiety subtypes. Thus I claimed that identification of the attentional vigilance-avoidance bias is more probable in the case of the Arousal Type of anxiety, whereas recognition of attentional control biases is more likely in the case of the Apprehension Type of anxiety. The question is whether examining the indirect associations between anxiety types (through their interactions and intercorrelations with temperament) and attentional processing provides an opportunity to observe the same attentional biases.

Making predictions here seems to be a complicated task. However, it can be postulated that behavioral output depends on (a) the level of functional simplicity (coherence) or complexity (incoherence); (b) the category of interaction between dominant controlling functions in a certain type of temperament and a certain type of anxiety; and (c) the experimental procedure and kind of stimulation.

Considering point (a) the intercorrelation among controlling functions of focal types, composing a particular structure of coherent/incoherent structures, should be analyzed. One may identify a functional distinctness between temperament type and anxiety (depression) type—for example, reactive for temperament and regulative for anxiety (depression). This informs us about a lack of correspondence between controlling functions, functional complexity, or incoherence. It might also reveal a functional overlap between temperament type and anxiety (depression) type—for example, reactive for both temperament type and anxiety (depression) type. This reflects a correspondence between controlling functions, functional simplicity, or coherence. Analysis of functional complexity/simplicity refers to the quality of stimulation processing. Put another way, it tells us about improving/worsening the quality of stimulation processing on the basis of comparing the quality of processing identified in coherent/incoherent personality structures with elevated anxiety (depression), with the quality of processing identified in particular coherent/incoherent personality structures with low anxiety (depression). This may be achieved by utilizing a multi-multivariable analysis of regressions.

Considering point (b) functional interaction analysis informs us about changes on the process level and changes in patterns of stimulation processing. It is operationalized as contrasting the attentional processes involved in stimulation processing with patterns of stimulation processing, identified in types of temperament and anxiety (depression) studied separately with those received for types of temperament and anxiety (depression) studied in interaction.

In other words, we have three different categories of functional interactions (cf. Chapter 2) and in order to assess which of these three categories of interactions occurred, we should compare the effects of interaction between a particular temperament type and a particular anxiety (depression) type on stimulation processing (e.g., attentional vigilance to threat, enhanced attentional control over negativity), with the effects of that specific temperament type and that specific anxiety (depression) type on stimulation processing when they are examined independently. This may be estimated with analysis of variance. Thus additive functional interactions here means that the same manner of stimulation regulation in both elements of coherent/incoherent structure (e.g., reactive x reactive) produces a pattern of processing typical for both of them. For example, the effect of reactive Arousal Type and reactive Choleric Type on attentional processing remains the same (e.g., attentional vigilance to threat), although studied through interaction.

Synergistic functional interactions denote that both elements of coherent/incoherent personality structure process information in the same (e.g., reactive x reactive) or different (e.g., reactive x regulative) ways, which results in maintaining a pattern of stimulation processing that is typical for one of them. Of course one should expect that the intensity of this pattern might be changed and observed in such conditions as the extension of behavioral indices or scope of emotional targets. For example, the reactive Arousal Type produces vigilance toward threat, while the regulative Sanguine Type creates effective happiness processing, but interaction between these types reveals effective processing of all emotional targets. Thus, if arousal anxiety interacts with the Sanguine Type, attentional effectiveness of processing extends to all emotions and might be observed across most behavioral indices.

Finally, antagonistic functional interactions signify that both elements of coherent/incoherent personality structure produce the same (e.g., reactive x reactive) or different (e.g., reactive x regulative) ways of processing stimulation, which results in an entirely new pattern of stimulation processing that is not identified in even one of them. For example, attentional vigilance toward threat in reactive arousal anxiety and attentional insensitivity toward threat in the regulative Sanguine Type diminish if they interact with each other. Instead, we observe impaired attentional control over emotional material.

With respect to the nature of stimulation, point (c) above, different theoretical perspectives converge on the notion that anxiety should be characterized by preferential attention to threat-relevant stimuli (e.g., Ioannou, Mogg, & Bradley, 2004; Lau & Pine, 2008; MacLeod, Mathews, & Tata, 1986; MacLeod, Soong, Rutherford, & Campbell, 2007). Although most studies have focused primarily on words as the stimuli, both theory and research suggest that attentional biases to emotional faces—rather than verbal stimuli—provide a more accurate and ecologically valid test of biased information processing in anxiety (e.g., Hankin, Gibb, Abela, & Flory, 2010; McNally, Riemann, & Kim, 1990).

Thus facial stimuli are utilized across all the experimental procedures presented in the next sections. Several behavioral indices of attentional biases to affective faces are taken into account: attentional vigilance/reduced attentional vigilance, assigned by (respectively) a high or low speed of processing emotional material (RT: reaction time; TN: total number of processed items in the limited time); impaired/enhanced attentional control, reflected in (respectively) a high or low level of false alarms (FA); attentional avoidance, marked by a high level of omissions (OM); and finally (in)effectiveness of attentional processing, expressed in (in)accuracy or (respectively) a low or high number of hits, indicative of the quality of attentional selectiveness.

### 5.2.1. Attentional biases in coherent/incoherent personality structures built upon temperament types in Pavlovian perspective and anxiety types

In an attempt to predict the quality and dynamics of attentional processing in coherent/incoherent personalities, built upon the four temperament types in Pavlov's approach and arousal anxiety or apprehension anxiety, the intercorrelations and interactions among these elements were analyzed. The findings are presented below.

*Intercorrelations: Temperament Type and Anxiety Type*

Temperament properties were assessed ($N$ = 254, 142 females, $M$ = 22.14 years, $SD$ = 2.93) by the PTS (Strelau & Zawadzki, 1998) and trait (apprehension) anxiety and state (arousal) anxiety by the STAI (Spielberger, 1983; Wrześniewski & Sosnowski, 1996). Then participants were asked to complete the Emotional Faces Attention Test (modification of the Attention Test by Moroń; Fajkowska, 2009; see Figure 5.1). The task was to detect (by crossing out) as quickly as possible a target threatening (Th), friendly (F), and sad (S) face, (respectively) in a matrix of faces within two minutes. Performance on this task imposed substantial demands on

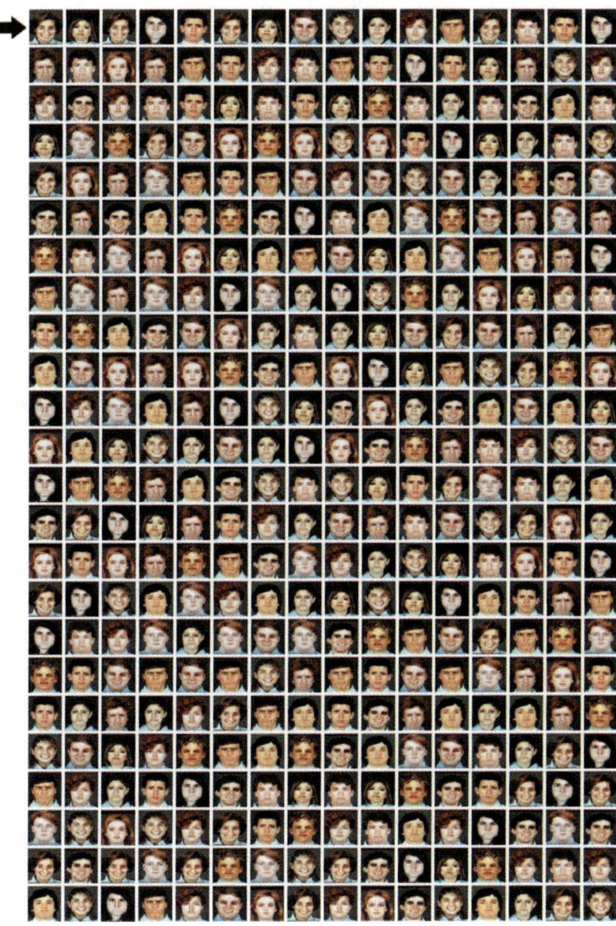

**Figure 5.1.** The Emotional Faces Attention Test: Ekman's faces, 384 stimuli arranged in 24 x 16 blocks on a standard sheet of paper, with threatening, friendly, and sad target expressions (Fajkowska, 2009).

the voluntary attentional control system (similar to those formed by the prolonged visual search design; cf. Mackworth, 1948, 1957), thus activating the temperament properties as sensitive to challenging conditions (cf. Strelau, 2008).

Figure 5.2 presents findings that provide information on how coherent/incoherent personality structures composed of the four temperament types and the Arousal Type of anxiety are associated with facial affect processing.

Figure 5.2A demonstrates that the incoherent high-arousal anxious Sanguine Type ($INPT_{\text{Sanguine: strong, mobile, balanced type of NS}}^{\text{high-arousal anxiety}}$) is connected with effective threat processing (low number of errors to Th), while the coherent low-arousal anxious Sanguine Type ($CPT_{\text{Sanguine: strong, mobile, balanced type of NS}}^{\text{low-arousal anxiety}}$) is connected with ineffective threat processing (high number of errors to Th). This implies that arousal anxiety is linked to effectiveness (good selectiveness) of threat processing in sanguines.

As Figure 5.2B illustrates, the coherent high-arousal anxious Melancholic Type ($CPT_{\text{Melancholic: weak type of NS}}^{\text{high-arousal anxiety}}$) is associated with ineffective happiness and sadness processing (low number of hits to F and S faces; high number of total errors to F faces) and reduced attentional vigilance to happiness and sadness (TN: processing speed; low level of total number of F and S faces processed correctly or incorrectly), whereas the incoherent low-arousal anxious Melancholic Type ($INPT_{\text{Melancholic: weak type of NS}}^{\text{low-arousal anxiety}}$) is linked to effective happiness and sadness processing (high number of hits to F and S faces; low number of total errors to F faces) and attentional vigilance to happiness and sadness (high level of TN of F and S faces processed). These results imply that a high level of arousal anxiety mixed with the Melancholic Type is associated with worse attentional selectiveness in processing F and S facial stimuli.

**Figure 5.2.**

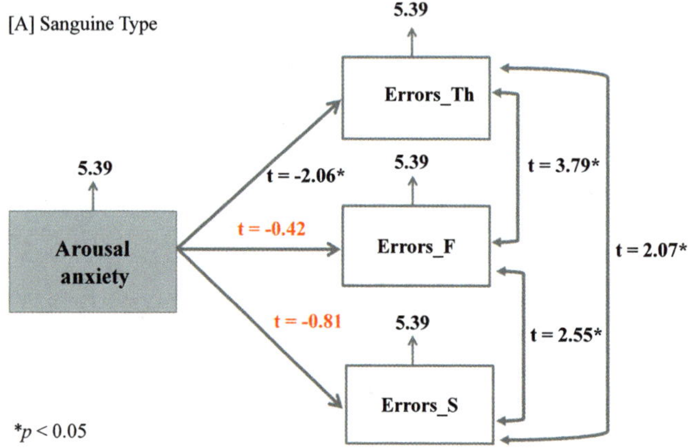

**Figure 5.2.** *(continued)*

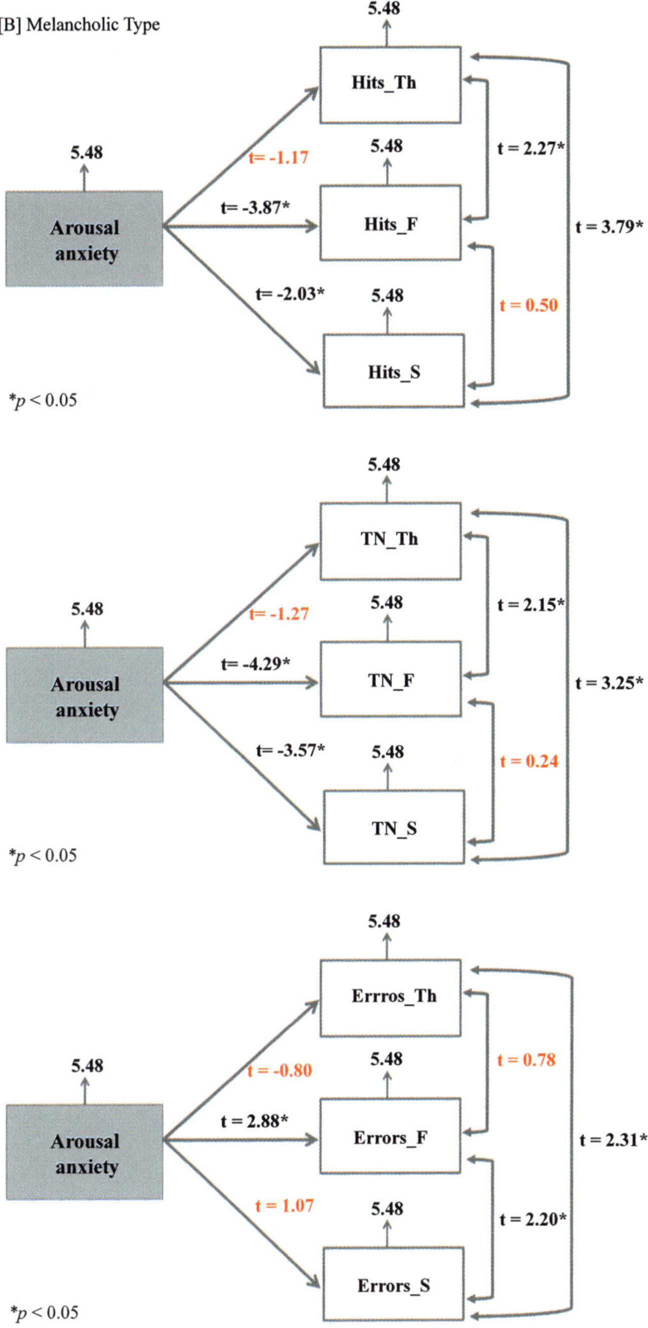

**Figure 5.2.** *(continued)*

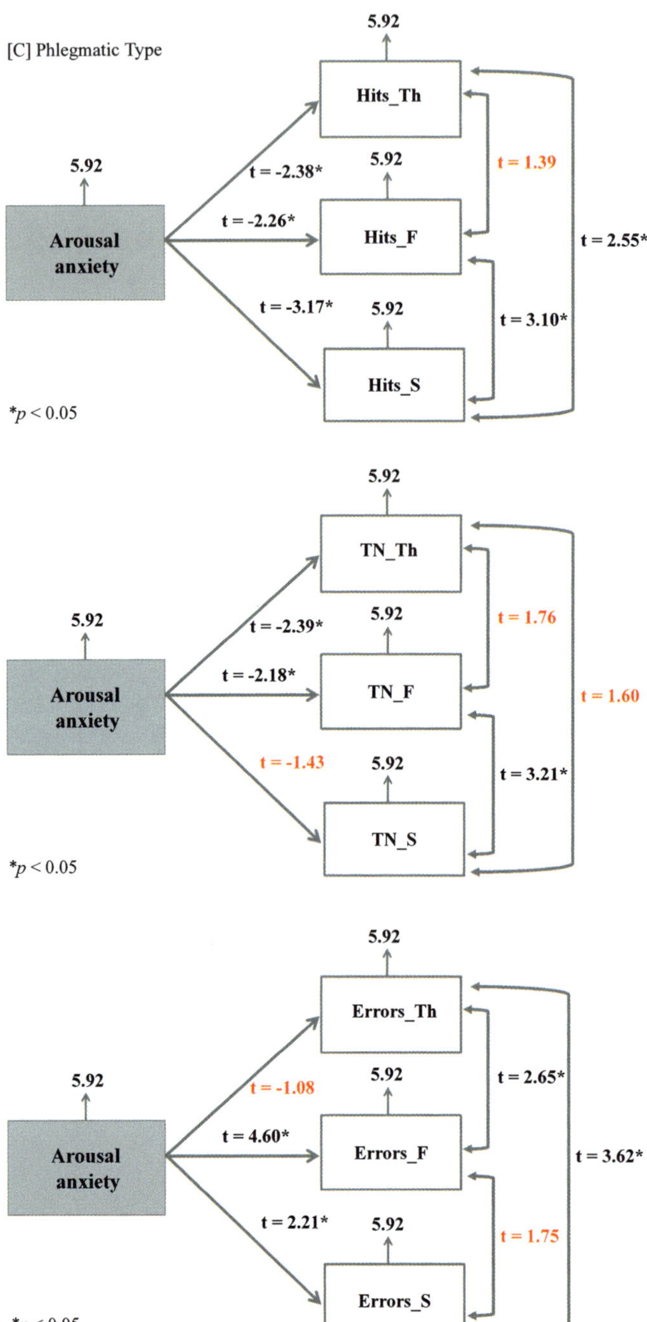

**Figure 5.2.** *(continued)*

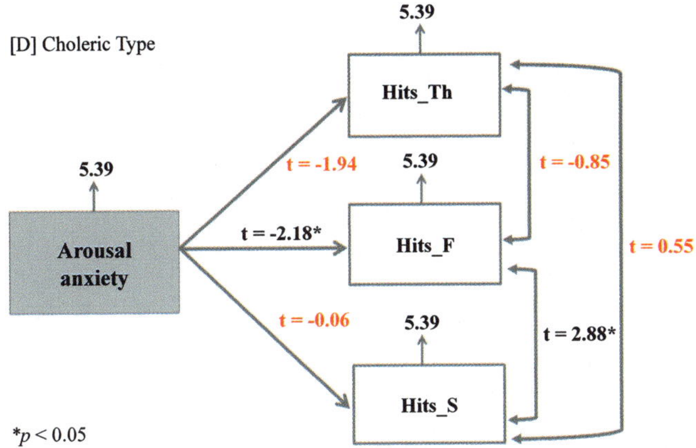



**Figure 5.2.** Results of the exploratory multi-multivariable analysis of regression (structural equations estimated by LISREL 8.51) for [A] errors in Sanguine Type ($N = 60$); [B] hits, total number of items processed, and errors in Melancholic Type ($N = 62$); [C] hits, total number of items processed, and errors in Phlegmatic Type ($N = 72$); and [D] hits in Choleric Type ($N = 60$) and arousal anxiety. TN = total number of items processed. Nonsignificant results are written in red.

In Figure 5.2C one can see that the incoherent high-arousal anxious Phlegmatic Type ($INPT_{Phlegmatic:\ strong,\ slow,\ balanced\ type\ of\ NS}^{high\text{-}arousal\ anxiety}$) is connected with ineffective emotions processing (low number of hits to Th, F, and S faces; high number of total errors to F and S faces) and reduced attentional vigilance to threat and happiness (low level of TN of Th and F faces processed). By contrast, the coherent low-arousal anxious Phlegmatic Type ($CPT_{Phlegmatic:\ strong,\ slow,\ balanced\ type\ of\ NS}^{low\text{-}arousal\ anxiety}$) goes with effective emotions processing (high number of hits to Th, F, and S; low number of total errors to F and S faces) and attentional vigilance to threat and happiness (high level of TN of Th and F faces processed). This means that the Arousal Type of anxiety is a factor in worsening attentional selectiveness of emotional material in the Phlegmatic Type.

The coherent high-arousal anxious Choleric Type ($CPT_{Choleric:\ strong,\ unbalanced\ type\ of\ NS}^{high\text{-}arousal\ anxiety}$) is linked to ineffective happiness processing (low number of hits to F faces), but the incoherent low-arousal anxious Choleric Type ($INPT_{Choleric:\ strong,\ unbalanced\ type\ of\ NS}^{low\text{-}arousal\ anxiety}$) is linked to effective happiness processing (high number of hits to F faces; see Figure 5.2D). This evidence indicates that the Arousal Type of anxiety contributes to declining attentional processing of positive faces in the Choleric Type.

The results demonstrated in Figure 5.3 are on the quality of facial emotions processing in coherent/incoherent personality structures, built upon temperament types and the Apprehension Type of anxiety.

**Figure 5.3.**

[A] Sanguine Type
Apprehension anxiety
5.39
TN_Th
TN_F
TN_S
5.39
5.39
5.39
t = -1.81
t = 1.18
t = -2.18*
t = 2.30*
t = 3.87*
t = 2.57*
*p < 0.05

[B] Melancholic Type
Apprehension anxiety
5.48
Errors_Th
Errors_F
Errors_S
5.48
5.48
5.48
t = 2.34*
t = 1.43
t = 1.75
t = 1.22
t = 2.06*
t = 2.77*
*p < 0.05

[C] Phlegmatic Type
Apprehension anxiety
5.92
Errors_Th
Errors_F
Errors_S
5.92
5.92
5.92
t = -3.31*
t = 1.51
t = 0.79
t = 2.94*
t = 2.34*
t = 3.37*
*p < 0.05

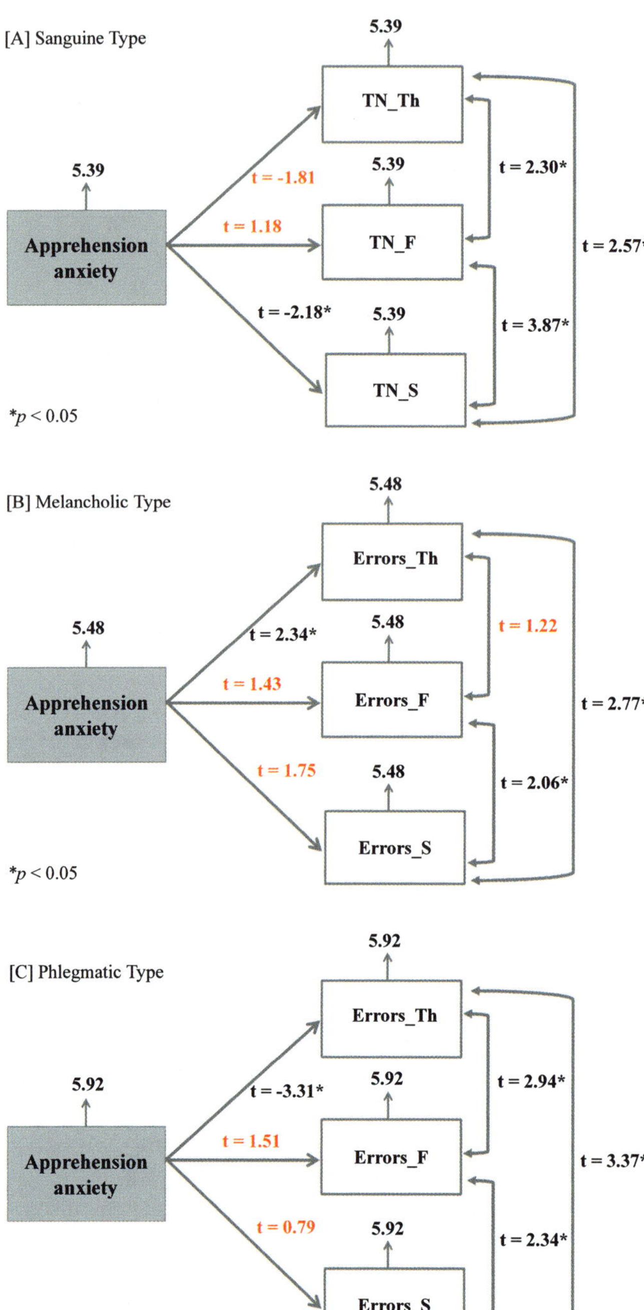

**Figure 5.3.** *(continued)*

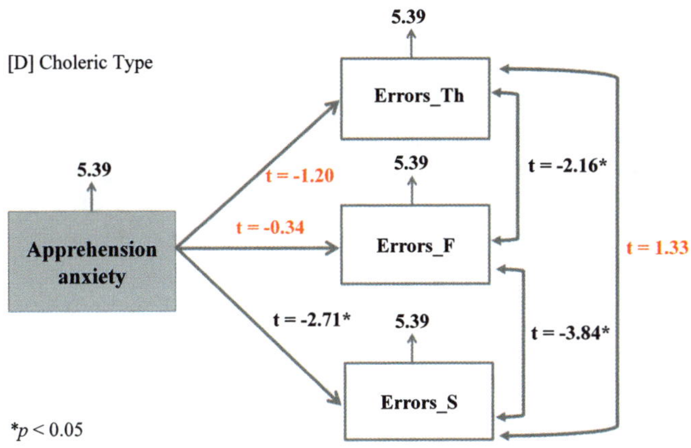


**Figure 5.3.** Results of the exploratory multi-multivariable analysis of regression (structural equations estimated by LISREL 8.51) for [A] total number of items processed in Sanguine Type ($N = 60$); [B] errors in Melancholic Type ($N = 62$); [C] errors in Phlegmatic Type ($N = 72$); and [D] errors in Choleric Type ($N = 60$) and apprehension anxiety. TN = total number of items processed. Nonsignificant results are written in red.

According to Figure 5.3A, the coherent high-apprehension anxious Sanguine Type ($CPT_{Sanguine:\ strong,\ mobile,\ balanced\ type\ of\ NS}^{high\text{-}apprehension\ anxiety}$) is connected with low speed of sadness processing (TN of S faces processed), while the coherent low-apprehension anxious Sanguine Type ($CPT_{Sanguine:\ strong,\ mobile,\ balanced\ type\ of\ NS}^{low\text{-}apprehension\ anxiety}$) is associated with high speed of sadness processing. This suggests that high-apprehension anxiety is linked to reduced attentional vigilance to sadness in sanguines.

As can be seen in Figure 5.3B, the incoherent high-apprehension anxious Melancholic Type ($INPT_{Melancholic:\ weak\ type\ of\ NS}^{high\text{-}apprehension\ anxiety}$) is associated with high number of total errors to Th faces, whereas the coherent low-apprehension anxious Melancholic Type ($CPT_{Melancholic:\ weak\ type\ of\ NS}^{low\text{-}apprehension\ anxiety}$) is linked to low number of errors to Th faces. These results imply that a high level of apprehension anxiety, when associated with the Melancholic Type, is connected with ineffective processing of Th stimuli.

Figure 5.3C presents that the coherent high-apprehension anxious Phlegmatic Type ($CPT_{Phlegmatic:\ strong,\ slow,\ balanced\ type\ of\ NS}^{high\text{-}apprehension\ anxiety}$) is connected with low number of errors to Th faces, but that the coherent low-apprehension anxious Phlegmatic Type ($CPT_{Phlegmatic:\ strong,\ slow,\ balanced\ type\ of\ NS}^{low\text{-}apprehension\ anxiety}$) goes with high number of errors to Th faces. This means that Apprehension Type of anxiety improves attentional selectiveness of threat processing in the Phlegmatic Type.

Finally, the incoherent high-apprehension anxious Choleric Type ($INPT_{Choleric:\ strong,\ unbalanced\ type\ of\ NS}^{high\text{-}apprehension\ anxiety}$) is linked to low number of errors to S faces, but the coherent low-apprehension anxious Choleric Type ($CPT_{Choleric:\ strong,\ unbalanced\ type}$

$_{of\,NS}^{\ low\text{-}apprehension\ anxiety}$) is linked to high number of errors to S faces (Figure 5.3D). This evidence indicates that the Apprehension Type of anxiety fosters attentional selectiveness over sadness in the Choleric Type.

Results from this study suggest that:

- A high level of arousal anxiety mediates in enhancing attentional selectiveness over threat in the Sanguine Type, and in weakening selective processing of emotional stimulation in the other three temperament structures (happiness and sadness in the Melancholic Type, all emotions in the Phlegmatic Type, and happiness in the Choleric Type).
- A high level of apprehension anxiety mediates in worsening processing of negative stimulation in harmonious types of temperaments with effective stimulation processing (sadness in the Sanguine Type and threat in the Melancholic Type), while improving selective processing of negative stimulation in disharmonious types of temperament with ineffective stimulation processing (threat in the Phlegmatic Type and sadness in the Choleric Type).

*Interactions: Temperament Type x Anxiety Type*

Across two separate sessions, participants ($N = 58$ undergraduate students, 42 females, $M = 26.43$ years, $SD = 7.77$) were presented with self-report questionnaires for assessing Pavlovian temperament traits (PTS; Strelau & Zawadzki, 1998) and for assessing state (arousal) and trait (apprehension) anxiety (STAI; Spielberger, 1983; Wrześniewski & Sosnowski, 1996). One week after the questionnaire period, subjects were administered a modified Emotional Go/NoGo task (Figure 5.4). Participants were instructed to respond as quickly and accurately as possible when a Go stimulus appeared and to withhold their reactions when a NoGo stimulus was displayed (for a detailed description of the task, see Fajkowska, Eysenck, Zagórska, & Jaśkowski, 2011).

Generally, the results obtained[1] showed that interaction between the Arousal Type of anxiety and the Melancholic Type is associated with impaired attentional control over happiness, but that interaction between the Arousal Type and Choleric Type is linked to effective happiness processing. More false alarms to F/NoGo trials were observed in coherent high-arousal anxious melancholics ($CPT_{\ Melancholic:\ weak\ type\ of\ NS}^{\ high\text{-}arousal\ anxiety}$) than incoherent low-arousal anxious melancholics ($INPT_{\ Melancholic:\ weak\ type\ of\ NS}^{\ low\text{-}arousal\ anxiety}$).[2] In addition, coherent high-arousal anxious cholerics ($CPT_{\ Choleric:\ strong,\ unbalanced\ type\ of\ NS}^{\ high\text{-}arousal\ anxiety}$) present more accuracy in

---

[1] All results reported from this experimental procedure are based on the log-transformed and arcsin-transformed data. Two-factor multivariate repeated MANOVAs using facial affect as within-subject factor were performed on accuracy, RT, OM, and FA.

[2] *Melancholic Type x Arousal anxiety.* FA: $F(2,51) = 6.60$, $p < 0.001$, $\eta^2 = 0.21$, F/NoGo—coherent high-arousal anxious melancholics ($0.04 \pm 0.01$) > incoherent low-arousal anxious melancholics ($0.02 \pm 0.01$), $p < 0.01$.

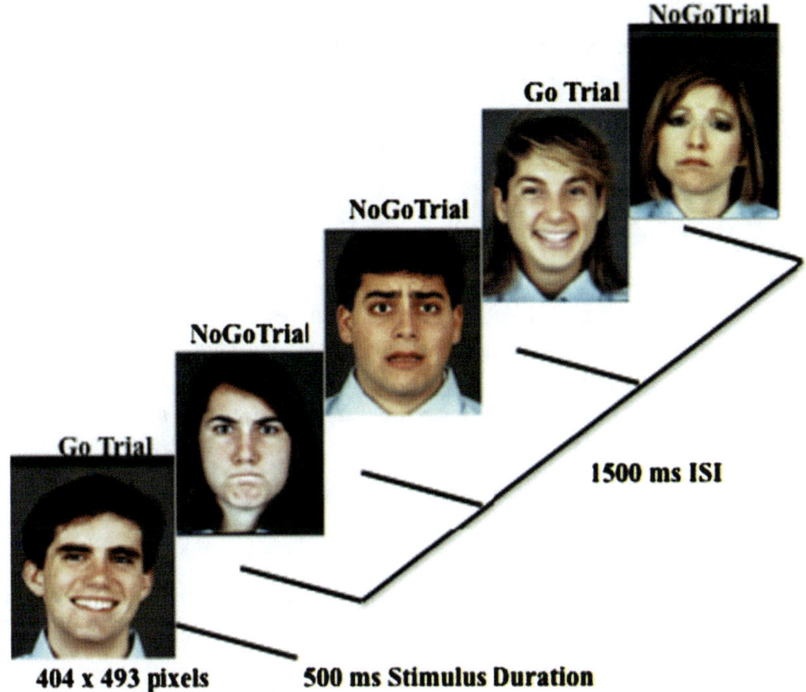


**Figure 5.4.** Illustration of the emotional Go/NoGo task. Stimuli: threatening, friendly, sad, and neutral faces (Ekman & Friesen, 1976), taken from 27 individuals (18 males); equiprobable frequency of the Go and NoGo trials (cf. Eimer, 1993; Todd et al., 2008). Task organization: a total of 720 trials, three blocks of 240 trials each—120 Go trials (Th/Go, F/Go, S/Go, respectively), 120 NoGo (40 Ne/NoGo trials, and two sets of 40 Th/NoGo, 40 F/NoGo, or 40 S/NoGo trials, respectively). ISI = interstimulus interval. Reprinted from "ERP Responses to Facial Affect in Low-Anxious, High-Anxious, Repressors and Defensive High-Anxious Individuals" by M. Fajkowska, M. W. Eysenck, A. Zagórska, and P. Jaśkowski, 2011, *Personality and Individual Differences, 50*, p. 964. Copyright 2011 by Elsevier. Reprinted with permission.

processing happiness than incoherent low-arousal anxious cholerics ($INPT_{Choleric:\ strong,\ unbalanced\ type\ of\ NS}^{low\text{-}arousal\ anxiety}$).[3]

Concerning the findings on interactions between the Apprehension Type of anxiety and the four temperament types, it was revealed that these interactions have an affect on reduced attentional vigilance to happiness and impaired attentional control over happiness in melancholics, and vigilance to happiness and effective happiness processing in cholerics. On a more elaborated level, incoherent high-apprehension anxious melancholics ($INPT_{Melancholic:\ weak\ type\ of\ NS}^{high\text{-}apprehension}$

---

[3] *Choleric Type x Arousal anxiety.* <u>Accuracy</u>: $F(2,51) = 8.38$, $p < 0.001$, $\eta^2 = 0.25$, F/Go—coherent high-arousal anxious cholerics ($1.57 \pm 0.07$) > incoherent low-arousal anxious cholerics ($1.21 \pm 0.65$), $p < 0.001$.

*anxiety*) have been found to be slower in processing F faces, and also with more false alarms to happiness, than coherent low-apprehension anxious melancholics (*CPT* $_{Melancholic:\ weak\ type\ of\ NS}$ $^{low\text{-}apprehension\ anxiety}$).[4] Incoherent high-apprehension anxious cholerics (*INPT* $_{Choleric:\ strong,\ unbalanced\ type\ of\ NS}$ $^{high\text{-}apprehension\ anxiety}$) detect happiness faster and more accurately than coherent low-apprehension anxious cholerics (*CPT* $_{Choleric:\ strong,\ unbalanced\ type\ of\ NS}$ $^{low\text{-}\ apprehension\ anxiety}$).[5]

The regularity emerging from these findings points to the fact that the Melancholic Type interacting with both the Arousal Type (coherent structure) and Apprehension Type (incoherent structure) produces reduced attentional vigilance to happiness and impaired attentional control over happiness processing. By contrast, attentional vigilance to happiness and effectiveness of happiness processing was obtained with interaction between the Choleric Type and Arousal Type (coherent structure) or Apprehension Type (incoherent structure). There were no significant results on the effects of interactions among sanguines or phlegmatics and anxiety types on facial processing.

*Summary and interpretation*

The data presented in Table 5.1 suggest that the intercorrelational and interactional relations among the Arousal Type and Apprehension Type of anxiety and the four temperament types significantly differentiated the attentional patterns of stimulation processing across coherent/incoherent personality types defined within the Pavlovian approach.

*Personality coherence and quality of processing stimulation*

The results evidenced in Table 5.1 indicate that overlapping reactive functions in coherent personality structures—namely, in the (reactive) Melancholic Type + (reactive) Arousal Type—go with reduced attentional vigilance and impaired attentional selectiveness in cases of happiness and sadness, while in the (reactive) Choleric Type + (reactive) Arousal Type they are linked to ineffective happiness processing. When we compare these findings with those for low-arousal anxious melancholics and cholerics, it is evident that functional simplicity (coherence) worsens attentional processing of happiness and sadness in both personality structures. Moreover,

---

[4] *Melancholic Type x Apprehension anxiety.* R̲T̲: $F(3,53) = 4.51$, $p < 0.01$, $\eta^2 = 0.15$, F/Go—incoherent high-apprehension anxious melancholics $(2.65 \pm 0.01)$ > coherent low-apprehension anxious melancholics $(2.61 \pm 0.02)$, $p < 0.05$; F̲A̲: $F(2,51) = 3.87$, $p < 0.001$, $\eta^2 = 0.09$, F/NoGo—incoherent high-apprehension anxious melancholics $(0.04 \pm 0.01)$ > coherent low-apprehension anxious melancholics $(0.02 \pm 0.01)$, $p < 0.05$.

[5] *Choleric Type x Apprehension anxiety.* R̲T̲: $F(3,53) = 4.51$, $p < 0.01$, $\eta^2 = 0.15$, F/Go—incoherent high-apprehension anxious cholerics $(2.59 \pm 0.03)$ < coherent low-apprehension anxious cholerics $(2.67 \pm 0.02)$, $p < 0.05$; A̲ccuracy̲: $F(2,51) = 10.37$, $p < 0.001$, $\eta^2 = 0.29$, F/Go—incoherent high-apprehension anxious cholerics $(1.57 \pm 0.07)$ > coherent low-apprehension anxious cholerics $(1.21 \pm 0.05)$, $p < 0.001$.

**Table 5.1.** Attentional biases in coherent/incoherent personality structures built upon temperament types in Pavlovian approach and anxiety types

| Processes-level of stimulation processing | Traits-level of stimulation processing | | | | | | | | | | | | | | | |
| --- | --- | --- | --- | --- | --- | --- | --- | --- | --- | --- | --- | --- | --- | --- | --- | --- |
| | **Nervous system control** *(Pavlovian approach)* | | | | | | | | | | | | | | | |
| **Attentional patterns of stimulation processing** | **Sanguine Type** | | | | **Melancholic Type** | | | | **Phlegmatic Type** | | | | **Choleric Type** | | | |
| | *CPT* | | | *INPT* | *CPT* | | | *INPT* | *CPT* | | | *INPT* | *CPT* | | *INPT* | |
| | Low-arousal anxiety | Low-appre. anxiety | High-appre. anxiety | High-arousal anxiety | High-arousal anxiety | Low-appre. anxiety | High-appre. anxiety | Low-arousal anxiety | Low-arousal anxiety | Low-appre. anxiety | High-appre. anxiety | High-arousal anxiety | High-arousal anxiety | Low-appre. anxiety | High-appre. anxiety | Low-arousal anxiety |
| **Vigilance** *(low RT, high TN)* | | S | | | | | | F&S | Th&F | | | | | | F | |
| **Reduced vigilance** *(high RT, low TN)* | | | S | | F&S | | F | | | | | Th&F | | | | |
| **Avoidance** *(high OM)* | | | | | | | | | | | | | | | | |
| **Impaired attentional control** *(high FA)* | | | | | F | | F | | | | | | | | | |
| **Enhanced attentional control** *(low FA)* | | | | | | | | | | | | | | | | |
| **Attentional effectiveness** *(high Accuracy and Hits)* | | | | Th | | Th | | F&S | All emotions | | Th | | F | | S / F | F |
| **Attentional ineffectiveness** *(low Accuracy and Hits)* | Th | | | | F&S | | Th | | | Th | | All emotions | F | S | | |

*Note.* RT = reaction time; TN = total number of items processed; OM = omissions; FA = false alarms; Th = threatening faces; F = friendly faces; S = sad faces. Intercorrelational relations are highlighted in blue for arousal anxiety and green for apprehension anxiety; interactive relations are highlighted in pink.

according to Table 5.1, overlapping regulative functions observed in coherent personalities—namely, in the (regulative) Sanguine Type + (regulative) Apprehension Type—lessen attentional vigilance to sadness, and in the (regulative) Phlegmatic + (regulative) Apprehension Type increase attentional selectivity over threat. When we contrast these data with the data for low-apprehension anxious sanguines or phlegmatics, we clearly see that functional simplicity based on elevated apprehension anxiety worsens attentional processing of sadness in the Sanguine Type but improves attentional processing of threat in the Phlegmatic Type.

*Personality incoherence and quality of processing stimulation*

The exploration of distinctness between controlling functions registered in incoherent personalities, built upon the (regulative) Sanguine Type + (reactive) Arousal Type, pointed at the enhanced attentional selectiveness over threat, and building upon the (regulative) Phlegmatic Type + (reactive) Arousal Type revealed reduced attentional vigilance and ineffective processing of all facial expressions. Coherent low-arousal anxious sanguines present worse attentional selectiveness over threat and coherent low-arousal anxious phlegmatics reveal better attentional processing of emotional stimuli. Hence functional complexity (incoherence) is connected on the one hand with improved processing in sanguines, and on the other with weakened processing in phlegmatics.

But distinctness between controlling functions seen in incoherent personalities—that is, in the (reactive) Melancholic Type + (regulative) Apprehension Type—reduces attentional selectiveness over threat, and in the (reactive) Choleric Type + (regulative) Apprehension Type enhances attentional selectiveness over sadness processing. Again, if we set these results side by side with those illustrated in Table 5.1 for low-apprehension anxious melancholics and cholerics, we receive information indicating that this functional complexity weakens processing of threat in the Melancholic Type but enhances sadness processing in the Choleric Type.

On the basis of these findings, one can see that a few interesting facts emerge from the analysis of intercorrelations among the Arousal Type and Apprehension Type of anxiety and the four temperament types in the Pavlovian model.

- The level of functional complexity (higher-level organization—that is, personality coherence/incoherence) specifically relates to the quality of attentional processing; however, it is difficult to extract any consistent patterns of results reflecting that particular type of personality, that is coherence or incoherence, is constantly associated either with improving or with worsening of processing stimulation.
- Yet, splitting personality coherence/incoherence into this constructed upon low or high level of anxiety some regularity emerges in results obtained: (a) personality coherence with high level of anxiety generally goes with worsening of attentional processing (except in phlegmatics), while (b) personality incoherence with low level of anxiety increases attentional processing (in

temperaments with low-SPC, that is melancholics and cholerics). But there is no such clarity for personality coherence with low level of anxiety and personality incoherence with elevated level of anxiety as they are equally connected with both worsening or improving of attentional processing of emotional material.

- However, more regular patterns of results relating to the quality of processing might be identified at the lower-level personality structures (harmoniousness of temperament and strength of nervous system control in temperaments).

- Those composing harmonious temperaments—sanguines and melancholics— present detachment of quality of processing across the strength of nervous system control differently distributed between these two temperaments.

- Those composing temperament with the strongest nervous system control over stimulation are sanguines in cases when arousal anxiety is concerned. Hypothetically, the reactive dominant in arousal anxiety increases sensitivity to threat in sanguines, which results in effective threat processing. Effective selectiveness over social threat seems to be adaptive (cf. Öhman, Lundqvist, & Esteves, 2001).

- Those composing temperament with the weakest nervous system control over stimulation are melancholics in cases when both types of anxiety are concerned. Both reactive and regulative dominants in arousal or apprehension anxiety worsen attentional selectiveness over emotional material in the Melancholic Type.

- Those composing disharmonious temperaments—phlegmatic and choleric— go with good attentional selectiveness over negativity in cases when they coexist with high-apprehension anxiety and with increased quality of emotional stimulation processing when they are associated with low-arousal anxiety; one possible explanation is that these two structures benefit from the regulative dominant in apprehension anxiety and absence of reactive dominant as the arousal anxiety is low, and  together improve their effectiveness of processing stimulation. In other words, a nonoptimal level of stimulation and ineffectiveness of stimulation processing typical for these two types of temperament may be altered into effective emotional stimulation processing thanks to presence of regulative anxious apprehension and absence of reactive anxious arousal.

*Personality coherence/incoherence and dynamics of processing stimulation*

The interpretation of interactional analysis of functions between arousal and apprehension anxiety and four temperament types (Table 5.1) has to be reinforced by data from Table 5.2. Findings included in Table 5.2 illustrate patterns of processing emotional material in temperament types and anxiety types, studied separately. They are taken from the research reported in the previous sections.

Considering the data in Table 5.2A, we have evidence that high-arousal anxiety produces impaired attentional control over happiness. The melancholic temperament goes with reduced attentional vigilance toward happiness and effective happiness processing. In the Choleric Type we find attentional vigilance toward happiness coupled with impaired attentional control over happiness, attentional

**Table 5.2.** Melancholic and choleric types (Pavlovian approach) and [A] Arousal Type of anxiety and [B] Apprehension Type of anxiety in attentional processing of facial affect

[A][1]

| Personality types | Behavioral indices of facial processing | | | |
| --- | --- | --- | --- | --- |
| | *RT* | *Accuracy* | *OM* | *FA* |
| **Melancholic** | ↑ F | ↑ F | ↓ F | ns |
| **Choleric** | ↓ F ↓ S | ↑ S | ↓ S | ↑ Th ↑ F |
| **High-arousal anxiety** | ns | ns | ns | ↑ F |

[B][2]

| Personality types | Behavioral indices of facial processing | | | |
| --- | --- | --- | --- | --- |
| | *RT* | *Accuracy* | *OM* | *FA* |
| **Melancholic** | ns | ↓ Th ↑ F ↑ S | ↓ F ↓ S | ns |
| **Choleric** | ↓ F | ↑ S | ↓ S | ↑ Th |
| **High-apprehension anxiety** | ns | ↓ F | ns | ↑ F |

*Note.* RT = reaction time; OM = omissions; FA = false alarms; Th = threatening faces; F = friendly faces; S = sad faces.

[1] RT: $F(3,53) = 7.91$, $p < 0.001$, $\eta^2 = 0.31$, F/Go – melancholics ($2.80 \pm 0.02$) > phlegmatics ($2.73 \pm 0.02$), $p < 0.001$, F/Go – cholerics ($2.63 \pm 0.02$) < phlegmatics ($2.73 \pm 0.02$), $p < 0.001$; $F(3,53) = 6.74$, $p < 0.001$, $\eta^2 = 0.28$, S/Go – cholerics ($2.71 \pm 0.01$) < phlegmatics ($2.80 \pm 0.02$), $p < 0.001$. Accuracy: $F(3,51) = 5.12$, $p < 0.001$, $\eta^2 = 0.23$, F/Go – melancholics ($1.34 \pm 0.03$) > phlegmatics ($1.19 \pm 0.04$), $p < 0.05$; $F(3,51) = 5.51$, $p < 0.001$, $\eta^2 = 0.30$, S/Go – cholerics ($1.01 \pm 0.08$) > phlegmatics ($0.61 \pm 0.08$), $p < 0.001$. OM: $F(3,51) = 3.89$, $p < 0.01$, $\eta^2 = 0.19$, F/Go –melancholics ($0.03 \pm 0.01$) < phlegmatics ($0.67 \pm 0.01$), $p < 0.05$; $F(3,51) = 5.60$, $p < 0.001$, $\eta^2 = 0.25$, S/Go – cholerics ($0.15 \pm 0.07$) < phlegmatics ($0.48 \pm 0.07$), $p < 0.001$. FA: $F(3,51) = 4.63$, $p < 0.001$, $\eta^2 = 0.21$, Th/NoGo – sanguines ($0.05 \pm 0.01$) < cholerics ($0.11 \pm 0.01$), $p < 0.05$, Th/NoGo – melancholics ($0.05 \pm 0.01$) < cholerics ($0.11 \pm 0.01$), $p < 0.05$; $F(3,51) = 4.89$, $p < 0.001$, $\eta^2 = 0.22$, F/NoGo – melancholics ($0.15 \pm 0.03$) < cholerics ($0.21 \pm 0.05$), $p < 0.05$; $F(1,51) = 27.30$, $p < 0.001$, $\eta^2 = 0.35$, F/NoGo – low-arousal anxious ($0.02 \pm 0.01$) < high-arousal anxious ($0.07 \pm 0.01$), $p < 0.001$.

[2] RT: $F(3,53) = 6.69$, $p < 0.001$, $\eta^2 = 0.27$, F/Go – cholerics ($2.63 \pm 0.02$) < phlegmatics ($2.77 \pm 0.03$), $p < 0.001$. Accuracy: $F(3,51) = 2.92$, $p < 0.05$, $\eta^2 = 0.15$, Th/Go – sanguines ($1.31 \pm 0.05$) > melancholics ($1.14 \pm 0.03$), $p < 0.05$; F/Go – melancholics ($1.34 \pm 0.03$) > cholerics ($1.21 \pm 0.03$), $p < 0.05$; $F(3,51) = 11.14$, $p < 0.001$, $\eta^2 = 0.40$, S/Go – melancholics ($0.81 \pm 0.05$) > phlegmatics ($0.18 \pm 0.13$), $p < 0.001$, S/Go – cholerics ($1.01 \pm 0.08$) > phlegmatics ($0.18 \pm 0.13$), $p < 0.001$; $F(1,51) = 11.13$, $p < 0.001$, $\eta^2 = 0.18$, F/Go – low-apprehension anxious ($1.48 \pm 0.04$) > high-apprehension anxious ($1.26 \pm 0.03$), $p < 0.001$. OM: $F(3,51) = 4.42$, $p < 0.001$, $\eta^2 = 0.21$, F/Go – melancholics ($0.03 \pm 0.01$) < phlegmatics ($0.11 \pm 0.02$), $p < 0.001$; $F(3,51) = 19.53$, $p < 0.001$, $\eta^2 = 0.53$, S/Go – melancholics ($0.30 \pm 0.04$) < phlegmatics ($0.95 \pm 0.09$), $p < 0.001$, S/Go – cholerics ($0.15 \pm 0.06$) < phlegmatics ($0.95 \pm 0.09$), $p < 0.001$. FA: $F(3,51) = 7.07$, $p < 0.001$, $\eta^2 = 0.29$, Th/NoGo – sanguines ($0.04 \pm 0.01$) < cholerics ($0.11 \pm 0.01$), $p < 0.001$; $F(1,51) = 14.41$, $p < 0.001$, $\eta^2 = 0.22$, F/NoGo – low-apprehension anxious ($0.01 \pm 0.01$) < high-apprehension anxious ($0.06 \pm 0.01$), $p < 0.001$.

vigilance and effectiveness in sadness processing, and impaired attentional control over threat. Linking these results to those from Table 5.1, one can perceive that interaction between the (reactive) Melancholic Type and (reactive) Arousal Type of anxiety causes impaired attentional control over happiness, while interaction between the (reactive) Arousal Type of anxiety and (reactive) Choleric Type results in effective happiness processing. Thus, with reference to the synergistic functional interaction, the relation between arousal anxiety and the Melancholic Type leads to the pattern of happiness processing that is typical for arousal anxiety. The antagonistic functional interaction explains the effect of interaction between arousal anxiety and the Choleric Type, which is a new pattern of happiness processing—attentional selectiveness over happiness.

Analyzing the data from Table 5.2B, we see that high-apprehension anxiety is connected with ineffective happiness processing and impaired attentional control over happiness. The Melancholic Type is effective in processing happiness and sadness, but ineffective in processing threat. The Choleric Type is associated with vigilance to happiness, effective processing of sadness, and impaired attentional control over threat. Comparing this evidence with the data from Table 5.1, one can notice that the interaction between the (regulative) Apprehension Type of anxiety and (reactive) Melancholic Type results in reduced vigilance and impaired attentional control over happiness, but that the interaction between the (regulative) Apprehension Type of anxiety and (reactive) Choleric Type produces attentional vigilance to happiness and attentional effectiveness in happiness processing. The synergistic interaction explains the fact that the patterns of attentional processing identified in the (regulative) Apprehension Type of anxiety displaced or superseded the patterns of attentional processing identified in the (reactive) Melancholic Type of temperament. In addition, the antagonistic interaction justifies the emergence of a quite new pattern of attentional processing when the relation between the (regulative) Apprehension Type of anxiety and (reactive) Choleric Type is concerned.

In conclusion, there is evidence that interactional analysis of personality coherence/incoherence reveals:

- The synergistic interactions between the Melancholic Type and both anxieties and the antagonistic interactions between the Choleric Type and both anxieties, narrowing attentional processes engaged in processing when all focal types are studied separately and reducing the set of emotions to a more specific one—here, happiness.
- The reactive Melancholic Type (a relatively weak nervous system signifying low strength of excitation and low strength of inhibition), when it interacts with arousal anxiety or apprehension anxiety, is dominated by patterns of adverse happiness processing typical for these anxieties—reflected in reduced attentional vigilance and impaired attentional control (which are the effects of synergistic interactions).

- The reactive Choleric Type (a relatively strong nervous system representing by high strength of excitation and moderate or low strength of inhibition), when it interacts with arousal anxiety or apprehension anxiety, produces a new, harmless happiness processing—reflected in good attentional selectiveness (which are the effects of antagonistic interactions).

Thus, according to the obtained results from interactional analysis, it appears that the synergistic and antagonistic interactions do not specifically explain how personality coherence or incoherence modify dynamics of attentional processes, but rather how elevated arousal or apprehension anxiety in temperaments with low SPC influence these dynamics. These data, combined with those from interactional analysis, extend our understanding of the quality and dynamics of attentional stimulation processing in these personality constellations.

### 5.2.2. Attentional biases in coherent/incoherent personality structures built upon temperament types in Eysenckian perspective and anxiety types

The evidence on the quality and dynamics of attentional processing of facial affect in coherent/incoherent personality structures, composed of the four temperament types in the Eysenckian perspective and anxiety types, is presented below.

*Intercorrelations: Temperament Type and Anxiety Type*

Across two separate sessions, participants ($N = 168$, 83 females, $M = 25.15$ years, $SD = 7.11$) first completed two questionnaires—evaluating extraversion and neuroticism (EPQ-R; Brzozowski & Drwal, 1995; Eysenck & Eysenck, 1994) and state and trait anxiety (STAI; Spielberger, 1983; Wrześniewski & Sosnowski, 1996); and second, they were administered the same Emotional Go/NoGo Task (cf. Figure 5.4).

Figure 5.5 presents evidence on affect processing in coherent/incoherent personality structures composed of three temperament types and arousal anxiety. The significant results were found for sanguines, melancholics, and phlegmatics.

Figures 5.5A and 5.5C demonstrate that in the incoherent high-arousal anxious Sanguine Type ($INPT_{\text{Sanguine: emotionally stable extrovert}}^{\text{high-arousal anxiety}}$) and incoherent high-arousal anxious Phlegmatic Type type ($INPT_{\text{Phlegmatic: emotionally stable introvert}}^{\text{high-arousal anxiety}}$), impaired attentional control over sadness is observed (high level of FAs to S/NoGo), while the coherent low-arousal anxious Sanguine Type ($CPT_{\text{Sanguine: emotionally stable extrovert}}^{\text{low-arousal anxiety}}$) and coherent low-arousal anxious Phlegmatic Type ($CPT_{\text{Sanguine: emotionally stable introvert}}^{\text{low-arousal anxiety}}$) present enhanced attentional control over sadness (low level of FAs to S/NoGo).

According to Figure 5.5B, the coherent high-arousal anxious Melancholic Type ($CPT_{\text{Melancholic: emotionally unstable introvert}}^{\text{high-arousal anxiety}}$) reveals ineffective sadness processing (low accuracy for S/Go trials), but the incoherent low-arousal anxious Melancholic Type ($INPT_{\text{Melancholic: emotionally unstable introvert}}^{\text{low-arousal anxiety}}$) shows effective sadness processing (high accuracy for S/Go trials).

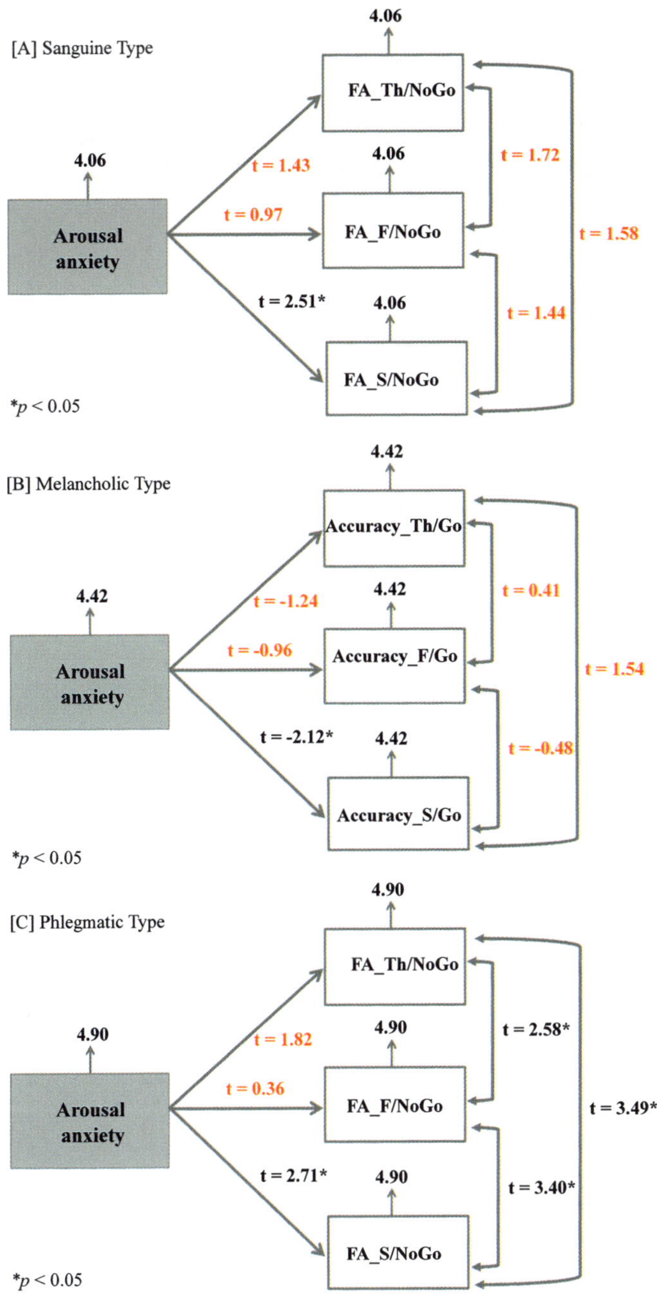


**Figure 5.5.** Results of the exploratory multi-multivariable analysis of regression (structural equations estimated by LISREL 8.51) for [A] false alarms to NoGo trials in Sanguine Type ($N = 35$); [B] accuracy to Go trials in Melancholic Type ($N = 41$); and [C] false alarms to NoGo trials in Phlegmatic Type ($N = 50$) and arousal anxiety. FA = false alarms. Nonsignificant results are written in red.

**Figure 5.6.**

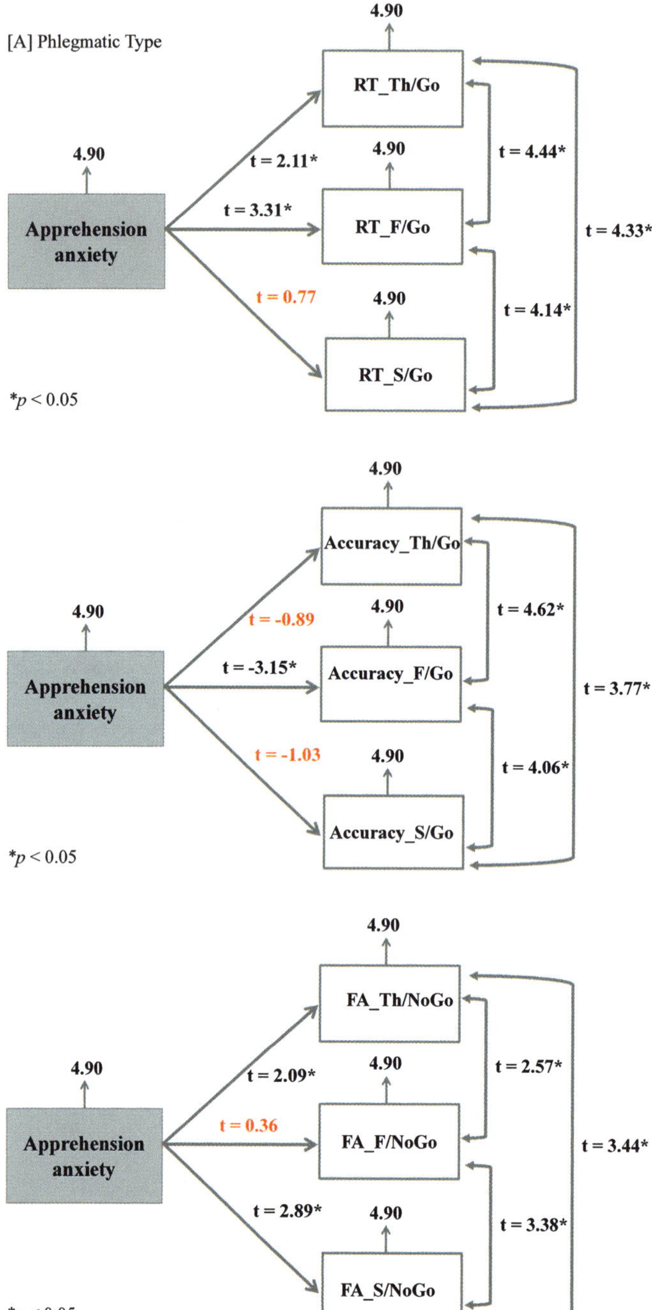

**Figure 5.6.** *(continued)*

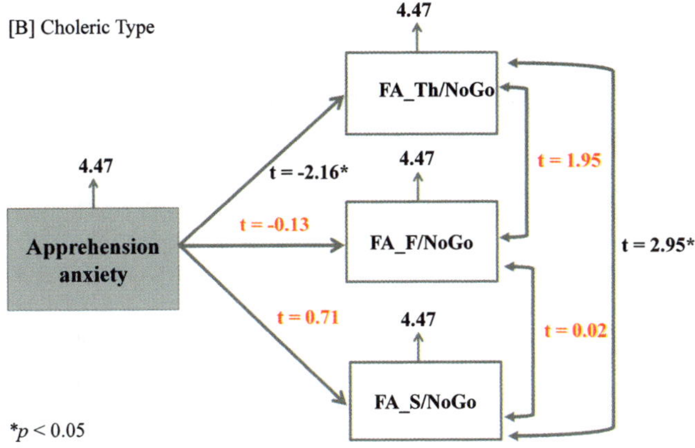


**Figure 5.6.** Results of the exploratory multi-multivariable analysis of regression (structural equations estimated by LISREL 8.51) for [A] reaction times, accuracy to Go trials, and false alarms to NoGo trials in Phlegmatic Type ($N = 50$); and [B] false alarms to NoGo trials in Choleric Type ($N = 42$) and apprehension anxiety. RT = reaction times; FA = false alarms. Nonsignificant results are written in red.

The significant findings on attentional processing of facial affect in coherent/ incoherent personality structures built of certain temperament types and apprehension anxiety are shown in Figure 5.6. In the aspects studied, there were nonsignificant results for the sanguine and melancholic types of temperament mixed with apprehension anxiety.

As illustrated in Figure 5.6A, in the case of the coherent high-apprehension anxious Phlegmatic Type ($CPT_{Phlegmatic:\ emotionally\ stable\ introvert}^{high\text{-}apprehension\ anxiety}$) reduced attentional vigilance (slow detection) to friendly and threatening faces is registered (F/Go; Th/Go), but in the case of the coherent low-apprehension anxious Phlegmatic Type ($CPT_{Phlegmatic:\ emotionally\ stable\ introvert}^{low\text{-}apprehension\ anxiety}$) attentional vigilance (fast detection) to these emotions is recorded. Also, in the coherent high-apprehension anxious Phlegmatic Type ($CPT_{Phlegmatic:\ emotionally\ stable\ introvert}^{high\text{-}apprehension\ anxiety}$) ineffectiveness (low accuracy) in detection of friendly faces (F/Go) is observed, whereas in the coherent low-apprehension anxious Phlegmatic Type ($CPT_{Phlegmatic:\ emotionally\ stable\ introvert}^{low\text{-}apprehension\ anxiety}$) high accuracy of happiness detection is observed (F/Go). And the coherent high-apprehension anxious Phlegmatic Type ($CPT_{Phlegmatic:\ emotionally\ stable\ introvert}^{high\text{-}apprehension\ anxiety}$) shows weakened attentional control over negative emotions (high level of FAs to Th/NoGo and S/NoGo); at the same time, the coherent low-apprehension anxious Phlegmatic Type ($CPT_{Phlegmatic:\ emotionally\ stable\ introvert}^{low\text{-}apprehension\ anxiety}$) presents good attentional control over negativity (low level of FAs to Th/NoGo and S/NoGo).

As shown in figure 5.6B, the incoherent high-apprehension anxious Choleric Type ($INPT_{Choleric:\ emotionally\ unstable\ extrovert}{}^{high\text{-}apprehension\ anxiety}$) displays good attentional control over threat (lower level of FAs to Th/NoGo), while the coherent low-apprehension anxious Choleric Type ($CPT_{Choleric:\ emotionally\ unstable\ extrovert}{}^{low\text{-}apprehension\ anxiety}$) demonstrates a weaken attentional control over threat (higher level of FAs to Th/NoGo).

Taken together, these results suggest that:

- The Arousal Type of anxiety is connected with decreased processing of emotional material, which is reflected in reduced attentional control over sadness in sanguine and phlegmatic types (with high SPC) and in ineffective sadness processing in the Melancholic Type (low SPC).
- The Apprehension Type of anxiety differentiates quality of attentional processing in two temperament types: in the Phlegmatic Type it is connected with reduced attentional vigilance to processing "arousing" emotions, ineffective happiness processing, and decreased attentional control over negativity processing, and in the Choleric Type it is linked to good attentional control over processing threat.

*Interactions: Temperament Type x Anxiety Type*

One hundred ninety-nine participants (156 females, $M = 24.80$ years, $SD = 6.50$) completed the same procedure as described above. To summarize the results of the multivariate analysis of variance, the Arousal Type of anxiety actively participates in stimulation processing in the phlegmatic temperament type (by avoidance of happiness processing and impaired attentional control over negativity) and choleric temperament type (by enhanced attentional control over negativity). The findings revealed that incoherent high-arousal anxious phlegmatics ($INPT_{Phlegmatic:\ emotionally\ stable\ introvert}{}^{high\text{-}arousal\ anxiety}$) process F faces with a higher level of omissions, and Th/NoGo and S/NoGo trials with more false alarms, than coherent low-arousal anxious phlegmatics ($CPT_{Phlegmatic:\ emotionally\ stable\ introvert}{}^{low\text{-}arousal\ anxiety}$)[6]. In addition, coherent high-arousal anxious cholerics ($CPT_{Choleric:\ emotionally\ unstable\ extravert}{}^{high\text{-}arousal\ anxiety}$) revealed fewer false alarms in processing negativity (Th/NoGo and S/NoGo trials) than incoherent low-arousal anxious cholerics ($INPT_{Choleric:\ emotionally\ unstable\ extravert}{}^{low\text{-}arousal\ anxiety}$).[7]

---

[6] *Phlegmatic Type x Arousal anxiety.* <u>OM</u>: $F(3,186) = 3.10$, $p < 0.05$, $\eta^2 = 0.05$, F/Go—coherent low-arousal anxious phlegmatic ($0.04 \pm 0.02$) < incoherent high-arousal anxious phlegmatics ($0.09 \pm 0.02$), $p < 0.05$; <u>FA</u>: $F(6,186) = 2.69$, $p < 0.01$, $\eta^2 = 0.08$, Th/NoGo—coherent low-arousal anxious phlegmatics ($0.05 \pm 0.01$) < incoherent high-arousal anxious phlegmatics ($0.10 \pm 0.01$), $p < 0.001$; $F(6,186) = 5.27$, $p < 0.001$, $\eta^2 = 0.14$, S/NoGo—coherent low-arousal anxious phlegmatics ($0.04 \pm 0.04$) < incoherent high-arousal anxious phlegmatics ($0.20 \pm 0.03$), $p < 0.01$.

[7] *Choleric Type x Arousal anxiety.* <u>FA</u>: $F(6,186) = 2.69$, $p < 0.01$, $\eta^2 = 0.08$, Th/NoGo—coherent high-arousal anxious cholerics ($0.05 \pm 0.01$) < incoherent low-arousal anxious cholerics ($0.09 \pm 0.01$), $p < 0.001$; $F(6,186) = 5.27$, $p < 0.001$, $\eta^2 = 0.14$, S/NoGo—coherent high-arousal anxious cholerics ($0.17 \pm 0.03$) < incoherent low-arousal anxious cholerics ($0.28 \pm 0.03$), $p < 0.001$.

The interaction between trait anxiety indicating the Apprehension Type and Phlegmatic Type of temperament affects the attentional avoidance, inefficiency, and impaired attentional control in detection of happiness, whereas the interaction between apprehension anxiety and the Choleric Type of temperament influences efficiency of happiness processing and better attentional control over threat. Thus less accuracy and more omissions and false alarms in processing happy faces have been found in the coherent high-apprehension anxious Phlegmatic Type ($CPT_{Phlegmatic:\ emotionally\ stable\ introvert}^{high-apprehension\ anxiety}$) compared with the coherent low-apprehension anxious Phlegmatic Type ($CPT_{Phlegmatic:\ emotionally\ stable\ introvert}^{low-apprehension\ anxiety}$).[8] More accuracy, fewer omissions in happiness processing, and lower level of false alarms in Th/NoGo trials were observed in the incoherent high-apprehension anxious Choleric Type ($INPT_{Choleric:\ emotionally\ unstable\ extravert}^{high-apprehension\ anxiety}$) than in the coherent low-apprehension anxious Choleric Type ($CPT_{Choleric:\ emotionally\ unstable\ extravert}^{low-apprehension\ anxiety}$).[9]

The results for influence of interactions between the Sanguine Type x both types of anxiety and the Melancholic Type x both types of anxiety on processing facial stimuli were nonsignificant.

### Summary and interpretation

Table 5.3 summarizes the results received for correlational and interactional analysis, done for individuals with coherent/incoherent personality structures composed of the four temperament types within the Eysenckian approach and arousal or apprehension anxiety and attentional processing.

### Personality coherence and quality of stimulation processing

As illustrated in Table 5.3, overlapping reactive functions in coherent structures built upon (reactive) Melancholic Type + (reactive) Arousal Type are connected with ineffective sadness processing. The opposite pattern presents in the low-arousal anxious Melancholic Type. Thus in this case functional simplicity

---

[8] *Phlegmatic Type x Apprehension anxiety.* <u>Accuracy</u>: $F(2,189) = 6.79$, $p < 0.001$, $\eta^2 = 0.07$, F/Go coherent low-apprehension anxious phlegmatics ($1.27 \pm 0.04$) > coherent high-apprehension anxious phlegmatics ($1.14 \pm 0.04$), $p < 0.05$; <u>OM</u>: $F(2,189) = 11.96$, $p < 0.001$, $\eta^2 = 0.11$, F/Go—coherent low-apprehension anxious phlegmatics ($0.05 \pm 0.02$) < coherent high-apprehension anxious phlegmatics ($0.14 \pm 0.02$), $p < 0.001$; <u>FA</u>: $F(5,189) = 3.87$, $p < 0.001$, $\eta^2 = 0.09$, F/NoGo—coherent low-apprehension anxious phlegmatics ($0.02 \pm 0.01$) < coherent high-apprehension anxious phlegmatics ($0.07 \pm 0.01$), $p < 0.001$.

[9] *Choleric Type x Apprehension anxiety.* <u>Accuracy</u>: $F(2,189) = 6.79$, $p < 0.001$, $\eta^2 = 0.07$, F/Go—incoherent high-apprehension anxious cholerics ($1.29 \pm 0.03$) > coherent low-apprehension anxious cholerics ($1.12 \pm 0.05$), $p < 0.001$; <u>OM</u>: $F(2,189) = 11.96$, $p < 0.001$, $\eta^2 = 0.11$, F/Go—incoherent high-apprehension anxious cholerics ($0.05 \pm 0.01$) < coherent low-apprehension anxious cholerics ($0.13 \pm 0.02$), $p < 0.001$; <u>FA</u>: $F(5,189) = 3.18$, $p < 0.001$, $\eta^2 = 0.08$, Th/NoGo—incoherent high-apprehension anxious cholerics ($0.05 \pm 0.01$) < coherent low-apprehension anxious cholerics ($0.07 \pm 0.01$), $p < 0.001$.

**Table 5.3.** Attentional biases in coherent/incoherent personality structures built upon temperament types in Eysenckian approach and anxiety types

| Processes-level of stimulation processing | Traits-level of stimulation processing | | | | | | | | | | | | | | | |
| --- | --- | --- | --- | --- | --- | --- | --- | --- | --- | --- | --- | --- | --- | --- | --- | --- |
| | Content (emotional and social) characteristics of activity *(Eysenckian approach)* | | | | | | | | | | | | | | | |
| Attentional patterns of stimulation processing | Sanguine Type | | | | Melancholic Type | | | | Phlegmatic Type | | | | Choleric Type | | | |
| | *CPT* | | | *INPT* | *CPT* | | | *INPT* | *CPT* | | | *INPT* | *CPT* | | *INPT* | |
| | Low-arousal anxiety | Low-appre. anxiety | High-appre. anxiety | High-arousal anxiety | High-arousal anxiety | Low-appre. anxiety | High-appre. anxiety | Low-arousal anxiety | Low-arousal anxiety | Low-appre. anxiety | High-appre. anxiety | High-arousal anxiety | High-arousal anxiety | Low-appre. anxiety | High-appre. anxiety | Low-arousal anxiety |
| **Vigilance** *(low RT, high TN)* | | | | | | | | | | Th&F | | | | | | |
| **Reduced vigilance** *(high RT, low TN)* | | | | | | | | | | | Th&F | | | | | |
| **Avoidance** *(high OM)* | | | | | | | | | | | F | F | | | | |
| **Impaired attentional control** *(high FA)* | | | | S | | | | | | | Th&S / F | S / Th&S | | Th | | |
| **Enhanced attentional control** *(low FA)* | S | | | | | | | | S | Th&S | | | Th&S | | Th / Th | |
| **Attentional effectiveness** *(high Accuracy and Hits)* | | | | | | | | S | | F | | | | | F | |
| **Attentional ineffectiveness** *(low Accuracy and Hits)* | | | | | S | | | | | | F / F | | | | | |

*Note.* RT = reaction time; TN = total number of items processed; OM = omissions; FA = false alarms; Th = threatening faces; F = friendly faces; S = sad faces. Intercorrelational relations are highlighted in blue for arousal anxiety and green for apprehension anxiety; interactive relations are highlighted in pink.

(coherence) is connected with weakened sadness processing. Moreover, as seen in Table 5.3, overlapping regulative functions in coherent structures built upon the (regulative) Phlegmatic Type + (regulative) Apprehension Type are associated with reduced attentional vigilance to threat and happiness, ineffectiveness of happiness processing, and impaired inhibitory control over negativity. Data from Table 5.3 for low-apprehension anxiety phlegmatics suggests a better quality of processing: early attentional vigilance toward thereat and happiness, effectiveness of happiness processing and enhanced inhibitory control over negativity.

*Personality incoherence and quality of stimulation processing*

Distinctness between controlling functions—seen in incoherent structures—consisting of the (regulative) Sanguine Type + (reactive) Arousal Type and (regulative) Phlegmatic + (reactive) Arousal Type, is linked to impaired attentional control over sadness. When we compare this evidence with data for low-arousal anxious sanguine and low-arousal anxious phlegmatic types, it seems obvious that functional complexity (incoherence) decreases attentional control over sadness. Next distinctness between controlling functions—seen in incoherent structures—consisting of the (reactive) Choleric Type + (regulative) Apprehension Type, is linked to enhanced attentional control over threat. This time results suggest the improvement in threat processing in the incoherent high-apprehension anxious Choleric Type compared with the coherent low-apprehension anxious Choleric Type (see Table 5.3).

Taken together, these results allow for some interesting conclusions.

- Similar to the results received within the Pavlovian approach, the level of functional complexity (higher-level organization—that is, personality coherence/incoherence) is specifically associated with the quality of attentional processing. However it is problematic to isolate any consistent patterns of results due to the insufficient significant results received.
- After dividing personality coherence/incoherence into this built upon low or high level of anxiety, one can identify a few regular patterns of results for some coherent structures: (a) personality coherence with a low level of anxiety enhances quality of attentional stimulation processing (in sanguines and phlegmatics); and (b) personality coherence with a high level of anxiety lessens quality of attentional stimulation processing (in melancholics and phlegmatics). But there is no such regularity for incoherent structures, since personality incoherence with a low level of anxiety improves quality of attentional stimulation processing in melancholics, while personality incoherence with a high level of anxiety advances quality of attentional stimulation processing in cholerics and reduces it in sanguines and phlegmatics.
- Thus both personality coherence and incoherence maintain high-quality attentional stimulation processing when low levels of both types of anxiety are involved, but also act counter to high-quality attentional processing of facial

affect when high levels of both types of anxiety are concerned. Nonetheless, it happens that personality incoherence with a high level of anxiety supports high-quality attentional processing of emotional material. It is the case for cholerics and I attempt to explain this finding below.

- More regular patterns of results relating to the quality of processing might be identified at the lower-level structures than personality coherence/incoherence.
- Harmonious temperaments—sanguine and melancholic—are linked to impaired attentional control and attentional selectiveness over sadness in cases when they coexist with arousal anxiety. However, one may speculate that the reactive nature of arousal anxiety diminishes effective stimulation processing in these two types of temperament in respect to sadness.
- For disharmonious temperaments (phlegmatic and choleric), however, dissociation is seen across quality of stimulation processing distributed between these two temperaments.
- Phlegmatic structure goes with low-quality stimulation processing (impaired attentional control over negativity, reduced vigilance toward threat and happiness) when it correlates with both types of anxieties. Choleric structure relates to high-quality stimulation processing (increased attentional control over threat) when apprehension anxiety is involved.
- One can expect that this dissociation may be attributed to general sensitivity to social and emotional stimulation in phlegmatics and cholerics. The Phlegmatic Type is not predisposed to be specifically responsive to emotional and social material; its correlation with both anxieties may "freeze" this low responsiveness. But the Choleric Type is predisposed to be specifically reactive to affective and social stimulation; its correlation with apprehension anxiety may only specify the attentional control system to work effectively with threatening stimuli.

With reference to the level of functional complexity and quality of stimulation processing, I have proposed the consideration of results from the other study, which to some extent support the findings presented above and also allow for their more extensive analysis. Fajkowska and Eysenck (2008) designed a study based on the assumption that the extraversion and neuroticism dimensions, together with trait anxiety, influence the level of arousal and amount of effort invested in performance and predispose individuals to preferentially process facial emotional information that is congruent with these traits (see Fox, 2008) and with coping styles relating to defensiveness (e.g., Brosschot, de Ruiter, & Kindt, 1999; Dawkins & Furnham, 1989; Derakshan, Feldman, Campbell, & Lipp, 2003; Fox, 1993; Loney, Kline, Joiner, Frick, & LaRowe, 2005; Myers & Derakshan, 2004; Newman & McKinney, 2002).

Thus the goal presented in the above study was validated with the face-in-the-crowd paradigm (Öhman et al., 2001) and the measurement of personality traits added (EPQ-R: Brzozowski & Drwal, 1995; Eysenck & Eysenck, 1994; STAI: Spielberger, 1983; Wrześniewski & Sosnowski, 1996; Social Desirability Scale: Crowne & Marlowe, 1960; Drwal & Wilczyńska, 1980). Individuals across two

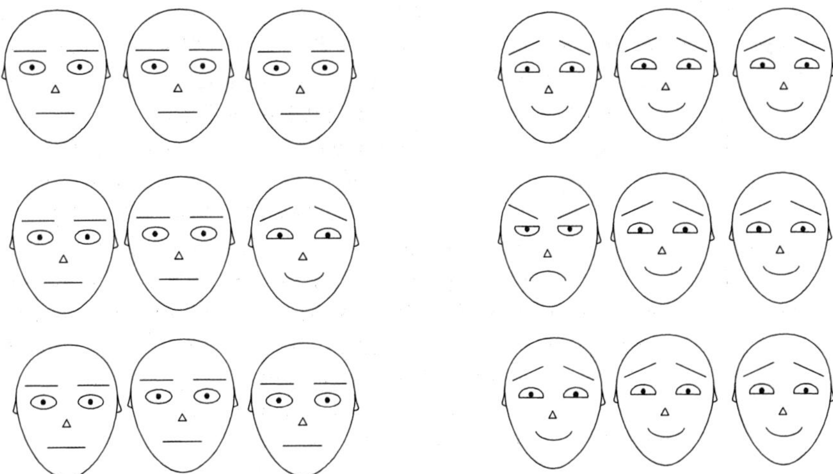

**Figure 5.7.** Samples of 3 x 3 matrices with threatening, friendly, and neutral target faces used in Experiment 1, adapted from Öhman, Lundqvist, and Esteves (2001). Reprinted from "Personality and Cognitive Performance" by M. Fajkowska and M. W. Eysenck, 2008, *Polish Psychological Bulletin, 39,* p. 183. Copyright 2008 by Polish Academy of Sciences. Reprinted with permission.

experiments searched for discrepant faces in matrices of otherwise identical faces. However, only Experiment 1 (cf. Figure 5.7) provided the most interesting data from the perspective analyzed here.

The exploratory multi-multivariable analysis of regression revealed that the incoherent high-trait (apprehension) anxious Melancholic Type ($INPT_{Melancholic:\ emotionally\ unstable\ introvert}^{high\text{-}apprehension\ anxiety}$)[10] with nondefensive coping style showed reduced attentional vigilance (slow detection) to neutral target faces with threatening distractors (Ne/Th) and threatening target faces with friendly distractors (Th/F), and had impaired attentional control (high level of false responses) in these two conditions. The coherent low-trait (apprehension) anxious sanguine individuals ($CPT_{Sanguine:\ emotionally\ stable\ extravert}^{low\text{-}apprehension\ anxiety}$) with repressive style of coping presented attentional vigilance toward these emotions (were fast in detection of Ne/Th and Th/F), and increased attentional control (few false responses) over these conditions.

The evidence from this research indicated that apprehension anxiety, when "hidden" in repressive coping in the coherent sanguine personality, enhances the

---

[10] In the original paper, this type was considered as a coherent one. In our previous papers, personality coherence/incoherence was built without reference to the consistency or inconsistency between functions in focal traits or types (e.g. Fajkowska & Eysenck, 2008; Fajkowska & Krejtz, 2007; Fajkowska & Marszał-Wiśniewska, 2005). Here I interpret this type according to my revised approach to personality coherence/incoherence.

processing quality of threatening and neutral stimuli; on the other hand, when it is part of the incoherent nondefensive melancholic structure of personality, apprehension anxiety is connected with the inferior processing of threatening and neutral stimuli. This pattern of findings suggests that in repressors the regulative "apprehension component" of anxiety is associated with efficient processing and good attentional selectivity (searching and inhibition) by managing its "arousal component," expressed here in more "reactive" characteristics of behavior—for example, by enhancing speed of processing and sensitivity to particular emotional stimuli. However, it might be the case that providing repressiveness is a part of coherent personality structure and is supported by high temperament capacities of stimulation processing (here connected with the Sanguine Type).

As expected, repressive coping is connected with the coherent low-trait anxious Sanguine Type (cf. Table 4.2). It seems probable that it represents the Balanced Type of anxiety composed of the apprehension component (the regulative one, *per definitionem*, representing strategic processing) and arousal component (more reactive, connected with attentional vigilance) being observed in behavioral reactions to emotional stimulation.

In closing, evidence from the studies presented here suggests that the relations between level of functional complexity and quality of stimulation processing deserve further investigation.

*Personality coherence/incoherence and dynamics of stimulation processing*

According to the data in Table 5.4A, high-arousal anxiety influences impaired inhibitory control over threat. The Phlegmatic Type is associated with reduced attentional vigilance to happiness and sadness and ineffective sadness processing, while the Choleric Type is associated with vigilance to happiness and sadness, effective sadness processing, and ineffective threat processing.

Contrasting these findings with data from Table 5.3, one can notice that on the basis of antagonistic functional interaction in the incoherent personality type, composed of (regulative) Phlegmatic Type and (reactive) Arousal Type, we received "a new product": attentional avoidance of happiness processing and impaired attentional control over negativity. Analogically, on the basis of antagonistic functional interaction in coherent personality structure, composed of the (reactive) Choleric Type and (reactive) Arousal Type, we obtained enhanced inhibitory control over negativity.

Data presented in Table 5.4B show that high-apprehension anxiety affects impaired attentional control over happiness and sadness. In both cases the Phlegmatic Type and Choleric Type have been found ineffective in processing emotional faces.

The avoidance of happiness, ineffective happiness processing, and impaired attentional control over happiness are observed in the coherent personality type consisting of the (regulative) Phlegmatic Type and (regulative) Apprehension Type. But when we examine the incoherent personality type organized around the (reactive) Choleric Type and (regulative) Apprehension Type, we find enhanced control

**Table 5.4.** Phlegmatic and choleric types (Eysenckian approach) and [A] Arousal Type of anxiety and [B] Apprehension Type of anxiety in attentional processing of facial affect

[A][1]

| Personality types | Behavioral indices of facial processing | | | |
|---|---|---|---|---|
|  | *RT* | *Accuracy* | *OM* | *FA* |
| **Phlegmatic** | ↑ F ↑ S | ↓ S | ↑ S | ns |
| **Choleric** | ↓ F ↓ S | ↓ Th ↑ S | ↑ Th | ns |
| **High-arousal anxiety** | ns | ns | ns | ↑ Th |

[B][2]

| Personality types | Behavioral indices of facial processing | | | |
|---|---|---|---|---|
|  | *RT* | *Accuracy* | *OM* | *FA* |
| **Phlegmatic** | ns | ↓ Th ↓ F ↓ S | ↑ Th ↑ F ↑ S | ns |
| **Choleric** | ns | ↓ Th ↓ F | ↑ Th ↑ F ↑ S | ns |
| **High-apprehension anxiety** | ns | ns | ns | ↑ F ↑ S |

*Note.* RT = reaction time; OM = omissions; FA = false alarms; Th = threatening faces; F = friendly faces; S = sad faces.

[1] RT: $F(3,190) = 5.32$, $p < 0.001$, $\eta^2 = 0.08$, F/Go – sanguines ($2.65 \pm 0.01$) < phlegmatics ($2.71 \pm 0.01$), $p < 0.001$, F/Go – phlegmatics ($2.71 \pm 0.01$) > cholerics ($2.66 \pm 0.01$), $p < 0.01$; $F(3,190) = 4.13$, $p < 0.001$, $\eta^2 = 0.06$, S/Go – sanguines ($0.69 \pm 0.05$) < phlegmatics ($2.76 \pm 0.01$), $p < 0.001$, S/Go – phlegmatics ($2.76 \pm 0.01$) > cholerics ($2.72 \pm 0.01$), $p < 0.01$. Accuracy: $F(3,186) = 4.08$, $p < 0.001$, $\eta^2 = 0.06$, S/Go sanguines ($0.91 \pm 0.03$) > phlegmatics ($0.69 \pm 0.05$), $p < 0.001$, S/Go – sanguines ($0.69 \pm 0.05$) < cholerics ($0.91 \pm 0.05$), $p < 0.05$; $F(3,186) = 4.18$, $p < 0.001$, $\eta^2 = 0.06$, Th/Go – sanguines ($1.14 \pm 0.02$) > cholerics ($1.04 \pm 0.03$), $p < 0.01$. OM: $F(3,186) = 3.22$, $p < 0.05$, $\eta^2 = 0.05$, S/Go – sanguines ($0.24 \pm 0.03$) < phlegmatics ($0.27 \pm 0.04$), $p < 0.01$; $F(3,186) = 4.08$, $p < 0.001$, $\eta^2 = 0.06$, Th/Go – sanguines ($0.10 \pm 0.01$) < cholerics ($0.15 \pm 0.01$), $p < 0.01$. FA: $F(1,186) = 27.30$, $p < 0.001$, $\eta^2 = 0.35$, Th/NoGo – low-arousal anxious ($0.02 \pm 0.01$) < high-arousal anxious ($0.07 \pm 0.01$), $p < 0.001$.

[2] Accuracy: $F(3,189) = 8.09$, $p < 0.001$, $\eta^2 = 0.14$, Th/Go – sanguines ($1.16 \pm 0.02$) > phlegmatics ($1.02 \pm 0.03$), $p < 0.001$, Th/Go – sanguines ($1.16 \pm 0.02$) > cholerics ($1.01 \pm 0.03$), $p < 0.001$; $F(3,189) = 6.32$, $p < 0.001$, $\eta^2 = 0.09$, F/Go – sanguines ($1.34 \pm 0.02$) > phlegmatics ($1.21 \pm 0.03$), $p < 0.001$, F/Go – sanguines ($1.34 \pm 0.02$) > cholerics ($1.21 \pm 0.03$), $p < 0.001$; $F(3,189) = 4.45$, $p < 0.001$, $\eta^2 = 0.07$, S/Go – sanguines ($0.92 \pm 0.04$) > phlegmatics ($0.71 \pm 0.05$), $p < 0.01$. OM: $F(3,189) = 7.32$, $p < 0.001$, $\eta^2 = 0.10$, Th/Go – sanguines ($0.09 \pm 0.01$) < phlegmatics ($0.16 \pm 0.01$), $p < 0.001$, Th/Go – sanguines ($0.09 \pm 0.01$) < cholerics ($0.17 \pm 0.01$), $p < 0.001$; $F(3,189) = 7.88$, $p < 0.001$, $\eta^2 = 0.11$, F/Go – sanguines ($0.03 \pm 0.01$) < phlegmatics ($0.09 \pm 0.01$), $p < 0.001$, F/Go – sanguines ($0.03 \pm 0.01$) < cholerics ($0.09 \pm 0.01$), $p < 0.001$; $F(3,189) = 3.57$, $p < 0.01$, $\eta^2 = 0.05$, S/Go – sanguines ($0.23 \pm 0.04$) < phlegmatics ($0.34 \pm 0.04$), $p < 0.05$, S/Go – sanguines ($0.23 \pm 0.04$) < cholerics ($0.29 \pm 0.04$), $p < 0.05$. FA: $F(1,189) = 4.80$, $p < 0.05$, $\eta^2 = 0.02$, F/NoGo – low-apprehension anxious ($0.04 \pm 0.01$) < high-apprehension anxious ($0.06 \pm 0.01$), $p < 0.05$; $F(1,189) = 6.24$, $p < 0.01$, $\eta^2 = 0.03$, S/NoGo – low-apprehension anxious ($0.15 \pm 0.02$) < high-apprehension anxious ($0.21 \pm 0.01$), $p < 0.01$.

over threat and effective happiness processing (see Table 5.3). This suggests antagonistic functional interactions for coherent phlegmatic and incoherent choleric.

To sum up, the interactional analysis of personality coherence/incoherence within the Eysenckian approach revealed:

- The antagonistic interaction does not specifically explain how personality coherence or incoherence affect the dynamics of attentional processes, but rather how elevated arousal or apprehension anxiety in disharmonious temperaments impact on these dynamics.
- The antagonistic interactions Phlegmatic Type x Arousal Type or Choleric Type x Arousal Type reduce the range of attentional processes and the range of processed emotional stimuli. The antagonistic interactions Phlegmatic Type x Apprehension Type or Choleric Type x Apprehension Type intensify and widen the range of attentional processes involved in processing, and also specify the processed affect.
- The antagonistic interactions Phlegmatic Type x Arousal Type and Phlegmatic Type x Apprehension Type imply impaired top-down attentional processes (avoidance, attentional control, and attentional ineffectiveness) when processing happiness and threat. Hypothetically, happiness and threat seem to be too arousing for coherent/incoherent phlegmatics (with tendencies not to seek stimulation in order to maintain the optimal arousal level) to perform effectively.
- The antagonistic interactions Choleric Type x Arousal Type and Choleric Type x Apprehension Type reveal themselves in enhanced top-down attentional processes (good attentional control and attentional effectiveness) in processing facial affect. This time emotional stimulation seems to be adequately arousing for coherent/incoherent cholerics (with tendencies to seek stimulation in order to maintain the optimal arousal level) to perform effectively.
- These results complement those obtained from the intercorrelational analysis, and taken together inform us about the quality and dynamics of attentional processing in disharmonious types of temperaments with elevated levels of both anxieties.

### 5.2.3. Attentional biases in coherent/incoherent personality structures built upon temperament types in RTT perspective and anxiety types

Results of studies that aimed to identify the quality and dynamics of attentional processing of emotional material in coherent/incoherent personality structures composed of the four temperament types in the RTT and anxiety types are demonstrated in the following sections.

*Intercorrelations: Temperament Type and Anxiety Type*

Research was also conducted ($N$ = 164, 104 females, $M$ = 25.15, $SD$ = 7.09) on processing emotional faces within the Emotional Go/NoGo procedure described earlier, in the context of four temperament types defined by the RTT (FCB-TI;

Zawadzki & Strelau, 1997) and arousal anxiety and apprehension anxiety (STAI; Spielberger, 1983; Wrześniewski & Sosnowski, 1996). Significant results were obtained for sanguine, melancholic, and phlegmatic types mixed with arousal (see Figure 5.8) or apprehension (see Figure 5.9) anxieties.

Figure 5.8A shows that the incoherent high-arousal anxious Sanguine Type ($INPT_{Sanguine:\ high\ SPC\ +\ high\ AC}{}^{high\text{-}arousal\ anxiety}$) presents impaired attentional control over happiness and sadness (high number of FAs to F/NoGo and S/NoGo trials), while the coherent low-arousal anxious Sanguine Type ($CPT_{Sanguine:\ high\ SPC\ +\ high\ AC}{}^{low\text{-}arousal\ anxiety}$) reveals increased attentional control over happiness and sadness (low number of FAs to F/NoGo and S/NoGo trials).

As seen in Figure 5.8B, in the coherent high-arousal anxious Melancholic Type ($CPT_{Melancholic:\ low\ SPC\ +\ low\ AC}{}^{high\text{-}arousal\ anxiety}$) increased attentional control over negativity (low number of FAs to Th/NoGo and S/NoGo trials) is observed, but in the incoherent low-arousal anxious Melancholic Type ($INPT_{Melancholic:\ low\ SPC\ +\ low\ AC}{}^{low\text{-}arousal\ anxiety}$) decreased attentional control over negativity (high number of FAs to Th/NoGo and S/NoGo trials) is noted.

According to Figure 5.8C, it might be concluded that the incoherent high-arousal anxious Phlegmatic Type ($INPT_{Phlegmatic:\ high\ SPC\ +\ low\ AC}{}^{high\text{-}arousal\ anxiety}$) reveals reduced attentional vigilance to threat (slow detection of Th/Go trials); by contrast, the coherent low-arousal anxious Phlegmatic Type ($CPT_{Phlegmatic:\ high\ SPC\ +\ low\ AC}{}^{low\text{-}arousal\ anxiety}$) shows attentional vigilance to threat (fast detection of Th/Go trials).

In conclusion, the Incoherent Type of personality presents worse attentional processing of emotional stimulation, whereas in the Coherent Type the opposite pattern of results was identified.

Based on Figure 5.9, one can see that poor attentional control over friendly faces (high level of FAs to F/NoGo) is associated with the coherent high-apprehension anxious Sanguine Type ($CPT_{Sanguine:\ high\ SPC\ +\ high\ AC}{}^{high\text{-}apprehension\ anxiety}$), while the coherent low-apprehension anxious Sanguine Type ($CPT_{Sanguine:\ high\ SPC\ +\ high\ AC}{}^{low\text{-}apprehension\ anxiety}$) demonstrates better attentional control over happiness (low level of FAs to F/NoGo).

Taken together, these results revealed that:

- The Arousal Type of anxiety is connected with reduced attentional control over happiness and sadness and reduced attentional vigilance to threat in sanguines and phlegmatics (respectively), and is also linked to improved attentional control over negativity in melancholics.
- The Apprenehsion Type of anxiety mediates the quality of attentional processing in sanguines and reduces attentional control over happiness.

*Interactions: Temperament Type x Anxiety Type*

To investigate the interactions among the four temperament types defined by the RTT and types of anxiety ($N = 84$, 54 females, $M = 24.36$ years, $SD = 4.78$ years), the same procedures—the Emotional Go/NoGo task boosted with self-report measures

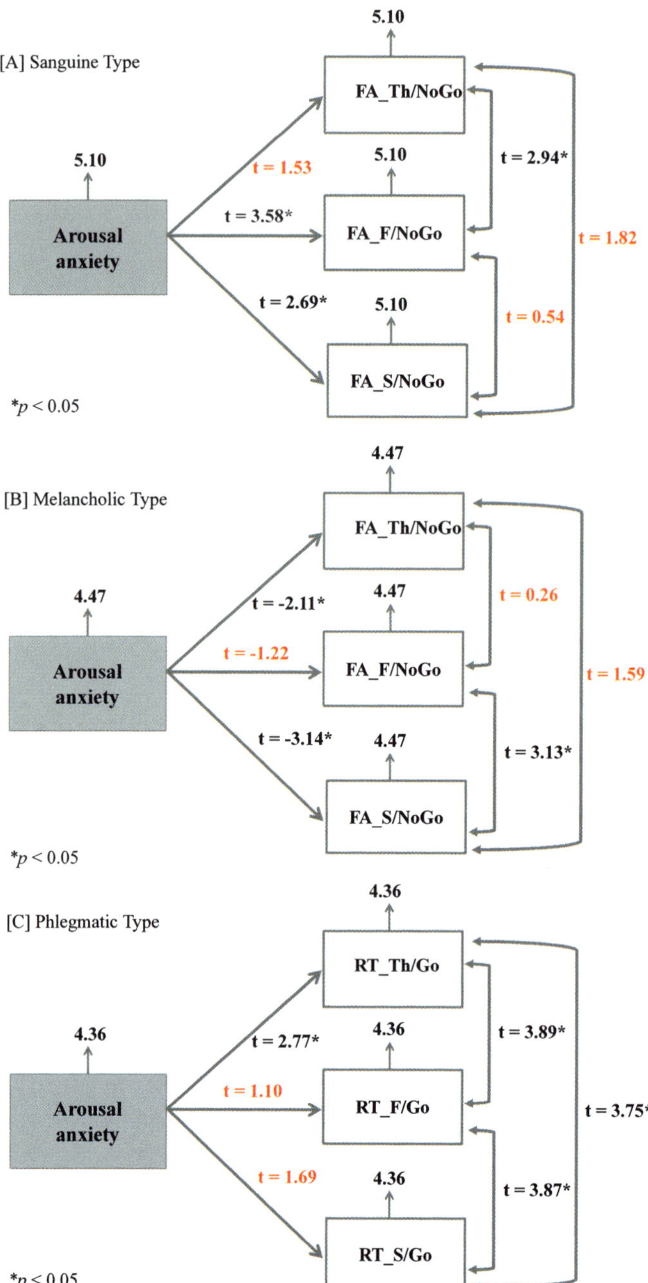



**Figure 5.8.** Results of the exploratory multi-multivariable analysis of regression (structural equations estimated by LISREL 8.51) for [A] false alarms to NoGo trials in Sanguine Type ($N = 60$); [B] false alarms to NoGo trials in Melancholic Type ($N = 40$); and [C] reaction times to Go trials in Phlegmatic Type and arousal anxiety. FA = false alarms; RT = reaction times. Nonsignificant results are written in red.

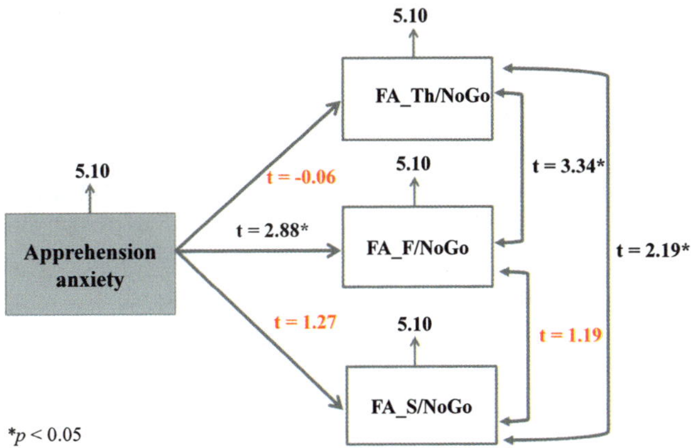


**Figure 5.9.** Results of the exploratory multi-multivariable analysis of regression (structural equations estimated by LISREL 8.51) for false alarms in NoGo trials in Sanguine Type ($N$ = 54) and apprehension anxiety. FA = false alarms. Nonsignificant results are written in red.

(FCB-TI: Zawadzki & Stelau, 1997; STAI: Spielberger, 1983; Wrześniewski & Sosnowski, 1996)—were conducted and the data were statistically analyzed in the same manner.

The analysis yielded that the interaction between temperament type and the Arousal Type of anxiety is connected with impaired attentional control (over S) in sanguine and increased attentional control (over F) in melancholic types. In addition, state anxiety participates in effective attentional processing of Th faces in phlegmatics, but in ineffective attentional processing of Th and F faces and avoidance of F faces processing in cholerics. More precisely, the incoherent high-arousal anxious Sanguine Type ($INPT_{Sanguine:\ high\ SPC\ +\ high\ AC}^{high\text{-}arousal\ anxiety}$) presents higher level of false alarms to sadness than the coherent low-arousal anxious Sanguine Type ($CPT_{Sanguine:\ high\ SPC\ +\ high\ AC}^{low\text{-}arousal\ anxiety}$).[11] Then the coherent high-arousal anxious Melancholic Type ($CPT_{Melancholic:\ low\ SPC\ +\ low\ AC}^{high\text{-}arousal\ anxiety}$) shows better attentional control over F faces (fewer false alarms) than the incoherent low-arousal anxious Melancholic Type ($INPT_{Melancholic:\ low\ SPC\ +\ low\ AC}^{low\text{-}arousal\ anxiety}$).[12] Better accuracy of Th processing was identified in the incoherent high-arousal anxious Phlegmatic Type ($INPT_{Phlegmatic:\ high\ SPC\ +\ low\ AC}^{high\text{-}arousal\ anxiety}$) than in the coherent low-arousal anxious Phlegmatic Type

---

[11] *Sanguine Type x Arousal anxiety.* FA: $F(6,76) = 3.99$, $p < 0.001$, $\eta^2 = 0.24$, S/NoGo—incoherent high-arousal anxious sanguines (0.41 ± 0.06) > coherent low-arousal anxious sanguines (0.25 ± 0.04), $p < 0.05$.

[12] *Melancholic Type x Arousal anxiety.* FA: $F(6,76) = 3.99$, $p < 0.001$, $\eta^2 = 0.24$, F/NoGo—coherent high-arousal anxious melancholics (0.06 ± 0.01) < incoherent low-arousal anxious melancholics (0.11 ± 0.01), $p < 0.001$.

$(CPT_{Phlegmatic:\ high\ SPC\ +\ low\ AC}{}^{low\text{-}arousal\ anxiety})$.[13] Finally, the coherent high-arousal anxious Choleric Type $(CPT_{Choleric:\ low\ SPC\ +\ high\ AC}{}^{high\text{-}arousal\ anxiety})$ exhibits less accuracy in Th and F faces processing and more omissions to F faces processing than the incoherent low-arousal anxious Choleric Type $(INPT_{Choleric:\ low\ SPC\ +\ high\ AC}{}^{low\text{-}arousal\ anxiety})$.[14]

The interaction between temperament type and the Apprehension Type of anxiety occurred to be involved in stimulation processing in the Melancholic Type of temperament. Hence the incoherent high-apprehension anxious Melancholic Type $(INPT_{Melancholic:\ low\ SPC\ +\ low\ AC}{}^{high\text{-}apprehension\ anxiety})$ processes threat more accurately than the coherent low-apprehension anxious Melancholic Type $(CPT_{Melancholic:\ low\ SPC\ +\ low\ AC}{}^{low\text{-}apprehension\ anxiety})$.[15]

*Summary and interpretation*

Table 5.5 provides condensed results achieved for functional intercorrelations and interactions between elements composing personality coherence/incoherence—temperament types within the RTT and types of anxiety—and their relations with attentional processing of facial affect.

*Personality coherence and quality of stimulation processing*

According to the data summarized in Table 5.5, overlapping reactive functions observed in coherent personality structures build upon the (reactive) Melancholic Type + (reactive) Arousal Type and are connected with enhanced attentional control over negativity. Contrasting this result with the finding for the incoherent low-arousal anxious Melancholic Type shows that functional simplicity (coherence) produces improved processing over negativity in the Melancholic Type. In addition, the available data established that overlapping regulative functions observed in coherent personality structures built upon the (regulative) Sanguine Type + (regulative) Apprehension Type components result in impaired attentional control over happiness (see Table 5.5). Comparing this result with the finding for coherent low-apprehension anxious sanguines suggests that this time functional simplicity results in worsening happiness processing in the Sanguine Type.

---

[13] *Phlegmatic Type x Arousal anxiety.* <u>Accuracy</u>: $F(3,76) = 4.15$, $p < 0.001$, $\eta^2 = 0.16$, Th/Go—incoherent high-arousal anxious phlegmatics ($1.39 \pm 0.09$) > coherent low-arousal anxious phlegmatics ($1.12 \pm 0.03$), $p < 0.01$.

[14] *Choleric Type x Arousal anxiety.* <u>Accuracy</u>: $F(3,76) = 4.15$, $p < 0.001$, $\eta^2 = 0.16$, Th/Go—coherent high-arousal anxious cholerics ($1.05 \pm 0.04$) < incoherent low-arousal anxious cholerics ($1.20 \pm 0.01$), $p < 0.01$; $F(3,76) = 2.56$, $p < 0.001$, $\eta^2 = 0.14$, F/Go—coherent high-arousal anxious cholerics ($1.25 \pm 0.03$) < incoherent low-arousal anxious cholerics ($1.37 \pm 0.03$), $p < 0.001$; <u>OM</u>: $F(3,76) = 3.08$, $p < 0.05$, $\eta2 = 0.11$; F/Go—coherent high-arousal anxious cholerics ($0.05 \pm 0.01$) > incoherent low-arousal anxious cholerics ($0.03 \pm 0.03$), $p < 0.05$.

[15] *Melancholic Type x Apprehension anxiety.* <u>Accuracy</u>: $F(2,75) = 3.95$, $p < 0.05$, $\eta^2 = 0.09$, Th/Go—incoherent high-apprehension anxious melancholics ($1.02 \pm 0.03$) > coherent low-apprehension anxious melancholics ($0.88 \pm 0.06$), $p < 0.05$.

**Table 5.5.** Attentional biases in coherent/incoherent personality structures built upon temperament types in RTT approach and anxiety types

| Processes-level of stimulation processing | Traits-level of stimulation processing | | | | | | | | | | | | | | | |
| --- | --- | --- | --- | --- | --- | --- | --- | --- | --- | --- | --- | --- | --- | --- | --- | --- |
| | Formal (energetic and temporal) characteristics of activity (RTT) | | | | | | | | | | | | | | | |
| **Attentional patterns of stimulation processing** | **Sanguine Type** | | | | **Melancholic Type** | | | | **Phlegmatic Type** | | | | **Choleric Type** | | | |
| | *CPT* | | | *INPT* | *CPT* | | | *INPT* | *CPT* | | | *INPT* | *CPT* | | *INPT* | |
| | Low-arousal anxiety | Low-appre. anxiety | High-appre. anxiety | High-arousal anxiety | High-arousal anxiety | Low-appre. anxiety | High-appre. anxiety | Low-arousal anxiety | Low-arousal anxiety | Low-appre. anxiety | High-appre. anxiety | High-arousal anxiety | High-arousal anxiety | Low-appre. anxiety | High-appre. anxiety | Low-arousal anxiety |
| **Vigilance** (low RT, high TN) | | | | | | | | | Th | | | | | | | |
| **Reduced vigilance** (high RT, low TN) | | | | | | | | | | | | Th | | | | |
| **Avoidance** (high OM) | | | | | | | | | | | | | F | | | |
| **Impaired attentional control** (high FA) | | | F | F&S S | | | | Th&S | | | | | | | | |
| **Enhanced attentional control** (low FA) | F&S | F | | | Th&S F | | | | | | | | | | | |
| **Attentional effectiveness** (high Accuracy and Hits) | | | | | | | | Th | | | | Th | | | | |
| **Attentional ineffectiveness** (low Accuracy and Hits) | | | | | | | | | | | | | Th&F | | | |

*Note.* RT = reaction time; TN = total number of items processed; OM = omissions; FA = false alarms; Th = threatening faces; F = friendly faces; S = sad faces. Intercorrelational relations are highlighted in blue for arousal anxiety and green for apprehension anxiety; interactive relations are highlighted in pink.

*Personality incoherence and quality of stimulation processing*

Distinctness between controlling functions observed in incoherent personality structures built upon the (regulative) Sanguine Type + (reactive) Arousal Type and (regulative) Phlegmatic Type + (reactive) Arousal Type accompanies impaired attentional control over happiness and sadness and reduced attentional vigilance to threat, respectively. Again, associating this evidence with the data for coherent low-arousal anxious sanguines and coherent low-arousal anxious phlegmatics, we see that worsening of attentional processing might be attributed to personality incoherence.

The data received from the analysis of interrcorelational relations between both types of anxieties and the four temperament types formulated in the RTT allow for the following conclusions.

- Corresponding to the results received within the Pavlovian and Eysenckian models, the level of functional complexity (higher-level organization—that is, personality coherence/incoherence) is specifically associated with the quality of attentional processing. However, it is complicated to identify a regular pattern of results.
- Personality coherence with a low level of anxiety generally goes with improvement of attentional processing (in sanguines and phlegmatics), while personality incoherence with a high level of anxiety is connected with worsening (in saguines and phlegmatics) attentional processing of emotional material. The data obtained for personality coherence with high anxieties and personality incoherence with low anxieties are deficient and produce vagueness.
- Again, more regular patterns of results relating to the quality of processing might be identified at the lower-level structures.
- However, here those composing high stimulation-processing capacities represent a lower-level structure than harmonious/disharmonious ones (sanguine and phlegmatic). The Sanguine Type is associated with decreased attentional control over happiness and sadness in cases when it coexists with arousal (and apprehension) anxiety. The Phlegmatic Type relates to reduced attentional vigilance to threat in cases when it coexists with arousal anxiety. It seems that the reactive dominant in arousal anxiety has negative affects on high SPC in sanguines and phlegmatics, which is reflected in adverse top-down and bottom-up attentional processing of emotional material, respectively. Moreover, a low level of arousal anxiety in sanguines and phlegmatics enhances attentional processing of emotional material in these two temperaments.
- This composing temperament with low SPC is melancholic in cases when arousal anxiety is concerned. It is possible that the reactive dominant in arousal anxiety has positive affects on low SPC in melancholics, which in turn is seen as positive top-down attentional processing of facial negative emotions.

However, these results are particularly insufficient for apprehension anxiety to draw any conclusions. That is why I would like to present results from other studies in this area.

Across three different studies, Fajkowska and colleagues (Fajkowska & Krejtz, 2006, 2007; Fajkowska et al., 2009) investigated how interaction between temperament properties formulated by the RTT and apprehension anxiety differentiate the attentional processing of facial emotions. In all three studies, individuals completed two questionnaires—the FCB-TI (Zawadzki & Strelau, 1997) and STAI (Spielberger, 1983; Wrześniewski & Sosnowski, 1996)—and then participated in the experimental sessions.

In the first study (Fajkowska & Krejtz, 2006), the computer task was designed by using the visual search paradigm boosted by some elements of the divided attention procedure (DIVA; cf. Nęcka, 2000; Öhman et al., 2001). The emotional version of the DIVA test (Fajkowska & Krejtz, 2006) was composed of two tasks: in the primary task, subjects were instructed to press the appropriate key as rapidly as possible to indicate whether the discrepant target was present in the display (see Figure 5.10); the secondary task was aimed at detecting as quickly as possible the face with a particular emotion within a matrix of faces, and to keep the falling line on the computer screen within the boundaries of the boxes located on both sides of the screen as close to the middle of the box as possible (see Figure 5.11).

**Figure 5.10.** Sample trial of primary task from the emotional version of the DIVA test (elaborated by Fajkowska & Krejtz, 2006). From "Temperament, lęk i uwagowe przetwarzanie informacji emocjonalnych" [Temperament, anxiety, and attentional processing of emotional stimuli] by M. Fajkowska and I. Krejtz, 2006. In M. Fajkowska, M. Marszał-Wiśniewska, & G. Sędek (Eds.), *Podpatrywanie myśli i uczuć. Zaburzenia i optymalizacja procesów emocjonalnych i poznawczych. Nowe kierunki badań*, p. 53. Copyright 2006 by Gdańskie Wydawnictwo Psychologiczne. Reprinted with permission.

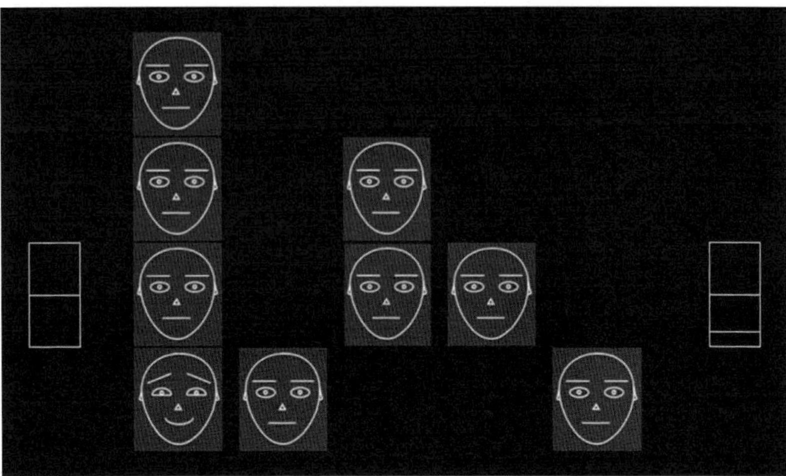

**Figure 5.11.** Sample trial of secondary task from the emotional version of the DIVA test (elaborated by Fajkowska & Krejtz, 2006). From "Temperament, lęk i uwagowe przetwarzanie informacji emocjonalnych" [Temperament, anxiety, and attentional processing of emotional stimuli] by M. Fajkowska and I. Krejtz, 2006. In M. Fajkowska, M. Marszał-Wiśniewska, & G. Sędek (Eds.), *Podpatrywanie myśli i uczuć. Zaburzenia i optymalizacja procesów emocjonalnych i poznawczych. Nowe kierunki badań*, p. 53. Copyright 2006 by Gdańskie Wydawnictwo Psychologiczne. Reprinted with permission.

In the second study (Fajkowska & Krejtz, 2007), the experiments replicated the design of Öhman et al. (2001) with the measurement of personality traits added (Fajkowska & Krejtz, 2007). Finally, in the third study participants were given a spatial memory task while eye movement was registered (Fajkowska et al., 2009). In an initial two-phase task, subjects were instructed to remember a localization of pairs of faces while eye movements were recorded; then they were expected to recall the localization of presented pairs of faces by pressing a button (see Figure 5.12).

In these three studies, all possible interactions among temperament types and traits and apprehension anxiety were analyzed. Taken together, the findings compose very consistent patterns of attentional processing.

Interestingly, across the three studies it was found that a consistency between anxiety intensity (Apprehension Type) and emotional reactivity (low anxiety, low emotional reactivity; high anxiety, high emotional reactivity) relates to attentional vigilance (faster and more accurate detection) of emotional material, particularly threat, while inconsistency between these traits (low anxiety, high emotional reactivity; high anxiety, low emotional reactivity) produces the reverse pattern. However, emotional reactivity—rather than anxiety—modifies the eye movements in processing the position of threatening faces.

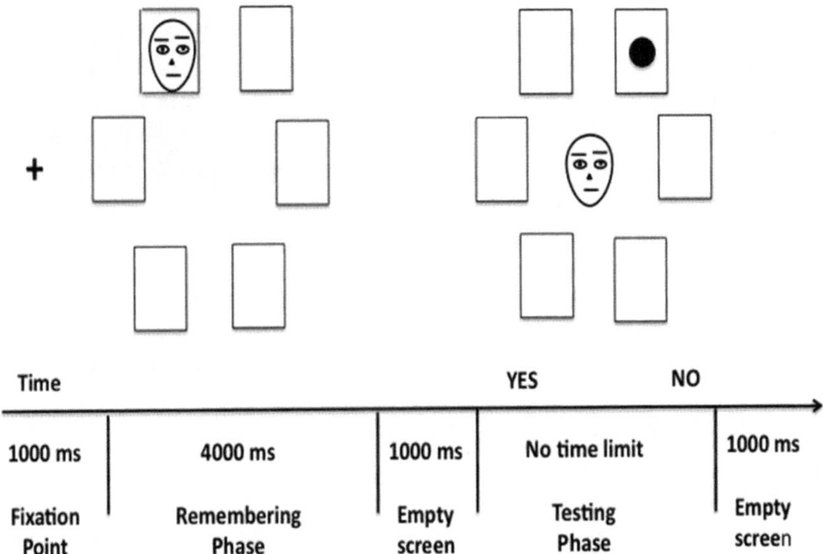


**Figure 5.12.** Illustration of the spatial memory task. Adapted from "Lęk, temperament i przetwarzanie bodźców emocjonalnych na podstawie ruchów gałek ocznych i procesów pamięci" [Anxiety, temperament, and emotional stimuli processing based on eye movement and memory] by M. Fajkowska, I. Krejtz, and K. Krejtz, 2009. In M. Fajkowska & B. Szymura (Eds.), *Lęk. Geneza–Mechanizmy–Funkcje*, p. 325. Copyright 2009 by Wydawnictwo Naukowe Scholar. Reprinted with permission.

Turning to an analysis of the structures,[16] although the incoherent high-trait anxious Melancholic Type ($INPT_{Melancholic:\ low\ EN\ high\ PE\ low\ AC}^{high\text{-}apprehension\ anxiety}$) has been found as attentionally vigilant (faster) to facial threat, the opposite pattern was identified in the coherent high-trait anxious Sanguine Type ($CPT_{Sanguine:\ high\ EN\ low\ PE\ high\ AC}^{high\text{-}apprehension\ anxiety}$). Moreover, findings reveal effective attentional processing (high accuracy) of emotional material in the incoherent high-trait anxious Melancholic Type ($INPT_{Melancholic:\ high\ ER\ high\ PE\ low\ AC}^{high\text{-}apprehension\ anxiety}$) and the incoherent high-trait anxious Choleric Type ($INPT_{Choleric:\ high\ ER\ high\ PE}^{high\text{-}apprehension\ anxiety}$). Contradictory configuration of results related to the coherent high-trait anxious Sanguine Type ($CPT_{Sanguine:\ low\ ER\ low\ PE\ high\ AC}^{high\text{-}apprehension\ anxiety}$) and coherent high-trait anxious Phlegmatic Type ($CPT_{Phlegmatic:\ low\ ER\ low\ PE}^{high\text{-}apprehension\ anxiety}$).

In closing, these studies encouraged the development of a new perspective on the functions of the Apprehension Type of anxiety. Explicitly, anxiety positively affects attentional vigilance to threat and attentional effectiveness of facial affect processing

---

[16] I interpret these findings in light of my revised approach to personality coherence/incoherence presented in this book.

in incoherent structures (high trait anxiety + Melancholic Type; high trait anxiety + Choleric Type) but does not facilitate processing of emotional material in coherent types (high trait anxiety + Sanguine Type; high trait anxiety + Phlegmatic Type). One possible explanation is that (in)consistency between intensity of trait anxiety and emotional reactivity may speak for these results. The other possible explanation is that the low capacities of stimulation processing in incoherent structures are "fueled by the regulative power" of trait anxiety to cope effectively with affective stimulation, whereas the high capacities of stimulation processing in coherent structures with regulative trait anxiety co-occur with ineffective stimulation processing. This suggests that more regulation does not necessarily contribute to better processing.

*Personality coherence/incoherence and dynamics of stimulation processing*

Measures of interactional relations between the Arousal Type of anxiety or Apprehension Type of anxiety and the four temperament types defined within the RTT revealed many results with contribution of arousal anxiety and only one with contribution of apprehension anxiety (see Table 5.6).

According to data presented in Table 5.6A, high-arousal anxiety affects impaired attentional control over threat. Sanguines, phlegmatics, and cholerics present effective threat processing, but melancholics process threat ineffectively. Thus, on the basis of synergistic functional interaction, the incoherent personality consisting of the (regulative) Sanguine Type + (reactive) Arousal Type goes with impaired inhibitory control over sadness. Enhanced attentional control over happiness in the coherent structure built of (reactive) Melancholic Type + (reactive) Arousal Type results in antagonistic functional interaction. The attentional effectiveness of threat processing identified in the incoherent personality combined with the (regulative) Phlegmatic Type + (reactive) Arousal Type has its source in synergistic functional interaction. The happiness avoidance, attentional ineffectiveness of threat, and happiness processing observed in the coherent personality structure—rooted in the (reactive) Choleric Type + (reactive) Arousal Type—spring from the antagonistic functional interaction.

Table 5.6B shows that high-apprehension anxiety influences impaired attentional control over happiness and sadness and that the Melancholic Type is associated with ineffective threat processing. Thus the incoherent personality composed of the (reactive) Melancholic + (regulative) Apprehension Type promotes effective threat processing (Table 5.6). This implies that interaction between these two components produces a new pattern of attentional processing (antagonistic functional interaction).

To sum up, the interactional analysis of personality coherence/incoherence within the Strelauvian approach showed:

- Both the Arousal Type of anxiety and Apprehension Type of anxiety, combined with the four temperaments, are associated with the recruitment of attentional processes connected with a top-down attentional system (e.g., attentional control,

**Table 5.6.** RTT temperament types and [A] Arousal Type of anxiety and [B] Apprehension Type of anxiety in attentional processing of facial affect

[A][1]

| **Personality types** | **Behavioral indices of facial processing** | | | |
|---|---|---|---|---|
| | *RT* | *Accuracy* | *OM* | *FA* |
| **Sanguine** | ns | ↑ Th | ↓ Th | ns |
| **Melancholic** | ns | ↓ Th | ↑ Th | ns |
| **Phlegmatic** | ns | ↑ Th | ↓ Th | ns |
| **Choleric** | ns | ↑ Th | ↓ Th | ns |
| **High-arousal anxiety** | ns | ns | ns | ↑ Th |

[B][2]

| **Personality types** | **Behavioral indices of facial processing** | | | |
|---|---|---|---|---|
| | *RT* | *Accuracy* | *OM* | *FA* |
| **Melancholic** | ns | ↓ Th | ↑ Th | ns |
| **High-apprehension anxiety** | ns | ns | ns | ↑ F ↑ S |

*Note.* RT = reaction time; OM = omissions; FA = false alarms; Th = threatening faces; F = friendly faces; S = sad faces.

[1] Accuracy: $F(3,76) = 11.26$, $p < 0.001$, $\eta^2 = 0.31$, Th/Go – sanguines $(1.19 \pm 0.03)$ > melancholics $(0.96 \pm 0.03)$, $p < 0.001$, Th/Go – phlegmatics $(1.25 \pm 0.05)$ > melancholics $(0.96 \pm 0.03)$, $p < 0.001$, Th/Go – cholerics $(1.13 \pm 0.03)$ > melancholics $(0.96 \pm 0.03)$, $p < 0.001$. OM: $F(3,76) = 13.43$, $p < 0.001$, $\eta^2 = 0.35$, Th/Go – sanguines $(0.07 \pm 0.01)$ < melancholics $(0.20 \pm 0.02)$, $p < 0.001$, Th/Go – phlegmatics $(0.06 \pm 0.02)$ < melancholics $(0.20 \pm 0.02)$, $p < 0.001$, Th/Go – cholerics $(0.11 \pm 0.01)$ < melancholics $(0.20 \pm 0.02)$, $p < 0.001$. FA: $F(1,76) = 27.30$, $p < 0.001$, $\eta^2 = 0.35$, Th/NoGo – low-arousal anxious $(0.02 \pm 0.01)$ < high-arousal anxious $(0.09 \pm 0.01)$, $p < 0.001$.

[2] Accuracy: $F(3,75) = 7.61$, $p < 0.001$, $\eta^2 = 0.23$, Th/Go – sanguines $(1.19 \pm 0.04)$ > melancholics $(0.95 \pm 0.03)$, $p < 0.001$. OM: $F(3,75) = 8.49$, $p < 0.001$, $\eta^2 = 0.25$, Th/Go – sanguines $(0.07 \pm 0.02)$ < melancholics $(0.20 \pm 0.02)$, $p < 0.001$, Th/Go- phlegmatics $(0.11 \pm 0.02)$ < melancholics $(0.20 \pm 0.02)$, $p < 0.001$. FA: $F(1,75) = 3.59$, $p < 0.05$, $\eta^2 = 0.05$, F/NoGo – low-apprehension anxious $(0.05 \pm 0.01)$ < high-apprehension anxious $(0.07 \pm 0.01)$, $F(1,75) = 6.20$, $p < 0.05$, $\eta^2 = 0.08$, S/NoGo – low-apprehension anxious $(0.15 \pm 0.02)$ < high-apprehension anxious $(0.24 \pm 0.03)$.

processing effectiveness). The synergistic or antagonistic interactions do not participate here in narrowing or widening the range of attentional processes or stimuli processed in analyzed coherent and incoherent structures.

- The mode of processing in the Sanguine Type is dominated by the anxious pattern of attentional processing typical for this type of anxiety—impaired attentional control over sadness. The Phlegmatic Type, when it interacts with arousal anxiety, "preserves" the pattern of attentional processing typical for itself—attentional effectiveness of threat processing. Both patterns of attentional processing result from the synergistic interaction between the studied components of personality.

- The antagonistic interaction between arousal anxiety and the melancholic or choleric types, and apprehension anxiety and the Melancholic Type, imply increased top-down attentional control in melancholics and impaired top-down attentional processes in cholerics.

- The synergistic and antagonistic interactions do not exactly explain how personality coherence or incoherence affect the dynamics of attentional processes, but rather how elevated arousal or apprehension anxiety in temperaments with low SPC (melancholics and cholerics) or high SPC (sanguines and phlegmatics) impact on these dynamics.

## *Conclusions*

I have analyzed the complex and somewhat puzzling links among the Arousal Type and Apprehension Type of anxiety and the four temperaments (across three theoretical models), and attentional processing. However, the findings revealed some common patterns.

In contrast to the fairly widespread evidence for attentional biases toward threat in anxiety, usually occurring at the early stages of processing, I obtained results showing that impaired attentional control over facial happiness and threat are typical attentional biases for the Arousal Type of anxiety, but that impaired attentional control over happiness and sadness—and ineffective happiness processing—are specific to the Apprehension Type of anxiety (see Tables 5.2, 5.4, and 5.6). These findings may be a consequence of the strategic nature of positive and sad information, which consists in less automatic and more voluntary properties of attention to happiness and sadness than to threat (cf. Fajkowska & Derryberry, 2010). This indicates that these attentional biases might represent a more regulative than reactive function in the situations studied, and is consistent with my earlier statement that both types of anxieties are characterized by reactive and regulative functions—but that only one is permanently dominant in a specific type of anxiety. However, the activation of a specific function in any given type of anxiety is situation-dependent. All our experimental procedures were prolonged and effort demanding, which suggests activation of regulative (rather than reactive) functions in a particular anxiety type. To some extent this might explain why regular patterns of results for quality of stimulation processing related to personality coherence/incoherence were not obtained.

It was expected that higher-level personality coherence/incoherence would explain changes in the range of quality of processing (mediating effects of the Arousal Type of anxiety and Apprehension Type of anxiety). In other words, personality coherence/incoherence would be consistently associated with improvement or worsening of attentional processing across all types of temperaments defined within Pavlovian, Eysenckian and Strelauvian theories. However, the studies discussed have failed to find solid evidence for this. Interestingly, it was demonstrated that the lower-integrated personality structures relate to the quality of stimulation processing—harmonious/disharmonious temperament structures in the Pavlovian and Eysenckian approaches, and stimulation-processing capacities in the RTT. More precisely, the regularity appeared for (a) Pavlovian approach, in the disharmonious structures of temperament revealing enhancement of attentional effectiveness, when coupled with elevated apprehension anxiety, (b) for Eysenckian model, in the harmonious structures of temperament revealing worsening of attentional control and effectiveness of processing, when go with elevated level of arousal anxiety, and (c) for Strelauvian theory, in temperaments with high-SPC showing weakening of attentional vigilance and control, when coupled with elevated level of arousal anxiety.

One possible explanation refers to the type of attentional tasks, which do not activate the performance of highly integrated personality structures such as personality coherence/incoherence. This suggests the importance of studying personality coherence/incoherence within the context of complex behaviors, not simple reactions. Moreover, it seems that activation of the personality structures within a certain approach—and their specific association with the quality of attentional processing—depend on the type of anxiety that is related to them and the variations in patterns of regulation stimulation identified across these three theories.

However, analysis of findings across theories provided a regular pattern of results that personality coherence/incoherence relates to quality of stimulation processing. Incoherent high-arousal sanguines and phlegmatics demonstrate adverse stimulation processing (impaired attentional control) when the Eysenckian and Strelauvian approaches are involved. High stimulation-processing capacities link Eysenckian and Strelauvian regulative sanguines and phlegmatics, having more strategic ways of stimulation processing and are in conflict with the "reactive nature" of arousal anxiety, predisposing them to respond more automatically to stimulation. Hypothetically, this conflicting constellation harms the attentional control system and impairs effective performance.

Coherent high-arousal anxious melancholics and cholerics present deteriorated stimulation processing (poor attentional selectiveness) when the Pavlovian and Eysenckian approaches are involved. Low stimulation-processing capacities—having more automatic ways of stimulation processing—link Pavlovian and Eysenckian reactive melancholics and cholerics and are congruent with the "reactive nature" of arousal anxiety, biasing processing toward a more automatic response to stimulation. Surprisingly, this consistent constellation harms the attentional selectiveness and impairs effective performance. Speculatively, it may be explained by the rule that an excess of reactivity negatively affects quality of performance.

Interestingly, incoherent high-apprehension anxious cholerics display good attentional control over stimulation processing across these two approaches. It seems probable that cholerics may produce effective performance when supported by the "regulative nature" of apprehension anxiety.

In sum, all these results advocate for generalized adverse and beneficial effects of (respectively) arousal anxiety and apprehension anxiety on attentional stimulation processing. These effects of both anxieties are permanent and not related to the level of personality integration to which these two anxieties belong.

Finally, another significant theme in the research presented addresses the kind of interaction between focal types and their relation to dynamics of attentional processes. Thus regular patterns reflecting specific correspondence between type interaction and personality coherence and incoherence were not identified. However, it was revealed that on the basis of synergistic and antagonistic interactions, top-down attentional processes were activated in all structures studied across the three theoretical perspectives. Evidence showed that both types of anxieties introduced regulative (not reactive) functions to these interactions; this may also be the case for temperament types and is reflected in the effortful, strategic top-down processing associated with coherent/incoherent personality structures.

## 5.3.
## How attentional stimulation processing relates to coherent/incoherent personality types built upon temperament and depression

The relationship between attentional biases and depression does not receive enough space in empirical studies. Thus it is difficult to present a consistent trend for attentional biases in depression, and far more difficult to find it for subtypes of depression. However, I tried to do this in Chapter 3. I have utilized some direct and indirect evidence and proposed attentional avoidance when depression is dominated by valence (in)sensitivity and reduced attentional control when depression is dominated by anhedonia (cf. Figure 3.5).

Just to briefly summarize the attentional patterns of reactions to emotional material, which might be attributable to valence (in)sensitivity specific for the Valence Type of depression. Thus, consistent with cognitive models (e.g., Beck, Brown, Steer, Eidelson, & Riskind, 1987; Clark, Beck, & Alford, 1999; Williams, Watts, MacLeod, & Mathews, 1997), affect theories postulate that positive and negative emotions play a prominent role in depression (e.g., Clark, 2005; Cole, Luby, & Sullivan, 2008; Watson, 2000, 2005). Generally, many studies of information processing are systematic in showing that depressed individuals exhibit attentional biases for sad and threatening facial expressions (cf. (Beevers & Carver, 2003; Gibb, Benas, Grassia, & McGeary, 2009; Hankin et al., 2010; Joorman & Gotlib, 2007; Scher, Ingram, & Segal, 2005), selective avoidance of processing sad faces and orienting attention toward positive material (cf. Bradley, Mogg, Falla, & Hamilton, 1998; Bradley, Mogg, & Millar, 2000), or impaired distractor inhibition on a selective attention task (Lemelin et al., 1996; MacQueen et al., 2000), the magnitude of which depends on a valence of stimuli (Jormann, 2004, 2005).

Regarding the Anhedonic Type of depression, the data reviewed imply that depressed individuals in particular—who tend to be low in subjective energy—are likely to be deficient in attentional resources as a result (for a review see Matthews, 1992; Matthews & Southall, 1991; Thayer, 1989; Wells & Matthews, 1999). The Anhedonic Type of depression does not relate to investment in effort (which is generally used to regulate a potential imbalance between activation and arousal) and initiation of motivation. Accordingly, individuals with the Anhedonic Type of depression initially direct their attention to emotional material, but then easily avoid processing it in an attempt to minimize energy expenditure. This suggests impaired attentional control in anhedonic depression.

These findings inform us about direct effects of depression subtypes on processing emotional material. Indirect analysis, when interactions or intercorrelations between temperament types and depression types are used, may potentially change these patterns (cf. section 5.2, speculations on anxiety types). The subsequent sections provide evidence on this issue; however, for several reasons I am only presenting data on the Anhedonic Type of depression. The conceptual reason includes measurement by self-report instruments such as the Beck Depression Inventory (BDI) and a trait-like definition of this type of depression; the practical reason deals with fact that my studies on the Valence Type of depression are in process.

### 5.3.1. Attentional biases in coherent/incoherent personality structures built upon temperament types in Pavlovian perspective and anhedonic depression

Below are presented the results on the quality and dynamics of attentional processing of affective stimuli in coherent/incoherent personality structures built upon the temperament types in the Pavlovian perspective and anhedonic depression.

*Intercorrelations: Temperament Type and Anhedonic Type*

The present study assessed how interrelations among the four temperament types defined in Pavlovian terms and the Anhedonic Type of depression relate to the quality of attentional processing. First, participants ($N = 254$, 142 females, $M = 22.14$, $SD = 2.93$) were administered the PTS (Strelau & Zawadzki, 1998) and BDI (Beck et al., 1987; Parnowski & Jernajczyk, 1977). Next the Emotional Faces Attention Test (Fajkowska, 2009; see Figure 5.1) was conducted. The results are demonstrated in Figure 5.13.

Thus, according to Figure 5.13A, the coherent high-anhedonic depressed Sanguine Type ($CPT_{Sanguine:\ strong,\ mobile,\ balanced\ type\ of\ NS}^{high\text{-}anhedonic\ depression}$) presents ineffective happiness processing (low level of hits to F faces), while the coherent low-anhedonic depressed Sanguine Type ($CPT_{Sanguine:\ strong,\ mobile,\ balanced\ type\ of\ NS}^{low\text{-}anhedonic\ depression}$) shows effective happiness processing (high level of hits).

Figure 5.13B reveals that the incoherent high-anhedonic depressed Melancholic Type ($INPT_{Melancholic:\ weak\ type\ of\ NS}^{high\text{-}anhedonic\ depression}$) is characterized by

 

**Figure 5.13.**

[A] Sanguine Type
5.39
Hits_Th
5.39
Anhedonic depression
5.39
Hits_F
5.39
Hits_S
t = -0.26
t = -2.03*
t = 0.22
t = 2.20*
t = 4.02*
t = 3.10*
*p < 0.05

[B] Melancholic Type
5.48
Hits_Th
5.48
Anhedonic depression
5.48
Hits_F
5.48
Hits_S
t = 0.41
t = -2.39*
t = 0.41
t = 2.63*
t = 1.56
t = 3.85*
*p < 0.05

5.48
Errors_Th
5.48
Anhedonic depression
5.48
Errors_F
5.48
Errors_S
t = -0.14
t = 2.69*
t = 0.32
t = 0.44
t = 2.41*
t = 2.18*
*p < 0.05

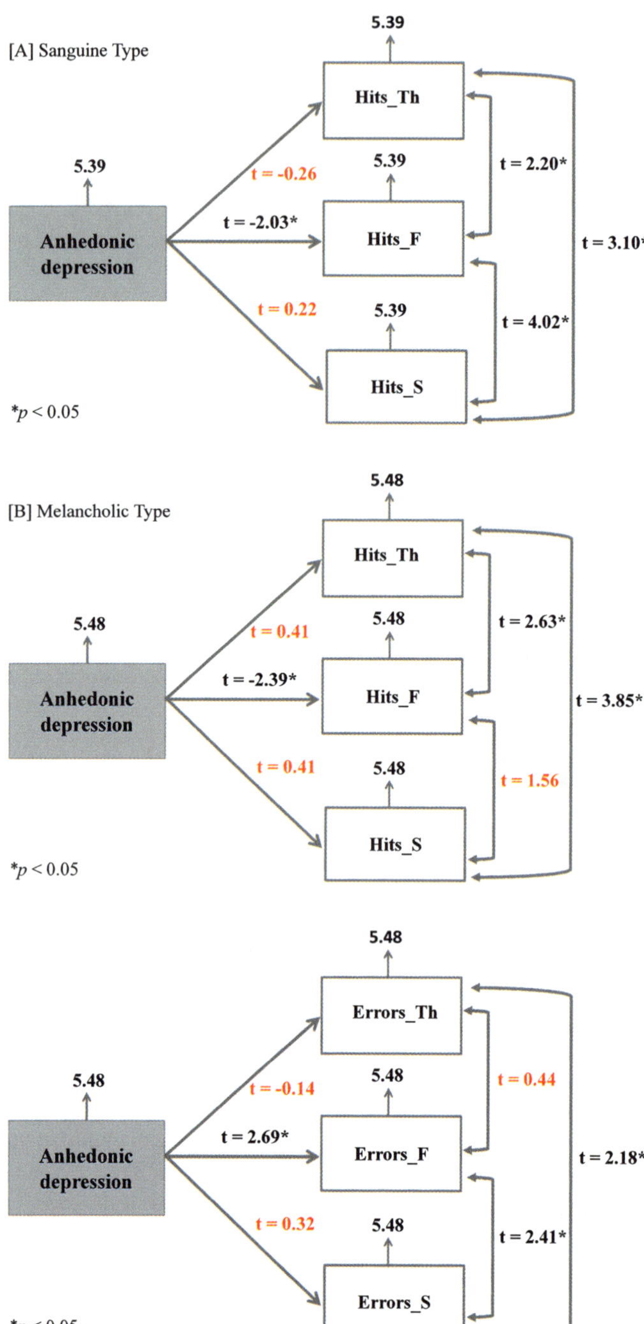

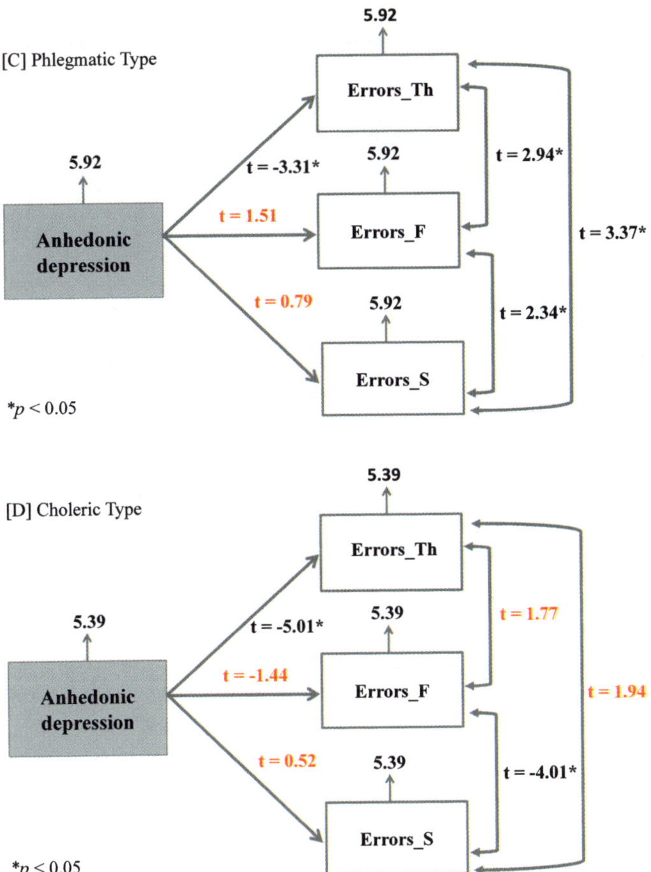


**Figure 5.13.** Results of the exploratory multi-multivariable analysis of regression (structural equations estimated by LISREL 8.51) for [A] hits in Sanguine Type ($N = 60$); [B] hits and errors in Melancholic Type ($N = 62$); [C] errors in Phlegmatic Type ($N = 72$); and [D] errors in Choleric Type ($N = 60$) and Anhedonic Type of depression. Nonsignificant results are written in red.

ineffective happiness processing (low level of hits; high number of errors), but that the coherent low-anhedonic depressed Melancholic Type ($CPT_{Melancholic:\ weak\ type\ of\ NS}^{low\text{-}anhedonic\ depression}$) is characterized by effective happiness processing (high level of hits; low number of errors).

In Figure 5.13C it is seen that the coherent high-anhedonic depressed Phlegmatic Type ($CPT_{Phlegmatic:\ strong,\ slow,\ balanced\ type\ of\ NS}^{high\text{-}anhedonic\ depression}$) shows effective threat processing (low number of total errors), but that the coherent low-anhedonic depressed Phlegmatic Type ($CPT_{Phlegmatic:\ strong,\ slow,\ balanced\ type\ of\ NS}^{low\text{-}anhedonic\ depression}$) has decreased effectiveness of threatening stimuli processing (high number of errors).

Figure 5.13D shows that the incoherent high-anhedonic depressed Choleric Type ($INPT_{Choleric:\ strong,\ unbalanced\ type\ of\ NS}^{high\text{-}anhedonic\ depression}$) shows effective threat processing (low number of total errors), whereas the coherent low-anhedonic Choleric Type ($CPT_{Choleric:\ strong,\ unbalanced\ type\ of\ NS}^{low\text{-}anhedonic\ depression}$) shows ineffective processing of threatening faces (higher number of errors).

It is clear from all these results that the Anhedonic Type of depression mediates worsening of attentional processing of happiness in sanguines and melancholics, but increases processing of threat in phlegmatics and cholerics.

*Interactions: Temperament Type x Anhedonic Type*

The extent to which interactions among the Anhedonic Type of depression and temperament types specifically affect processing of emotional material has been examined with the Emotional Go/NoGo task (cf. Figure 5.4). Using this paradigm, participants ($N = 244$, 150 females, $M = 25.56$, $SD = 7.66$) completed two self-report instruments: the PTS for assessing Pavlovian temperament traits (Strelau & Zawadzki, 1998) and the BDI for evaluating depressive syndromes (Beck et al., 1987; Parnowski & Jernajczyk, 1977).

Significant results were obtained only for the incoherent high-anhedonic depressed Choleric Type ($INPT_{Choleric:\ strong,\ unbalanced\ type\ of\ NS}^{high\text{-}anhedonic\ depression}$) and indicated impaired attentional control over happiness. For the coherent low-anhedonic Choleric Type ($CPT_{Choleric:\ strong,\ unbalanced\ type\ of\ NS}^{low\text{-}anhedonic\ depression}$), the opposite pattern of results was found.[17]

*Summary and interpretation*

The findings from Table 5.7 illustrate that intercorrelational and interactional relations among the Anhedonic Type of depression and the four temperaments formulated within Pavlovian theory significantly discriminated the attentional patterns of stimulation processing in coherent/incoherent personality structures.

*Personality coherence and quality of stimulation processing*

On the basis of the data obtained, it appears that having constellations with overlapping functions—coherent personality structures composed of the (regulative) Sanguine Type + (regulative) Anhedonic Type and coherent personality structures built of the (regulative) Phlegmatic Type + (regulative) Anhedonic Type—we received a lessening in effectiveness of happiness processing and an intensifying of effectiveness of threat processing, respectively (Table 5.7).

---

[17] *Choleric Type x Anhedonic depression.* FA: $F(1, 240) = 15.37$, $p < 0.001$, $\eta^2 = 0.20$, F/Go—incoherent high-anhedonic depressed cholerics ($0.12 \pm 0.02$) > coherent low-anhedonic depressed cholerics ($0.01 \pm 0.01$), $p < 0.001$.

**Table 5.7.** Attentional biases in coherent/incoherent personality structures built upon temperament types in Pavlovian approach and anhedonic depression

| Processes-level of stimulation processing | Traits-level of stimulation processing | | | | | | | |
|---|---|---|---|---|---|---|---|---|
| | Nervous system control activity<br>*(Pavlovian approach)* | | | | | | | |
| **Attentional patterns of stimulation processing** | Sanguine Type | | Melancholic Type | | Phlegmatic Type | | Choleric Type | |
| | *CPT* | | *CPT* | *INPT* | *CPT* | | *CPT* | *INPT* |
| | Low-anhedonic depression | High-anhedonic depression | Low-anhedonic depression | High-anhedonic depression | Low-anhedonic depression | High-anhedonic depression | Low-anhedonic depression | High-anhedonic depression |
| **Vigilance**<br>*(low RT, high TN)* | | | | | | | | |
| **Reduced vigilance**<br>*(high RT, low TN)* | | | | | | | | |
| **Avoidance**<br>*(high OM)* | | | | | | | | |
| **Impaired attentional control**<br>*(high FA)* | | | | | | | | F |
| **Enhanced attentional control**<br>*(low FA)* | | | | | | | | |
| **Attentional effectiveness**<br>*(high Accuracy and Hits)* | F | | F | | | Th | | Th |
| **Attentional ineffectiveness**<br>*(low Accuracy and Hits)* | | F | | F | Th | | Th | |

*Note.* RT = reaction time; TN = total number of items processed; OM = omissions; FA = false alarms; Th = threatening faces; F = friendly faces. Intercorrelational relations are highlighted in green; interactive relations are highlighted in pink.

                                                          

*Personality incoherence and quality of stimulation processing*

The noteworthy finding is that functional distinctness, reflected in incoherent personality systems organized by the (reactive) Melancholic Type + (regulative) Anhedonic Type and (reactive) Choleric Type + (regulative) Anhedonic Type, have found the ineffective happiness processing and effective threat processing, respectively (Table 5.7).

Comparing these results with the data contained in Table 5.7 for coherent low-anhedoninc depressed sanguines and coherent low-anhedonic depressed phlegmatics, and for coherent low-anhedonic depressed melancholics and coherent low-anhedonic depressed cholerics, it is clear that personality coherence built upon a low level of anhedonic depression is associated with the quality of processing—worsening happiness processing in high-anhedonic depressed sanguines and melancholics (harmonious temperaments with effective stimulation processing) and improving threat processing in high-anhedonic depressed phlegmatics and cholerics (disharmonious temperaments with ineffective stimulation processing). Thus we have similar data constellations to that received for apprehension anxiety. In contrast to the results for anxiety, here disharmonious types of temperament are connected with decreased happiness processing, not negativity processing. This informs us that negative affective content attracts the attention of high-trait anxious individuals, but that positive affect content attracts the attention of high-anhedonic depressed individuals. In addition, it confirms the tripartiate model of anxiety and depression disorders (see Watson, 2000, for a review).

However, the results obtained are in conflict with results from studies of Marszał-Wiśniewska and Fajkowska-Stanik (2005). They analyzed the relationship among depressive tendencies (BDI; Beck et al., 1987; Parnowski & Jernajczyk, 1977), Pavlovian temperament properties (PTS; Strelau & Zawadzki, 1998), and detection of emotional signals (controlled visual search; paper-and-pencil attention test; cf. Szymura & Słabosz, 2002). Using the exploratory multi-multivariable analysis of regression, insufficient significant correlations between independent variables (depression and temperament properties) have been found to allow for building coherent/incoherent personality structures. But it was observed that both high depression and high strength of inhibition (typical for sanguines, phlegmatics, and in some cases in a moderate level for cholerics) lead to the same result—namely, a lower level of false alarms to happiness and the more careful strategy of reactions to signals of happiness. This implies that both characteristics are associated with good attentional control over happiness. In the studies presented in this book, none of these traits participated in increased attentional control over happiness.

*Personality coherence/incoherence and dynamics of stimulation processing*

As demonstrated in Table 5.8, high-anhedonic depression affects impaired attentional control over happiness. Attentional vigilance toward happiness, effective happiness and sadness processing, and impaired attentional control over threat

**Table 5.8.** Choleric Type (Pavlovian approach) and Anhedonic Type of depression in attentional processing of facial affect

| Personality types | Behavioral indices of facial processing | | | |
|---|---|---|---|---|
|  | *RT* | *Accuracy* | *OM* | *FA* |
| **Choleric** | ↓ F | ↑ F ↑ S | ↓ S | ↑ Th |
| **High-anhedonic depression** | ns | ns | ns | ↑ F |

*Note.* RT = reaction time; OM = omissions; FA = false alarms; Th = threatening faces; F = friendly faces; S = sad faces.

RT: $F(3,62) = 6.50$, $p < 0.001$, $\eta^2 = 0.24$, F/Go – cholerics ($2.63 \pm 0.02$) < phlegmatics ($2.72 \pm 0.02$), $p < 0.001$. Accuracy: $F(3,60) = 5.37$, $p < 0.001$, $\eta^2 = 0.21$, F/Go – cholerics ($1.39 \pm 0.05$) > phlegmatics ($1.19 \pm 0.04$), $p < 0.01$; $F(3,60) = 7.19$, $p < 0.001$, $\eta^2 = 0.26$, S/Go – cholerics ($1.01 \pm 0.08$) > phlegmatics ($0.55 \pm 0.08$), $p < 0.001$; OM: $F(3,60) = 4.38$, $p < 0.001$, $\eta^2 = 0.18$, S/Go – cholerics ($0.15 \pm 0.06$) < phlegmatics ($0.55 \pm 0.08$), $p < 0.001$. FA: $F(3,60) = 4.25$, $p < 0.001$, $\eta^2 = 0.17$, Th/NoGo – sanguines ($0.05 \pm 0.01$) < cholerics ($0.11 \pm 0.01$), $p < 0.01$, Th/NoGo – melancholics ($0.05 \pm 0.01$) < cholerics ($0.11 \pm 0.01$), $p < 0.001$; $F(1,60) = 31.30$, $p < 0.001$, $\eta^2 = 0.34$, F/NoGo – low-anhedonic depressed ($0.02 \pm 0.05$) < high-anhedonic depressed ($0.09 \pm 0.01$), $p < 0.001$

have been found in the Choleric Type. Thus it seems that on the basis of synergistic functional interactions, the incoherent high-anhedonic Choleric Type revealed impaired attentional control over happiness.

### 5.3.2. Attentional biases in coherent/incoherent personality structures built upon temperament types in Eysenckian perspective and anhedonic depression

The study of how the quality and dynamics of attentional processing of facial expressions might be connected with coherent/incoherent personality structures built upon the temperament types in the Eysenckian perspective and anhedonic depression are presented below.

*Intercorrelations: Temperament Type and Anhedonic Type*

In this study participants ($N = 170$, 83 females, $M = 25.15$, $SD = 7.11$) completed questionnaires (BDI: Beck et al., 1987; Parnowski & Jernajczyk, 1977; EPQ-R: Brzozowski & Drwal, 1995; Eysenck & Eysenck, 1994) and took part in the Emotional Go/NoGo task (cf. Figure 5.4). Figure 5.14 presents significant results on correlational relations obtained for the Phlegmatic Type, Choleric Type, and Anhedonic Type of depression.

According to Figure 5.14A, the coherent high-anhedonic depressed Phlegmatic Type (*CPT* $_{Phlegmatic:\ emotionally\ stable\ introvert}^{high\text{-}anhedonic\ depression}$) demonstrates ineffective sadness processing (low accuracy in S/Go), while the coherent low-anhedonic depressed Phlegmatic Type ($CPT_{Phlegmatic:\ emotionally\ stable\ introvert}^{low\text{-}anhedonic\ depression}$) demonstrates high accuracy in sadness detection (S/Go).

Figure 5.14B reveals that the incoherent high-anhedonic depressed Choleric Type ($INPT_{Choleric:\ emotionally\ unstable\ extravert}^{high\text{-}anhedonic\ depression}$) is connected with vigilance to happiness (faster detection of F/Go), but that the coherent low-anhedonic depressed Choleric Type ($CPT_{Choleric:\ emotionally\ unstable\ extravert}^{low\text{-}anhedonic\ depression}$) is connected with reduced vigilance to happiness (slower detection of F/Go).

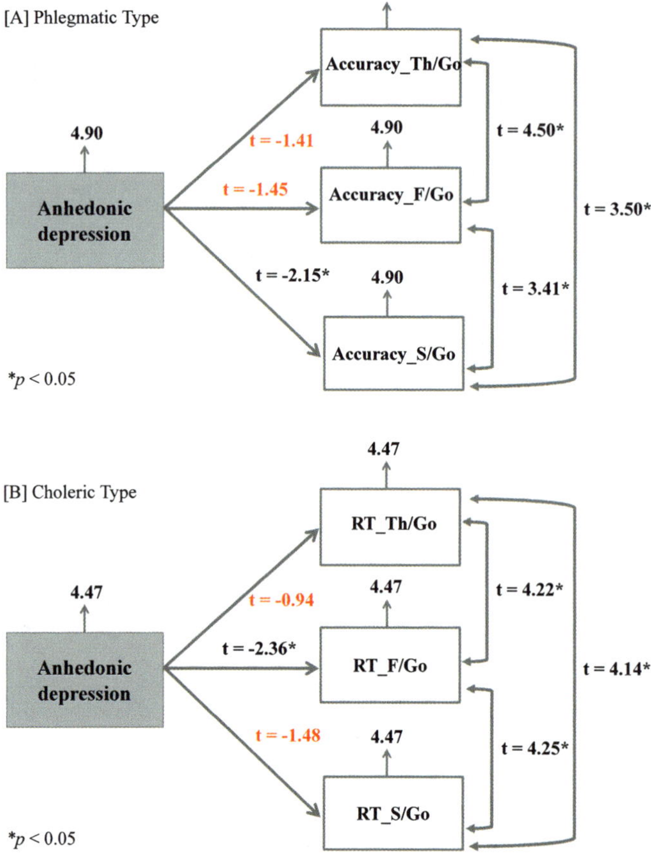


**Figure 5.14.** Results of the exploratory multi-multivariable analysis of regression (structural equations estimated by LISREL 8.51) for [A] accuracy to Go trials in Phlegmatic Type ($N = 50$) and [B] reaction times to Go trials in Choleric Type ($N = 42$) and Anhedonic Type of depression. RT = reaction times. Nonsignificant results are written in red.

Thus the Anhedonic Type of depression and Phlegmatic Type and the Anhedonic Type of depression and Choleric Type are connected with impairment in sadness processing and enhanced processing of happiness, respectively.

*Interactions: Temperament Type x Anhedonic Type*

The evidence, obtained with the same procedure as above ($N = 250$, 150 females, $M = 25.18$ years, $SD = 7.09$), suggests that interactions between the Anhedonic Type of depression and (a) the Sanguine Type, affect vigilance to sadness; (b) the Melancholic Type, produce vigilance to happiness; (c) the Phlegmatic Type, result in vigilance to sadness and happiness and effective happiness processing; and (d) the Choleric Type, give vigilance to happiness and sadness. More precisely, the coherent high-anhedonic depressed Sanguine Type ($CPT_{Sanguine:\ emotionally\ stable\ extravert}^{high\text{-}anhedonic\ depression}$) has been found to be faster in sadness detection than the coherent low-anhedonic depressed Sanguine Type ($CPT_{Sanguine:\ emotionally\ stable\ extravert}^{low\text{-}anhedonic\ depression}$).[18] The incoherent high-anhedonic depressed Melancholic Type ($INPT_{Melancholic:\ emotionally\ unstable\ introvert}^{high\text{-}anhedonic\ depression}$) is faster in happiness detection than the coherent low-anhedonic depressed Melancholic Type ($CPT_{Melancholic:\ emotionally\ unstable\ introvert}^{low\text{-}anhedonic\ depression}$).[19] Further, the coherent high-anhedonic depressed Phlegmatic Type ($CPT_{Phlegmatic:\ emotionally\ stable\ introvert}^{high\text{-}anhedonic\ depression}$) is faster and more accurate in happiness processing, and faster in sadness processing, than the coherent low-anhedonic depressed Phlegmatic Type ($CPT_{Phlegmatic:\ emotionally\ stable\ introvert}^{low\text{-}anhedonic\ depression}$).[20] Finally, the incoherent high-anhedonic depressed Choleric Type ($INPT_{Choleric:\ emotionally\ unstable\ extravert}^{high\text{-}anhedonic\ depression}$) is faster in happiness and sadness processing than the coherent low-anhedonic depressed Choleric Type ($CPT_{Choleric:\ emotionally\ unstable\ extravert}^{low\text{-}anhedonic\ depression}$).[21]

---

[18] *Sanguine Type x Anhedonic depression.* RT: $F(3,247) = 4.48$, $p < 0.001$, $\eta^2 = 0.05$, S/Go—coherent high-anhedonic depressed sanguines ($2.72 \pm 0.03$) < coherent low-anhedonic depressed sanguines ($2.78 \pm 0.01$), $p < 0.05$.

[19] *Melancholic Type x Anhedonic depression.* RT: $F(3,242) = 3.52$, $p < 0.01$, $\eta^2 = 0.04$, F/Go—incoherent high-anhedonic depressed melancholics ($2.64 \pm 0.01$) < coherent low-anhedonic depressed melancholics ($2.69 \pm 0.01$), $p < 0.01$.

[20] *Phlegmatic Type x Anhedonic depression.* RT: $F(3,242) = 3.52$, $p < 0.01$, $\eta^2 = 0.04$, F/Go—coherent high-anhedonic depressed phlegmatics ($2.67 \pm 0.02$) < coherent low-anhedonic depressed phlegmatics ($2.72 \pm 0.01$), $p < 0.05$; $F(3,247) = 4.48$, $p < 0.001$, $\eta^2 = 0.05$, S/Go—coherent high-anhedonic depressed phlegmatics ($2.71 \pm 0.02$) < coherent low-anhedonic depressed phlegmatics ($2.78 \pm 0.01$), $p < 0.001$; Accuracy: $F(3,236) = 2.75$, $p < 0.05$, $\eta^2 = 0.04$, F/Go—coherent high-anhedonic depressed phlegmatics ($1.30 \pm 0.06$) > coherent low-anhedonic depressed phlegmatics ($1.13 \pm 0.03$), $p < 0.001$.

[21] *Choleric Type x Anhedonic depression.* RT: $F(3,242) = 3.52$, $p < 0.01$, $\eta^2 = 0.04$, F/Go—incoherent high-anhedonic depressed cholerics ($2.62 \pm 0.01$) < coherent low-anhedonic depressed cholerics ($2.69 \pm 0.01$), $p < 0.01$; $F(3,247) = 4.48$, $p < 0.001$, $\eta^2 = 0.05$, S/

As these results suggest, interactions among the Anhedonic Type of depression and the four temperament types affect the early attentional functions and attentional effectiveness in the processing of emotional material.

*Summary and interpretation*

Table 5.9 presents the results obtained for correlational and interactional analysis in coherent/incoherent personality structures built upon the four temperament types within Eysenckian theory and anhedonic depression.

*Personality coherence/incoherence and quality of stimulation processing*

Thus data taken from Table 5.9 show that functional overlaps in the coherent (regulative) Phlegmatic Type + (regulative) Anhedonic Type are connected with ineffective sadness processing. When the functions are distinct—incoherent (reactive) Choleric Type + (regulative) Anhedonic Type—vigilance to happiness is observed. When we combine these data with those for low-anhedonic depressed phlegmatics and low-anhedonic depressed cholerics, we see effectiveness of sadness processing and reduced vigilance to happiness, respectively (Table 5.9).

*Personality coherence/incoherence and dynamics of stimulation processing*

From Table 5.9 it is clear that Eysenckian traits, married with depressed mood traits, activate mostly bottom-up attentional processes and attentional effectiveness in stimulation processing. Given the presence of social and emotional material across all experiments used in my studies, it should come as no surprise that both neuroticism and extraversion, reflected in the particular type of temperament, would be involved and specifically sensitive to this type of stimulation. However, as Table 5.10 shows, neither neuroticism nor extraversion in sanguines, melancholics, phlegmatics, and cholerics were engaged in stimulation processing. Only anhedonic depression revealed itself as connected with attentional vigilance to all emotional targets and with attentional effectiveness to happiness. This implies that all received effects of interactions between anhedonic depression and the four temperament types emerged on the basis of synergistic functional interaction. This type of interaction produces attentional vigilance to sadness in coherent sanguines, to happiness in incoherent melancholics, to happiness and sadness in coherent phlegmatics and incoherent cholerics, and (in addition) to effective happiness processing in coherent phlegmatics.

By contrast, for both types of anxieties combined with temperament types, we obtained results suggesting an activation of the top-down attentional processes in facial affect processing.

---

Go—incoherent high-anhedonic depressed cholerics (2.67 ± 0.01) < coherent low-anhedonic depressed cholerics (2.74 ± 0.01), $p < 0.001$.

**Table 5.9.** Attentional biases in coherent/incoherent personality structures built upon temperament types in Eysenckian approach and anhedonic depression

| Processes-level of stimulation processing | Traits-level of stimulation processing | | | | | | | |
| --- | --- | --- | --- | --- | --- | --- | --- | --- |
| | Content (emotional and social) characteristics of activity *(Eysenckian approach)* | | | | | | | |
| | Sanguine Type | | Melancholic Type | | Phlegmatic Type | | Choleric Type | |
| | CPT | | CPT | INPT | CPT | | CPT | INPT |
| Attentional patterns of stimulation processing | Low-anhedonic depression | High-anhedonic depression | Low-anhedonic depression | High-anhedonic depression | Low-anhedonic depression | High-anhedonic depression | Low-anhedonic depression | High-anhedonic depression |
| **Vigilance** *(low RT, high TN)* | | S | | F | | F&S | | F F&S |
| **Reduced vigilance** *(high RT, low TN)* | | | | | | | F | |
| **Avoidance** *(high OM)* | | | | | | | | |
| **Impaired attentional control** *(high FA)* | | | | | | | | |
| **Enhanced attentional control** *(low FA)* | | | | | | | | |
| **Attentional effectiveness** *(high Accuracy and Hits)* | | | | | S | F | | |
| **Attentional ineffectiveness** *(low Accuracy and Hits)* | | | | | | S | | |

*Note.* RT = reaction time; TN = total number of items processed; OM = omissions; FA = false alarms; F = friendly faces; S = sad faces. Intercorrelational relations are highlighted in green; interactive relations are highlighted in pink.

**Table 5.10.** Temperament types in Eysenckian approach and Anhedonic Type of depression in attentional processing of facial affect

| Personality types | Behavioral indices of facial processing | | | |
| --- | --- | --- | --- | --- |
| | *RT* | *Accuracy* | *OM* | *FA* |
| **Sanguine** | ns | ns | ns | ns |
| **Melancholic** | ns | ns | ns | ns |
| **Phlegmatic** | ns | ns | ns | ns |
| **Choleric** | ns | ns | ns | ns |
| **High-anhedonic depression** | ↓ Th ↓ F ↓ S | ↑ F | ns | ns |

*Note.* RT = reaction time; OM = omissions; FA = false alarms; Th = threatening faces; F = friendly faces; S = sad faces.

RT: $F(1,242) = 5.17$, $p < 0.01$, $\eta^2 = 0.02$, Th/Go – low-anhedonic depressed $(2.70 \pm 0.01) >$ high-anhedonic depressed $(2.67 \pm 0.01)$, $p < 0.05$; $F(1,242) = 7.70$, $p < 0.001$, $\eta^2 = 0.03$, F/Go – low-anhedonic depressed $(2.69 \pm 0.01) >$ high-anhedonic depressed $(2.65 \pm 0.01)$, $p < 0.001$; $F(1,242) = 4.11$, $p < 0.05$, $\eta^2 = 0.02$, S/Go – low-anhedonic depressed $(2.75 \pm 0.01) >$ high-anhedonic depressed $(2.72 \pm 0.01)$, $p < 0.05$. Accuracy: $F(1,236) = 9.23$, $p < 0.001$, $\eta^2 = 0.04$, F/Go – low-anhedonic depressed $(1.23 \pm 0.01) <$ high-anhedonic depressed $(1.33 \pm 0.03)$, $p < 0.05$.

### 5.3.3. Attentional biases in coherent/incoherent personality structures built upon temperament types in RTT perspective and anhedonic depression

This section presets data on the quality and dynamics of attentional processing of facial affect in coherent/incoherent personality structures composed of the four temperament types in the RTT perspective and anhedonic depression.

*Intercorrelations: Temperament type and Anhedonic Type*

Utilizing the same procedure ($N = 170$, 83 females, $M = 25.15$, $SD = 7.11$) based on the Emotional Go/NoGo task (cf. Figure 5.4) boosted with personality measures, I explored the mediating effects of the Anhedonic Type of depression in the four temperament types defined within the RTT. Figure 5.15 presents the significant results.

According to Figure 5.15A, the coherent high-anhedonic depressed Sanguine Type ($CPT_{Sanguine:\ high\ SPC\ +\ high\ AC}{}^{high\text{-}anhedonic\ depression}$) shows increased attentional control over happiness (low level of FAs to F/NoGo), while the coherent low-anhedonic depressed Sanguine Type ($CPT_{Sanguine:\ high\ SPC\ +\ high\ AC}{}^{low\text{-}anhedonic\ depression}$) shows decreased attentional control over happiness (high level of FAs to F/NoGo).

From Figure 5.15B we learn that the coherent high-anhedonic depressed Phlegmatic Type ($CPT_{Phlegmatic:\ high\ SPC\ +\ low\ AC}{}^{high\text{-}anhedonic\ depression}$) demonstrates increased attentional control over happiness and sadness (low level of FAs for F/NoGo and S/NoGo trials), but that the coherent low-anhedonic depressed Phlegmatic Type ($CPT_{Phlegmatic:\ high\ SPC\ +\ low\ AC}{}^{low\text{-}anhedonic\ depression}$) has decreased attentional control over happiness and sadness (high level of FAs for F/NoGo and S/NoGo trials). This

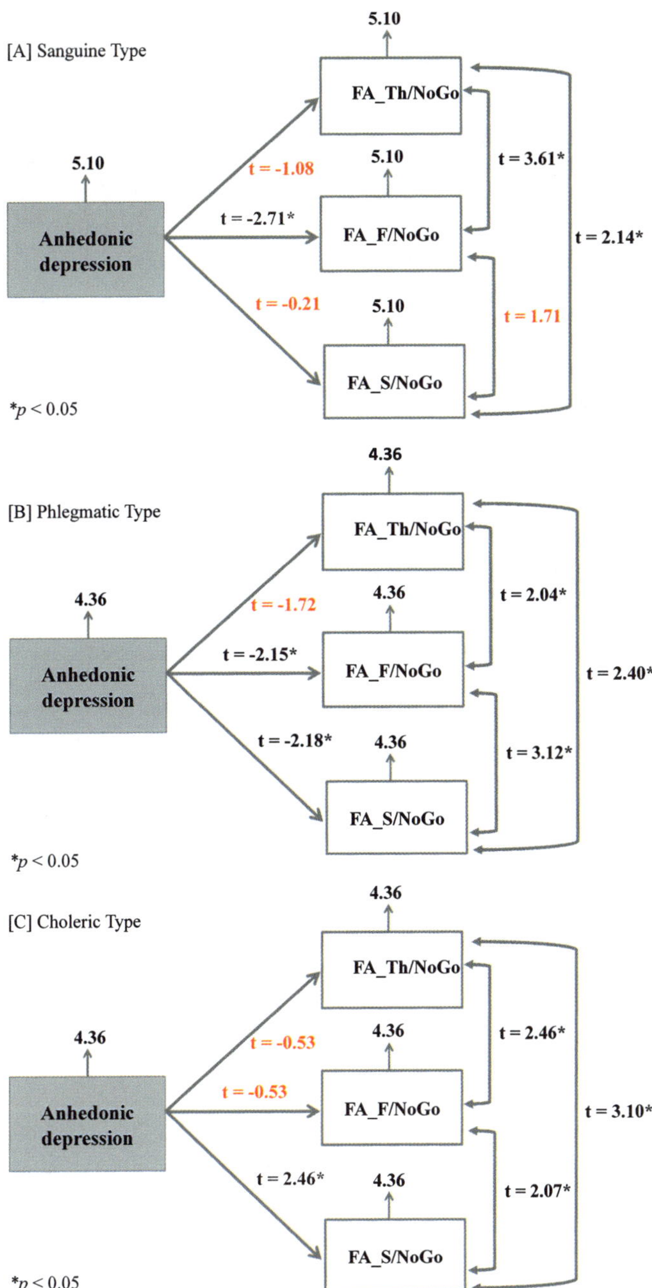



**Figure 5.15.** Results of the exploratory multi-multivariable analysis of regression (structural equations estimated by LISREL 8.51) for [A] false alarms to NoGo trials in Sanguine Type ($N = 54$); [B] false alarms to NoGo trials in Phlegmatic Type ($N = 40$); and [C] false alarms to NoGo trials in Choleric Type ($N = 40$) and Anhedonic Type of depression. FA = false alarms. Non-significant results are written in red.

implies that the Anhedonic Type of depression modulates increased attentional control over happiness and sadness in phlegmatics.

As can be seen in Figure 5.15C, in the case of the incoherent high-anhedonic depressed Choleric Type ($INPT_{Choleric:\ low\ SPC\ +\ high\ AC}^{high\text{-}anhedonic\ depression}$), we see decreased attentional control over sadness (high level of FAs for S/NoGo trials), but in the coherent low-anhedonic depressed Choleric Type ($CPT_{Choleric:\ low\ SPC\ +\ high\ AC}^{low\text{-}anhedonic\ depression}$) we see increased attentional control over sadness (low level of FAs for S/NoGo trials). These results suggest that the Anhedonic Type of depression mediates impairment of attentional control over sadness in cholerics.

*Interactions: Temperament Type x Anhedonic Type*

Studies ($N = 114$, 98 females, $M = 24.75$, $SD = 6.21$) on relations among depression (BDI; Beck et al., 1987; Parnowski & Jernajczyk, 1977) and RTT temperament properties (FCB-TI; Zawadzki & Strelau, 1997) within the Emotional Go/NoGo task (cf. Figure 5.4) provided a small number of significant results.

It has been found that interaction between the Anhedonic Type of depression and Melancholic Type, and between the Anhedonic Type of depression and Choleric Type, affects impaired attentional control over sadness. Thus the incoherent high-anhedonic depressed Melancholic Type ($INPT_{Melancholic:\ low\ SPC\ +\ low\ AC}^{high\text{-}anhedonic\ depression}$) presented more false alarms to sadness than the coherent low-anhedonic depressed Melancholic Type ($CPT_{Melancholic:\ low\ SPC\ +\ low\ AC}^{low\text{-}anhedonic\ depression}$).[22] Also, a higher number of false alarms to sadness have been identified in the incoherent high-anhedonic depressed Choleric Type ($INPT_{Choleric:\ low\ SPC\ +\ high\ AC}^{high\text{-}anhedonic\ depression}$) than in the coherent low-anhedonic depressed Choleric Type ($CPT_{Choleric:\ low\ SPC\ +\ high\ AC}^{low\text{-}anhedonic\ depression}$).[23]

*Summary and interpretation*

Table 5.11 informs us about intercorrelations and interactions between elements composing coherent/incoherent structures—the four temperament types within the RTT and anhedonic depression—and how they relate to patterns of attentional processing of facial expressions.

*Personality coherence/incoherence and quality of stimulation processing*

Analyzing the data for coherent low-anhedonic depressed sanguines and coherent low-anhedonic depressed phlegmatics, we see that functional overlapping—when

---

[22] *Melancholic Type x Anhedonic depression.* FA: $F(5,103) = 8.44$, $p < 0.001$, $\eta^2 = 0.29$, S/NoGo—incoherent high-anhedonic depressed melancholis ($0.24 \pm 0.04$) > coherent low-anhedonic depressed melancholics ($0.14 \pm 0.03$), $p < 0.05$.

[23] *Choleric Type x Anhedonic depression.* FA: $F(5,103) = 8.44$, $p < 0.001$, $\eta^2 = 0.29$, S/NoGo—incoherent high-anhedonic depressed cholerics ($0.33 \pm 0.05$) > coherent low-anhedonic depressed cholerics ($0.15 \pm 0.03$), $p < 0.001$.

**Table 5.11.** Attentional biases in coherent/incoherent personality structures built upon temperament types in RTT approach and anhedonic depression

| Attentional patterns of stimulation processing | Traits-level of stimulation processing | | | | | | | |
| --- | --- | --- | --- | --- | --- | --- | --- | --- |
| | Formal (energetic and temporal) characteristics of activity (RTT) | | | | | | | |
| | Sanguine Type | | Melancholic Type | | Phlegmatic Type | | Choleric Type | |
| | CPT | | CPT | INPT | CPT | | CPT | INPT |
| | Low-anhedonic depression | High-anhedonic depression | Low-anhedonic depression | High-anhedonic depression | Low-anhedonic depression | High-anhedonic depression | Low-anhedonic depression | High-anhedonic depression |
| **Vigilance** (low RT, high TN) | | | | | | | | |
| **Reduced vigilance** (high RT, low TN) | | | | | | | | |
| **Avoidance** (high OM) | | | | | | | | |
| **Impaired attentional control** (high FA) | F | | | S | F&S | | | S S |
| **Enhanced attentional control** (low FA) | | F | | | | F&S | S | |
| **Attentional effectiveness** (high Accuracy and Hits) | | | | | | | | |
| **Attentional ineffectiveness** (low Accuracy and Hits) | | | | | | | | |

*Note.* RT = reaction time; TN = total number of items processed; OM = omissions; FA = false alarms; F = friendly faces; S = sad faces. Intercorrelational relations are highlighted in green; interactive relations are highlighted in pink.

high-anhedonic depression is involved—improves quality of processing in the coherent (regulative) Sanguine Type + (regulative) Anhedonic Type and in the coherent (regulative) Phlegmatic Type + (regulative) Anhedonic Type. Examining the data for incoherent high-anhedonic depressed cholerics (vs. coherent low-anhedonic depressed cholerics), we see that functional distinctness in the incoherent (reactive) Choleric + (regulative) Anhedonic Type leads to a decrement in quality of processing (cf. Table 5.11). With these results one can conclude that a high quality of stimulation processing is connected with personality coherence with elevated anhedonic depression, but that a low quality of stimulation processing is connected with personality incoherence also accompanied by high anhedonic depression.

*Personality coherence/incoherence and dynamics of stimulation processing*

The findings considering interactional analysis between the Anhedonic Type of depression and the four temperament types defined within the RTT clearly demonstrated that this type of depression moderates attentional control over emotional material. More precisely, we observe decreased inhibitory control over sadness in incoherent melancholics and cholerics. Interestingly, it was found that high-anhedonic depression affects the decreased attentional control over sadness, while the results obtained for melancholics and cholerics were nonsignificant (see Table 5.12). This suggests that on the basis of synergistic functional interaction, we observe the effects of interaction between melancholics and choleric types and anhedonic depression.

To some extent these findings conflict with those presented by Fajkowska and Marszał-Wiśniewska (2006). These authors studied the relations among depressive tendencies (BDI; Beck et al., 1987; Parnowski & Jernajczyk, 1977) and the four RTT temperament traits (FCB-TI; Zawadzki & Strelau, 1997) using the face-in-the-crowd procedure. Among other findings, they discovered that the incoherent high-anhedonic depressed Melancholic Type ($INPT_{Melancholic:\ low\ SPC}^{high\text{-}anhedonic\ depression}$) and incoherent high-anhedonic depressed Choleric Type ($INPT_{Choleric:\ low\ SPC}^{high\text{-}anhedonic\ depression}$) were slower in detecting friendly faces, but that the coherent low-anhedonic depressed Sanguine Type ($CPT_{Sanguine:\ high\ SPC}^{low\text{-}anhedonic\ depression}$) and coherent low-anhedonic depressed Phlegmatic Type ($CPT_{Phlegmatic:\ high\ SPC}^{low\text{-}anhedonic\ depression}$)[24] were faster in happiness detection. The discrepancies embrace different attentional functions engaged in processing emotional material; attentional control was identified as primarily engaged in my studies, but in their studies attentional vigilance was identified. Contrary to Fajkowska and Marszał-Wiśniewska (2006), I have collected data suggesting attentional biases to sadness in incoherent melancholics and cholerics.

---

[24] I interpret these data according to my revised approach to personality coherence/incoherence presented in this book.

**Table 5.12.** Melancholic Type, Choleric Type (RTT approach), and Anhedonic Type of depression in attentional processing of facial affect

| Personality types | Behavioral indices of facial processing | | | |
| --- | --- | --- | --- | --- |
| | *RT* | *Accuracy* | *OM* | *FA* |
| **Melancholic** | ns | ns | ns | ns |
| **Choleric** | ns | ns | ns | ns |
| **High-anhedonic depression** | ns | ns | ns | ↑ S |

*Note.* RT = reaction time; OM = omissions; FA = false alarms; S = sad faces.

FA: $F(1,103) = 5.61$, $p < 0.05$, $\eta^2 = 0.05$, S/NoGo – low-anhedonic depressed $(0.18 \pm 0.01) <$ high-anhedonic depressed $(0.28 \pm 0.04)$, $p < 0.05$.

*Conclusions*

What overall conclusions can be drawn regarding the relationships among the Anhedonic Type of depression, temperament characteristics, and attentional processing of stimulation?

The findings obtained are difficult to explain purely in terms of typical attentional biases for the Anhedonic Type of depression. On one hand, there is evidence that anhedonic depression is associated with impaired inhibitory control over happiness and sadness; but on the other hand, it is also associated with vigilance to emotional material and effective happiness processing (see Tables 5.8, 5.10, and 5.12). These results point to the fact that attentional biases might represent both reactive and regulative functions of anhedonic depression in the situations examined. However, the all-emotion bias reflects the minor reactive function (bottom-up attentional processes), while happiness and sadness biases reflect the dominating regulative function (top-down attentional processes) of anhedonic depression. This may explain why any regular pattern concerning the quality of processing is not obtained for coherent and incoherent personality structures. This general conclusion is identical for both types of anxieties and suggests the usefulness of conducting a pilot study before the main study, aimed at identifying the task-specific dominant controlling function—in particular, subtypes of mood traits.

The studies presented are important because the evidence shows a differentiation in personality structures involved in the quality of stimulation processing across two theoretical approaches—from the more integrated personality structures within the Pavlovian approach to the less integrated personality structures within the Strelauvian approach. The small number of results obtained does not allow for any conclusions in this aspect for the Eysenckian approach. Thus in the Pavlovian approach personality harmony/disharmony is addressed to the quality of stimulation processing. In harmonious types (sanguines and melancholics) is observed the worsening of attentional effectiveness, when high-anhedonic depression is concerned; in disharmonious types (phlegmatics and cholerics) is registered enhancement of attentional effectiveness, when high-anhedonic depression is involved. In the Strelauvian approach, the high stimulation-processing capacities relate to the quality of processing stimulation: improving processing in sanguines and phlegmatics with elevated level of anhedonic depression. Interestingly, a differentiation in personality structures involved in the quality of stimulation processing across these two theories of temperament is specific to attentional processes: attentional effectiveness corresponds to the Pavlovian approach, and attentional control matches to the RTT. Hypothetically, specific personality structures with different levels of integration have a specific role for the operating quality of particular attentional process when anhedonic depression is involved. However, this speculation should be left for future studies.

With regard to the kind of interaction between focal types, relating them to attentional processes revealed a decrease of attentional control in incoherent cholerics (the Pavlovian approach), which reflects the synergistic type of intereaction. Also thanks to synergistic interactions, bottom-up and top-down attentional processes were activated across the Eysenckian and RTT approaches, respectively. A typical pattern of processing emotional material for anhedonic depression dominated those patterns that are typical for temperament types across all three theories. Within the Pavlovian approach top-down attentional processes showed themselves in incoherent cholerics. Within the Eysenckian approach, bottom-up attentional processes displayed themselves as vigilance to emotional material in all coherent (sanguines and phlegmatics) and incoherent (melancholics and cholerics) temperament types. Within the RTT approach, top-down attentional processes exhibited themselves as impaired attentional control in incoherent melancholics and cholerics. It seems likely that this differentiation is due to the specific aspects emphasized by each temperament theory in maintaining an optimal level of stimulation, combined with a regulative role of anhedonic depression in stimulation processing.

5.4.
## Summing up

Research on anxiety and depressed mood as elements of the coherent and incoherent personalities structures reviewed above allows us to compose a probable picture of their effects on attentional processing. These effects are analyzed across two important questions—namely, (a) how the level of functional complexity reflected in coherent/incoherent personality structures affects quality of processing stimulation; and (b) how functional interactions in coherent/incoherent personality structures relate to the dynamics of attentional processes engaged in stimulation processing.

With reference to the first question, clearly the accumulation of data reveals that personality coherence (functional overlapping) or incoherence (functional distinctness) does not elucidate the quality of stimulation processing in the context studied. Generally, the lower-integrated personality structures (e.g., SPC, disharmonious, or harmonious temperaments) relate to the quality of stimulation processing. One possible explanation is that higher-level integrated traits (e.g., personality coherence/incoherence) are useful for predicting quality of performance of more complex behaviors, but at the same time seem are inadequate for predicting patterns of simple reactions to attentional tasks. Also, it seems probable that these traits might be activated more in complex situations than experimental ones. The conclusion is that the complex, multilevel traits or personality types should be studied through more complex behaviors and more ecologically valid situations. In addition, it is believed that the tasks administered were not adequate to cover all controlling functions in focal types—which is considered a main drawback of these studies.

However, two exceptions were identified. First, a quite regular pattern for quality of processing and personality coherence/incoherence with elevated level of arousal anxiety was found. Incoherent high-arousal sanguines and phlegmatics produce poor processing of affective stimulation, whereas coherent high-arousal melancholics and cholerics present weak stimulation processing. The possible explanation for these data was provided earlier, with reference to the generalized deteriorating impact of arousal anxiety on attentional processing, which seems to be relatively stable and independent from the intercorrelational relations among arousal anxiety and temperament types. Second, incoherent cholerics with elevated apprehension anxiety or elevated level of anhedonic depression present increased attentional processing. One possible explanation is that reactive choleric type benefits from the "regulative nature" of these two affective traits, which acting together produce effective stimulation processing.

Considering the second question, it appeared that regular patterns of results suggesting relatively stable correspondence between the type of interaction and personality coherence/incoherence were not provided. In other words, it was found that synergistic and antagonistic interactions do not specifically explain how personality coherence or incoherence modify dynamics of attentional processes, but rather how elevated arousal or apprehension anxiety and anhedonic depression—as elements of lower-integrated personality structures—influence these dynamics. Actually, it was found that synergistic and antagonistic interactions related to the dynamics of the top-down attentional processes across most personality structures when both types of anxieties were considered. Also, these two types of functional interactions were connected with activation of bottom-up and top-down attentional processes across most personality structures when anhedonic depression was considered. For example, the synergistic interaction is connected with the activation of bottom-up attentional processes (cf. data for anhedonic depression in the Eysenckian approach) and top-down attentional processes (cf. data for arousal anxiety or anhedonic depression in the RTT approach). It is worth noting that the synergistic type of interaction emerged from the dominance of typical patterns of stimulation processing for two types of anxiety and anhedonic depression over the temperament mode of stimulation processing.

To conclude, (a) with reference to the quality and dynamics of attentional stimulation processing, except for very few situations no solid, regular, or specific patterns of results for (respectively) personality coherence and personality incoherence were shown within or across the temperament models studied here; (b) as regards the quality of attentional stimulation processing, it was demonstrated that this is more frequently connected with personality structures of lower integration level than personality coherence/incoherence (this conclusion is valid for all of three models of temperament; it was also evidenced that personality coherence or incoherence do not always mean good or poor stimulation processing, respectively); and (c) in relation to the dynamics of attentional stimulation processing, it appeared that these dynamics originate from two types of interactions—synergistic (responsible for maintaining attentional processes engaged in stimulation processing specific for types of mood, not for types of temperament) or antagonistic (evoking totally new attentional processes engaged in stimulation processing).

These studies had several limitations. First, they utilized the self-report instrument for assessing subtypes of anxiety and depression. My recommendation for the future is to use more sophisticated measures for assessing subtypes of anxiety and depression, including physiological ones. Second, they focused on relatively simple experimental procedures rather than on more complex real-life situations, which probably explains the weak activation of more integrated personality structures in stimulation processing. (However, an advantage of this situation is to show that personality system operates as an "effective investor" and does not engage its highly integrated structures when it is not necessary.) And finally, they applied experimental procedures addressed to the regulative aspect of traits. Further studies should be designed to also measure reactive aspects of traits—for example, by a temporal distribution (at different points in time) approach to stimulation processing.

# Part III

## Epilogue

# Chapter 6

# Looking to the future: A need for integrative models of personality



## The Complex–System Approach to Personality versus selected integrative theories of personality

We have seen that personality psychology is moving toward integrative theories that address personality at multiple levels. Of course this integration is possible only as a result of what we have learned in recent years. Nevertheless, the integrative approach attempts to offer a promise for comprehensive personality theories that account for within-person organization as well as between-person comparisons. The unique challenge for integrative approaches is not only to formulate a cohesive theory, but also to hold to rigorous standards of evidence and to identify causal chains, developmental processes, and correlates with established variables in addition to effect sizes (cf. Campbell, 2008).

Recently, some very interesting propositions of integrative theories of personality have appeared that also subsume many of the insights from earlier models. I have selected three of them, which differ among themselves but inspired me very much in shaping my own vision of an integrative theory of personality—that is, social cognitive theories, personal narratives and the life story approach, and a systems framework for personality. Thus Table 6.1 presents comparisons among these approaches, the aim being to outline the specificity of the Complex–System Approach to Personality (C-SAP) in the context of other designated theories.

### 6.1.1. Personality organization

The social cognitive approaches are an interrelated family of different theoretical perspectives; however, the contributions of four investigators (Albert Bandura, Walter Mischel, Yuichi Shoda, and Daniel Cervone) have been fundamental. Naturally, these scholars turn their attention to distinct scientific challenges. Nevertheless, a highly correlated body of theory and research exists that may constitute a common denominator.

In social cognitive theory, personality organization consists of affective and cognitive systems that contribute causally to the patterns of behavior (cf. Cervone,

**Table 6.1.** Comparison of selected integrative approaches to personality

| Theory / Criterion | Social cognitive theories (e.g., Cervone & Shoda, 1999a, 1999b; Mischel, Shoda, & Smith, 2004) | Personal narratives and the life story (e.g., McAdams, 1999, 2006; McAdams & Pals, 2006) | Systems framework for personality (e.g., Mayer, 2006, 2007a, 2007b) | Complex–System Approach to Personality (Fajkowska, this volume) |
|---|---|---|---|---|
| **Personality organization** | Affective and cognitive systems | Three different vantage points/levels to study individuality | Three-dimensional system | Compositional hierarchy: three-level organization |
| **Personality development** | Human experience and learning | Four developmental milestones | Stability Cyclical change Normative stages Prescriptive change | Personality as the subsumptive hierarchy |
| **Crucial components of personality** | Knowledge and appraisals | Self structuralized through the four main stages of development | Enablers Establishments Themes Agencies | System of Regulation and Integration Stimulation |
| **Traits and processes** | Personal determinants (behavioral signatures); dynamic, affective, and cognitive processes | Dispositional signatures (traits) | Structural forms and dynamic formations | Relatively stable structures (traits) and dynamic processes |
| **Personality coherence/ incoherence** | Personality coherence | Personality coherence/narrative identity | Personal consistency | Personality coherence and incoherence |
| **Methodology** | Idiographic approach to the study of personality | Idiographic and nomothetic approaches to the study of personality | Person- and test-centered approaches to the study of personality | Idiographic and nomothetic approaches to the study of personality |

2008; Cervone & Bartoszek, 2013). These elements of personality structure develop in social settings and are activated by elements of social settings. Cognitive and affective systems consist of a set of functionally distinct systems that interact with one another in the flow of experience and behavior. In a personality system, it is the stable organization of cognitive and affective elements that characterizes the individual and constitutes the structure of one's personality. Of course different individuals develop different interrelations among cognitive and affective elements that underlie the behavioral expressions that distinguish one person from another. The specific personality variables are contextualized; thus the social cognitive units of analysis are person-in-context variables (Caprara & Cervone, 2000).

As social cognitive theories postulate, the processual organization of personality—and to some extent, to reduce it to dynamic mind functioning, the approach of personal narratives and the life story—introduces dispositional characteristics to personality organization. However, they do not correspond directly to particular behaviors or individual strategies. More precisely, it is postulated to study personality from three levels. Level 1 indicates dispositional traits. Level 2 captures what individuals want and the strategies that they employ and includes motives, defenses, cognitive styles, beliefs, values, plans, and goals. All these are characteristic adaptations: characteristic because they are ways in which the character is expressed; adaptations because they are unique to the individual contextualized in time and space, and triggered by specific roles and social demands. This is one level where change happens and where we operate as coaches, mothers, and change agents. Characteristic adaptations fill in the details of human individuality. The Level 2 variables relate loosely to the variables of Level 1; they are established empirically rather than assumed, and they are not necessarily derivatives of Level 1 traits.

In addition, contrary to the social cognitive theories in which personality organization is determined by the external world, this approach leaves room for a very internal part of personality—the self. Level 3 addresses a narrative life story that synthesizes behavior and provides unity and purpose in one's life. These life stories "construe his or her life in narrative terms with the implicit goal of creating an internalized story of the self that binds together the reconstructed past, perceived present, and anticipated future in such a way as to confer upon adult life a sense of unity and purpose" (McAdams, 1999, p. 485). Life stories change substantially over time, reflecting personality development. Integrative life narratives tell what a person's life means in time and culture (McAdams & Pals, 2006).

In contrast to previous approaches, the next one—a systems framework for personality—explicitly emphasizes the systemic organization of personality. It allows for analyzing—and not merely systematizing—mutual connections and influences among distinguished personality elements. Personality has typically been considered from four perspectives: (a) as an open  system that exchanges information with the environment; (b) as distributed across different psychological  subsystems that process information in partial independence of one another; (c) as organized in a hierarchical pattern controlled by a conscious executive; and (d) as developing to meet a particular goal (Mayer, 1998, 2000).

Personality is seen as a three-dimensional system.

- The vertical, molecular-molar dimension separates the more molecular enablers (mental mechanisms: floor of personality cube) from the establishments (mental models: second level), themes (traits: third level), and agencies (processing areas: fourth level).
- The horizontal, internal-external dimension separates those systems most internal to personality (such as consciousness, the self, conscious themes, and the

self-as-knower dimension) from those components more external in orientation (such as conation, affect, cognition, models of the world, and cognitive themes).

- The third dimension—depth—separates those components of personality most enmeshed with the organism (such as conation) from those most independent (such as cognition).

The three dimensions also position the systems surrounding personality, such as the nervous system, external situation, and larger groups/systems (Mayer, 1998, 2000).

According to Mayer (1998, 2000, 2006), the personality system is organized under three different types of control: (a) outside control (e.g., hypnotic states); (b) distributed control (e.g., cognition and affect); and (c) hierarchical control (e.g., conscious control).

The Complex–System Approach to Personality capitalizes on some of the theoretical contributions presented above. Taken together, they allow for conceptualizing personality organization as a system comprising both processes and dispositions. With reference to the compositional hierarchy, it is claimed that the personality system is organized into three levels (subsystems): Level L-1 denotes biological, psychological, and environmental mechanisms and processes; Level L represents structures; and Level L+1 indicates behaviors and actions.

The first level covers personality components such as energetic capacities and different abilities. The second level covers emergent properties such as traits, personality types, or personality patterns. Finally, the third level covers relatively stable behavioral tendencies, strategies, or styles. However, there are more components—besides those identified across the three levels—that are components of control based on regulative and integrative mechanisms. Integrative mechanisms refer to upward causation and produce stability of the system, which allows for an optimal level of system variability. Regulative mechanisms refer to downward causation and maintain a system's stability and optimum level of variability. These mechanisms give rise to intralevel and interlevel emergent properties.

In saying this, I take a position similar to that of Mayer (2000, 2006, 2007a) who theorizes about personality within a systems framework, but I differ from his approach in my emphasis on the compositional hierarchical organization of personality. In addition, I differ from social cognitive theorists in my emphasis on personality traits as the emergent properties of the dynamic personality system and a very important element of personality organization. Instead, in the social cognitive approach, traits as elements of personality organization promote a profile of information indicating the person's responses across an array of psychologically significant situations (also see Mischel, 2009). I also differ from the narrative approach by minimizing the role of the self in integrative processes. In closing, a complete account of personality structure clearly requires a more in-depth focus on situational factors than that proposed in my own approach.

### 6.1.2. Personality development

Within social cognitive theories, human experience (rather than human nature) is the primary cause of personality growth and development—to be more precise, on the social (role of experiences) and cognitive (interpretations and expectations about the events we experience) levels that determine what we learn. However, this theory does not provide details on how personality develops. Additionally, it fails to emphasize biological and genetic, unconscious, or emotional factors in personality development (cf. Cervone, 2008). Also, it does not clarify what is stable in personality. By contrast, the theories discussed below attempt to present the mechanisms or stages of personality development and relatively stable elements of personality.

Thus personal narratives and the life story approach proposes that Erikson's eight psychosocial stages may be seen as the successive stages in a generic story of human life, with basic crises as plot lines (cf. McAdams, 1999). However, four particular periods in the human life course are highlighted here as the most theoretically important. These four milestones are the movement from the attachment to the emergence of an agentic, autobiographical self; the difficult transition between late childhood and early adolescence; emerging adulthood; and tipping points in the midlife years. Each of these four developmental milestones may be viewed from the standpoint of dispositional traits, characteristic adaptations, and integrative life stories (McAdams & Adler, 2006).

A systems framework for personality emphasizes that certain aspects of personality (traits such as level of neuroticism or intelligence) remain relatively stable throughout the life span, while some portions of personality follow rhythms (e.g., cyclical changes are typical for moods). It is also acceptable that personality develops over time according to certain "normative" patterns—for example, stages of development. Finally, prescriptive change of personality is associated with growth according to a prescribed, optimal plan. Sometimes this is called self-actualization (cf. Mayer, 1993b, 2006).

The Complex–System Approach to Personality employs the subsumptive hierarchy to explain personality changes over time and situations. Obviously, some portions of personality remain much the same (e.g., traits, behavioral tendencies), but the other perspective is that personality follows rhythms, developmental stages, and self-actualization. The subsumptive hierarchy denotes stages of development, which is modeled as the accumulation of greater specification (as via growth and/or differentiation). However, the main reasons why personality develops and changes are mutual, dynamic interrelations and interactions between personality components representing different functional roles within system. I would like to emphasize that my approach postulates high plasticity and long-term stability in personality development, but does not refer to the mechanisms of maintaining a stable personal identity.

### *6.1.3. Crucial components of personality*

Within social cognitive theories, personality is understood by reference to basic cognitive and affective structures and processes that have social foundations (e.g., Baltes & Staudinger, 1996; Bandura, 1986; Levine, Resnick, & Higgins, 1993). The term "personality architecture" refers to the intraindividual, overall design and operating characteristics of those mental systems that contribute to behavioral and experiential expressions of personality (Cervone, 2005). Here, in a theoretical model of personality architecture, constructs are designed to model psychological systems in the mind of individuals, not individual differences in the population (Cervone & Bartoszek, 2013). Social cognitive theory differentiates among a number of distinct cognitive capacities that contribute to personality functioning (Bandura, 1986), and recognizes that cognitive and affective processes are closely linked and that a central feature of personality functioning is the deployment of cognitive strategies to regulate affective states (e.g., Metcalfe & Mischel, 1999). Differentiation between knowledge and appraisal processes (Lazarus, 1991; Smith & Lazarus, 1990) seems to be the most important factor to capture personality architecture.

Appraisals are evaluations of a particular encounter or type of encounter and may directly regulate experience and action in any given setting, whereas knowledge refers to general beliefs about personal characteristics or characteristics of the environment (Lazarus, 1991). People's appraisals of a given encounter, however, may be substantially shaped by the knowledge that they bring to that setting. Salient knowledge structures, then, may contribute to stability and coherence in personality functioning by creating coherent patterns of appraisal (Cervone, 1997).

Elements of personality architecture are activated, and express themselves, in appropriate context. Features of the social environment activate knowledge structures, affective reactions, and the links among them. Behavioral expressions of personality architecture, then, include not only average-level responses, but above all patterns of variability in action across social context (Cervone & Bartoszek, 2013).

Personality architecture is anchored in social context or in personal development according to the social cognitive theories or personal narratives and the life story approach, respectively. It seems that the self, which is structuralized through the four main stages of development, is the main element of personality architecture within the personal narratives and the life story approach. Thus the first stage brings the emergence of temperament traits (extraversion, neuroticism; Level 1); attachment as a psychological goal; and the subsequent emergence of an agentic, goal-directed self, showing a rudimentary understanding of human personality (Level 2) and self-composing life stories (Level 3). The next stage, transition to adolescence, brings a new dispositional trait, which here is self-esteem (Level 1), influencing the characteristic adaptations associated with utilizing strategies like compensations or personal fables (Level 2); thus the life stories may be unrealistic and incoherent. Emerging adulthood, the third stage, brings increases in agreeableness and conscientiousness but level of openness to experience may begin to decline—indicating more focus on consolidating different commitments (Level 1). In personality development Level 2 (emerging adulthood) marks taking different social roles and making commitments to new life goals, while at Level 3 new narratives reflect integration of different internalized personifications of the self (McAdams & Adler, 2006).

The next approach, the systems framework for personality, argues that personality is captured by four elements (Mayer, 1998, 2000, 2006). First, mental mechanisms (enablers) are addressed to near-biological mental modules—such as the neural circuitry for emotional facial expression, attentional selectiveness, or working memory—that carry out specific tasks central to personality functioning. Enablers can be divided into four subtypes: conative, affective, cognitive, and consciousness. Second, mental models (establishments) indicate learned mental representations of significant objects or concepts (e.g., representations of the self, the structure of a university). Establishments are mental contents that are so named because they are established by the individual through learning. Third, traits (themes) refer to thematic combinations of mental mechanisms and mental models forming a pattern that can be identified internally (e.g., a mood state) or behaviorally (e.g., a social role). And finally, processing areas (agencies)—which are a composite of enablers, establishments, and themes—are connected with the broad portions of mental operations unified by their focus on a specific, related set of information/stimulation. A particular processing area typically coordinates the actions of metal mechanisms, mental models, and traits that emerge from them or describe them (Mayer, 1998, 2000, 2006).

The Complex–System Approach to Personality postulates that the crucial element of personality architecture is the System of Regulation and Integration Stimulation (SRIS). It consists of the subclasses with (a) the physiological mechanisms of temperament traits—which determine one's need for stimulation—and attentional processes, which regulate the receptivity to signals (reception) and readiness to respond (action), related to emotional and motivational systems; (b) other internal stimulation-related elements—that is, personality characteristics, cognitive and affective mechanisms, and self-regulatory processes; and also (c) external stimulation-related elements like environment and its subsystems. The SIRS accounts for and allocates effort to attain and maintain an optimal level of personality system functioning by regulating the level of activation and arousal, intraindividual coherence, and behavioral integrity.

Thus attempts to understand individual differences in behaviors and within-person organization, with reference to the relations between stimulation-related components of personality, are relevant for my model. These variables do not represent the theories described above.

### 6.1.4. Traits and processes

As we review these theories, we see how they explain dispositional tendencies versus processes. The social cognitive approach contrasts personal determinants with individual differences and dispositions. Here surface-level dispositions are understood in a nontraditional way. Traditionally, traits or dispositions capture consistent behavioral tendencies, while in the social cognitive perspective traits are not viewed as personality structures. Instead, personality structures consist of affective and cognitive systems, which causally produce patterns of behaviors that are an individual's dispositional tendencies. Hence dispositions are effects, not causes.

In social cognitive theory, standard dispositional taxonomies are seen as inadequate for fully describing the individual or for explaining one's personality functioning (cf. Wright & Mischel, 1987), particularly when attempting to explain both the consistency and variability of personality. Unlike a traditional dispositional approach, social cognitive theory assesses not only individual differences, but also the within-person system of psychological attributes that contribute to personal identity and uniqueness. In a bottom-up approach such as social cognitive theory, the individual structures of personality do not correspond in any direct, one-to-one way with dispositional tendencies. Instead, multiple structures and processes act in concert to give rise to overt psychological qualities. This type of theorizing has very different implications for assessment than a top-down approach.

On the other hand, in the next approach—personal narratives and the life story—one defines traits as global tendencies to exhibit one versus another class of response (cf. McAdams & Pals, 2006). Thus variations on a small set of broad dispositional traits (dispositional signatures) constitute the most stable and recognizable aspect of psychological individuality. The main function of these dispositional traits is to sketch a behavioral outline. Traits are nonconditional, decontextualized, and implicitly comparative dimensions; they capture average tendencies across a range of settings, are useful in making between-persons distinctions, show long-term stability, and have strong heritability quotients. Personality trait scores predict observed behavioral trends across situations and over time and predict important life outcomes. For example, the Big Five itself has proven to be a useful and coherent framework for organizing traits, maintaining its validity across cultures. Similar trait labels and systems are found in many different cultures and languages, and culture influences how traits are expressed. Moreover, links between certain traits and the functioning of the brain are emerging (cf. McAdams & Pals, 2006).

Similarly, traits are understood within a systems framework for personality. Traits are seen as the structural forms of a personality system. Traits refer to the relatively static arrangements of a system. They might be seen as supercomponents (or superfactors)—that is, a superordinate variable that can be divided into smaller, highly intercorrelated variables. Thus structural formation is basically a list of formations of supercomponents. Although themes are used here interchangeably with traits, they are defined as the internal manifestations of traits (Mayer, 1995). Thus traits/structures/themes involve features of enablers and establishments that are interwoven to form a coherent program of action (Mayer, 1998). In addition, in the personality system, dynamic forms/dynamic processes involve units that are mutually causal. By their influence on one another, they produce something unique within personality (Mayer, 1999).

Actually, in both social cognitive theory and the personal narratives and life story approach, traits are thought to be psychological systems that less or more directly correspond to broad behavioral tendencies. From my perspective traits are not hypothetical constructs or merely a contextualized profile of responses. The Complex–System Approach to Personality postulates that processes and structures (traits) do not represent antagonistic concepts, but rather exist as harmonious and deeply interrelated constructs. Here processes correspond to dynamic changes in personality and contribute to the structures' formation, and at the same time are subjected to the structures—the stronger the structure, the less flexible the process, and vice-versa (Smith, 1999). Traits, in turn, denote underlying, recurrent mechanisms that form a stable pattern and account for the stability of individual characteristics. Thus traits might be described as processes with a slow rate of change, and might be substituted for structures. This understanding of trait includes the ongoing habituation (automatization) responsible for binding underlying mechanisms and processes in fixed paths; however, such relatively fixed processual patterns have their history and may be subject to change (Smith, 1999).

A few more issues should be explicitly stated. Traits—as denoting underlying, recurrent biological, cognitive, affective, motivational, and situational mechanisms—reflect related content. Moreover, there is no direct correspondence between traits and behavioral tendencies. Instead, transactional relations between manifold structures and processes induce overt behaviors. And it is claimed that behavioral tendencies are more stable than traits. This is because behavioral tendencies are more integrated properties and are located on a higher level of personality than traits. Higher integration and higher level mean more stability.

### 6.1.5. Personality coherence and incoherence

Personality coherence is a central issue for personality psychology, specifically for integrative approaches. However, the theories discussed here differ in understanding personality coherence.

The social cognitive theories underlie coherence in overt psychological responses. In other words, they study how individuals exhibit patterns of behavior that cohere across both time and situation. On a more advanced level, they study how distinct subsystems of personality—such as those involving mood and mental representations of oneself—commonly function as systems that are coherently linked. Coherence is linked to overt psychological response; this means that across circumstances and time, individuals exhibit patterns of behaviors that are meaningfully interconnected or that cohere. In addition, despite life transitions and varying social roles, personality coherence involves continuity in personal identity (cf. Cervone & Shoda, 1999a; Scott & Cervone, 2002).

One can see that coherence is explored here through a behavioral unit. The next approach transports personality coherence into the inner world. Personal narratives and life stories promote consistency and coherence of healthy, normal personality and view the individual organism as an organized and complexly structured whole living in a social context (McAdams, 1997). However, here personality coherence is seen as a narrative identity, which refers to an individual's internalized, evolving, and integrative story of the self. The most important function of stories is integration in two ways. The first is a synchronic one: it expresses how an individual person, who seems to incorporate so many different things in a complex social world, is—at the same time—unique. In other words, an individual is complex and even contradictory, but is still unique. The second reason is diachronic integration (integration in time), which provides causal accounts regarding how a person moved from A to B to C in life—showing, for example, how from a rebellious teenager somebody became a respectable adult (McAdams, 2008).

A more comprehensive vision of personality coherence promotes a systems framework for personality. What is really attractive here is that the analysis of personality coherence is a multilevel one. Personal consistency is seen from four perspectives (Mayer, 1993a, 1993b). Personality as an open system exchanges information with the environment. It might be claimed that some situations (e.g., threatening ones) elicit consistent individual differences in behavior, but that others (e.g., ambiguous ones) do not. Also, personality is a system distributed across different psychological systems that process information in partial independence of one another, which suggests that consistency is likely to be present in many instances and not necessarily easily detected in behavior. In addition, personality is a hierarchical organization with a mostly unchanging executive exerting control over the personality subsystems. This executive control is seen as consciousness. Moreover, from a hierarchical perspective an individual's conscious awareness is constant from birth to death. Finally, personality is a developing system that meets a particular goal and is self-governing, which seems to be critical for consistency (Mayer, 1993a, 1993b).

In my approach personality coherence is a central issue. A unique characteristic of the Complex–System Approach to Personality is that it provides defining features of personality coherence and introduces personality incoherence. In the first three models, these themes cannot be identified. Thus personality coherence versus incoherence emerges as a high-ordered property that is a relatively stable, organized structure formed by a specific set of internal mechanisms. It expresses itself in overt responses and behaviors. An implication is that distinct subsystems in personality might include both coherent as well as incoherent functional relations. To be more specific, personality coherence/incoherence consists of highly interrelated bodies, involving functional consistency or inconsistency of complex personality traits or types.

Personality coherence/incoherence is a substantial element of the SRIS. Thus it is assumed that personality coherence is composed of traits consistent in their controlling functions over stimulation, and that personality incoherence constitutes traits inconsistent in their controlling functions over stimulation. The basic traits forming personality coherence/incoherence are temperament ones. Intraindividual coherence is therefore understood as intraindividual consistency between temperament traits associated with one's need for stimulation, and other traits related to self-providing doses of stimulation, adequate to one's need for stimulation determined by physiological mechanisms of temperament. By contrast, intraindividual incoherence means intraindividual inconsistency between temperament traits associated with one's need for stimulation, and other traits related to self-providing doses of stimulation, not adequate to one's need for stimulation determined by physiological mechanisms of temperament.

In my opinion, my approach presents a deeper and more nuanced understanding of personality coherence, which potentially allows for enhanced operationalization in empirical analysis.

### *6.1.6. Methodology*

Social cognitivists commonly bring both correlational and experimental methods to bear on questions of personality functioning. Here laboratory methods are used to experimentally manipulate psychological structures that underlie phenotypic individual differences. Thus strong tests of theoretical hypotheses are acquired by studying social cognitive processes—correlationally to connect chronic levels of a given variable with a target outcome, and experimentally to clarify causal relations among personality processes and outcomes (e.g., Caprara & Cervone, 2000). Using correlational and experimental methods, Cervone, Shadel, and Jencius (2001) propose five assessment principles for analyzing personality.

- Distinguish between the assessment of internal personality structures and dynamics, whose assessment would be guided by a conceptual model of personality architecture and overt behavioral tendencies, which may be presented in a variety of ways that may be prove useful to the examiner or examinee.
- Assess personal determinants of action to tap those competencies and self-regulatory systems that contribute causally to people's experiences and actions, and finally to people's development.
- Since complex constructs incorporate a number of subconstructs (or facets) that are conceptually distinct, keep distinct response systems (cognition, affection, overt social action) separate.
- Employ assessments that are sensitive to individual idiosyncrasy.
- Assess persons-in-context.

Within this approach a bottom-up strategy of explanation of personality functioning is offered. This means that the attempt is to specify the psychological mechanisms that account not only for common psychological patterns, but also the idiosyncratic tendencies expressed by unique individuals (Caprara & Cervone, 2000).

A different methodological perspective provides personal narratives and the life story approach. Most narrative-based studies rely on quantitative analysis of data. Within this approach structured protocols have been developed for obtaining life narrative data and many procedures have been validated for coding the psychological dimensions of life stories (e.g., life story interview protocols, guided autobiography questionnaires; McAdams, 2008). However, the narrative study of lives is supported by (and has inspired) case-based, idiographic research. In sum, narrative studies show how idiographic and nomothetic studies of personality can complement and enrich each other (McAdams, 2008).

Within a systems framework for personality, Mayer (2006, 2007a) proposes a systems framework for data classification, which begins with the premise that all data about personality must come from the personality itself or from the systems surrounding personality—the brain, social situations, or groups. Thus in this new classification, system data about personality are first divided according to whether they originate outside the personality system (external source data) or inside it (personal report data). Personal report data are divided into life-, world-, self-, and process-report data. Data are further subdivided by the mental processes that produce each type (e.g., convergent thinking, divergent thinking) and are then connected to the measurement procedures that elicit the specific type. These provide a comprehensive collection of data types of both historical and contemporary interest, which span from standard questionnaire data—such as those found in the Big Five—to act-frequency and life-space data categories (Buss & Craik, 1983; Goldberg & Rosolack, 1994; Mayer, 1998).

The methodological aspect is the "Achilles's heel" of the Complex–System Approach to Personality. Generally, I postulate the idiographic and nomothetic approach to study personality, a utilization of self-report measures, experimental procedures, and physiological measures. Data from different response systems are analyzed quantitatively and the responses collected are indicators of common constructs or distinct yet functionally related constructs. However, what is needed is a precise elaboration of a methodological credo that might contribute to better validation of the theory presented here, and to solving some methodological problems that emerged from the studies presented in Chapter 5—for example, lack of measurement sensitive to the functional role of personality traits.

### 6.2.
### Four sins in the study of anxiety and depression: Correctives from the Complex–System Approach to Personality

I have identified four main sins in the studies of anxiety and depression and argue that developments in the C-SAP model presented here can help correct some of them. These sins are shown in Table 6.2.

**Table 6.2.** Sins identified in studies on anxiety and depression

| Sin 1 | Anxiety and depression divorced from the personality system |
|---|---|
| Sin 2 | Neglecting the complexity of anxiety and depression |
| Sin 3 | Research on anxiety and depression hampered by the excessive number of procedures |
| Sin 4 | Lack of purity in studies on anxiety and depression |

Sin 1 is the examination of affective traits as elements distinct from the whole personality system, but especially from temperament. Of course it is easier to analyze these affective disorders if they are isolated from other personality structures; however, the evidence presented in this book shows that each of these phenomena is deeply integrated with other personality elements involved in stimulation processing. There is no doubt that the most important task is the analysis of the mutual relationships among anxiety, depression, and temperament structure as they relate to the arousal processes. Also, it is obvious from the foregoing chapters that specificity of these relations is associated uniquely with the attentional system, an important element of the SRIS.

There is limited empirical evidence indicating temperament risk factors for anxiety and depression and looking at the extent to which they can be linked to attentional biases (e.g., Helzer, Connor-Smith, & Reed, 2009; Peers & Lawrence, 2009; Reeb-Sutherland et al., 2009; Spievak & Murtagh, 2009; Susa & Benga, 2009). Although some researchers (e.g., Longian, Vasey, Philips, & Hazen, 2004) offer proposals for integrating these three areas, these are not directed at promoting a more clear understanding of the relations between anxiety/depression and temperament structure (e.g., formulated in the context of personality coherence and incoherence) and their links to attentional biases. In addition, in these studies temperament is usually understood as behavioral inhibition (Kagan & Snidman, 1999), negative affect (including trait anxiety; Watson, 2000), or reactivity and effortful attentional control (Derryberry & Rothbart, 1997).

In these approaches affect, attention, or withdrawal are components of temperament; they cannot be classified as specific theories of temperament because they limit temperament to emotions or extend temperament characteristics over all behaviors (cf. Strelau, 1998). While temperament refers mainly to formal characteristics of behavior or reactions, it also has a biological basis (cf. Strelau, 2008). Thus the absence of a clear theoretical distinction between affective traits and temperament structure potentially leads to the production of artifacts. Finally, a construct of arousal is entered as a one of the core concepts in most theories of temperament, but unfortunately without guidelines about how to operationalize it for empirical validation.

Thus these facts cannot be ignored. Related to this, these theories of temperament—which I have introduced into my approach—clearly define on operational and theoretical levels the concept of arousal and temperament traits and clearly establish relations among anxiety, depression, and temperament traits. This allowed me to build coherent and incoherent personality structures of anxiety/depression and temperament subtypes and study them in the context of attentional biases.

This leads us to Sin 2: the assumption that anxiety and depression are homogeneous traits. Traditionally, anxiety has been examined as a homogeneous phenomenon—or sometimes, in a perspective of defensive coping, as heterogeneous (e.g., Derakshan & Eysenck, 2001; Eysenck, 2006; Fajkowska & Eysenck, 2008)—whereas depression is usually studied as a structurally noncomplex trait. This approach, especially in the case of depression, enhances a number of inconsistencies in attentional processing in these moods that are widely documented in the literature.

A promising attempt reported in the literature for elucidating these discrepancies in both depression and anxiety is the introduction of their subtypes. Perhaps the most useful distinction in research on anxiety has been the comparison of arousal anxiety (characterized by symptoms of physiological hyperarousal and somatic tension) with apprehension anxiety (involving worry and is characterized by verbal rumination, typically about future events). For depression, on the other hand, the distinction proposed is between anhedonic depression—with the defining feature of anhedonia, which is the inability to experience pleasure—and valence depression, which is characterized by (in)sensitivity to valence of emotional stimulation (cf. Heller & Nitschke, 1998).

We have seen throughout this book that investigators examining anxiety and depression from a psychophysiological standpoint often adopt this view (e.g., Compton, Heller, Banich, Palmieri, & Miller, 2000; Engels et al., 2007). I believe that distinguishing types of anxiety and depression may clarify inconsistent findings in research on attentional biases by linking these subtypes of anxiety and depression to their specific functions associated with controlling stimulation—namely, their reactive and regulative functions over emotional stimulation. Evidence shows that activation of the specific functional role of anxiety or depression subtypes (as a part of coherent/incoherent personality structures) might be situation-dependent (cf. Heller & Nitschke, 1998).

Sin 3 relates to the fact that attentional biases in anxiety and depression are analyzed through a growing number of experimental procedures. For convenience we loosely group these procedures into visual search paradigms, attentional probe tasks, dual-task paradigm Stroop tests, attentional blink, and eye-gaze cueing accompanied by a variety of related specific tasks (cf. Fox, 2008; Wells & Matthews, 1999). Obviously, there is nothing wrong with the variety of experimental paradigms that have been used to investigate attentional biases in anxiety and depression. The main points of interest are whether the choice of procedures allows for examining anxiety or depression as multilayer phenomena, and in consequence to provide a more integrative and comprehensive picture of attentional functioning in these two disorders. In other words, how is stimulation processed across different systems of responses (e.g., physiological, behavioral, cognitive, self-report) in the case of anxiety and depression? This book has presented a description of anxiety and depression from the self-report and processes levels. Each level is important for the other (which justifies the systemic approach) but cannot be reduced (or amplified) at one level or another. By contrast, a description of anxiety and depression from the same level—but with the use of different experimental procedures—does not specifically broaden our understanding of these affective disorders. (However, a drawback to my study is that the procedure is not sensitive to the reactive functional role of these two phenomena).

Sin 4 is the assumption that depression and anxiety are orthogonal phenomena. Most studies have examined attentional biases to emotional stimulation in a group of comorbid anxious and depressed individuals. Indeed, some scholars noted that it is unclear how attentional biases function in individuals with comorbid depression and anxiety, along with diagnostically pure depressed, pure anxious, and healthy individuals (e.g., Bar-Haim, Lamy, Pergamin, Bakersmans-Kranenburg, & van Ijzendoorn, 2007; Hankin, Gibb, Abela, & Flory, 2010). For example, in the studies of Hankin et al. (2010), it was shown that pure depressed and pure anxious individuals exhibited attentional biases specifically to sad and angry faces, (respectively), whereas comorbid ones exhibited attentional biases to both facial expressions. In addition, control healthy individuals exhibited attentional avoidance of sad faces and comorbid male subjects avoided happy faces. Thus the assumption that anxiety and depression are distinct phenomena clearly remains a sin. However, the question is how to rectify this sin.

Obviously, one reasonable scenario is to introduce "clinically pure" groups into the study. But most studies relate to nonclinical forms of anxiety and depression. This raises another question: can these pure types be identified among subclinically anxious and depressed subjects? It seems more probable to select pure anxiety than pure depression (see Davidson, 2000, for a review). On several occasions, utilizing questionnaires in different experimental groups, I have tried to identify such a pure group; however, it was almost impossible to find depressed individuals without anxiety. By contrast, it was possible to identify pure anxiety without depressive symptoms.

In conclusion, having this information, the specificity of biased information processing in anxiety should be considered for those connected with anxiety, while the specificity of biased information processing in depressed mood should be considered for those connected with depression and anxiety co-occurrence.

6.3.

**Toward future directions**

In closing, I would like to identify three problems as top priorities in future research and theorizing—that is, (a) continuation of empirical validation of the theory presented; (b) neurophysiological perspective within the C-SAP; and (c) applicative utility of the model.

With reference to the first issue, I am aware that a large part of the C-SAP model embraces theoretical assumptions, the necessity of further long-term empirical validations, and exclusion of the limitations of the studies presented in this book. First, the studies utilized the self-report instrument for assessing subtypes of anxiety and depression. My recommendation for the future is to use more sophisticated measures for assessing subtypes of anxiety and depression, including physiological ones. Second, they focused on relatively simple experimental procedures rather than on more complex real-life situations, which probably explains the weak activation of more integrated personality structures while performing such simple tasks. However, an advantage of this situation is to show that the personality system operates as an "effective investor"; it does not engage its highly integrated structures when it is not necessary. And finally, they applied experimental procedures addressed to the regulative aspect of traits. Further studies should be designed to also measure the reactive aspects of traits.

Thus my suggestion would be to replicate the studies described in this book and explore these theoretical speculations in a more complex situation—but above all, to formulate the methodological principles allowing for valid measurement and valid data analysis. Having these methodological principles, it is obligatory to empirically validate the postulated controlling functions over stimulation in affective traits and temperament types. It is also important to study the (in)compatibility between intraindividual coherence/incoherence and coherence/incoherence in overt behaviors.

Considering the second problem, the study of anxiety/depression within coherent/incoherent personality structures will also likely benefit from the incorporation of evolving developments in the biological bases of personality and individual differences, such as those made available through advances in neurotechniques. For example, examining the contributions of the brain acting in response to differentiated types of stimulation in more complex settings might be useful for the development of truly predictive markers that account for the majority of variance in dominant functions in stimulation processing in affective and temperament types.

With reference to the third problem, one of the crucial questions facing therapists is understanding why people change and what can be done to enhance this process of needed change. One approach is to treat a specific symptom as complex and related to more complex structures; this is particularly true in the case of anxiety and depression. Specifically, in the empirical part of the book, I demonstrated how affective traits operate differently when related to particular temperament structure. I also showed that occasionally the mixture of anxiety/depression types with temperament produces effective performance on a very basic cognitive level. For example, when connected with apprehension anxiety or anhedonic depression, the Choleric Type is a "champion" temperament structure in regard to effective attentional performance. (However, this is only the case when it is analyzed within the Eysenckian approach). In addition, from the discussion of the results it is clear that personality coherence/incoherence seems to be an important subject of analysis in more complex situations (e.g., in marital conflicts or job dissatisfaction). Thus the predictive utility of the higher-level, more integrated personality constructs in (a) minimizing the negative outcomes of hyperintensive nonclinical anxiety and depression or (b) curing clinical anxiety or depression should be expected. All of this points to the need for further studies and theory development in these areas.

# References


Allen, T. F. H, & Hoekstra, T. W. (1984). Nested and non-nested hierarchies: A significant distinction for ecological systems. In A. W. Smith (Ed.), *Proceedings of the Society for General Systems Research: I. Systems methodologies and isomorphies* (pp. 175–180). Lewiston, NY: Intersystems Publications.

Allen, T. F. H., & Starr, T. B. (1982). *Hierarchy: Perspectives for ecological complexity*. Chicago: University of Chicago Press.

Allport, G. W. (1937). *Personality: A psychological interpretation*. New York: Holt.

Alonso, J., Bruffaerts, R., Gabilondo, A., Haro, J. M., Kovess, V., & Vilagut, G. (2008). Depression. In *Major and chronic diseases report 2007*. Luxembourg: European Comission.

American Psychiatric Association [APA]. (2000). *Diagnostic and statistical manual of mental disorders* (4th ed., Text revision). Washington, DC: Author.

Anderson, A. K., Christoff, K., Stappen, I., Panitz, D., Ghahremani, D., G., Glover, G., et al. (2003). Dissociated neural representations of intensity and valence in human olfaction. *Nature Neuroscience, 6*, 196–202.

Anderson, M. C., Ochsner, K. N., Kuhl, B., Cooper, J., Robertson, E., Gabrieli, et al. (2004). Neural systems underlying the suppression of unwanted memories. *Science, 303*, 232–235.

Angold, A., Costello, E. J., & Erkanli, A. (1999). Comorbidity. *Journal of Child Psychology and Psychiatry and Allied Disciplines, 40*, 57–87.

Applehans, B. M., & Luecken, L. J. (2006). Attentional processes, anxiety, and the regulation of cortisol reactivity. *Anxiety, Stress, and Coping, 19*, 81–92.

Aronson, L. R. (1984). Levels of integration and organization: A reevaluation of the evolutionary scale. In G. Greenberg & E. Tobach (Eds.), *Behavioral evolution and integrative levels* (pp. 57–81). Hillsdale, NJ: Erlbaum.

Asendorpf, J. A., & Denissen, J. J. (2006). Predictive validity of personality types versus personality dimensions from early childhood to adulthood: Implications for the distinction between core and surface traits. *Merrill-Palmer Quarterly, 52*, 486-513.

Asendorpf, J. A., & Scherer, K. R. (1983). The discrepant repressor: Differentiation between low anxiety, high anxiety, and repression of anxiety by autonomic-facial-verbal patterns of behavior. *Journal of Personality and Social Psychology, 45*, 1334–1344.

Bak, P., & Chen, K. (1991). Self-organized criticality. *Scientific American, 262*, 92–99.

Balakrishnan, J. D., & MacDonald, J. A. (2001). Alternatives to signal detection theory. In W. Karwowski (Ed.), *International encyclopedia of ergonomics and human factors* (Vol. 1, pp. 546–550). London: Taylor & Francis.

Ball, S. A. (2005). Personality traits, problems, and disorders: Clinical applications to substance use disorders. *Journal of Research in Personality, 39*, 84–102.

Baltes, P. B., & Staudinger, U. (1996). Interactive minds in a life-span perspective: Prologue. In P. B. Baltes & U. Staudinger (Eds.), *Interactive minds* (pp.1–32). New York: Cambridge University Press.

Bandura, A. (1986). *Social foundations of thought and action*. Englewood Cliffs, NJ: Prentice-Hall.

Bandura, A. (1997). *Self-efficacy: The exercise of control*. New York: Freeman.

Bandura, A. (1999). Social cognitive theory of personality. In L. A. Pervin & O. P. John (Eds.), *Handbook of personality: Theory and research* (2nd ed., pp. 154–196). New York: Guilford Press.

Bandura, A. (2006). Toward a psychology of human agency. *Perspectives on Psychological Science, 1,* 164–180.

Bar-Haim, Y., Lamy, D., Pergamin, L., Bakersmans-Kranenburg, M. J., & van Ijzendoorn, M. H. (2007). Threat-related attentional bias in anxious and nonanxious individuals in a meta-analytic study. *Psychological Bulletin, 133,* 1–24.

Bargh, J. A., Lombardi, W. J., & Higgins, E. T. (1988). Automaticity of chronically accessible constructs in person X situation effects on person perception: It's just a metter of time. *Journal of Personality and Social Psychology, 55,* 599–605.

Barlow, D. H. (1991). Disorders of emotion. *Psychological Inquiry, 2,* 58–71.

Barlow, D. H. (2002). *Anxiety and its disorders: The nature and treatment of anxiety and panic* (2nd ed.). New York: Guilford Press.

Barton, S. (1994). Chaos, self-organization, and psychology. *American Psychologist, 49,* 5–14.

Bateson, G. (1972). *Steps to an ecology of mind: Collected essays in anthropology, psychiatry, evolution, and epistemology*. San Francisco: Chandler Publishing.

Bateson, G. (1979). *Mind and nature: A necessary unity*. New York: Dutton.

Baxter, L. R., Phelps, M. E., Mazziotta, J. C., Guze, B. H., Schwartz, J. M., & Selin, C. E. (1987). Local cerebral glucose metabolic rates in obsessive-compulsive disorder. *Archives of General Psychiatry, 44,* 211–218.

Beavers, W. R. (1976). A theoretical basis for family evaluation. In J. M. Lewis, W. R. Beavers, J. T. Gossett, & V. A. Philips (Eds.), *No single threat: Psychological health in the family system* (pp. 46–82). New York: Brunner/Mazel.

Beck, A. T., Brown, G., Steer, R. A., Eidelson, J. I., & Riskind, J. H. (1987). Differentiating anxiety and depression: A test of the cognitive content-specificity hypothesis. *Journal of Abnormal Psychology, 96,* 179–183.

Beck, A. T., & Clark, D. A. (1997). An information processing model of anxiety: Automatic and strategic processes. *Behaviour Research and Therapy, 35,* 49–58.

Beck, A., Hammen, C. L., Hollon, S. D., Ingram, R. E., & Kendall, P. C. (1987). Issues and recommendations regarding use of the Beck Depression Inventory. *Cognitive Therapy and Research, 11,* 289–299.

Beck, A. T., Rush, A. J., Shaw, B. E, & Emery, G. (1979). *Cognitive therapy of depression*. New York: Guilford.

Beevers, C. G., & Carver, C. S. (2003). Attentional bias and mood persistence as prospective predictors of dysphoria. *Cognitive Therapy and Research, 27,* 619–637.

Bellew, M., & Hill, A. B. (1990). Negative bias as a predictor of susceptibility to induced depressive mood. *Personality and Individual Differences, 11,* 471–480.

Bench, C. J., Friston, K. J., Brown, R. G., Scott, L. C., Frackowiak, R. S. J., & Dolan, R. J. (1992). The anatomy of melancholia: Focal abnormalities of cerebral blood flow in major depression. *Psychological Medicine, 22,* 60–615.

Berlyne, D. E. (1960). *Conflict, arousal, and curiosity*. New York: McGraw-Hill.

Bishop, S., Duncan, J., Brett, M., & Lawrence, A. D. (2004). Prefrontal cortical function and anxiety: controlling attention to threat-related stimuli. *Nature Neuroscience, 7,* 184–188.

Block, J. (1971). *Lives through time*. Berkeley, CA: Bancroft Books.

Block, J. (1993). Studying personality the long way. In D. C. Funder, R. D. Parke, C. Tomlinson-Keasey, & K. Widaman (Eds.), *Studying lives through time: Personality and development* (pp. 9–41). Washington, DC: American Psychological Association.

Blowers, G. H. (1979). The Archimedes spiral after-effect as a test of arousability. *British Journal of Psychology, 70*, 59–64.

Blum, G. S, Geiwitz, P. J., & Stewart, C. G. (1967). Cognitive arousal: The evolution of a model. *Journal of Personality and Social Psychology, 5*, 138–154.

Boorom, M. L., Goolsby, J. R., & Ramsey, R. P. (1998). Relational communication traits and their effect on adaptiveness and sales performance. *Journal of the Academy of Marketing Science, 26*, 13–30.

Borkovec, T. D. (1994). The nature, functions, and origins of worry. In G. C. L. Davey & F. Tallis (Eds.), *Worrying: Perspectives on theory, assessment, and treatment* (pp. 5–33). New York: Wiley.

Borkovec, T. D., Ray, W. J., & Stober, J. (1998). Worry: A cognitive phenomenon intimately linked to affective, physiological, and interpersonal behavioral processes. *Cognitive Therapy and Research, 22*, 561–576.

Borkovec, T. D., & Roemer, L. (1995). Perceived functions of worry among generalized anxiety disorder subjects: Distraction from more emotionally distressing topics? *Journal of Behaviour Therapy and Experimental Psychiatry, 26*, 25–30.

Bourke, C., Douglas, K., & Porter, R. (2010). Processing of facial emotion expression in major depression: A review. *Australian and New Zealand Journal of Psychiatry, 44*, 681–696.

Bradley, B. P., Mogg, K., Falla S. J., & Hamilton, L. R. (1998). Attentional bias for threatening facial expressions in anxiety: Manipulation of stimulus duration. *Cognition and Emotion, 12*, 737–753.

Bradley, B. P., Mogg, K., & Millar, N. H. (2000). Covert and overt orienting of attention to emotional faces in anxiety. *Cognition and Emotion, 14*, 789–808.

Brandstätter, H. (1994). Well-being and motivational person-environment fit: A time sampling study of emotions. *European Journal of Personality, 8*, 75–93.

Broomfield, N. M., & Turpin, G. (2005). Covert and overt attention in trait anxiety: A cognitive psychophysiological analysis. *Biological Psychology, 68*, 179–200.

Brosschot, J. F, de Ruiter, C., & Kindt, M. (1999). Processing bias in anxious subjects and repressors, measured by emotional Stroop interference and attention allocation. *Personality and Individual Differences, 26*, 777–793.

Brown, T. A., Chorpita, B. F., & Barlow, D. H. (1998). Structural relationships among dimensions of the *DSM–IV* anxiety and mood disorders and dimensions of negative affect, positive affect, and autonomic arousal. *Journal of Abnormal Psychology, 107*, 179–192.

Bruder, G. E. (1995). Cerebral laterality and psychopathology: Perceptual and event-related potential asymmetries in affective and schizophrenic disorders. In R. J. Davidson & K. Hugdahl (Eds.), *Brain asymmetry* (pp. 661–691). Cambridge, MA: MIT Press.

Brzozowski, P., & Drwal, R. Ł. (1995). *Kwestionariusz Osobowości Eysencka. Polska adaptacja EPQ-R. Podręcznik.* [Eysenck Personality Questionnaire: Polish adaptation of the EPQ-R. Manual]. Warsaw: Pracownia Testów Psychologicznych PTP.

Buss, A. H. (2012). Style. In A. H. Buss (Ed.), *Pathways to individuality: Evolution and development of personality traits*. Washington: American Psychological Association.

Buss, D. M., & Craik, K. H. (1983). The act frequency approach to personality. *Psychological Review, 90*, 105–126.

Calvo, M. G., & Eysenck, M. W. (2000). Early vigilance and late avoidance of threat processing: Repressive coping versus low/high anxiety. *Cognition and Emotion, 14*, 763–787.

Campbell, J. B. (2008). Modern personality theories: What have we gained? What have we lost? In G. J. Boyle, G. Matthews, & D. H. Saklofske (Eds.), *The SAGE handbook of personality theory and assessment: Vol. 1. Personality theories and models* (pp. 191–212). London: Sage.

Canli, T. (2008). Toward a neurogenetic theory of neuroticism. In D. W. Pfaff & B. L. Kieffer (Eds.), *Molecular and biophysical mechanisms of arousal, alertness, and attention* (pp. 153–174). Malden, MA: Blackwell.

Canli, T., Zhao, Z., Desmond, J. E., Kang, E. J., Gross, J., & Gabrieli, J. H. (2001). An fMRI study of personality influences on brain reactivity to emotional stimuli. *Behavioural Neuroscience, 115*, 33–42.

Caprara, G. V. (1996). Structures and processes in personality psychology. *European Psychologist, 1*, 14–26.

Caprara, G. V., & Cervone, D. (2000). *Personality: Determinants, dynamics, and potentials.* New York: Cambridge University Press.

Carlson, N. R. (2001). *Physiology of behavior* (7th ed.). Boston: Allyn & Bacon.

Carlson, N. R. (2002). *Foundations of physiological psychology* (5th ed.). Boston: Allyn & Bacon.

Carver, C. S. (2004). Self-regulation of action and affect. In R. F. Baumeister & K. D. Vohs (Eds.), *Handbook of self-regulation: Research, theory, and applications* (pp. 13–39). New York: Guilford Press.

Carver, C. S., & Scheier, M. F. (1998). *On the self-regulation of behavior.* New York: Cambridge University Press.

Carver, C. S., & Scheier, M. F. (2002). Control processes and self-organization as complementary principles underlying behavior. *Personality and Social Psychology Review, 6*, 304–315.

Carver, C. S., Scheier, M. F., & Weintraub, J. K. (1989). Assessing coping strategies: A theoretically based approach. *Journal of Personality and Social Psychology, 56*, 267–283.

Carver, C. S., & White, T. L. (1994). Behavioral inhibition, behavioral activation, and affective responses to impending reward and punishment: The BIS/BAS scales. *Journal of Personality and Social Psychology, 67*, 319–333.

Caspi, A. (1998). Personality development across the life course. In W. Damon (Series Ed.) & N. Eisenberg (Vol. Ed.), *Handbook of child development: Vol. 3. Social, emotional, and personality development* (5th ed., pp. 311–388). New York: Wiley.

Cassimjee, N. (2003). *Neuropsychological symptoms and premorbid temperament traits in Alzheimer's dementia.* Unpublished doctoral dissertation, University of Pretoria, Pretoria, South Africa.

Cervone, D. (1991). The two disciplines of personality psychology. *Psychological Science, 2*, 371–377.

Cervone, D. (1997). Social-cognitive mechanisms and personality coherence: Self-knowledge, situational beliefs, and cross-situational coherence in perceived self-efficacy. *Psychological Science, 8*, 43–50.

Cervone, D. (1999). Bottom-up explanation in personality psychology: the case of cross-situational coherence. In D. Cervone & Y. Shoda (Eds.), *The coherence of personality: Social-cognitive bases of consistency, variability, and organization* (pp. 303–341). New York: Guilford Press.

Cervone, D. (2000). Evolutionary psychology and explanation in personality psychology: How do we know which module to invoke? *American Behavioral Scientist, 43,* 1001–1014.

Cervove, D. (2004). The architecture of personality. *Psychological Review, 111,* 183–204.

Cervone, D. (2005). Personality architecture: Within-person structures and processes. *Annual Review of Psychology, 56,* 423–452.

Cervone, D. (2008). Explanatory models of personality: Social-cognitive theories and the knowledge-and-appraisal model of personality architecture. In G. J. Boyle, G. Matthews, & D. H. Saklofske (Eds.), *The SAGE handbook of personality theory and assessment: Vol. 1. Personality theories and models* (pp. 191–212). London: Sage.

Cervone, D., & Bartoszek, G. (2013). Knowledge, appraisal, and personality dynamics. In D. Cervone, M. Fajkowska, M. W. Eysenck, & T. Maruszewski (Eds.), *Personality dynamics: Meaning construction, the social world, and the embodied mind.* Clinton Corners, NY: Eliot Werner Publications.

Cervone, D., Shadel, W. G., & Jencius, S. (2001). Social-cognitive theory of personality assessment. *Personality and Social Psychology Review, 5,* 33–51.

Cervone, D., & Shoda, Y. (1999a). Beyond traits in the study of personality coherence. *Current Directions in Psychological Science, 8,* 27–32.

Cervone, D. & Shoda, Y. (1999b). Social-cognitive theories and the coherence of personality. In D. Cervone & Y. Shoda (Eds.), *The coherence of personality: Social-cognitive bases of consistency, variability, and organization* (pp. 3–33). New York: Guilford Press.

Chapman, B. P., & Goldberg, L. R. (2011). Replicability and 40-year predictive power of childhood ARC types. *Journal of Personality and Social Psychology, 101,* 593–606.

Chioqueta, A. P. & Stiles, T. C. (2005). Personality traits and the development of depression, hopelessness, and suicide ideation. *Personality and Individual Differences, 38,* 1283–1291.

Claridge, G. S. (1967). *Personality and arousal: A psychophysiological study of psychiatric disorders.* London: Pergamon Press.

Claridge, G. S. (1985). *Origins of mental illness: Temperament, deviance, and disorder.* New York: Blackwell.

Clark, D. A., Beck, A. T., & Alford, B. A. (1999). *Scientific foundations of cognitive theory and therapy of depression.* New York: Wiley.

Clark, L. A. (2005). Temperament as a unifying basis for personality and psychopathology. *Journal of Abnormal Psychology, 114,* 505–521.

Clark, L. A., & Watson, D. (1991). Tripartite model of anxiety and depression: Psychometric evidence and taxonomic implications. *Journal of Abnormal Psychology, 100,* 316–336.

Clarke, D. (2004). Neuroticism: Moderator or mediator in the relation between locus of control and depression? *Personality and Individual Differences, 37,* 245–258.

Coan, J. A., & Allen, J. J. B. (2003). Frontal EEG asymmetry and the behavioral activation and inhibition systems. *Psychophysiology, 40,* 106–114.

Coan, J. A., & Allen, J. J. B. (2004). Frontal EEG asymmetry as a moderator and mediator of emotion. *Biological Psychology, 67,* 7–49.

Coifman, K. G., Bonanno, G. A., Ray, R. D., & Gross, J. J. (2007). Does repressive coping promote resilience? Affective-automatic response discrepancy during bereavement. *Journal of Personality and Social Psychology, 92,* 745–758.

Cole, P. M., Luby, J., & Sullivan, M. W. (2008). Emotions and the development of childhood depression: Bridging the gap. *Child Development Perspectives, 2*, 141–148.

Collier, J. (1989). Supervenience and reduction in biological hierarchies. *Canadian Journal of Philosophy, 14*, 209–23

Compton, R. J. (2003). The interface between emotion and attention: A review of evidence from psychology and neuroscience. *Behavioral and Cognitive Neuroscience Reviews, 2*, 115–129.

Compton, R. J., Banich, M. T., Mohanty, A., Milham, M. P., Miller, G. A., Scalf, P. E., et al. (2003). Paying attention to emotion: An fMRI investigation of cognitive and emotional Stroop tasks. *Cognitive, Affective, and Behavioral Neuroscience, 3*, 81–96.

Compton, R. J., Heller, W., Banich, M. T., Palmieri, P. A., & Miller, G. A. (2000). Responding to threat: Hemispheric asymmetries and interhemispheric division of input. *Neuropsychology, 14*, 254–264.

Corbetta, M., & Shulman, G. L. (2002). Control of goal-directed andstimulus-driven attention in the brain. *Nature Reviews Neuroscience, 3*, 201–215.

Corr, P. J. (2008). Reinforcement Sensitivity Theory (RST): Introduction. In P. J. Corr (Ed.), *The reinforcement sensitivity theory of personality* (pp.1–43). Cambridge, UK: Cambridge University Press.

Corr, P. J., & Fajkowska, M. (2011). Introduction to special issue on anxiety. *Personality and Individual Differences, 50*, 885–888.

Crost, N. W., Pauls, C. A., & Wacker, J. (2008). Defensiveness and anxiety predict frontal EEG asymmetry only in specific situational contexts. *Biological Psychology, 78*, 43–52.

Crowne, D. P., & Marlowe, D. A. (1960). A new scale of social desirability independent of psychopathology. *Journal of Consulting Psychology, 24*, 349–354.

Curtindale, L., Laurie-Rose, C., Bennett-Murphy, L., & Hill, S. (2007). Sensory modality, temperament, and the development of sustained attention: A vigilance study in children and adults. *Developmental Psychology, 43*, 576–589.

Damasio, A. R. (1999). *The feeling of what happens: Body and emotion in the making of consciousness*. New York: Harcourt Brace.

Daum, I., Hehl, F. J., & Schugens, M. M. (1988). Construct validity and personality correlates of the Strelau Temperament Inventory. *European Journal of Personality, 2*, 205–216.

Davidson, R. J. (1992a). Anterior cerebral asymmetry and the nature of emotion. *Brain and Cognition, 20*, 125–151.

Davidson, R. J. (1992b). Emotion and affective style: Hemispheric substrates. *Psychological Science, 3*, 39–43.

Davidson, R. J. (1994). Asymmetric brain function, affective style and psychopathology: The role of early experience and plasticity. *Development and Psychopathology, 6*, 741–758.

Davidson, R. J. (2000). Affective style, mood, and anxiety disorders: An affective neuroscience approach. In R. J. Davidson (Ed.), *Anxiety, depression, and emotion* (pp. 88–108). New York: Oxford University Press.

Davidson, R. J., Larson, C., & Abercrombie, H. (1995, October). *Prefrontal electrophysiological asymmetries differentiate between melancholic and non-melancholic depression.* Paper presented at the annual meeting of the Society for Research in Psychopathology, Iowa City, IO.

Davidson, R., Pizzagalli, D., Nitschke, J., & Putnam, K. (2002). Depression: Perspectives from affective neuroscience. *Annual Review of Psychology, 53*, 545–574.

Dawkins, K., & Furnham, A. (1989). The colour naming of emotional words. *British Journal of Psychology, 80*, 383–389.

Deary, I. J., Battersby, S., Whiteman, M. C., Connor, J. M., Fowkes, F. G., & Harmar, A. (1999). Neuroticism and polymorphism in the serotonin transporter gene. *Psychological Medicine, 29*, 735–739.

de Brabander, B., Declerck, C. H., & Boone, C. (2002). Tonic and phasic activation and arousal effects as a function of feedback in repetitive-choice reaction time tasks. *Behavioral Neuroscience, 116*, 397–402.

de Fruyt, F., & Denollet, J. (2002). Type D personality: A five-factor model perspective. *Psychology and Health, 17*, 671–683.

Deldin, P. J., Naidu, S. K., Shestyuk, A. Y., & Casas, B. R. (2009). Nerophysiological indices of free recall memory biases in major depression: The impact of stimulus arousal and valence. *Cognition and Emotion, 23*, 1002–1020.

Delgado, P. L., Price, L. H., Miller, H. L., Salomon, R. M., Heminger, G. H., & Charney, D. S. (1994). Serotonin and the neurobiology of depression: Effects of tryptophan depletion in drug-free depressed patients. *Archives of General Psychiatry, 51*, 865–874.

Dennis, T. A., & Chen, C. (2009). Trait anxiety and conflict monitoring following threat: An ERP study. *Psychophysiology, 46*, 122–131.

Denny, E. R., & Hunt, R. R. (1992). Affective valence and memory in depression: Dissociation of recall and fragment completion. *Journal of Abnormal Psychology, 101*, 575–580.

Denollet, J. (1997). Personality, emotional distress and coronary heart disease. *European Journal of Personality, 11*, 343–357.

de Pascalis, V., Strelau, J., Zawadzki, B. (1999). The effect of temperamental traits on event-related potentials, heart rate and reaction time. *Personality and Individual Differences, 26*, 441–465.

Derakshan, N., & Eysenck, M. W. (2001). Effects of focus of attention on physiological, behavioral, and reported state anxiety in repressors, low-anxious, high-anxious, and defensive high-anxious individuals. *Anxiety, Stress, and Coping, 14*, 285–299.

Derakshan, N., Eysenck, M. W., & Myers, L. B. (2007). Emotional information processing in repressors: The vigilance-avoidance theory. *Cognition and Emotion, 21*, 1585–1614.

Derakshan, N., Feldman, M., Campbell, T., & Lipp, O. V. (2003). Can I have your attention please: Repressors and enhanced P3 to emotional stimuli. *Psychophysiology, 40*, 36.

Derakshan, N., Myers, L. B., Hansen, J., & O'Leary, M. (2004). Defensiveness and attempted thought suppression of negative material. *European Journal of Personality, 18*, 521–535.

Derryberry, D. (2002). Attention and voluntary self-control. *Self and Identity, 1*, 105–111.

Derryberry, D., & Reed, M. (2002). Anxiety-related attentional biases and their regulation by attentional control. *Journal of Abnormal Psychology, 111*, 225–236.

Derryberry, D., & Rothbart, M. K. (1988). Affect, arousal, and attention as components of temperament. *Journal of Personality and Social Psychology, 55*, 958–966.

Derryberry, D., & Rothbart, M. K. (1997). Reactive and effortful processes in the organization of temperament. *Development and Psychopathology, 9*, 633–652.

Deveney, C. M., & Deldin, P. J. (2004). Memory of faces: A slow wave ERP study of depression. *Emotion, 4*, 295–304.

Dichter, G. S., & Tomarken, A. (2008). The chronometry of affective startle modulation in unipolar depression. *Journal of Abnormal Psychology, 117*, 1–15.

Dichter, G. S., Tomarken, A. J., Shelton, R. C., & Sutton, S. K. (2004). Early- and late-onset startle modulation in unipolar depression. *Psychophysiology, 41*, 433–-440.

Dickens, W. T., & Flynn, J. R. (2001). Heritability estimates versus large environmental effects: The IQ paradox resolved. *Psychological Review, 108*, 346–369.

Dillon, D. G., & La Bar, K. S. (2005). Startle modulation during conscious emotion regulation is arousal-dependent. *Behavioural Neuroscience, 119*, 1118–1124.

Dolan, R. (2002). Emotion, cognition, and behavior. *Science, 298*, 1191–1194.

Dolcos, F., La Bar, K. S., & Cabeza, R. (2004). Dissociable effects of arousal and valence on prefrontal activity indexing emotional evaluation and subsequent memory: An event-related fMRI study. *NeuroImage, 23*, 64–74.

Drwal, R. Ł., & Wilczyńska, J. T. (1980). Opracowanie Kwestionariusza Aprobaty Społecznej [The elaboration of the Social Desirability Questionnaire]. *Przegląd Psychologiczny, 23*, 569–583.

Duffy, E. (1957). The psychological significance of the concept of arousal or activation. *Psychological Review, 64*, 262–275.

Duffy, E. (1962). *Activation and behavior.* New York: Wiley.

Dugas, M. J., Freeston, M. H., Ladouceur, R., Rheaume, J., Provencher, M., & Boisvert, J. M. (1998). Worry themes in primary GAD, secondary GAD, and other anxiety disorders. *Journal of Anxiety Disorders, 12*, 253–261.

Dunn, D. D., Dalgleish, T., Ogilvie, A. D., Lawrence, A. D., & Cusack, R. (2004). Categorical and dimensional reports of experienced affect to emotion-inducing pictures in depression. *Journal of Abnormal Psychology, 113*, 654–660.

Dusenbery, D. B. (1992). *Sensory ecology: How organisms acquire and respond to information.* New York: Freeman.

Easterbrook, J. A. (1959). The effect of emotion on cue utilization and the organization of behavior. *Psychological Review, 66*, 183–201.

Eaves, L., Eysenck, H. J., & Martin, N. (1988). *Genes, culture, and personality: An empirical approach.* New York: Academic Press.

Egeland, J., Rund, B. R., Sundet, K., Landro, N. I., Asbjornsen, A., Lund, A., et al. (2003). Attention profile in schizophrenia compared with depression: Differential effects of processing speed, selective attention and vigilance. *Acta Psychiatrica Scandinavica, 108*, 276–284.

Eimer, M. (1993). Effects of attention and stimulus probability on ERPs in a Go/NoGo task. *Biological Psychology, 35*, 123–138.

Eisenberg, N., Smith, C. L., Sadovsky, A., & Spinrad, T. L. (2004). Effortful control: Relations with emotion regulation, adjustment, and socialization in childhood. In R. F. Baumeister & K. D. Vohs (Eds.), *Handbook of self-regulation: Research, theory, and applications* (pp. 259–282). New York: Guilford Press.

Ekman, P. (1992). An argument for basic emotions. *Cognition and Emotion, 6*, 169–200.

Ekman, P., & Friesen, W. V. (1976). *Pictures of facial affect.* Palo Alto, CA: Consulting Psychologists Press.

Eliasz, A. (1980). Temperament and trans-situational stability of behaviour in the physical and social environment. *Polish Psychological Bulletin, 11*, 143–153.

Eliasz, A. (1981). *Temperament a system regulacji stymulacji* [Temperament and system of regulation of stimulation]. Warsaw: Państwowe Wydawnictwo Naukowe.

Eliasz, A. (1985). Transactional model of temperament. In J. Strelau (Ed.), *Temperamental bases of behavior: Warsaw studies on individual differences* (pp. 41–78). Lisse, The Netherlands: Swets & Zeitlinger.

Eliasz, A. (1988). *Właściwości temperamentu i środowiska sprzyjające rozwojowi zachowania A* [Characteristic of temperament and environment conducive to a development of Type A behavior pattern]. Wrocław, Poland: Ossolineum.

Eliasz, A. (1990). Broadening the concept of temperament: From disposition to hypothetical construct. *European Journal of Personality, 4*, 287–302.

Eliasz, A. (1992). Rola interakcji temperamentu i środowiska w rozwoju człowieka [Role of temperament and environment interaction in human development]. In A. Eliasz & M. Marszał-Wiśniewska (Eds.), *Temperament a rozwój młodzieży* (pp. 11–27). Warsaw: Instytut Psychologii, Polska Akademia Nauk.

Eliasz, A. (1993). *Psychologia ekologiczna* [Ecological psychology]. Warsaw: Instytut Psychologii, Polska Akademia Nauk.

Eliasz, A. (1995). Podmiotowe i środowiskowe czynniki utrudniające efektywną regulację stymulacji [Personal and environmental factors disturbing the effective regulation of stimulation]. *Czasopismo Psychologiczne, 1*, 129–141.

Eliasz, A. (2001). Temperament, Type A, and motives: A time sampling study. In H. Brandstätter & A. Eliasz (Eds.), *Persons, situations, and emotions: An ecological approach* (pp. 55–73). Oxford, UK: Oxford University Press.

Eliasz, A. (2004). Transakcyjny Model Temperamentu. Analiza właściwości temperamentu z perspektywy nomotetycznego oraz idiograficznego badania osobowości [Transactional Model of Temperament: The analysis of temperament from the nomothetic and idiographic perspective of personality]. In Z. Chlewiński & A. Sękowski (Eds.), *Psychologia w perspektywie XXI wieku* (pp. 49–95). Lublin, Poland: Towarzystwo Naukowe KUL.

Eliasz, A., & Klonowicz, T. (2001). Top-down and bottom-up approaches to personality and their application to temperament. In A. Eliasz & A. Angleitner (Eds.), *Advances in research on temperament* (pp. 14–42). Lengerich, Germany: Pabst Science Publishers.

Eliasz, A., & Wrześniewski, K. (1991). Two kinds of Type A behavior pattern. In C. D. Spielberger, J. G. Sarason, J. Strelau, & M.T. Brebner (Eds.), *Stress and anxiety* (Vol. 13, pp. 275–282). New York: Hemisphere.

Ellis, H. C., & Moore, B. A. (2000). Mood and memory. In T. Dalgleish & M. Power (Eds.), *Handbook of cognition and emotion* (pp. 193–210). Chichester, UK: Wiley.

Ellsworth, P.C., & Scherer, K. R. (2003). Appraisal processes in emotion. In R. J. Davidson, K. Scherer, & H. H. Goldsmith (Eds.), *Handbook of affective sciences* (pp. 572–595). New York: Oxford University Press.

Endler, N.S. (1977). The role of person-by-situation interactions in personality theory. In I. C. Uzgiris & F. Weizmann (Eds.), *The structuring of experience* (pp. 343–369). New York: Plenum Press.

Endler, N. S. (1983). *Interactionism: A personality model, but not yet a theory.* Lincoln, NE: University of Nebraska Press.

Engels, A. S., Heller, W., Mohanty, A., Herrington, J. D., Banich, M. T., Webb, A. G., & Miller, G. A. (2007). Specificity of regional brain activity in anxiety types during emotion processing. *Psychophysiology, 44*, 352–363.

Epstein, S. (1979). The stability of behavior: On predicting most of the people much of the time. *Journal of Personality and Social Psychology, 37*, 1097–1126.

Eysenck, H. J. (1957). *Dynamics of anxiety and hysteria*. London: Routledge & Kegan Paul.

Eysenck, H. J. (1967). *The biological basis of personality*. Springfield, IL: Charles C. Thomas.

Eysenck, H. J. (1970). *The structure of human personality* (3rd ed.). London: Methuen.

Eysenck, H. J. (1972). Human typology, higher nervous activity, and factor analysis. In V. D. Nebylitsyn & J. A. Gray (Eds.), *Biological bases of individual behavior* (pp. 165–181). New York: Academic Press.

Eysenck, H. J. (1981). General features of the model. In H. J. Eysenck (Ed.), *A model of personality* (pp. 1–37). Berlin: Springer-Verlag.

Eysenck, H. J. (1987). Special review of *Temperamental bases of behavior: Warsaw studies on individual differences* (J. Strelau, Ed.) and *The biological bases of personality and behavior, Volumes 1 and 2* (J. Strelau, F. H. Farley, and A. Gale, Eds.). *Personality and Individual Differences, 8*, 289–290.

Eysenck, H. J. (1991). Dimensions of personality: The biosocial approach to personality. In J. Strelau & A. Angleitner (Eds.), *Explorations in temperament: International perspectives on theory and measurement* (pp. 87–103). New York: Plenum Press.

Eysenck, H. J. (1994). Cancer, personality, and stress: Prediction and prevention. *Advanced Behaviour Research and Therapy, 16*, 167–215.

Eysenck, H. J. (1998). *Dimensions of personality*. London: Transaction. (Original work published in 1947)

Eysenck, H. J., & Eysenck, M. W. (1985) *Personality and individual differences: A natural science approach*. New York: Plenum Press.

Eysenck, H. J., & Eysenck, S. B. G. (1968). *Manual of the Eysenck Personality Inventory*. San Diego, CA: Educational and Industrial Testing Service.

Eysenck, H. J., & Eysenck, S. B. G. (1991). *Manual of the Eysenck Personality Scales*. London: Hodder & Stoughton.

Eysenck H. J., & Eysenck S. B. G. (1994). *Manual of the Eysenck Personality Questionnaire*. San Diego, CA: EdITS Publishers.

Eysenck, M. W. (1982). *Attention and arousal: Cognition and performance*. Berlin: Springer-Verlag.

Eysenck, M. W. (1992). The nature of anxiety. In A. Gale & M. W. Eysenck (Eds.), *Handbook of individual differences: Biological perspectives* (pp. 157–178). Chichester, UK: Wiley.

Eysenck, M. W. (1997). *Anxiety and cognition: A unified theory*. Hove, UK: Psychology Press.

Eysenck, M. W. (2006). Teorie lęku i wykonanie zadań poznawczych [Theories of anxiety and cognitive performance]. In M. Fajkowska, M. Marszał-Wiśniewska, & G. Sędek (Eds.), *Podpatrywanie myśli i uczuć. Zaburzenia i optymalizacja procesów emocjonalnych i poznawczych. Nowe kierunki badań* (pp. 45–62). Gdańsk, Poland: Gdańskie Wydawnictwo Psychologiczne.

Eysenck, M. W., & Calvo, M. G. (1992). Anxiety and performance: The processing efficiency theory. *Cognition and Emotion, 6*, 409–434.

Eysenck, M. W., & Derakshan, N. (2011). New perspectives in attentional control theory. *Personality and Individual Differences, 50*, 955–960.

Eysenck, M. W., Derakshan, N., Santos, R., & Calvo, M. (2007). Anxiety and cognitive performance: Attentional control theory. *Emotion, 7*, 336–353.

Eysenck, M. W., & Fajkowska, M. (2009). Teoria efektywności przetwarzania informacji i jej rozwój [Efficient processing theory and beyond]. In M. Fajkowska & B. Szymura

(Eds.), *Lęk. Geneza–Mechanizmy–Funkcje* (pp. 138–157). Warsaw: Wydawnictwo Naukowe Scholar.

Fahrenberg, J. (1987). Concepts of activation and arousal in the theory of emotionality (neuroticism): a multivariate conceptualization. In J. Strelau & H. J. Eysenck (Eds.), *Personality dimensions and arousal* (pp. 99–120). New York: Plenum Press.

Fajkowska, M. (2009). The Emotional Faces Attentional Test (EFAT). Unpublished manuscript.

Fajkowska-Stanik, M. (2001). *Transseksualizm i rodzina. Przekaz pokoleniowy wzorów relacyjnych w rodzinach transseksualnych kobiet* [Transsexualism and families: Intergenerational transmission of relational patterns in families of transsexual women]. Warsaw: Wydawnictwo Instytutu Psychologii, Polska Akademia Nauk & SWPS.

Fajkowska, M., & Derryberry, D. (2010). Psychometric properties of Attentional Control Scale: The preliminary study on a Polish sample. *Polish Psychological Bulletin, 41*, 1–7.

Fajkowska, M., & Eysenck, M. W. (2008). Personality and cognitive performance. *Polish Psychological Bulletin, 39*, 178–191.

Fajkowska, M., Eysenck, M. W., Zagórska, A., & Jaśkowski, P. (2011). ERP responses to facial affect in low-anxious, high-anxious, repressors and defensive high-anxious individuals. *Personality and Individual Differences, 50*, 961–976.

Fajkowska, M., & Krejtz, I. (2006). Temperament, lęk i uwagowe przetwarzanie informacji emocjonalnych [Temperament, anxiety, and attentional processing of emotional stimuli]. In M. Fajkowska, M. Marszał-Wiśniewska, & G. Sędek (Eds.), *Podpatrywanie myśli i uczuć. Zaburzenia i optymalizacja procesów emocjonalnych i poznawczych. Nowe kierunki badań* (pp. 45–62). Gdańsk, Poland: Gdańskie Wydawnictwo Psychologiczne.

Fajkowska M., & Krejtz, I. (2007). Właściwości indywidualne i "efekt twarzy tłumie" [Individual differences and the "face-in-the-crowd effect"]. *Przegląd Psychologiczny, 50*, 401–433.

Fajkowska, M., Krejtz, I., & Krejtz, K. (2009). Lęk, temperament i przetwarzanie bodźców emocjonalnych na podstawie ruchów gałek ocznych i procesów pamięci [Anxiety, temperament, and emotional stimuli processing based on eye movement and memory] In M. Fajkowska & B. Szymura (Eds.), *Lęk. Geneza—Mechanizmy–Funkcje* (pp. 311–342). Warsaw: Wydawnictwo Naukowe Scholar.

Fajkowska, M., & Marszał-Wiśniewska, M. (2006). Depresja i temperament: Efekt smutnej twarzy w tłumie [Depressed mood and temperament: The sad-face-in-the-crowd effect]. In M. Fajkowska, M. Marszał-Wiśniewska, & G. Sędek (Eds.). *Podpatrywanie myśli i uczuć. Zaburzenia i optymalizacja procesów emocjonalnych i poznawczych. Nowe kierunki badań* (pp. 63–84). Gdańsk, Poland: Gdańskie Wydawnictwo Psychologiczne.

Fajkowska, M., & Marszał-Wiśniewska, M. (2009). Właściwości psychometryczne Skali Pozytywnego i Negatywnego Afektu–Wersja Rozszerzona (PANAS-X). Wstępne wyniki badań w polskiej próbie [Psychometric properties of the Positive and Negative Affect Schedule–Expanded Form (PANAS-X): Study of a Polish sample]. *Przegląd Psychologiczny, 52*, 355–388.

Fajkowska, A., Zagórska, A., Strelau, J., & Jaśkowski, P. (2012). ERP responses to facial affect and temperament types in Eysenckian and Strelauvian theories. *Journal of Individual Differences, 33*, 212–226.

Feibleman, J. K. (1954). Theory of integrative levels. *British Journal for the Philosophy of Science, 5*, 59–66.

Feldman Barrett, L. (2006). Valence as a basic building block of emotional life. *Journal of Research in Personality, 40*, 35–55.

Feldman Barrett, L., Mesquita, B., Ochsner, K. N., & Gross, J. J. (2007). The experience of emotion. *Annual Review of Psychology, 58*, 373–403.

Fisher, J. E., Sass, S. M., Heller, W., Silton, R. L., Edgar, C., Stewart, J. L., et al. (2010). Time course of processing emotional stimuli as a function of perceived emotional intelligence, anxiety, and depression. *Emotion, 10*, 486–497.

Fletcher, P. C., & Henson, R. N. (2001). Frontal lobes and human memory: Insights from functional imaging. *Brain, 124*, 849–881.

Foa, E. B., Rothbaum, B. O., & Kozak, M. J. (1989). Behavioral treatments for anxiety and depression. In P. C. Kendall & D. Watson (Eds.), *Anxiety and depression: Distinctive and overlapping features* (pp. 413–454). San Diego, CA: Academic Press.

Fox, E. (1993). Attentional bias in anxiety: Selective or not? *Behaviour Research and Therapy, 31*, 487–493.

Fox, E. (1994). Attentional bias in anxiety: A defective inhibition hypothesis. *Cognition and Emotion, 8*, 165–195.

Fox, E. (2008). *Emotion science: Cognitive and neuroscientific approaches to understanding human emotions.* Basingstoke, UK: Palgrave Macmillian.

Fox, E., Russo, R., Bowles, R., & Dutton, K. (2001). Do threatening stimuli draw or hold visual attention in subclinical anxiety? *Journal of Experimental Psychology: General, 130*, 681–700.

Fox, E., Russo, R., & Dutton, K. (2002). Attentional biases for threat: Evidence for delayed disengagement from emotional faces. *Cognition and Emotion, 16*, 355–379.

Fox, E., Russo, R., & Georgiou, G. A. (2005). Anxiety modulates the degree of attentive resources required to process emotional faces. *Cognitive, Affective, and Behavioral Neuroscience, 5*, 396–404.

Fowles, D. C. (1988). Psychophysiology and psychopathology: A motivational approach. *Psychophysiology, 25*, 373–392.

Friedman, M. (1996). *Type A behavior: Its diagnosis and treatment.* New York: Plenum Press.

Funder, D. C. (1987). Errors and mistakes: Evaluating the accuracy of social judgment. *Psychological Bulletin, 101*, 75–90.

Funder, D. C. (2008). Persons, situations, and person-situation interactions. In O. P. John, R. W. Robins, & L. A. Pervin (Eds.), *Handbook of personality: Theory and research* (3rd ed., pp. 568–583). New York: Guilford Press.

Galynker, I. I., Cai, J., Ongseng, F., Finestone, H., Dutta, E., & Serseni, D. (1998). Hypofrontaliti and negative symptoms in major depressive disorders. *Journal of Nuclear Medicine, 39*, 608–612.

Garlow, S. J., & Nemeroff, C. B. (2003). Neurobiology of depressive disorders. In R. J. Davidson, K. R. Scherer, & H. H. Goldsmith (Eds.), *Handbook of affective sciences.* Oxford, UK: Oxford University Press.

Garnefski, N., van den Kommer, T., Kraaij, V., Teerds, J., Legerstee, J., & Onstein, E. (2002). The relationship between cognitive emotion regulation strategies and emotional problems: Comparison between a clinical and non-clinical sample. *European Journal of Personality, 5*, 403–420.

Gibb, B. E., Benas, J. S., Grassia, M., & McGeary, J. (2009). Children's attentional biases and 5-HTTLPR genotype: Potential mechanisms linking mother and child depression. *Journal of Clinical Child and Adolescent Psychology, 38*, 415–426.

Główny Urząd Statystyczny, GUS [Central Statistical Office, GUS]. (2007). *Stan zdrowia ludności Polski w roku 2004 r* [Health conditions in the Polish population in 2004]. Warsaw: Author.

Główny Urząd Statystyczny, GUS [Central Statistical Office, GUS]. (2011). *Stan zdrowia ludności Polski w roku 2009 r.* [Health conditions in the Polish population in 2009]. Warsaw: Author.

Goldberg, L. R., & Rosolack, T. K. (1994). The Big Five factor structure as an integrative framework: An empirical comparison with Eysenck's P-E-N model. In C. F. Halverson, Jr., G. A. Kohnstamm, & R. P. Martin (Eds.), *The developing structure of temperament and personality from infancy to adulthood* (pp. 7–35). Hillsdale, NJ: Erlbaum.

Goldstein, K. (1995). *The organism: A holistic approach to biology derived from pathological data in man.* New York: Zone Books. (Original work published in 1939)

Gorman, J. M. (1996). Comorbid depression and anxiety spectrum disorders. *Depression and Anxiety, 4,* 160–168.

Gotlib, I. H., & Cane, D. B. (1987). Construct accessibility and clinical depression: A longitudinal investigation. *Journal of Abnormal Psychology, 96,* 199–204.

Gotlib, I. H., Gilboa, E., & Sommerfeld, B. K. (2000). Cognitive functioning in depression: Nature and origins, In R. J. Davidson (Ed.), *Anxiety, depression, and emotion* (pp.133–163). New York: Oxford University Press.

Gotlib, I. H., Krasnoperova, E., Yue, D. N., & Joormann, J. (2004). Attentional biases for negative interpersonal stimuli in clinical depression. *Journal of Abnormal Psychology, 113,* 127–135.

Gotlib, I. H., & MacLeod, C. (1997). Information processing in anxiety and depression: A cognitive developmental perspective. In J. Burack & J. Enns (Eds.), *Attention, development, and psychopathology* (pp. 350–378). New York: Guilford Press.

Gray, J. A. (1964). Strengh of the nervous system and levels of arousal: A reinterpretation. In J. A. Gray (Ed.), *Pavlov's typology: Recent theoretical and experimental developments from the laboratory of B. M. Teplov* (pp. 289–364). Oxford, UK: Pergamon Press.

Gray, J. A. (1971). *The psychology of fear and stress.* London: Weidenfeld & Nicolson.

Gray, J. A. (1972). The psychophysiological nature of introversion-extraversion: A modification of Eysenck's theory. In V. D. Nebylitsyn & J. A. Gray (Eds.), *Biological bases of individual behavior* (pp. 182–205). New York: Academic Press.

Gray, J. A. (1981). A critique of Eysenck's theory of personality. In H. J. Eysenck (Ed.), *A model for personality* (pp. 246–276). Berlin: Springer-Verlag.

Gray, J. A. (1982). *The neuropsychology of anxiety: An enquiry into the functions of the septo-hippocampal system.* Oxford, UK: Oxford University Press.

Gray, J. A. (1994). Three fundamental emotion systems. In P. Ekman & R. J. Davidson (Eds.), *The nature of emotion: Fundamental questions* (pp. 243–247). New York: Oxford University Press.

Gray, J. A., & McNaughton, N. (2000). *The neuropsychology of anxiety: An enquiry into the functions of the septo-hippocampal system* (2nd ed.). Oxford, UK: Oxford University Press.

Green, D. M., & Swets, J. A. (1974). *Signal detection theory and psychophysics.* Huntington, NY: Krieger. (Original work published in 1966)

Grigorienko, E. L., & Sternberg, R. J. (1997). Styles of thinking, abilities, and academic performance. *Exceptional Children, 63,* 295–312.

Grigsby, J., & Stevens, D. (2000). *Neurodynamics of personality.* New York: Guilford Press.

Grimm, S., Schmidt, C. F., Bermpohl, F., Heinzel, A., Dahlem, Y., Wyss, M., et al. (2006). Segregated neural representation of distinct emotion dimensions in the prefrontal cortex: An fMRI study. *NeuroImage, 30,* 325–340.

Gruzelier, J. H., Lykken, D. T., & Venables, P. H. (1972). Schizophrenia and arousal revisited. *Archives of General Psychiatry, 26,* 427–432.

Habrat, E. (1997). *Reaktywność i zapotrzebowanie na stymulację w depresjach w przebiegu choroby afektywnej dwubieunowej* [Reactivity and the need for stimulation in bipolar depression]. Unpublished doctoral dissertation, Instytut Psychologii, Warsaw University, Warsaw.

Hankin, B. L., Gibb, B. E., Abela, J. R. Z., & Flory, K. (2010). Selective attention to affective stimuli and clinical depression among youths: Role of anxiety and specificity of emotion. *Journal of Abnormal Psychology, 119,* 491–501.

Hariri, A. R., & Holmes, A. (2006). Genetics of emotion regulation: The role of the serotonin transporter in neural function. *Trends in Cognitive Sciences, 10,* 182–191.

Hariri, A. R., & Weinberger, D R. (2003). Functional neuroimaging of genetic variation in serotogenic neurotransmissions. *Genes, Brain and Behavior, 2,* 341–349.

Hartagle, S., Alloy, L. B., Vazquez, C., & Dykman, B. (1993). Automatic and effortful processing in depression. *Psychological Bulletin, 110,* 215–236.

Hayes, S., MacLeod, C., & Hammond, G. (2009). Anxiety-linked task performance: Dissociating the influence of restricted working memory capacity and increased investment of effort. *Cognition and Emotion, 23,* 753–781.

Hebb, D. O. (1949). *The organization of behavior: A neuropsychological theory.* New York: Wiley.

Hebb, D. O. (1955). Drives and the C.N.S (conceptual nervous system). *Psychological Review, 62,* 243–254.

Hecht, D. (2010). Depression and the hyperactive right-hemisphere. *Neuroscience Research, 68,* 77–87.

Heilman, K. M., Schwartz, H. D., & Watson, R. T. (1978). Hypoarousal in patients with the neglect syndrome and emotional indifference. *Neurology, 28,* 229–232.

Heim-Dreger, U., Kohlmann, C.-W., Eschenbeck, H., & Burkhardt, U. (2006). Attentional biases for theratening faces in children: Vigilant and avoidant processes. *Emotion, 6,* 320–325.

Heller, W. (1986). *Cerebral organization of emotional function in children.* Unpublished doctoral dissertation, University of Chicago, Chicago.

Heller, W. (1990). The neuropsychology of emotion: Developmental patterns and implications for psychopathology. In N. L. Stein, B. Leventhal, & T. Trabasso (Eds.), *Psychological and biological approaches to emotion* (pp. 167–211). Hillsdale, NJ: Erlbaum.

Heller, W. (1993a). Gender differences in depression: Perspectives from neuropsychology. *Journal of Affective Disorders, 29,* 129–143.

Heller, W. (1993b). Neuropsychological mechanisms of individual differences in emotion, personality, and arousal. *Neuropsychology, 7,* 476–489.

Heller, W., Etienne, M. A., & Miller, G. A. (1995). Patterns of perceptual asymmetry in depression and anxiety: Implications for neuropsychological models of emotion and psychopathology. *Journal of Abnormal Psychology, 104,* 327–333.

Heller, W., & Nitschke, J. B. (1997). Regional brain activity in emotion: A framework for understanding cognition in depression. *Cognition and Emotion, 11,* 637–666.

Heller, W., & Nitschke, J. B. (1998). The puzzle of regional brain activity in depression and anxiety: The importance of subtypes and comorbidity. *Cognition and Emotion, 12,* 421–447.

Heller, W., Nitschke, J. B., Etienne, M. A., & Miller, G. A. (1997). Patterns of regional brain activity differentiate types of anxiety. *Journal of Abnormal Psychology, 106,* 376–385.

Helm, R., & Landschulze, S. (2009). Optimal stimulation level theory, explanatory consumer behaviour and product adoption: An analysis of underlying structures across product categories. *Review of Managerial Science, 3*, 41–73.

Helzer, E. G., Connor-Smith, J. K., & Reed, M. A. (2009). Traits, states, and attentional gates: Temperament and threat relevance as predictors of attentional bias to social threat. *Anxiety, Stress, and Coping, 22*, 57–76

Henriques, J. B., & Davidson, R. J. (1991). Left frontal hypoactivation in depression. *Journal of Abnormal Psychology, 100*, 535–545.

Henriques, J. B., & Davidson, R. J. (2000). Decreased responsiveness to reward in depression. *Cognition and Emotion, 14*, 711–724.

Herrington, J. D., Heller, W., Mohanty, A., Engels, A., Banich, M. T., Webb, A. G., et al. (2010). Localization of asymmetric brain function in emotion and depression. *Psychophysiology, 47*, 442–454.

Hertel, P. T. (1994). Depresive deficits in word identification and recall. *Cognition and Emotion, 8*, 313–327.

Hertel, P. T. (1997). On the contributions of deficient cognitive control to memory impariments in depression. *Cognition and Emotion, 11*, 569–583.

Hettema, P. J., Leidelmeijer, K. C., & Greenen, R. (2000). Dimensions of information processing: Physiological reactions to motion pictures. *European Journal of Personality, 14*, 39–63.

Heylighen, F., & Aerts, D. (Eds.). (1996). *The evolution of complexity*. Dordrecht, The Netherlands: Kluwer Academic Publishers.

Himmelhoch, J. M., Levine, J., & Gershon, S. (2001). Historical overview of the relationship between anxiety disorders and affective disorders. *Depression and Anxiety, 14*, 53–66.

Hock, M., & Krohne, H. W. (2004). Coping with threat and memory for ambiguous information: Testing the repressive discontinuity hypothesis. *Emotion, 4*, 65–86.

Hoehn-Saric, R., MacLeod, D., & Zimmerli, W. D. (1989). Somatic manifestations in women with generalized anxiety disorder: Psychophysiological responses to psychological stress. *Archives of General Psychiatry, 46*, 1113–1119.

Hofmann, S. G., Moscovitch, D. A., Litz, B. T., Kim, H.-J., Davis, L. L., & Pizzagalli, D. A. (2005). The worried mind: Autonomic and prefrontal activation during worrying. *Emotion, 5*, 464–475.

Holland, J. L. (1985). *Making vocational choices* (2nd ed.). Englewood Cliffs, NJ: Prentice-Hall.

Hume, W. I., & Claridge, G. S. (1965). A comparison of the measures of "arousal" in normal subjects. *Life Sciences, 4*, 545–553.

Humphreys, M. S., & Revelle, W. (1984). Personality, motivation, and performance: A theory of the relationship between individual differences and information processing. *Psychological Review, 91*, 153–184.

Humphreys, M. S., Revelle, W., Simon, L., & Gilliland, K. (1980). Individual differences in diurnal rhythms and multiple activation states: A reply to M. W. Eysenck and Folkard. *Journal of Experimental Psychology: General, 109*, 42–48.

Ioannou, M. C., Mogg, K., & Bradley, B. P. (2004). Vigilance for threat: Effects of anxiety and defensiveness. *Personality and Individual Differences, 36*, 1879–1891.

Isen, A. M. (2000). Positive affect. In T. Dalgleish & M. Power (Eds.), *Handbook of cognition and emotion* (pp. 521–539). Chichester, UK: Wiley.

Izard, C. E. (2007). Basic emotions, natural kinds, emotion schemas, and a new paradigm. *Perspectives in Psychological Science, 2*, 260–280.

Jahoda, M. (1961). A social-psychological approach to the study of culture. *Human Relations, 14*, 23–30.

James, W. (1890). *The principles of psychology* (2 vols.). New York: Henry Holt.

Jensen-Campbell, L. A., & Graziano, W. G. (2001). Agreeableness as a moderator of interpersonal conflict. *Journal of Personality, 69*, 323–361.

Johnson, A. M., Vernon, P. A., & Feiler, A. R. (2008). Behavioral genetic studies of personality: An introduction and review of the results of 50+ years of research. In G. J. Boyle, G. Matthews & D. H. Saklofske (Eds.), *The SAGE handbook of personality theory and assessment: Vol. 1. Personality theories and models* (pp. 145–173). London: Sage.

Joormann, J. (2004). Attentional bias in dysphoria: The role of inhibitory processes. *Cognition and Emotion, 18*, 125–147.

Joormann, J. (2005). Inhibition, rumination, and mood regulation in depression. In R. W. Engle, G. Sędek, U. von Hecker, & D. N. McIntosh (Eds.), *Cognitive limitations in aging and psychopathology* (pp. 275–312). New York: Cambridge University Press.

Joormann, J., & Gotlib, I.H. (2007). Selective attention to emotional faces following recovery from depression. *Journal of Abnormal Psychology, 116*, 80–85.

Kagan, J., & Snidman, N. (1999). Early childhood predictors of adult anxiety disorders. *Biological Psychiatry, 46*, 1536–1541.

Katsuragi, S., Kunugi, H., Sano, A., Tsutsumi, T., Isogawa, K., Nanko, S., et al. (1999). Association between serotonin transporter gene polymorphism and anxiety-related traits. *Biological Psychiatry, 45*, 368–370.

Kessler, R. C. (2001–2004). National Comorbidity Survey Replication (NCS-R).

Kessler, R. C., Birnbaum, H. G., Bromet, E., Hwang, I., Sampson, N., & Shahly, V. (2010a). Age differences in major depression: Results from the National Comorbidity Survey Replication (NCS-R). *Psychological Medicine, 40*, 225–237.

Kessler, R. C., Birnbaum, H. G., Shahly, V., Bromet, E., Hwang, I., McLaughlin, K. A., et al. (2010b). Age differences in the prevalence and comorbidity of DSM-IV major depressive episodes: Results from the WHO World Mental Health Survey Initiative. *Depression and Anxiety, 27*, 351–364.

King, A. W. (1997). Hierarchy theory: A guide to system structure for wildlife biologists. In J. A. Bissonette (Ed.), *Wildlife and landscape ecology: Effects of pattern and scale* (pp. 185–212). New York: Springer-Verlag.

Kitcher, P. (1985). Two approaches to explanations. *Journal of Philosophy, 82*, 632–639.

Kline, J. P., Allen, J. J. B., & Schwartz, G. E. (1998). Is left frontal brain activation in defensiveness gender specific? *Journal of Abnormal Psychology, 107*, 149–153.

Klirs, E. G., & Revelle, W. (1986). Predicting variability from perceived situational similarity. *Journal of Research in Personality, 20*, 34–50.

Klonowicz, T. (1973). *Reaktywność a przydatność do zawodu operatora* [Reactivity and fitness to the profession of operator]. Unpublished doctoral dissertation. Warsaw University, Warsaw.

Klonowicz, T. (1985). Temperament and performance. In J. Strelau (Ed.), *Temperamental bases of behavior: Warsaw studies on individual differences* (pp. 79–115). Lisse, The Netherlands: Swets & Zeitlinger.

Klonowicz, T. (1987). Reactivity and the control of arousal. In J. Strelau & H. J. Eysenck (Eds.), *Personality dimenstions and arousal* (pp. 183–196). New York: Plenum Press.

Klonowicz, T. (1992). *Stress w Wieży Babel. Różnice indywidualne a wysiłek inwestowany w trudną prace umysłową* [Stress in the Tower of Babel: Individual differences and allocation of effort during difficult mental work]. Wrocław, Poland: Ossolineum.

Kotov, R., Gamez, W., Schmidt, F., & Watson, D. (2010). Linking "big" personality traits to anxiety, depressive, and substance use disorders: A meta-analysis. *Psychological Bulletin, 136*, 768–821.

Krahé, B. (1990). *Situation cognition and coherence in personality.* Cambridge, UK: Cambridge University Press.

Krasnoperova, E., Neubauer, D. L., & Gotlib, I. H. (1998). Attentional biases for negative interpersonal stimuli in clinical depression and anxiety. Unpublished manuscript.

Kreitler, S., & Kreitler, H. (1990). *Cognitive foundations of personality traits.* New York: Plenum Press.

Krieger, J., Schröder, C., & Erhardt, C. (2003). Cortical arousal, autonomic arousal: Evaluation techniques and clinical importance. *Revue Neurologique, 159*, 1107–1112.

Laguna, L. B., Ham, L. S., Hope, D. A., & Bell, C. (2004). Chronic worry as avoidance of arousal. *Cognitive Therapy and Research, 28*, 269–281.

Lang, P. J. (1995). The emotion probe: Studies of motivation and attention. *American Psychologist, 50*, 372–385.

Lang, P. J. (2000). Emotion and motivation: Attention, perception, and action. *Journal of Sport and Exercise Psychology, 22*, S122–S140.

Lang, P. J., Bradley, M. M., & Cuthbert, B. N. (1997). Motivated attention: Affect, activation, and action. In P. J. Lang, R. F. Simons, & R. F. Balaban (Eds.), *Attention and orienting: Sensory and motivational processes* (pp. 97–135). Hillsdale, NJ: Lawrence Erlbaum.

Lang, P. J., Greenwald, M., Bradley, M. M., & Hamm, A. O. (1993). Looking at pictures: Affective, facial, visceral, and behavioral responses. *Psychophysiology, 30*, 261–273.

Larsen, R. J., & Diener, E. (1992). Promises and problems with the circumplex model of emotion. In M. S. Clark (Ed.), *Review of personality and social psychology: Emotion* (Vol. 13, pp. 25–59). Newbury Park, CA: Sage.

Latané, B., & L'Herrou, T. (1996). Spatial clustering in the conformity game: Dynamic social impact in electronic groups. *Journal of Personality and Social Psychology, 70*, 1218–1230.

Lau, J. Y. F., & Pine, D. S. (2008). Elucidating risk mechanisms of gene-environment interactions on pediatric anxiety: Integrating findings from neuroscience. *European Archives of Psychiatry and Clinical Neuroscience, 258*, 97–106.

Lavelle, C., Berry, H., Beslon, G., Ginelli, F., Giavitto, J.-L., Kapoula, Z., et al. (2008). From molecules to organisms: Towards multiscale integrated models of biological systems. *Theoretical Biology Insights, 1*, 13–22.

Lawson, C., MacLeod, C., & Hammond, G. (2002). Interpretation revealed in the blink of an eye: Depressive bias in the resolution of ambiguity. *Journal of Abnormal Psychology, 111*, 321–328.

Lazarus, R. S. (1991). *Emotion and adaptation.* New York: Oxford University Press.

LeDoux, J. E. (1996). *The emotional brain: The mysterious underpinnings of emotional life.* New York: Simon & Schuster.

Lemelin, S., Baruch, P., Vincent, A., LaPlante, L., Everett, J., & Vincent, P. (1996). Attention disturbance in clinical depression: Deficient distractor inhibition or processing resource deficit? *Journal of Nervous and Mental Disease, 184*, 114–121.

Lemke, J. L. (2000). Opening up closure: Semiotics across scales. In J. L. R. Chandler & G. van de Vijver (Eds.), *Closure: Emergent organizations and their dynamics* (pp. 100–111). New York: New York Academy of Sciences. (Annals of the New York Academy of Sciences, Vol. 901)

Levens, S. M., & Gotlib, I. H. (2009). Impaired selection of relevant positive information in depression. *Depression and Anxiety, 26,* 403–410.

Levenson, M. R., Aldwin, C. M., Bosse, R., & Spiro, A. (1988). Emotionality and mental health: Longitudinal findings from the normative aging study. *Journal of Abnormal Psychology, 97,* 94–96.

Levine, J. M., Resnick, L. B., & Higgins, H. T. (1993). Social foundations of cognition. *Annual Review of Psychology, 44,* 585–612.

Levy, J., Heller, W., Banich, M. T., & Burton, L. A. (1983). Are variations among right-handed individuals in perceptual asymmetries caused by characteristic arousal differences between hemispheres? *Journal of Experimental Psychology: Human Perception and Performance, 9,* 329–359.

Lewis, P. A., Critchley, H. D., Rothstein, P., & Dolan, R. J. (2007). Neural correlates of valence and arousal in processing affective words. *Cerebral Cortex, 17,* 742–748.

Loehlin, J. C. (1992). *Genes and environment in personality development.* Newbury Park, CA: Sage.

Loney, B. R., Kline, J. P., Joiner, T. E., Frick, P. J., & LaRowe, S. D. (2005). Emotional word detection and adolescent repressive-defensive coping style. *Journal of Psychopathology and Behavioral Assessment, 27,* 1–9.

Lonigan, C. J., Vasey, M. W., Phillips, B. M., & Hazen, R. A. (2004). Temperament, anxiety, and the processing of threat-relevant stimuli. *Journal of Clinical Child and Adolescent Psychology, 33,* 8–20.

Lovallo, W. R., & Gerin, W. (2003). Psychophysiological reactivity: Mechanisms and pathways to cardiovascular disease. *Psychosomatic Medicine , 65,* 36–45.

Lykken, D. T., & Maley, M. (1968). Autonomic versus cortical arousal in schizophrenics and non-psychotics. *Journal of Psychiatric Research, 61,* 21–32.

Mackworth, N. H. (1948). The breakdown of vigilance during prolonged visual search. *Quarterly Journal of Experimental Psychology, 1,* 6–21.

Mackworth, N. H. (1957). Some factors affecting vigilance. *Advancements in Science, 53,* 389–393.

MacLeod, A. K., & Cropley, M. L. (1995). Depressive future-thinking: The role of valence and specificity. *Cognitive Therapy and Research, 19,* 35–50.

MacLeod, C., Mathews, A., & Tata, P. (1986). Attentional bias in emotional disorders. *Journal of Abnormal Psychology, 95,* 15–20.

MacLeod, C., Soong, L. Y., Rutherford, E. M., & Campbell, L. W. (2007). Internet-delivered assessment and manipulation of anxiety-linked attentional bias: Validation of a free-access attentional probe software package. *Behavior Research Methods, 39,* 533–538.

MacQueen, G. M., Tipper, S. P., Young, L. T., Joffe, R. T., & Levitt, A. J. (2000). Impaired distractor inhibition on a selective attention task in unmedicated, depressed subjects. *Psychological Medicine, 30,* 557–564.

Magnusson, D. (1988). *Individual development from an interactional perspective: A longitudinal study.* Hillsdale, NJ: Erlbaum.

Magnusson, D. (1999). Holistic interactionism: A perspective for research on personality development. In L. A. Pervin & O. P. John (Eds.), *Handbook of personality: Theory and research* (2nd ed., pp. 219–247). New York: Guilford Press.

Magnusson, D., & Endler, N. S. (Eds.) (1977). *Personality at the crossroads: Current issues in interactional psychology.* Hillsdale, NJ: Erlabum.

Marszał-Wiśniewska, M., & Fajkowska-Stanik, M. (2005). *Temperament, tendencje depresyjne i detekcja sygnałów emocjonalnych* [Temperament, depressd mood, and detection of emotional signals]. *Czasopismo Psychologiczne 11*, 119–130.

Maruszewski, T., Fajkowska, M., & Eysenck, M. W. (2010). Introduction: An integrative view of personality. In T. Maruszewski, M. Fajkowska, & M. W. Eysenck (Eds.), *Personality from biological, cognitive, and social perspectives* (pp. 1–9). Clinton Corners, NY: Eliot Werner Publications.

Maslow, A. H. (1954). *Motivation and personality.* New York: Harper & Row.

Mathersul, D. Williams, L. M., Hopkinson, P. J., & Kemp, A. H. (2008). Investigating models of affect: Relationships among EEG alpha, asymmetry, depression, and anxiety. *Emotion, 8*, 560–572.

Mathews, A., & MacLeod, C. (2002). Induced processing biases have causal effects on anxiety. *Cognition and Emotion, 16*, 331–354.

Matt, G. E., Vazquez, C., & Campbell, W. K. (1992). Mood-congruent recall of affectively toned stimuli: A meta-analytic review. *Clinical Psychology Review, 12*, 227–255.

Matthews, G. (1992). Mood. In A. P. Smith & D. M. Jones (Eds.), *Handbook of human performance: Vol. 3. State and trait* (pp. 161–193). London: Academic Press.

Matthews, G. (2009). Komputacyjne modele lęku [Anxiety and computational modeling]. In M. Fajkowska & B. Szymura (Eds.), *Lęk. Geneza–Mechanizmy–Funkcje* (pp. 77–107). Warsaw: Wydawnictwo Naukowe Scholar.

Matthews, G., Davies, D. R., Westerman, S. J., & Stammers, R. S. (2004). *Human performance: Cognition, stress, and individual differences.* New York: Psychology Press.

Matthews, G., & Deary, I. J. (2002). *Personality traits.* Cambridge, UK: Cambridge University Press.

Matthews, G., & Southall, A. (1991). Depression and the processing of emotional stimuli: A study of semantic priming. *Cognitive Therapy and Research, 15*, 283–302.

Mayer, J. D. (1993a). A system-topics framework for the study of personality. *Imagination, Cognition, and Personality, 13*, 99–123.

Mayer, J. D. (1993b). Personality systems and personal consistency. *Psychological Inquiry, 4*, 295–297.

Mayer, J. D. (1998). A systems framework for the field of personality psychology. *Psychological Inquiry, 9*, 118–144.

Mayer, J. D. (2000). Understanding personality organization helps clarify mood regulation. *Psychological Inquiry, 11*, 196–199.

Mayer, J. D. (2006). A new vision of personality and of personality theory. *American Psychologist, 61*, 331–332.

Mayer, J. D. (2007a). *Personality: A systems approach.* Boston: Allyn & Bacon.

Mayer, J. D. (2007b). The big questions of personality psychology: Defining common pursuits of the discipline. *Imagination, Cognition, and Personality, 27*, 3–26.

McAdams, D. P. (1997). A conceptual history of personality psychology. In R. Hogan, J. Johnson, & S. Briggs (Eds.), *Handbook of personality psychology* (pp. 3–39). San Diego, CA: Academic Press.

McAdams, D. P. (1999). Personal narratives and the life story. In L. A. Pervin & O. P. John (Eds.), *Handbook of personality: Theory and research* (2nd ed., pp. 478–500). New York: Guilford Press.

McAdams, D. P. (2006). *The person: A new introduction to personality psychology* (4th ed.). New York: Wiley.

McAdams, D. P. (2008). Personal narratives and the life story. In O. P. John, R. W. Robins, R., & L. A. Pervin (Eds.), *Handbook of personality: Theory and research* (3rd ed., pp. 241–261). New York: Guilford Press.

McAdams, D. P., & Adler, J. M. (2006). How does personality develop? In D. Mroczek & T. Little (Eds.), *Handbook of personality development* (pp. 469–492). Mahwah, NJ: Erlbaum.

McAdams, D. P., & Pals, J. L. (2006). A new Big Five: Fundamental principles for an integrative science of personality. *American Psychologist, 61*, 204–217.

McCabe, S. B., & Gotlib, I. H. (1995). Selective attention and clinical depression: Performance on a deployment-of-attention task. *Journal of Abnormal Psychology, 104*, 241–245.

McGuinness, D., & Pribram, K. (1980). The neuropsychology of attention: Emotional and motivational controls. In M. C. Wittrock (Ed.), *The brain and psychology* (pp. 95–139). New York: Academic Press.

McManus, S., Meltzer, H., Brugha, T., Bebbington, P., &, Jenkins, R. (2009). *Adult psychiatric morbidity in England, 2007: Results of a household survey.* London: NHS Information Centre for Health and Social Care.

McNally, R. J., Riemann, B. C., & Kim, E. (1990). Selective processing of threat cues in panic disorder. *Behaviour Research and Therapy, 28*, 407–412.

Mehrabian, A., & O'Reilly, E. (1980). Analysis of personality measures in terms of basic dimensions of temperament. *Journal of Personality and Social Psychology, 38*, 492–503.

Mendolia, M., & Baker, G. A. (2008). Attentional mechanisms associated with repressive distancing. *Journal of Research in Personality, 42*, 546–563.

Merlin, V. S. (1986). *Outline of integral research on individuality.* Moscow: Pedagogika (in Russian).

Metcalfe, J., & Mischel, W. (1999). A hot/cool-system analysis of delay of gratification: Dynamics of willpower. *Psychological Review, 106*, 3–19.

Mineka, S., Rafaeli, E., & Yovel, I. (2003). Cognitive biases in emotional disorders: Information processing and social-cognitive perspectives. In R. J. Davidson, K. R. Scherer, & H. H. Goldsmith (Eds.), *Handbook of affective sciences* (pp. 976–1009). Oxford, UK: Oxford University Press.

Mischel, W. (1968). *Personality and assessment.* New York: Wiley.

Mischel, W. (2009). From *Personality and Assessment* (1968) to personality science, 2009. *Journal of Research in Personality, 43*, 282–290.

Mischel, W., & Peake, P. K. (1982). Beyond déjà vu in the search for cross-situational consistency. *Psychological Review, 89*, 730–755.

Mischel, W., Shoda, Y., & Smith, R. E. (2004). *Introduction to personality: Toward an integration* (7th ed.). New York: Wiley.

Mogg, K., Bradley, B. P., Williams, R., & Mathews, A. (1993). Subliminal processing of emotional information in anxiety and depression. *Journal of Abnormal Psychology, 102*, 304–311

Moruzzi, G., & Magoun, H. W. (1949). Brain stem reticular formation and activation of the EEG. *Electroencephalography and Clinical Neurophysiology, 1*, 455–473.

Muris, P., de Jong, P. J., & Englelen, S. (2004). Relationships between neuroticism, attentional control, and anxiety disorders symptoms in non-clinical children. *Personality and Individual Differences, 37*, 789–797.

Murray, H. A. (1938). *Explorations in personality.* New York: Oxford University Press.

Myers, L. B., & Derakshan, N. (2004). To forget or not forget: What do repressors forget and when do they forget? *Cognition and Emotion, 18,* 495–511.

Myers, L. B., Vetere, A., & Derakshan, N. (2004). Are suppression and repressive coping related? *Personality and Individual Differences, 36,* 1009–1013.

Naragon-Gainey, K., & Watson, D. (2011). Clarifying the dispositional basis of social anxiety: A hierarchical perspective. *Personality and Individual Differences, 50,* 926–934.

Naragon-Gainey, K., Watson, D., & Markon, K. E. (2009). Differential relations of depression and social anxiety symptoms to the facets of extraversion/positive emotionality. *Journal of Abnormal Psychology, 118,* 299–310.

Nebylitsyn, V. D. (1972). *Fundamental properties of the human nervous system* (G. L. Mangan, Trans.). New York: Plenum Press.

Nesse, R. M. (2000). Is depression an adaptation? *Archives of General Psychiatry, 57,* 14–20.

Netter, P. (1991). Biochemical variables in the study of temperament. In J. Strelau & A. Angleitner (Eds.), *Explorations in temperament: International perspectives on theory and measurement* (pp. 147–161). New York: Plenum Press.

Newberry, B. H., Clark, W. B., Crawford, R. L., Strelau, J., Angleitner, A., Jones, J. H., et al. (1997). An American English version of the Pavlovian Temperament Survey. *Personality and Individual Differences, 22,* 105–114.

Newman, L. S., & McKinney, L. C. (2002). Repressive coping and threat-avoidance: An idiographic Stroop study. *Personality and Social Psychology Bulletin, 28,* 409–422.

Newton, T. L., & Contrada, R. J. (1992). Repressive coping and verbal-autonomic response dissociation: The influence of social context. *Journal of Personality and Social Psychology, 62,* 159–167.

Nęcka, E. (2000). *Pobudzenie intelektu. Zarys formalnej teorii inteligencji* [Aroused intellect: Formal theory of intelligence]. Kraków, Poland: Towarzystwo Autorów and Wydawców Prac Naukowych UNIVERSITAS.

Nicolis, J. S. (1986). *Dynamics of hierarchical systems: An evolutionary approach.* New York: Springer-Verlag.

Nitschke, J. B., & Heller, W. (2002). The neuropsychology of anxiety disorders: Affect, cognition, and neural circuitry. In H. D'haenen, J. A. den Boer, H. Westenberg, & P. Willner (Eds.), *Textbook of biological psychiatry* (pp. 975–988). Chichester, UK: Wiley.

Nitschke, J. B., Heller, W., Imig, J. C., McDonald, R. P., & Miller, G. A. (2001). Distinguishing dimensions of anxiety and depression. *Cognitive Therapy and Research, 25,* 1–22.

Nitschke, J. B., Heller, W., & Miller, G. A. (2000). Anxiety, stress, and cortical brain function. In J. C. Borod (Ed.), *The neuropsychology of emotion* (pp. 298–319). New York: Oxford University Press.

Nitschke, J. B., Heller, W., Palmieri, P. A., & Miller, G. A. (1999). Contrasting patterns of brain activity in anxious apprehension and anxious arousal. *Psychophysiology, 36,* 628–637.

Nowak, A., & Vallacher, R. R. (1998). *Dynamical social psychology.* New York: Guilford Press.

Odum, H. T., & Odum, E. C. (2000). *Modeling for all scales: An introduction to system simulation.* San Diego, CA: Academic Press.

O'Gorman, J. G., & Lloyd, J. E. M. (1987). Extraversion, impulsiveness, and EEG alpha activity. *Personality and Individual Differences, 8,* 169–174.

Öhman, A. (1997). As fast as the blink of an eye: Evolutionary preparedness for pre-attentive processing of threat. In P. J. Lang, R. F. Simons, & M. Balaban (Eds.), *Attention and orienting: Sensory and motivational processes* (pp. 165–184). Mahwah, NJ: Erlbaum.

Öhman, A., Lundqvist, D., & Esteves, F. (2001). The face in the crowd revisited: A threat advantage with schematic stimuli. *Journal of Personality and Social Psychology, 80,* 381–396.

Öhman, A., & Mineka, S. (2001). Fears, phobias, and preparedness: Toward an evolved module of fear and fear learning. *Psychological Review, 108,* 231–240.

O'Neill, R. V., DeAngelis, D. L., Waide, J. B., & Allen, T. F. H. (1986). *A hierarchical concept of ecosystems.* Princeton, NJ; Princeton University Press.

Onnis, R., Dadds, M. R., & Bryant, R. A. (2011). Is there a mutual relationship between opposite attentional biases underlying anxiety? *Emotion, 3,* 582–594.

Orth, U. R., & Bourrain, A. (2005). Optimum stimulation level theory and the differential impact of olfactory stimuli on consumer exploratory tendencies. *Advances in Consumer Research, 32,* 613–619.

Panksepp, J. (1998). *Affective neuroscience: The foundations of human and animal emotions.* New York: Oxford University Press.

Panksepp, J. (2000). Emotions as natural kinds within the mammalian brain. In M. Lewis & J. M. Haviland-Jones (Eds.), *Handbook of emotions* (2nd ed., pp. 137–156). New York: Guilford Press.

Parker, G., Wilhelm, K., Mitchell P., Austin, M. P., Roussos, J., & Gladstone, G. (1999). The influence of anxiety as a risk to early onset major depression. *Journal of Affective Disorders, 52,* 11–17.

Parker, G., & Roy, K. (2002). Examining the utility of a temperamental model for modelling non-melancholic depression. *Acta Psychiatrica Scandinavica, 106,* 54–61.

Parnowski, T., & Jernajczyk, W. (1977). Inwentarz depresji Becka w ocenie nastroju osób zdrowych i chorych na choroby afektywne [The Beck Depression Inventory in mood assessment in healthy individuals and individuals with affective disorders]. *Psychiatria Polska, 4,* 416–421.

Pavlov, I. P. (1927). *Conditioned reflexes: An investigation of the physiological activity of the cerebral cortex* (G. V. Anrep, Ed. & Trans.). London: Oxford University Press.

Pavlov, I. P. (1928). *Lectures on conditioned reflexes: Twenty-five years of objective study of the higher nervous activity (behavior) of animals* (W. H. Gantt, Trans.). New York: Liveright Publishing.

Peers, P. V., & Lawrence, A. D. (2009). Attentional control of emotional distraction in rapid serial visual presentation. *Emotion, 9,* 140–145.

Pervin, L. A. (1976). Performance and satisfaction as a function of individual-environment fit. In N. S. Endler & D. Magnusson (Eds.), *Interactional psychology and personality* (pp. 71–89). New York: Wiley.

Piaget, J. (1955). *The child's construction of reality.* London: Routledge & Kegan Paul.

Piaget, J. (1983). Piaget's theory. In P. Mussen (Ed.), *Handbook of child psychology, Vol. 1* (4th ed., pp. 103–128). New York: Wiley.

Pivik, R. T., Stelmack, R. M. & Bylsma, F. W. (1988). Personality and individual differences in spinal motoneuronal excitability. *Psychophysiology, 25,* 16–24.

Posner, M. I. (1978). *Chronometric explorations of mind.* Hillsdale, NJ: Erlbaum.

Posner, M. I. (1980). Orienting of attention. *Quarterly Journal of Experimental Psychology, 32,* 3–25.

Posner, M. I. (1994). Attention: The mechanism of consciousness. *Psychological Review, 91*, 7398–7403.

Posner, M. I., & Petersen, S. E. (1990). The attention system of the human brain. *Annual Review of Neurosceince, 13*, 25–42.

Posner, M. I., & Rothbart, M. K. (1998). Attention, self-regulation and consciousness. *Philosophical Transactions of the Royal Society of London B, 353*, 1915–1927.

Pribram, K. H., & McGuiness, D. (1975). Arousal, activation, and effort in the control of attention. *Psychological Review, 82*, 116–149.

Prinz, J. J. (2004). *Gut reactions: A perceptual theory of emotion.* New York: Oxford University Press.

Rachman, S. (2004). *Anxiety* (2nd ed.). Hove, UK: Psychology Press.

Raju, P. S. (1980). Optimum stimulation level: Its relationship to personality, demographics, and exploratory behavior. *Journal of Consumer Research, 7*, 272–282.

Reeb-Sutherland, B. C, Vanderwert, R. E., Degnan, K. A., Marshall, P. J., Pérez-Edgar, K., Chronis-Tuscano, A., et al. (2009). Attention to novelty in behaviorally inhibited adolescents moderates risk for anxiety. *Journal of Child Psychology and Psychiatry 50*, 1365–1372.

Reiman, E. M., Raichle, M. E., Butler, F. K., Herscovitch, P., & Robins, E. (1984). A focal brain abnormality in panic disorder, a severe form of anxiety. *Nature, 310*, 683–685.

Ressler, K. J., & Mayberg, H. S (2007). Targeting abnormal neural circuits in mood and anxiety disorders: From the laboratory to the clinic. *Nature Neuroscience, 10*, 1116–1124.

Revelle, W. (1997) Extraversion and impulsivity. In H. Nyborg (Ed.), *The scientific study of human nature: Tribute to Hans J. Eysenck at eighty* (pp. 189–212). Amsterdam: Elsevier.

Revelle, W., Humphreys, M. S., Simon, L., & Gilliland, K. (1980). The interactive effect of personality, time of day, and caffeine: A test of the arousal model. *Journal of Experimental Psychology: General, 109*, 1–31.

Robbins, T. W. (1997). Arousal systems and attentional processes. *Biological Psychology, 45*, 57–71.

Robinson, M. D., & Compton, R. J. (2006). The automaticity of affective reactions: Stimulus valence, arousal, and lateral spatial attention. *Social Cognition, 24*, 469–495.

Robinson, M. D., Meier, B. P., Tamir, M., Wilkowski, B. M., & Ode, S. (2009). Behavioral facilitation: A cognitive model of individual differences in approach motivation. *Emotion, 9*, 70–82.

Robinson, T. N., Jr., & Zahn, T. P. (1985). Psychoticism and arousal: Possible evidence for a linkage of P and psychopathy. *Personality and Individual Differences, 6*, 47–66.

Rothbart, M. K. (1989a). Temperament in childhood: A framework. In G. Kohnstamm, J. Bates, & M. K Rothbart (Eds.), *Temperament in childhood* (pp. 59–73). Chichester, UK: Wiley.

Rothbart, M. K. (1989b). Temperament and development. In G. A. Kohnstamm, J. E. Bates, & M. K. Rothbart (Eds.), *Temperament in childhood* (pp. 187–247). Chichester, UK: Wiley.

Rothbart, M. K. & Ahadi, S. A. (1994). Temperament and the development of personality. *Journal of Abnormal Psychology, 103*, 55–66.

Rothbart, M. K., Derryberry, D., & Posner, M. I. (1994). A psychobiological approach to the development of temperament. In J. E. Bates & T. D. Wachs (Eds.), *Temperament: Individual differences at the interface of biology and behavior* (pp. 83–116). Washington, DC: American Psychological Association.

Rottenberg, J. (2007). Major depressive disorder: Emerging evidence for emotion context insensitivity. In J. Rottenberg & S. L. Johnson (Eds.), *Emotion and psychopathology: Bridging affective and clinical science* (p. 151–166). Washington, DC: American Psychological Association.

Rottenberg, J., Kasch, K. L., Gross, J. J., & Gotlib, I. H. (2002). Sadness and amusement reactivity differentially predict concurrent and prospective functioning in major depressive disorder. *Emotion, 2*, 135–146.

Routtenberg, A. (1968). The two-arousal hypothesis: Reticular formation and the limbic system. *Psychological Review, 75*, 51–80.

Rubino, A., Zanasi, M., Robone, C., & Siracusano, A. (2009). Personality differences between depressed melancholic and non-melancholic inpatients. *Australian and New Zealand Journal of Psychiatry, 43*, 145–148.

Russell, J. A. (1980). A circumplex model of affect. *Journal of Personality and Social Psychology, 39*, 1161–1178.

Russell, J. A. (1983). Pancultural aspects of the human conceptual organization of emotions. *Journal of Personality and Social Psychology, 45*, 1281–1288.

Russell, J. A. (1991). Culture and the categorization of emotion. *Psychological Bulletin, 110*, 426–450.

Russell, J. A. (2003). Core and the psychological construction of emotion. *Psychological Review, 110*, 145–172.

Russell, J. A., & Feldman Barrett, L. (1999). Core affect, prototypical emotional episodes, and other things called emotion: Dissecting the elephant. *Journal of Personality and Social Psychology, 76*, 805–819.

Russell, J. A., & Lemay, G. (2000). Emotion concepts. In M. Lewis & J. M. Haviland-Jones (Eds.), *Handbook of emotions* (2nd. ed., pp. 491–503). New York: Guilford Press.

Salthe, S. N. (1985). *Evolving hierarchical systems: Their structure and representation.* New York: Columbia University Press.

Salthe, S. N. (1988). Notes toward a formal history of the levels concept. In G. Greenberg & E. Tobach (Eds.), *Evolution of social behavior and integrative levels.* Hillsdale, NJ: Erlbaum.

Salthe, S. N. (1991). Two forms of hierarchy theory in Western discourses. *International Journal of General Systems, 18*, 251–264.

Salthe, S. N. (1993). *Development and evolution: Complexity and change in biology.* Cambridge, MA: MIT Press.

Salthe, S. N. (2006). Two frameworks for complexity generation in biological systems. In C. Gershenson & T. Lanaerts (Eds.), *Evolution of complexity: A life proceedings.* Bloomington, IN: Indiana University Press.

Salthe, S. N. (2009). A hierarchical framework for levels of reality: Understanding through representation. *Axiomathes, 19*, 87–99.

Sanders, A. F. (1980). Stage analysis of reaction processes. In G. Stelmach & J. Requin (Eds.), *Tutorials on motor behavior* (pp. 331–354). Amsterdam: North-Holland.

Sanders, A. F. (1983). Towards a model of stress and human performance. *Acta Psychologica, 53*, 61–97.

Sanders, A. F. (1997). A summary of resource theories from a behavioral perspective. *Biological Psychology, 45*, 5–18.

Sanders, A. F. (1998). *Elements of human performance: Reaction processes and attention in human skill.* Mahwah, NJ: Erlbaum.

Sanderson, W. C., & Barlow, D. H. (1990). A description of patients diagnosed with DSM-III-Revised generalized anxiety disorder. *Journal of Nervous and Mental Disease, 178,* 588–591.

Sapolsky, R. M. (1992). Neuroendocrinology of the stress response. In J. B. Becker, S. M. Breedlove, & D. Crews, *Behavioral endocrinology* (pp. 287–324). Cambridge, MA: MIT Press.

Sato, T., Narita, T., Hirano, S., Kusunoki, K., Sakado, K., & Uehara, T. (2003). Is interpersonal sensitivity specific to non-melancholic depressions? *Journal of Affective Disorders, 64,* 133–144.

Sava, F. A., & Popa, R. I. (2011). Personality types based on the Big Five model: A cluster analysis over the Romanian population. *Cognition, Brain, Behaviour: An Interdisciplinary Journal, 3,* 359–384.

Savostyanov, A. N., Tsai, A. C., Liou, M., Levin, E. A., Lee, J. D., Yurganov, A. V., et al. (2009). EEG-correlates of trait anxiety in the stop-signal paradigm. *Neuroscience Letters, 449,* 112–116.

Scher, C. D., Ingram, R. E., & Segal, Z. V. (2005). Cognitive reactivity and vulnerability: Empirical evaluation of construct activation and cognitive diatheses in unipolar depression. *Clinical Psychology Review, 25,* 487–510.

Schnabel, K., Asendorpf, J. B., & Ostendorf, F. (2002). Replicable types and subtypes of personality: German NEO-PI-R versus NEO-FFI. *European Journal of Personality, 16,* 7–24.

Schneirla, T. (1959). An evolutionary and developmental theory of biphasic processes underlying approach and withdrawal. In M. Jones (Ed.), *Nebraska Symposium on Motivation* (Vol. 7, pp. 144–171). Lincoln, NE: University of Nebraska Press.

Schock, L., Schwenzer, M., Strum, W., & Mathiak, K. (2011). Alertness and visuospatial attention in clinical depression. *BMC Psychiatry, 11,* 1–6.

Schwerdtfeger, A. (2004). Predicting autonomic reactivity to public speaking: Don't get fixed on self-report data! *International Journal of Psychophysiology, 52,* 217–224.

Shadel, W. G., Cervone, D., Niaura, R., & Abrams, D. B. (2004). Developing an integrative social-cognitive strategy for personality assessment at the level of the individual: An illustration with regular cigarette smokers. *Journal of Research in Personality, 38,* 394–419.

Shankman, S. A., Klein, D. N., Tenke, C. E., & Bruder, G. E. (2007). Reward sensitivity in depression: A biobehavioral study. *Journal of Abnormal Psychology, 116,* 95–104.

Sheperd, G. M., & Grillner, S. (Eds). (2010). *Handbook of brain microciruits.* New York: Oxford University Press.

Shestyuk, A. Y., Deldin, P. J., Brand, J. E., & Deveney, C. M. (2005). Reduced sustained brain activity during processing of positive emotional stimuli in major depression. *Biological Psychiatry, 57,* 1089–1096.

Shoda, Y. (1999). Behavioral expressions of a personality system: Generation and perception of behavioral signatures. In D. Cervone & Y. Shoda (Eds.), *The coherence of personality: Social-cognitive bases of consistency, variability, and organization* (pp. 155–181). New York: Guilford Press.

Shoda, Y., & Mischel, W. (1998). Personality as stable cognitive-affective activation network: Characteristic patterns of behavior variation emerge from a stable personality structure. In S. J. Read & L. C. Miller (Eds.), *Connectionist models of social reasoning and social behavior* (pp. 175–208). Mahwah, NJ: Erlbaum.

Simon, H. A. (1973). The organization of complex systems. In H. H. Pattee (Ed.), *Hierarchy theory: The challenge of complex systems* (pp. 1–27). New York: George Braziller.

Simonov, P. V. (1987). Individual characteristics of brain limbic structures interactions as the basis of Pavlovian/Eysenckian typology. In J. Strelau & H. J. Eysenck (Eds.), *Personality dimensions and arousal* (pp. 123–132). New York: Plenum Press.

Simonov, P. V. & Ershov, P. M. (1991). *Temperament, character, and personality: Biobehavioral concepts in science, art and social psychology* (A. Bastow, Trans.). Philadelphia: Gordon & Breach.

Skyttner, L. (2006). *General systems theory: Problems, perspectives, practice* (2nd ed.). Hackensack, NJ: World Scientific Publishing.

Sloan, D. M., Strauss, M. E., & Wisner, K. L. (2001). Diminished response to pleasant stimuli by depressed women. *Journal of Abnormal Psychology, 110,* 488–493.

Small, D. M., Gregory, M. D., Mak, Y. E., Gitelman, D., Mesulam, M. M., & Parrish T. (2003). Dissociation of neural representation of intensity and affective valuation in human gustation. *Neuron, 39,* 701–711.

Smith, C. A., & Lazarus, R. S. (1990). Emotion and adaptation. In L. A. Pervin (Ed.), *Handbook of personality: Theory and research* (pp. 609–637). New York: Guilford.

Smith, E. R., & Conrey, F. R. (2007). Agent-based modeling: A new approach for theory building in social psychology. *Personality and Social Psychology Review, 11,* 1–18.

Smith, G. J. W. (1999). Trait and process in personality theory: Defined within two contemporary research traditions. *Scandinavian Journal of Psychology, 40,* 269–276.

Spielberger, C. D. (1983). *State–Trait Anxiety Inventory for Adults: Sampler set manual, test, scoring key.* Redwood City, CA: Mind Garden.

Spielberger, C. D., Gorsuch, R. L., & Lushene, R. E. (1970). *The State–Trait Anxiety Inventory: Test manual.* Palo Alto, CA: Consulting Psychologists Press.

Spievak, E. R., & Murtagh, A.M. (2009). Temperament and attentional focus: Reaction time indicators of bias and cue salience. *Social Behavior and Personality, 37,* 289–298.

Stein, D. J., Ruscio, A. M., Lee, S., Petukhova, M., Alonso, J., Andrade, L. H., et al. (2010). Subtyping social anxiety disorder in developed and developing countries. *Depression and Anxiety, 27,* 390–403.

Stelmack, R. M. (1990). Biological basis of extraversion: Psychophysiological evidence. *Journal of Personality, 58,* 293–311.

Stelmack, R. B., & Houlihan, M. (1995). Event-related potentials, personality, and intelligence: Concepts, issues, and evidence. In D. H. Saklofske & M. Zeidner (Eds.) *International handbook of personality and intelligence.* (pp. 349–365). New York: Plenum Press.

Stern, W. (1935). *Allgemeine Psychologie auf personalisticher grundlage* [General psychology from the personalistic standpoint]. Dordrecht, The Netherlands: Nijhoff.

Sternberg, R. J. (2007). *Wisdom, intelligence, and creativity synthesized.* New York: Cambridge University Press.

Stober, J. (1998). Worry, problem elaboration, and suppression of imagery: The role of concreteness. *Behaviour Research and Therapy, 36,* 751–756.

Strelau, J. (1969). *Temperament i typ układu nerwowego* [Temperament and type of nervous system]. Warsaw: Państwowe Wydawnictwo Naukowe.

Strelau, J. (1974). Temperament as an expression of energy level and temporal features of behavior. *Polish Psychological Bulletin, 5,* 119–127.

Strelau, J. (1983). *Temperament, personality, activity.* London: Academic Press.

Strelau, J. (1987). The concept of temperament in personality research. *European Journal of Personality, 1*, 107–117.

Strelau, J. (1994). The concepts of arousal and arousability as used in temperament studies. In J. E. Bates & T. D. Wachs (Eds.), *Temperament: Individual differences at the interface of biology and behavior* (pp. 117–141). Washington, DC: American Psychological Association.

Strelau, J. (1995). Temperament and stress: Temperament as a moderator of stressors, emotional states, coping, and costs. In C. D. Speilberger & I. G. Sarason (Eds.), *Stress and emotion: Anxiety, anger, and curiosity* (Vol.15, pp. 215–254). Washington, DC: Hemisphere.

Strelau, J. (1998). *Temperament: A psychological perspective*. New York: Plenum Press.

Strelau, J. (2000). Temperament [Temperament]. In J. Strelau (Ed.), *Psychologia. Podręcznik akademicki. Vol. 2: Psychologia ogólna* (pp. 683–719). Gdańsk, Poland: Gdańskie Wydawnictwo Psychologiczne.

Strelau, J. (2001). The concept and status of trait in research on temperament. *European Journal of Personality, 15*, 311–325.

Strelau, J. (2006). *Psychologia różnic indywidualnych* [Psychology of individual differences]. Warsaw: Wydawnictwo Naukowe Scholar.

Strelau, J. (2008). *Temperament as a regulator of behavior: After fifty years of research*. Clinton Corners, NY: Eliot Werner Publications.

Strelau, J. (2009a). Miejsce lęku i zbliżonych konstruktów w badaniach nad temperamentem [Anxiety and related constructs in studies on temperament]. In M. Fajkowska & B. Szymura (Eds.), *Lęk. Geneza–Mechanizmy–Funkcje* (pp. 211–230). Warsaw: Wydawnictwo Naukowe Scholar.

Strelau, J. (2009b). *Psychologia temperamentu* [Psychology of temperament]. Warsaw: Wydawnictwo Naukowe PWN.

Strelau, J., & Angleitner, A. (Eds.). (1991). *Explorations in temperament: International perspectives on theory and measurement*. New York: Plenum Press.

Strelau, J., Angleitner, A., & Newberry, B. H. (1999). *Pavlovian Temperament Survey (PTS): An international handbook*. Göttingen, Germany: Hogrefe & Huber.

Strelau, J., & Zawadzki, B. (1995). The Formal Characteristics of Behaviour–Temperament Inventory (FCB-TI): Validity studies. *European Journal of Personality, 9*, 207–229.

Strelau, J., & Zawadzki, B. (1998). *Kwestionariusz Temperamentu PTS. Podręcznik* [PTS Temperament Questionnaire: Manual]. Warsaw: Pracownia Testów Psychologicznych PTP.

Susa, G., & Benga, O. (2009). Temperamental traits and attention to threat: A theoretical exploration of their joint contribution to childhood anxiety disorders. *Cognition, Brain, Behavior, 13*, 299–311.

Swedo, S. E., Schapiro, M. B., Grady, C. L., Cheslow, D. L., Leonard, H. L., Kumar, A., et al. (1989). Cerebral glucose metabolismin childhood-onset obsessive-compulsive disorder. *Archives of General Psychiatry, 46*, 518–523.

Szymura, B., & Słabosz, A. (2002). Uwaga selektywna a pozytywne i negatywne konsekwencje automatyzacji czynności [Selective attention and positive and negative consequences of automatic actions]. *Studia Psychologiczne, 2*, 161–183.

Tembler, S .E., & Schüssler, G. (2009). Differenzierung der nonmelancholic depression [Differential diagnosis of melancholic depression: A multidimensional study]. *Zeitschrift für Psychosomatische Medizin und Psychotherapie, 55*, 393–403.

Teplov, B. M. (1985). *Selected works* (2 vols.). Moscow: Pedagogica (in Russian).

Thayer, J., Friedman, B. H., & Borkovec, T. D. (1996). Autonomic characteristics of generalized anxiety disorder and worry. *Biological Psychiatry, 39*, 255–266.

Thayer, R. E. (1985). Activation (arousal): The shift from a single to a multidimensional perspective. In J. Strelau, F. H. Farley, & A. Gale (Eds.), *The biological bases of personality and behavior: Vol.1. Theories, measurement techniques, and developments* (pp. 115–127). Washington, DC: Hemisphere.

Thayer, R. E. (1989). *The biopsychology of mood and arousal.* New York: Oxford University Press.

Thayer, R. E. (1996). *The origin of everyday mood.* New York: Oxford University Press.

Thomas, J. C., Segal, D. L., & Hersen, M. (Eds.). (2006). *Comprehensive handbook of personality and psychopathology: Vol. 1. Personality and everyday functioning.* Hoboken, NJ: Wiley.

Tomarken, A. J., & Keener, A. D. (1998). Frontal brain asymmetry and depression: A self-regulatory perspective. *Cognition and Emotion, 12*, 387–420.

Toates, F. (2001). *Biological psychology: An integrative approach.* Harlow, UK: Prentice-Hall.

Todd, R. M., Lewis, M. D., Meusel L. A., & Zelazo, P. D. (2008). The time course of social-emotional processing in early childhood: ERP responses to facial affect and personal familiarity in a Go-Nogo task. *Neuropsychologia, 46*, 595–613.

Togo, F., Cherniack, N. S., & Natelson, B. H. (2006). Electroencephalogram characteristics of autonomic arousals during sleep in healthy men. *Clinical Neurophysiology, 117*, 2597–2603.

Tomarken, A. J., Shelton, R. C., & Hollon, S. D. (2007). Affective science as a framework for understanding the mechanisms and effects of antidepressant medication. In J. Rottenberg & S. L. Johnson (Eds.), *Emotion and psychopathology: Bridging affective and clinical science* (pp. 263–283). Washington, DC: American Psychological Association.

Tomaszewski, T. (1967). Aktywność człowieka [Human activity]. In T. Maruszewski, J. Reykowski, & T. Tomaszewski (Eds.), *Psychologia jako nauka o człowieku* (pp. 219–278). Warsaw: Książka i Wiedza.

Tooby, J., & Cosmides, L., Gallistel, C. R., Fernald, R. D., White, S. A., Sherry, D. F., et al. (2000). Toward mapping the evolved functional organization of mind and brain. In M. S. Gazzaniga (Ed.), *The new cognitive neurosciences* (2nd ed., pp. 1167–1270). Cambridge, MA: MIT Press.

Tran-Cao, D., Abran, A., & Lévesque, G. (2001). Functional complexity measurement. In R. Dumke & A. Abran (Eds.), *Current trends in software management* (pp. 173–181). Montreal: Shaker-Verlag.

Tucker, D. M. (1981). Lateral brain function, emotion, and conceptualization. *Psychological Bulletin, 89*, 19–46.

Tucker, D. M., Antes, J. R., Stenslie , C. E., & Barnhardt, T. M. (1978). Anxiety and lateral cerebral function. *Journal of Abnormal Psychology, 87*, 380–383.

Tucker, D. M., Roth, R. S., Arneson, B. A., & Buckingham, V. (1977). Right hemisphere activation during stress. *Neuropsychologia, 15*, 697–700.

Tucker, D. M., & Williamson, P. A. (1984). Asymmetric neural control systems in human self-regulation. *Psychological Review, 91*, 185–215.

Uehara, T., Sakado, K., Sakado, M., Sato, T., & Someya, T. (1999). Relationship between stress coping and personality in patients with major depressive disorder. *Psychotherapy and Psychosomatics, 68*, 26–30.

Vallacher, R. R. & Nowak, A. (Eds.) (1994). *Dynamic systems in social psychology.* San Diego, CA: Academic Press.

Vallacher, R. R. & Nowak, A. (1997). The emergence of dynamical social psychology. *Psychological Inquiry, 8,* 73–99.

van der Molen, M. W., & Keuss, P. J. G. (1981). Response selection and the processing of auditory intensity. *Quarterly Journal of Experimental Psychology, 31,* 95–102.

Venables, P. H. (1963). The relationship between the level of skin potential and fusion of paired light flashes in schizophrenics and normal subjects. *Journal of Psychiatric Research, 1,* 279–287.

Vendemia, J. M. C. (2006). *Repressors vs. low- and high-anxious coping styles: EEG, heart rate, and blood pressure differences during cognitive and cold pain stressors* (Doctoral dissertation, Virginia Polytechnic Institute and State University, Blacksburg, VA). Dissertation Abstracts International, Section B: The Sciences and Engineering, 67, 1177.

von Bertalanffy, L. (1950). An outline of general systems therapy. *British Journal of the Philosophy of Science, 1,* 134–165.

von Bertalanffy, L. (1955). An essay on the relativity of categories. *Philosophy of Science, 22,* 243–263.

von Bertalanffy, L. (1968a). *Organismic psychology and systems theory.* Worcester, MA: Clark University Press.

von Bertalanffy, L. (1968b). The meaning of general systems theory. In L. von Bertalanffy (Ed.), *General system theory: Foundations, development, applications* (pp. 30–53). New York: George Braziller.

von Bertalanffy, L. (1975). *Perspectives on general systems theory: Scientific-philosophical studies* (E. Taschdjian, Ed.). New York: George Braziller.

von Bertalanffy, L. (1981). *A systems view of man* (P. A. LaViolette, Ed.). Boulder, CO: Westview Press.

Wagner, A. D. (1999). Working memory contributions to human learning and remembering. *Neuron, 22,* 19–22.

Wallace, J. C. (2004). Confirmatory factor analysis of the cognitive failures questionnaire: Evidence for dimensionality and construct validity. *Personality and Individual Differences, 37,* 307–324.

Watkins, P. C., Vache, K., Verney, S. P., Mathews, A., & Muller, S. (1996). Unconsious mood-congruent memory bias in depression. *Journal of Abnormal Psychology, 105,* 34–41.

Watson, D. (2000). *Mood and temperament.* New York: Guilford Press.

Watson, D. (2005). Rethinking the mood and anxiety disorders: A quantitative hierarchical model for DSM-V. *Journal of Abnormal Psychology, 114,* 522–536.

Watson, D., Clark, L. A., Weber, K., Assenheimer, J. S., Strauss, M. E., & McCormick, R. A. (1995). Testing a tripartite model: II. Exploring the symptom structure of anxiety and depression in student, adult, and patient samples. *Journal of Abnormal Psychology, 104,* 15–25.

Watson, D., & Kendall, P. C. (1989). Common and differentiating features of anxiety and depression: Current findings and future directions. In P. C. Kendall & D. Watson (Eds.), *Anxiety and depression: Distinctive and overlapping features* (pp. 493–508). San Diego, CA: Academic Press.

Watson, D., & Tellegen, A. (1985). Toward a consensual structure of mood. *Psychological Bulletin, 98,* 219–235.

Watson, D., Weber, K., Assenmeimer, J. S., Clark, L. A., Strauss, M. E., & McCormick, R. A. (1995). Testing a tripartite model: I. Evaluating the convergent and discriminant validity of anxiety and depression symptom scales. *Journal of Abnormal Psychology, 104,* 3–14.

Watson, D., Wiese, D., Vaidya, J., & Tellegen, A. (1999). The two general activation systems of affect: Structural findings, evolutionary considerations, and psychobiological evidence. *Journal of Personality and Social Psychology, 76*, 820–838.

Weinberg, G. M. (2001) *An introduction to general systems thinking.* New York: Dorset House. (Silver Anniversary Edition)

Weinberger, D. A. (1990). The construct validity of the repressive coping style. In J. L. Singer (Ed.), *Repression and dissociation: Implications for personality theory, psychopathology, and health* (pp. 337–386). Chicago: University of Chicago Press.

Weinberger, D. A., Schwartz, G. E., & Davidson, J. R. (1979). Low-anxious, high-anxious, and repressive coping styles: Psychometric patterns and behavioral and physiological responses to threat. *Journal of Abnormal Psychology, 88*, 369–380.

Weiss, P. A. (1971). The basic concept of hierarchic systems. In P. A. Weiss (Ed.), *Hierarchically organized systems in theory and practice.* New York: Hafner Publishing.

Welford, A. T. (1973). Stress and performance. *Ergonomics, 16*, 567–580.

Wells, A., & Matthews, G. (1999). *Attention and emotion: A clinical perspective.* Hove, UK: Psychology Press.

Westra, H. A., & Kuiper, N. A. (1997). Cognitive content specificity in selective attention across four domains of maladjustment. *Behaviour Research and Therapy, 35*, 349–365.

Williams, J. M. G. (2004). Experimental cognitive psychology and clinical practice: Autobiographical memory as a paradigm case. In J. Yiend (Ed.), *Cognition, emotion and psychopathology: Theoretical, empirical and clinical directions.* Cambridge, UK: Cambridge University Press.

Williams, J. M. G., Watts, F. N., MacLeod, C., & Mathews, A. (1997). *Cognitive psychology and emotional disorders* (2nd ed.). New York: Wiley.

Willis, T. A., Sandy, J. M., & Yaeger, A. (2000). Temperament and adolescent substance use: An epigenetic approach to risk and protection. *Journal of Personality, 68*, 1127–1161.

Wilson, E., & MacLeod, C. (2003). Contrasting two accounts of anxiety-linked attentional bias: Selective attention to varying levels of stimulus threat intensity. *Journal of Abnormal Psychology, 112*, 212–218.

Wilt, J., Oehlberg, K., & Revelle, W. (2011). Anxiety in personality. *Personality and Individual Differences, 50*, 987–993.

Wintston, J. S, Gottfried, J. A., Kilner, J. M., Dolan, R. J. (2005). Integrated neural representations of odor intesity and affective valence in human amygdala. *Journal of Neuroscience, 25*, 8903–8907.

Withall, A., Harris, L. M., & Cumming, S. R. (2009). A longitudinal study of cognitive function in melancholic and non-melancholic subtypes of major depressive disorder. *Journal of Affective Disorders, 120*, 150–157.

Woodruff-Pak, D. S. (1997). Classical conditioning. In R. J. Bradley, R. A. Harris, & P. Jenner (Series Eds.) & J. D. Schmahmann (Vol. Ed.), *International review of neurobiology: Vol. 41. The cerebellum and cognition* (pp. 341–366). San Diego, CA: Academic Press.

World Health Organization [WHO]. (1992). *International statistical classification of diseases and related health problems, ICD-10.* Geneva: Author.

Wright, J. C., & Mischel, W. (1987). A conditional approach to dispositional constructs: The local predictability of social behavior. *Journal of Personality and Social Psychology, 53*, 1159–1177.

Wrześniewski, K., & Sosnowski, T. (1996). *Inwentarz Stanu i Cechy Lęku (ISCL). Polska adaptacja STAI. Podręcznik* [The State–Trait Anxiety Inventory: Polish adaptation of the STAI]. Warsaw: Pracownia Testów Psychologicznych PTP.

Wu, J. C., Buchsbaum, M. S., Hershey, T. G., Hazlett, E., Sicotte, N., & Johnson, J. C. (1991). PET in generalized anxiety disorder. *Biological Psychiatry, 29*, 1181--1199.

Yee, C. M., & Miller, G. A. (1988). Emotional information processing: Modulation of fear in normal and dysthymic subjects. *Journal of Abnormal Psychology, 97*, 54–63.

Yerkes, R. M., & Dodson, J. D. (1908). The relation of strength of stimulus to rapidity of habit-formation. *Journal of Comparative Neurology and Psychology, 18*, 459–482.

Yermolayeva-Tomina, L.B. (1964). Concentration of attention and strength of the nervous system. In J. A. Gray (Ed.), *Pavlov's typology: Recent theoretical and experimental developments from the laboratory of B. M. Teplov* (pp. 446–464). Oxford, UK: Pergamon Press.

Zagórska, A., Fajkowska, M., Strelau, J., & Jaśkowski, P. (2010, September). *Temperament traits and ERP responses to facial affect: Validation of the Regulative Theory of Temperament*. Poster presented at the Second Biennial Symposium on Personality and Social Psychology, Warsaw.

Zawadzki, B. (1992). *Cechy temperamentu w ujęciu Regulacyjnej Teorii Temperamentu i ich pomiar metodą kwestionariusza* [Temperament traits according to the Regulative Theory of Temperament and their measurement by means of a questionnaire]. Unpublished doctoral dissertation, Warsaw University, Warsaw.

Zawadzki, B. (2001). Temperamentalny czynnik ryzyka chorób somatycznych: Raka płuca i zawału serca [Temperament as a risk factor of somatic diseases: Lung cancer and myocardial infarction]. In W. Ciarkowska & A. Matczak (Eds.), *Różnice indywidualne. Wybrane badania inspirowane Regulacyjną Teorią Temperamentu Profesora Jana Strelaua* (pp. 27–52). Warsaw: Interdisciplinary Center for Behavior Genetic Research, Warsaw University.

Zawadzki, B. (2006). *Kwestionariusze osobowości. Strategie i procedura konstruowania* [Personality questionnaires: Strategies and procedures of construction]. Warsaw: Wydawnictwo Naukowe Scholar.

Zawadzki, B., Czarnota-Bojarska J., Strelau, J., & Sobolewski A. (2004). Wartość predyktywna cech i typów temperamentu. Analiza porównawcza [Predictive validity of traits and types of temperament: Comparative analysis]. *Psychologia–Etologia–Genetyka, 9*, 7–31.

Zawadzki, B., & Radzikowska, E. (2006). Próba kwestionariuszowej diagnozy potencjalnych osobowościowych czynników ryzyka raka płuca i choroby wieńcowej [Questionnaire diagnosis of risk factors of lung cancer and myocardial infarction]. *Psychologia–Etologia–Genetyka, 13*, 135–154.

Zawadzki B., & Strelau, J. (1997). *Formalna Charakterystyka Zachowania–Kwestionariusz Temperamentu (FCZ-KT). Podręcznik* [Formal Characteristics of Behavior–Temperament Inventory (FCB-TI): Manual]. Warsaw: Pracownia Testów Psychologicznych PTP.

Zawadzki, B., & Strelau, J. (2003). Identyfikacja trzech podstawowych prototypów osobowości w grupach polskich. Próba reorientacji badań nad osobowością z koncepcji cech w koncepcję typów [The replicability of three basic personality prototypes in Polish samples: An attempt to shift personality studies from the concept of traits to the concept of types]. *Studia Psychologiczne, 41*, 217–242.

Zawadzki, B., & Strelau, J. (2010). Structure of personality: Search for a general factor viewed from a temperament perspective. *Personality and Individual Differences, 49*, 77–82.

Zeidner, M. (2008). Anxiety revisited: Theory, research, applications. In G. J., Boyle, G. Matthews, & D. H. Saklofske (Eds.), *The SAGE handbook of personality theory and assessment: Vol. 1. Personality theories and models* (pp. 423–446). London: Sage.

Zentall, S. S., & Zentall, T. R. (1983). Optimal stimulation: A model of disordered activity and performance in normal and deviant children. *Psychological Bulletin, 94*, 446–471.

Zhang, L. F., & Sternberg, R. J. (2006). *The nature of intellectual styles.* Mahwah, NJ: Erlbaum.

Zimmerman, M., Coryell, W., & Pfohl, B. (1986). Melancholic subtyping: A qualitative or quantitative distinction? *American Journal of Psychiatry, 143*, 98–100.

Zuckerman , M. (1979). *Sensation seeking: Beyond the optimal level of arousal.* Hillsdale, NJ: Erlbaum.

Zuckerman, M. (1991). *Psychobiology of personality.* New York: Cambridge University Press.

Zuckerman, M. (1994). *Behavioral expressions and biosocial bases of sensation seeking.* New York: Cambridge University Press.

# Index

**F**